# A ROAD MAP FOR IMPROVEMENT OF STUDENT LEARNING AND SUPPORT SERVICES THROUGH ASSESSMENT

By the same authors:

*Asssessment Case Studies: Common Issues in Implementation with Various Campus Approaches to Resolution*

*The Departmental Guide and Record Book for Student Outcomes Assessment and Instituional Effectiveness*

*The Department Head's Guide to Assessment Implementation in Administrative and Educational Support Units*

*General Education Assessment for Improvement of Student Academic Achievement: Guidance for Academic Departments and Committees*

# A ROAD MAP FOR IMPROVEMENT OF STUDENT LEARNING AND SUPPORT SERVICES THROUGH ASSESSMENT

**James O. Nichols and Karen W. Nichols**

*with additional contributions by*
**Cheryl Cleaves, Paul Cunningham, Eliot Elfner, Margie Hobbs, Fred Trapp, and Daniel Weinstein**

**AGATHON PRESS**

**NEW YORK**

**Library of Congress Cataloging-in-Publication Data**

Nichols, James O. (James Oliver), 1941-

A road map for improvement of student learning and support services through assessment / James O.
Nichols and Karen W. Nichols, with additional contributions by Cheryl Cleaves ... [et al.].

p. cm.

Includes bibliographical references and index.

ISBN 0-87586-325-6 (alk. paper)

1. Universities and colleges--United States--Evaluation. 2. Educational tests and measurements--
United States. I. Nichols, Karen W. II. Title.

LB2331.63.N55 2005

378.73--dc22

2005048121

# Table of Contents

# Introduction

Since the publication of the third edition of a *Practitioner's Handbook for Institutional Effectiveness and Student Outcomes Assessment Implementation* (Agathon Press, 1995), assessment has matured to the point that within the field the current emphasis is no longer on assessment (the means) but upon the use of assessment results (the end) to improve student learning and administrative services. This work, which completely takes the place of *A Practitioner's Handbook* as the foundation volume in the series described in more detail below, is the result of the primary authors' desire to distill the lessons learned from their professional experiences over the span of some thirty combined years of service as consultants to more than 350 institutions ranging from two-year colleges to major research universities in every regional accrediting association. It has been a continuous process of refining and putting in place successful procedures for assessment-based improvements.

The authors developed this publication to be utilized as a road map for a number of reasons. First, while acknowledging there are a number of routes to the final destination (improvement of student learning and administrative services), a road map provided by an experienced traveler or "auto club" frequently highlights one suggested route (model) and describes that journey in considerable detail.

Second, as on a road map, such guidance identifies areas in which caution is advised along the route, areas under construction, obstacles which may impede progress, speed traps, and other detours. Finally, like a tour guide accompanying a road map, this publication provides a number of descriptions (models) of successful experiences by various types of travelers (institutions) using the route (model).

*Road Map* exhibits a number of characteristics of which the reader should be aware. First, it provides very practical suggestions for assessment or institutional effectiveness implementation and is not intended as a scholarly work. Second, this publication is decidedly proscriptive, offering a clear set of guidance for the campus journey toward improvement of student learning and administrative services, rather than a broad survey of various approaches. Finally, the model presents a process that has been shaped by requirements of regional accrediting agencies and the actual experiences in implementation of assessment activities by numerous campuses.

*Road Map* is intended for the individual or committee members at the institutional level who have been given the charge of development/support of the institutional effectiveness or assessment process at a campus for the purpose of making improvements in student learning and administrative services. Along with *Assessment Case Studies: Com-*

*mon Issues in Implementation with Various Campus Approaches to Resolution* (Agathon Press, 1995), *Road Map* provides the needed guidance for implementation at the institutional level. The three monographs below complete the family of publications regarding this subject from Agathon Press and are written to fulfill the need for guidance at the departmental level.

- *The Departmental Guide and Record Book for Student Outcomes Assessment and Institutional Effectiveness* (Agathon Press, 2000)
- *General Education Assessment for Improvement of Student Academic Achievement* (Agathon Press, 2001)
- *The Department Head's Guide to Assessment Implementation in Administrative and Educational Support* (Agathon Press, 2000)

*Road Map* is composed of three major parts and a series of resource sections and appendices. Part One (Chapters One to Five) addresses context and institutional level implementation decisions. Part Two (Chapters Six to Nine) describes implementation within academic and administrative departments and is in many ways the heart of the work. Part Three (Chapters Ten to Thirteen) illustrates implementation of the concepts described in Part Two, in particular institutional settings (general education, the two-year college, and at the graduate/professional level), and discusses the issues and need for documentation of the process. Next, two resource sections describe briefly a selection of standardized/commercial examination and surveys which the institution may wish to consider utilizing. Finally, the appendices provide examples of implementation activities as well as a limited commentary on assessment of Distance Learning.

While the contributing authors listed below each have areas of specialization, all are experienced practitioners who have contributed in one way or another to the development of all the chapters in the publication. It has been our pleasure to know and to work with these great professionals, and we appreciate their expertise, work, and contributions to this publication:

| Author/Contributor | Chapter/Section |
|---|---|
| Dr. Cheryl Cleaves<br>Chair, Developmental Studies<br>South West Tennessee Community College | *Chapter Eleven*: Contributing Author. Assessment in Two Year Colleges—(Developmental Studies Programs—Student Learning Outcomes Assessment) |
| Dr. Paul F. Cunningham<br>Professor of Psychology<br>Director, College Assessment<br>Riviera College | *Resource Section*: Standardized Assessment Tests |

| | |
|---|---|
| Dr. Eliot Elfner<br>Professor of Business Administration<br>St. Norbert College | *Chapter Seven*: Contributing Author. Means of Assessment and Criteria for Success for Instructional Programs— (Developing Rubrics as a Means of Assessment)<br><br>&<br><br>*Chapter Ten:* Contributing Author. Assessment in General Education |
| Dr. Margie Hobbs<br>Associate Director Institutional<br>    Research and Assessment<br>Assistant Professor of Mathematics<br>University of Mississippi | *Chapter Twelve*: Assessment Issues in Graduate and Professional Programs |
| Dr. Frederick P. Trapp<br>Dean, Research and Services<br>Long Beach City College | *Chapter Eleven*: Assessment in Two-Year Colleges |
| Dr. Daniel A. Weinstein<br>Assistant Provost Institutional Planning<br>    and Assessment<br>Millersville University | *Chapter Thirteen*: Assessment Documentation<br><br>&<br><br>*Resource Section*: Attitudinal Assessment Surveys |

Particular thanks needs to be given to Dr. Peggy Thomas, Oxford, Mississippi, for her editorial assistance as well as to Ms. Leslye Bloom, Blacksburg, Virginia, for the design of the cover and to Ms. Maureen Feller, Administrative Assistant, Millersville University, for her research assistance.

It is our desire that this work will serve the same purpose as does an automotive road map in providing a successful guide for getting your campus from its current status to its future destination a better institution. A route which has proven successful to many institutions in their journey toward improvement of student learning and administrative services through assessment is described for this purpose. While most of the curves have been pointed out and means suggested for safely negotiating these common obstacles, every bump in the road cannot be anticipated. At the end of the journey, it is not the particular route utilized in getting to your destination (improvement of student learning and administrative services) that is important, but that you have achieved that end and, in the process, built a stronger institution of greater service to society.

**Enjoy your trip!** It can be one of the most important and satisfying institutional journeys which your campus has experienced in quite some time.

**Jim and Karen Nichols**

Dr. James O. Nichols
Director Emeritus of University Plan-
     ning and Institutional Research
Assistant Professor Emeritus of
     Higher Education
University of Mississippi

Currently serves as Chief Executive
     Officer of Institutional Effective-
     ness Associates
www.iea-nich.com

Ms. Karen W. Nichols
Nationally Board Certified Counselor
     and Former Coordinator of Career
     Services
University of Mississippi

Currently serves as Executive Direc-
     tor of Institutional Effectiveness
     Associates
www.iea-nich.com

# Part One

# INSTITUTIONAL LEVEL PREPARATION FOR PROGRAM/UNIT ASSESSMENT IMPLEMENTATION

# CHAPTER ONE

# Development of the Institutional Effectiveness/ Assessment Movement

*A "road map" is only useful in relationship to its ability to get an individual (or in this case an institution) to a predetermined destination. That destination is shaped in part by its context and historical development. This chapter describes the purpose and historical development of the assessment movement.*

What is the purpose of implementation of educational (student learning) outcomes assessment or Institutional effectiveness activities? The answer to this seemingly relatively simple question has resulted in two related, but separate, streams in the development of the institutional effectiveness/assessment movement. On the one hand, campus faculty and administrators along with regional and professional accrediting associations have consistently emphasized that assessment activities on a campus are a means to an end—improvement in student learning and services provided by the institution to its constituents. On the other hand, many federal and state assessment initiatives have focused upon the notion of assessment being the means through which institutions are held accountable for their actions by the public. These two lines of development are not mutually exclusive in nature; however, they clearly have proceeded toward these different ends.

## Development of the Learning/Service Improvement Aspect of Institutional Effectiveness

The national focus on assessment began in the early 1980s when various commissions or committees completed and published a series of studies. These included the following:

- *To Strengthen Quality in Higher Education*: Summary recommendations of the National Commission on Higher Education Issues (1982)
- *A Nation at Risk: The Imperative for Educational Reform* (Bennett, 1983)
- *To Reclaim a Legacy*: A report on the humanities in higher education (Bennett, 1984)
- *Involvement in Learning: Realizing the Potential of American Higher Education* (NIE, 1984).

Each of these national commissions or committees called for a renaissance in American higher education and the development of "excellence," particularly in undergraduate education. Most of these studies also included some reference to "assessment" of undergraduate learning as a component of a program for enhancement of students' achievement.

These reports led to a basic change in 1987 in the manner in which the federal government approved regional accrediting associations Bill Bennett, in one of his last acts as Secretary of Education, changed the federal regulations for recognition of regional and professional accrediting associations to indicate that "the Secretary determines whether an accrediting agency in making its decisions places substantial emphasis on the assessment of student achievement by educational institutions or programs, by requiring that . . ." (5602.17 Subpara B, *Federal Register*, September 8, 1987).

This change has echoed throughout higher education for almost twenty years. Among the regional accrediting associations, the early leader in compliance with Secretary Bennett's change in requirements was the Southern Association of Colleges and Schools' Commission on Colleges. In 1986-87, the Commission on Colleges published its *Criteria for Accreditation*, which, after two years of discussion among the association's members concerning the measurability of some outcomes, firmly established the dominant position of educational (student learning) outcomes assessment and institutional effectiveness as the core of its requirements. Shortly after (1989) this initial assessment/institutional effectiveness mandated by SACS' COC, the North Central Association (NCA)'s Commission on Institutions of Higher Education (CIHE) (now Higher Learning Commission) put forward its first policy statement urging its institutions to implement assessment of "student academic achievement." This statement was followed very shortly by NCA's CIHE requiring assessment plans from a large proportion of its institutions. The final regional accrediting association within this initial wave of implementation was the Middle States Association of Colleges and Schools. Its work in this regard was initiated by its "Framework for Assessment," originally published in the early 1990's.

The second wave of regional accrediting association implementation took place during the period between 1998 and the years immediately following the turn of the century. It was geographically located primarily on the West Coast. The Northwest Association of Colleges and Schools (NWA) and the Western Association of Colleges: Junior Colleges (WASC: JC) have had within their accreditation requirements material concerning assessment of student outcomes and improvement of learning and services since the mid-1990s. During the period beginning 1998-99, both of these regional accrediting associations significantly increased their expectations concerning the extent of implementation which their reaffirmation committees expected of campuses. In 2003, the Western Association of Colleges: Junior Colleges published a substantially revised set of requirements, thoroughly grounded in outcomes assessment and institutional effectiveness, which became effective in the fall of 2004. The expectations of the Western Association of Colleges and Schools: Senior Colleges (WASC: SC) during the period of 1997-2000 could best be described as a "moving target" regarding assessment implementation. With the help of a large Pew Foundation grant, WASC: SC completely restyled its accreditation criteria during this period of time, and the resulting requirements are based primarily upon assessment of student learning.

The New England Association of Schools and Colleges (NEASC) has also recently begun to emphasize assessment of student learning or outcomes. Though the last regional accrediting association to begin active utilization of outcomes assessment as a primary portion of its accreditation processes, the New England Association of Schools and Colleges has made considerable progress in its development of requirements concerning assessment of general education.

Despite the efforts of the regional accrediting associations to incorporate outcomes assessment broadly into their requirements during the 1990s, the associations continued to receive criticism both at the national and institutional level concerning the appropriateness of the process. This criticism led to a third wave of student outcomes assessment integration into regional accrediting requirements. Its status as of the summer of 2000 can be seen in the figure shown below, summarizing an article in the *Chronicle of Higher Education*, entitled "Accreditors Revamp Policies to Stress Student Learning." (See Figure 1.)

---

## Figure 1
### *How the Regional Accreditors Are Changing*

**Middle States Associations of Colleges and Schools:** Revising standards to focus on student learning and other measures, such as the quality of student services. Will publish proposed changes in October.

**New England Associations of Schools and Colleges:** Developing better ways for colleges to measure student learning. Will do a complete review of standards in two to three years.

**North Central Association of Colleges and Schools:** Began alternative accreditation process this spring that replaces the 10-year review with continual self-analysis by colleges.

**Northwest Association of Schools and Colleges:** Drafted revisions in eligibility requirements to require evidence of student achievement and institutional effectiveness. Changes must still be voted on by the group. Revisions of standards to begin this fall.

**Southern Association of Colleges and Schools:** Revising standards to make them less prescriptive and more focused on measuring results, such as student achievement. Will publish proposed changes in December

**Western Association of Schools and Colleges, Commission for Community and Junior Colleges:** Plans to revise standards in 2001. Considering an alternative accreditation process similar to North Central's

**Commission for Senior Colleges and Universities:** Approved revised standards this spring that simplify the compliance process and stress evidence of student learning. Final version to be adopted in November.

---

Those actions resulted in the further strengthening during recent years of requirements for student learning assessment in institutional effectiveness implementation as reflected in:

- The Commission on Colleges, Southern Association of Colleges and Schools, "Principles of Accreditation: Foundation for Quality Enhancement," 2001
- Commission on Higher Education, Middle States Association of Colleges and Schools, "Characteristics of Excellence: Standards for Accreditation," 2001
- Western Association of Colleges: Junior Colleges, "Guide to Evaluating Institutions," 2003
- Higher Learning Commission, North Central Association of Colleges and Schools, "Program to Evaluate and Advance Quality (PEAQ)" and "Academic Quality Improvement Program (AQIP)," 2003

Additional guidance and requirements concerning assessment and institutional effectiveness will likely continue to be forthcoming from these regional accrediting associations in the foreseeable future. As these regional accrediting associations have matured, their focus has broadened to include services in the institution's administrative and educational support (AES) component. Hence, their requirements have become more comprehensive in nature, asking for evidence of a functioning and institution-wide program of continuous quality improvement based upon assessment results.

### Federal and State Interest in the Development of the Assessment Movement for Accountability Purposes

Federal interest in the assessment movement was initially established in the revised regulatory requirements concerning regional and professional accrediting associations referenced previously. This interest has continued as the National Advisory Committee on Institutional Quality and Integrity, the U.S. Department of Education's body through which regional accreditors are periodically reviewed and certified, has demanded more proof of student achievement in accreditation association reviews.

State agencies from one end of the country to the other have also been active in the establishment of assessment requirements for accountability or performance funding purposes during the last ten years. Many state agencies have in one form or another established assessment requirements for their institutions. Among these requirements are those allegedly established without input from institutions of higher learning, such as those established in South Carolina.

### Compatibility of Assessment Initiatives Concerning Accountability and Learning/Service Improvement

In the presence of governmental requirements for assessment information, one can be reasonably assured that these requirements will be met by public and most private institutions. Unfortunately, in doing so, a number of side effects related to assessment for improvement of student learning may occur. These include:

- Dictation of the "assessment" data required by the external agency, which often confuses the institution concerning the difference between outcomes or results of the educational process and measures of the process itself (numbers of classes, numbers of graduates, retention rates, etc.,)
- Commitment on the part of the institution to pleasing the external agency at virtually all costs, thus turning the process into a "game" in which the purpose is not improvement but improved perception of the institution by the public's representatives
- Loss of credibility among the faculty in the assessment data forwarded to the external agency and belief that it is intentionally slanted to please the external agency, and thus generally of little internal use
- Disassociation with the assessment process as a "responsibility of the administration"

Hence, in the opinion of the authors, the existence of state mandated assessment for accountability programs is a two-edged sword. While data of one type or another concerning the institution and student learning will be collected; on the other hand, the use of these data for the improvement of student learning or services is highly unlikely as the entire process is seen as "playing the game."

Although regional and professional accreditation requirements differ in terms of semantics, most now call for those components identified by the Council on Post Secondary Accreditation (COPA) in 1986:

1. A sharpened statement of institutional mission and objectives
2. Identification of intended departmental/programmatic outcomes or results
3. Establishment of effective means of assessing the accomplishment outcomes and results

Added to these components, implicitly, is the use of the assessment results to improve the function of the institution or program and enhanced student learning to complete the Institutional Effectiveness Paradigm.

**Figure 2**

*The Institutional Effectiveness Paradigm*

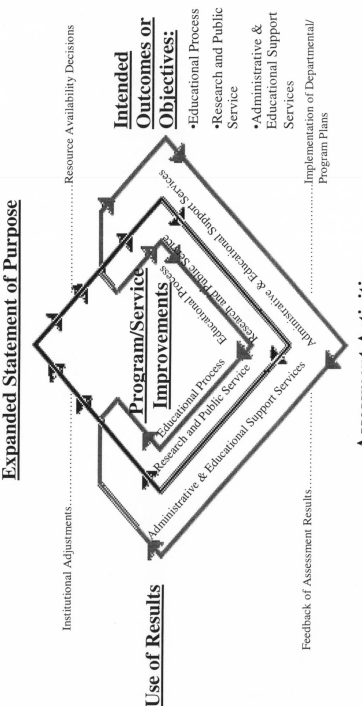

# CHAPTER TWO

# THE INSTITUTIONAL EFFECTIVENESS CONCEPT, ITS PLACE WITHIN A CONTEXT OF INSTITUTIONAL PLANNING ACTIVITIES, AND ITS IMPLEMENTATION THROUGH THE FIVE-COLUMN MODEL: AN OVERVIEW

*This book presents a detailed "road map" to implementation of the institutional effectiveness concept. However, before getting "too close to the trees to see the forest," an overview will prove useful in planning the specific actions proposed in the institutional context within which they must function.*

## The Institutional Effectiveness Paradigm

How then should an institution go about integrating the common institutional effectiveness components cited at the close of the preceding chapter into its ongoing academic and administrative operations so that they become a part of the institution's fabric? One answer to these questions is graphically portrayed in Figure 2, the "Institutional Effectiveness Paradigm," and is described in the following explanation.

This paradigm depicts activities that have been proposed, fostered, and occasionally practiced by some authors and institutions for a number of years. It is an important adaptation of the rational planning model that has existed and been discussed in the literature during the past. Skeptics will quickly ask, "Why this rational model when we know that campuses are essentially political entities and often act irrationally?" The answer is that its elements precisely fit those components required by most accreditation processes. Others will then ask, "How is **this** version of rational planning different from earlier ones that have been proposed and implemented, only to fail?" The primary differences in implementation of this paradigm are its focus on assessment of results (as opposed to processes and resource requirements) and the fact that our peers from other institutions serving on regional accrediting association visiting teams (representing the public directly or indirectly) are reviewing our campus periodically to see if the components of institutional effectiveness are indeed being practiced as well as they are professed.

The essential elements of the Institutional Effectiveness Paradigm (displayed in Figure 2), whose implementation is the subject of this publication, are as follows:

1.  Establishment of an Expanded Statement of Institutional Purpose
2.  Identification of Intended Educational (Student Learning), Research, and Service Outcomes/Administration Objectives
3.  Assessment of the extent to which the Intended Outcomes and Objectives are being accomplished
4.  Adjustment (improvement) of the Institution's Purpose, Intended Outcomes/ Objectives, or activities based on assessment findings

The reader should note in Figure 2 the separate bands or tracks of implementation activities depicted for the "Educational Process," "Research and Public Service," and "Administrative and Educational Support (AES) Services." While the "Educational Process" is the central core of any institution's operations, each aspect of its function (including "Research and Public Service" as well as "Administrative and Education Support Services") is expected to play an essential role in demonstrating institutional effectiveness.

In recent years, regional accreditation has focused on accomplishment of the institution's "statement of purpose" or mission. Yet, today the purpose or mission statements of many institutions are virtually interchangeable. Why is this the case? Many reasons exist, but two are most apparent. First, until recently, accreditation procedures have been primarily episodic. Every ten years, the institution's mission or statement of purpose has been studied by a faculty committee, reworded (usually retaining the same lack of substance), presented to the visiting committee, and afterward promptly filed and forgotten for another ten years. Second, such disregard for the influence of the statement of purpose was possible because of the assumption (some would call it a "leap of faith") that if the institution could demonstrate adequate educational and administrative processes as well as financial resources, then surely it must be accomplishing its purpose. The result has been the singular lack of meaning or importance to actual institutional functioning that characterizes many existing statements of purpose.

Institutional effectiveness (and outcomes assessment) is changing the role of the statement of purpose. Instead of assuming its accomplishment, institutions are being challenged to demonstrate their overall effectiveness through assessments of departmental/program outcomes and objectives linked closely to and supporting the institutions' statements of purpose. This requirement changes the mission or statement of purpose from a shelf document with little practical use to the basis for institutional actions that it was intended to be. In order to provide a useful basis for the assessment of institutional effectiveness, most existing statements of purpose must be substantially expanded and refocused to reflect institutional intentions. Further, a working relationship between the revised or expanded statement of purpose and the intended outcomes and objectives at program and departmental levels must be established.

Expansion and refinement of the institutional statement of purpose are described in more detail in Chapter Five as an essential early element of implementing institutional effectiveness. In addition, Appendix A contains an example of an expanded statement of purpose for a four-year college, for a two-year institution, and for a major research university.

Actual implementation of the institution's expanded statement of purpose will, in most instances, take place at the program and departmental levels through the identification of intended student learning outcomes and administrative and educational support (AES) outcomes/objectives linked closely to the expanded statement of purpose and focusing on the institution's planned impact on its constituents or external environment. This intent primarily consists of institutional assertions concerning its role regarding instruction, research, and public service. These institutional statements of intentions will principally be implemented by the institution's academic and administrative and educational support (AES) units through identification of their own intended educational (student learning), research, and public service outcomes. The institution's AES units also have a vital and direct role to play in demonstrating institutional effectiveness. This role is further described in Chapter Nine.

The formulation of statements of intended educational (student learning) outcomes and assessment of their accomplishments are described in Chapters Six and Seven, respectively. A number of specific examples of statements of intended educational (student learning) outcomes and means of assessment are included in Appendix B of *Assessment Case Studies: Common Issues in Implementation with Various Campus Approaches to Resolution*, Agathon Press, 1995. Once the expanded statement of institutional purpose and departmental statements of intended outcomes and administrative objectives/outcomes are in place, the institution (primarily through its departments) will implement activities to accomplish these ends.

Unquestionably, the single aspect of institutional effectiveness that has gained the highest level of public and institutional visibility is assessment. It is important to note that assessment, within the Institutional Effectiveness Paradigm, (a) occurs after establishment of the expanded statement of institutional purpose and its supporting departmental or program statements of intended educational (student learning) outcomes or administrative objectives/outcomes, (b) is entirely focused on ascertaining the extent of accomplishment of the outcomes and objectives identified, (c) does not attempt to assess every aspect of an institution's operations, and (d) is the foundation for improvement of student learning and services.

The feedback or reporting of assessment findings and the use of such findings in adjusting institutional and departmental actions were originally not emphasized in discussions of implementation strategies. Today, this "use of results" includes adjustment of the expanded statement of institutional purpose, modification to departmental/program statements of intended educational (student learning) outcomes and administrative objectives/outcomes, and changes in departmental operations designed to accomplish the purposes intended. This "use of results" or "closing the loop" is now the central focus or primary concern in the assessment movement and the principal intent of the Institutional Effectiveness Paradigm.

While each of the regional accrediting associations' ultimate expectations will include complete implementation of the paradigm shown in Figure 2, a considerable difference remains in their expectations as of this publication. Beyond any reasonable doubt, the Commission on Colleges of the Southern Association of Colleges and Schools expects each educational program (including general education and where appropriate developmental education), as well as every administrative and educational support (AES) unit, to have fully implemented the paradigm shown in Figure 2 and to be able to document substantive change or improvements resulting from that implementation. To a large extent, the same expectation is being called for by many visitation committees representing the North Central Association of Colleges and Schools.

Though the Middle States Association (MSA) of Colleges and Schools began expecting assessment plans from its member institutions over ten years ago, many MSA committees, as well as the association itself, were willing to continue acceptance of plans almost indefinitely. A dramatic, and many would say traumatic, change in expectations transpired with change of staff and publication of their most recent "Characteristics of Excellence" in 2002. Currently, expectations by MSA are quickly moving to complete and comprehensive use of results. The Northwest Association of Colleges and Schools and the Junior and Senior Colleges Divisions of the Western Association of Schools and Colleges are moving rapidly through their willingness to accept plans for assessment as sufficient progress. They are quickly escalating their expectations that institutions will have used the results of assessment activities to make substantive improvements in their academic programs as well as educational support and administrative services. While each of these associations on the West Coast approaches the subject from a slightly different perspective, they are all moving rapidly forward in their expectations regarding implementation through "closing the loop."

Despite recent substantive gains regarding assessment, the New England Association of Schools and Colleges (NEASC) remains the least rigorous in its expectation regarding implementation of the paradigm shown in Figure 2. For the most part, NEASC is willing to accept assessment plans through the bottom of the paradigm as of the date of this publication. Some expectation exists on the part of the association that a number of the programs at an institution (particularly general education) will have actually done assessment and will have begun to consider its results for improvement of student learning.

Regardless of their current status, evidence reveals that all of the regional accrediting associations are moving toward expectation of the complete implementation of the paradigm shown in Figure 2. The authors estimate that by 2008 expectations will be consistent in all regions.

## Relationship to Other Types of Institutional Planning and Management

A great deal of confusion exists regarding the relationship of institutional effectiveness activities to strategic planning and budgeting, administrative evaluations, TQM/CQI, and reengineering. These relationships are addressed next.

On many campuses both strategic planning and institutional effectiveness or assessment planning are conducted. They are necessary and often required by regional accrediting associations. However, they are different in their approaches to planning, and institutions must recognize and respect the different purpose which each serves. (See Figure 3.)

## Figure 3

## *Types of Planning at Colleges and Universities*

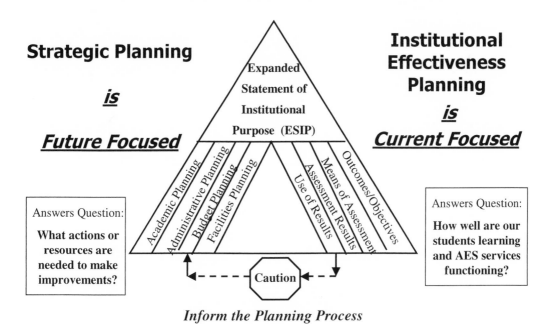

*Inform the Planning Process*

Strategic planning is frequently a product of presidential leadership or the requirements of the governing board. Regional accrediting associations also often require some form of strategic planning activity. Such planning focuses upon the question, "What actions should we take to implement the Expanded Statement of Institutional Purpose?" As such, strategic planning is "Future Focused," often resulting in a series of action plans (which are frequently long range) with resource requirements to put into action the necessary *processes* to accomplish the statement of purpose. Strategic planning is characterized by the following:

- Administrative planning
- Academic planning

- Physical facilities planning
- Budget planning

The unit action plans developed as part of strategic planning are, as illustrated in Figure 4, the results of many factors. Results of the assessment process which cannot be accomplished within existing departmental resources are only one of a number of factors taken into account in creation of these action plans and, frankly, may not be among the most important factors to the unit.

## Figure 4

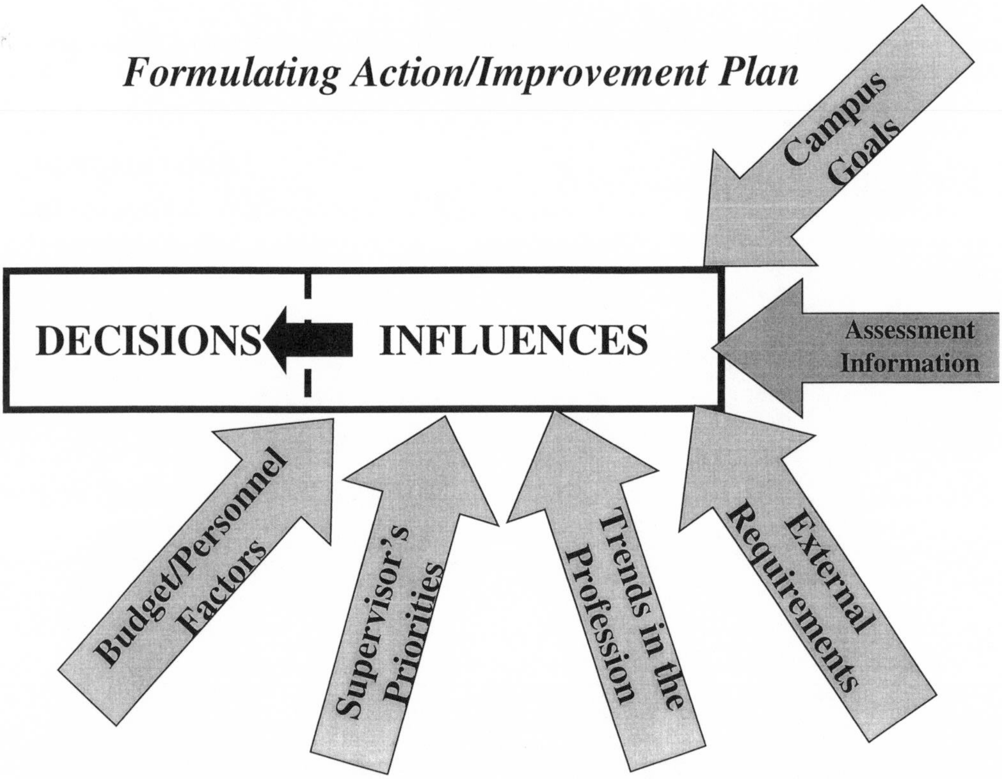

### *Formulating Action/Improvement Plan*

Strategic planning takes place in order for an institution to survive and/or go about its development and refinement. A number of institutions have assumed that since strategic planning was being well accomplished on their campuses and the success of these plans carefully evaluated (Figure 5) that these activities constitute effectiveness planning. This assumption has led to negative findings regarding institutional effectiveness planning by regional accrediting association reaffirmation review committees that have been a shock to many of these institutions.

Institutional effectiveness planning also relates to the expanded statement of purpose of the institution. However, it asks the basic question, "How well are our students learning and administrative (AES) services functioning?" Thus, institutional effectiveness is

# Figure 5

## *Evaluation of Strategic Planning Action Plans*

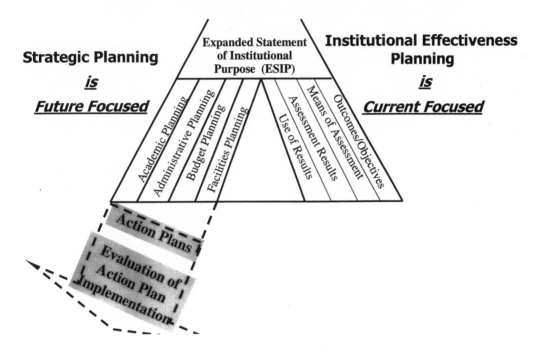

very *ends* or *outcomes* oriented, focusing upon the current results of the institution's efforts (as opposed to the processes implemented to bring about these results) as measured by services provided by AES units and student learning in educational programs. This "Current Focus" is also contrasted to the "Future Focus" of plans resulting from the institution's strategic planning activities. Institutional effectiveness is characterized by the following:

- Describing expected results through construction of educational (student learning) outcomes and administrative objectives/outcomes
- Selecting of the means of assessment that will best determine the accomplishment of those outcomes and objectives identified
- Actually conducting the assessment and recording of the data (results) of that assessment
- Describing of how the data collected from assessment activities were used to improve student learning and AES services

Though all of the regional accrediting associations support the use of assessment results, some explicitly suggest such use in strategic planning and budgeting. In the authors' opinion, if assessment activities are identified widely on the campus as the means through which to justify or drive budget requests, the use of these assessment results for learning and service improvements will substantially diminish. While a close relationship between planning and budgeting is certainly desirable, an equally close tie between assessment and budgeting undermines the process of learning and service improvement in several ways. First, if assessment results are seen as a primary justification for the request of additional resources, then the absence of additional resources will be widely utilized as a reason for not making learning and service improvements. Under these circumstances, many educational programs, as well as AES units, will never stop to consider what improvements could be made within existing resources but will move directly to make an assessment-justified request for additional learning or service resources which in many institutions stands little chance of funding. Second, in some programs and AES units, means of assessment and criteria for success will be crafted in such a way as to justify the request for additional resources rather than to improve learning or services. Third, both of the previously described circumstances will lead rapidly toward faculty and staff considering the assessment process as a means through which to "play the game" rather than to genuinely improve student learning and services.

The appropriate relationship between strategic planning and budgeting processes and institutional effectiveness or service or learning/service improvement activities is shown in Figure 3. Learning and service improvement activities should be primarily based upon the existing resources within each educational program and AES unit. However, upon rare occasion, it should be possible for assessment results to inform the strategic planning/budgeting process regarding resource requirements. Institutions are urged to give the manner or process through which this action may take place great consideration lest assessment become focused on resource acquisition rather than learning and service improvements.

Just as institutional effectiveness and assessment activities differ from strategic planning and budgeting, they also differ from personnel evaluation as well as CQI/TQM/Re-engineering. Since assessment activities in educational programs as well as administrative and educational support (AES) units are carried out by groups of individuals, the relationship to individual employee evaluation regarding either faculty or staff is inappropriate. There is little quicker way to kill assessment implementation than for the faculty or staff involved to believe that the process in which they are taking part for the formative purpose of learning or service improvement will be used against them for summative purposes or personnel evaluation. While both processes of employee evaluation and assessment are appropriate on a campus, they must be kept entirely separate, or those faculty and staff involved will only set intended outcomes/administrative objectives, means of assessment, and criteria for success which they are absolutely certain of accomplishing and, thereby, receiving pay increases, promotions, or tenure.

"If we are doing Continuous Quality Improvement/Total Quality Management (CQI/TQM) activities, do we also need to do assessment activities?" In those portions of a campus' administrative and educational support (AES) units where CQI/TQM activities are taking place, probably little more than slight reformatting of the work already being done will be necessary to satisfy the regional accrediting association's assessment requirements. On the other hand, even mentioning Total Quality Management or Continuous

Quality Improvement as a description of assessment activities will be greeted as anathema in all but a few academic disciplines, such as engineering and business. Clearly, these concepts do not travel well within the academic aspect of an institution.

Re-engineering is currently a popular "buzz word" on college and university campuses and one which has a number of potential meanings. In general, re-engineering describes the disassembly of existing administrative processes, the examination of each component of the process, improvement of each component (often through greater automation), and ultimately reassembly based upon the processes conducted at an institution. The basic assumption behind re-engineering is that all units taking part do so intensively. On the other hand, assessment activities in AES units primarily function based upon the assumption that "if it ain't broke, don't fix it" and focus upon those components of each administrative and educational support unit which the units believe are most in need of improvement. The concept of re-engineering is even less well received than TQM/CQI within the academic aspects of an institution.

## Description of the Five-Column Model

Transition from the theory of Institutional Effectiveness described earlier in Figure 2 to a model more applicable to the program and service unit level is accomplished through the Five Column Model. This model's relationship to the previously described Institutional Effectiveness Paradigm is illustrated in Figure 6.

Note that the descriptive titles on the model shown in Figure 2 have been replaced (or supplemented) by the column numbers depicted in Figure 7 which follows.

Shown in Figure 7 is the Five-Column Model (in this case for the Undergraduate English Program) which (a) meets regional accreditation requirements, (b) is the simplest manner through which to implement institutional effectiveness or assessment for learning/service improvement, and (c) is the result of implementation on hundreds of campuses throughout the country of the procedures described in this book.

The model was developed initially as the Three-Column Model, depicting an assessment plan for each educational program, as well as administrative and educational support units. During the mid-90s, the three-column model was expanded to five columns in order to show completed assessment results and the use of those results to improve learning/service improvement.

In the **first column** of the model, the relationship of the individual degree program or administrative and educational support (AES) unit to the expanded statement of institutional purpose is related. All regional accrediting associations require that assessment activities ultimately link to and provide evidence of the accomplishment of the institutional statement of purpose. This linkage is most often to a listing of institutional level goals.

The **second column** in the model provides the educational (student learning) outcomes identified by the English department faculty (in this example) for the undergraduate program in English. In the case of administrative and educational support (AES) units, these statements would have been administrative objectives/outcomes.

## FIGURE 6
### *The Institutional Effectiveness Paradigm and the Five-Column Model*

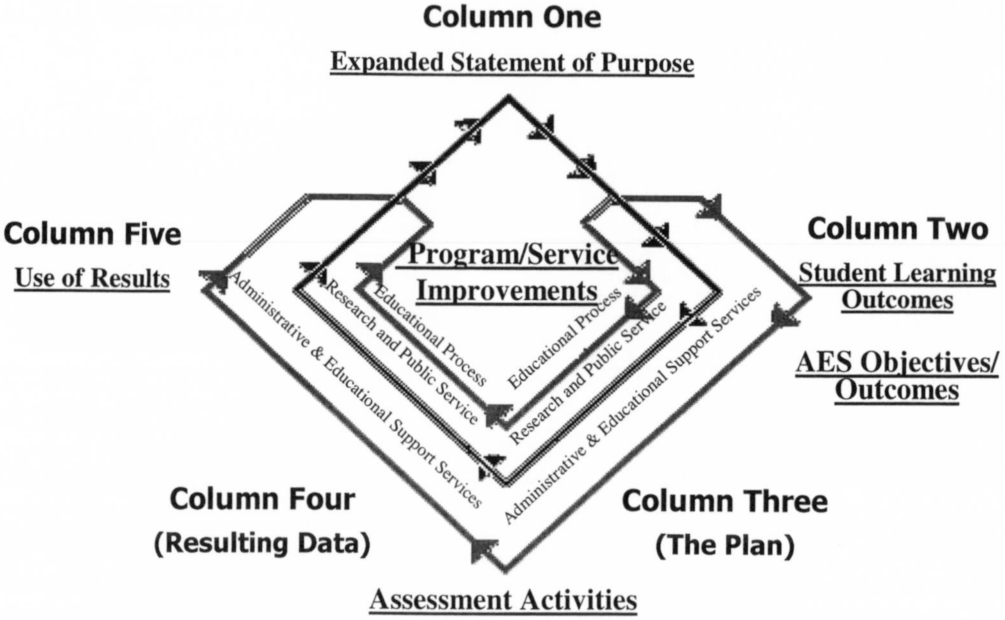

**Column One**

Expanded Statement of Purpose

**Column Five**

Use of Results

**Column Two**

Student Learning Outcomes

AES Objectives/ Outcomes

Program/Service Improvements

Administrative & Educational Support Services

Research and Public Service

Educational Process

Educational Process

Research and Public Service

Administrative & Educational Support Services

**Column Four**

(Resulting Data)

**Column Three**

(The Plan)

Assessment Activities

Not until the **third column** of the model are the specific means of assessment regarding each educational (student learning) outcome or administrative objective/outcomes identified. This apparent delay is in order to limit the amount of assessment activity at a campus and to focus that activity taking place only upon the intended outcomes or administrative objectives identified. In addition to the means of assessment, a specific "Criteria for Success" regarding each program or AES unit are provided. Identification of this "benchmark" by the faculty or staff in the program or unit is the single most important factor in the ultimate use of the data resulting from execution of the means of assessment for program/service improvement.

The **fourth column** of the model describes briefly the assessment data resulting from the actual implementation of the means of assessment described. This column provides credibility to the overall process and should focus upon the intended outcomes or administrative objectives/outcomes identified in the second column.

All of the previously described columns are intent upon focusing outcomes and means of assessment on the provision of data for ultimate use in the **fifth column** of the model. This "Use of Results" column is the most important portion of the five-column model and the center of regional accrediting association attention

# Figure 7

## Undergraduate English Program–Five-Column Model

| Expanded Statement of Institutional Purpose | Program Intended Educational Outcomes: | Means of Program Assessment and Criteria for Success: | Summary of Data Collected: | Use of Results: |
|---|---|---|---|---|
| **Institutional Mission Statement:**<br><br>The principal focus of Our University's curricular program is undergraduate education in the liberal arts and science… | 1. Students completing the baccalaureate program in English will compare very favorably in their knowledge of literature with those students completing a similar program nationally. | 1a. The average score of the graduates of the BA program in English on the MFAT "Literature in English" will be at or near the 50th percentile compared to national results and no subscale score will be below the 30th percentile.<br><br>1b. On the Graduating Student Questionnaire, 90% of the English BA program graduates will "agree" or "strongly agree" with the statement "In the field of literature, I feel as well prepared as the majority of individuals nation wide who have completed a similar degree during the past year." | 1a. MFAT score for year's graduates (18) found to be at the 37th percentile. This was due to a 23rd percentile score on the "American Literature" subscale.<br><br>1b. 93% responded "agree" or "strongly agree." | 1a. Course offerings in "American Literature" were reviewed to ascertain degree of match with MFAT "American Literature" subscale. Added additional course LIT 317 (Survey of American Lit) as requirement.<br><br>1b. Criteria met. At this time no action required. Question is deleted from next year's questionnaire. Faculty has added question relating to electronic reviews of literature. |
|  | 2. Graduates will be able to critique a brief draft essay. | 2. As part of a "capstone course" during the final semester, students will critique a short draft essay. 80% of the program's graduates will identify 90% of the errors in the draft essay. Additionally, none of the 14 rubrics utilized to evaluate the student's critique will appear to be consistently unmet. | 2. 92% of graduates identified 87% of errors. However, grammatical conventions regarding capitalization were not consistently applied. | 2. Faculty use of commonly accepted conventions regarding capitalization in reviewing upper division papers has been emphasized. |
| **Institutional Goal:**<br><br>…all graduates of baccalaureate level will have developed a depth of understanding in their major field. | 3. Students completing the baccalaureate program will be capable of writing an acceptable journal article. | 3a. A jury of English dept. faculty from an institution comparable to Our University will judge 80% of those journal articles submitted acceptable for publication based on commonly accepted standards.<br><br>3b. 20% of journal articles submitted will be published in student or other publications. | 3a. 55% of articles reviewed were found acceptable for publication.<br><br>3b. 10% of articles were published. | 3a. English 407 (advanced writing) modified to include journal article exercise.<br><br>3b. Additional outlets for student publishing have been identified. |

Each of these columns will be described in considerably more detail in the following chapters; however, this overview of the resulting Five-Column Model provides the reader with some sense of direction for the rest of the publication.

Implementation of the institutional effectiveness paradigm shown in Figure 2 is certainly much easier described than accomplished. Yet, countless institutions across the country are being successful in using the results of carefully designed assessment procedures to precisely accomplish the purposes described in the paradigm. The balance of this publication is designed so that your institution can also reap the benefits of this process. While much institutional attention will be centered on meeting regional accrediting association requirements, it is important to constantly return institutional attention to improvement of learning and services as the *reason* and the primary benefit of the process rather than satisfaction of accrediting association requirements, which is the *occasion* for highlighting what we are doing.

# CHAPTER THREE

# STRUCTURES, PLANS, AND STRATEGIES FOR INSTITUTIONAL EFFECTIVENESS OR ASSESSMENT IMPLEMENTATION

*Very few successful journeys begin without careful planning and preparation. The road to successful implementation of institutional effectiveness or assessment on a campus should likewise be taken only after thorough consideration of the route and challenges likely along the way. While no plans for assessment implementation can take into account all eventualities, many of the pitfalls which have ended other such journeys can be avoided with only a modest amount of forethought.*

Both external and internal reasons exist for an institution to carefully plan its assessment activities. As states or regions begin assessment processes, an institution may find itself required to submit an assessment plan to an external agency such as the legislature, state governing board, or regional accrediting association within a relatively short time frame. Often an institution is given little guidance and few suggestions about the specific format or content of the required plan. Unfortunately, such guidance may be provided only later when the reviewing agency explains why the institution's assessment plan has been found to be unacceptable. The other (internal) reason for comprehensive campus assessment planning is the genuine need to coordinate various institutional assessment activities that would otherwise be carried on independently.

Three general concepts underlie assessment planning. Assessment planning should be characterized by the following:

- Focus upon intended educational (student learning) outcomes or administrative objectives/outcomes
- Dynamic in nature
- Only secondarily involved in the preparation of a document which might bear the title "Assessment Plan"

The event immediately preceding evaluation of achievement or assessment in the Institutional Effectiveness Paradigm shown in Figure 2 is the identification of "Intended Outcomes and Objectives," which are linked to and support the expanded statement of institutional purpose. Therefore, the focus or target of assessment planning activities at the institution is the determination of the extent to which the outcomes and objectives identified have been achieved. Any other assessment planning or action at the institution not directly attributable to or connected with ascertaining the accomplishment of identified intended outcomes or objectives is superfluous and wasteful of institutional resources. Among the institutions taking part in *Assessment Case Studies*, it was estimated that almost half of their initial effort expended on assessment activities was not focused on intended educational (student learning) outcomes or administrative and educational support objectives and hence, in many cases, was wasted.

One of the great misconceptions about documents bearing the title "Assessment Plan" is that once conceived and, if necessary, approved by whatever external agency, they are "written in stone." In fact, assessment planning is exceedingly dynamic in nature and must respond rapidly to changes in intended outcomes or objectives as well as experiences with means of assessment.

Too often, the focus of assessment planning becomes the creation of the written document entitled "Assessment Plan." When the focus of attention is the written document, the emphasis frequently shifts to the acceptability of the Assessment Plan to off-campus authorities, rather than the coordination of on-campus operations. When this happens, the plan tends to be seen on campus as less important in terms of feasibility or workability. It is not uncommon for an Assessment Plan to be submitted and found to be entirely acceptable by off-campus authorities and then prove to be totally unworkable on the campus. The plan should focus on the subject of assessment implementation and not the attractiveness of the plan.

### Issues in Assessment Planning

A series of organizational and policy level issues initially need to be addressed in planning for assessment implementation. Philosophically, among the first issues to be addressed in implementation planning is the degree of centralized or decentralized assessment coordination and support to take place on campus. Many advantages exist to a highly centralized approach to assessment activities on a campus. These advantages include: (a) the ability to focus the best expertise available on assessment issues within departments, (b) relative efficiency as resident "experts" replace novices and as economies of scale reduce the per unit cost of assessment activities, such as questionnaires, and (c) the ability to control the process, thus insuring uniform and comprehensive implementation throughout all disciplines in the institution. On the other hand, the primary limitations of this approach are its very considerable and apparent additional cost resulting from the significant growth in budgets associated with centralized implementation and the probable lack of faculty interest, involvement, or responsibility for the assessment process.

The completely decentralized approach to assessment implementation (which some people might call the "dump it on the faculty and staff" approach), practiced at too many institutions in our opinion, has a number of apparent liabilities as well as benefits. From the administration's standpoint, little centralized cost escalation will be involved with such an effort, and faculty/staff involvement will be guaranteed since the responsibility is exclusively their own. On the other hand, such a totally decentralized approach (a) provides no assurance that individual academic departments and AES units will implement the desired assessment activities, (b) is extremely inefficient as few economies of scale can be realized and each lesson learned must be repeated in every department, and (c) distracts from instructional and service operations as departments are required to commit their already limited resources to support assessment activities.

On most campuses, a compromise between a totally centralized and totally decentralized approach to assessment implementation is put into place in recognition of the fact that neither the faculty nor the administration is capable of successful implementation on its own. A judgment is necessarily made regarding which aspects of implementation can best be handled at the institutional level and which at the departmental or unit level. Those activities frequently identified as best handled at the institutional level include: overall coordination, the conduct of survey research, and administration of standardized testing. Responsibility for locally developed cognitive testing, performance testing, and other matters is often decentralized to the departmental or unit level.

Initial assessment planning should be based upon determination of what assessment activities are currently taking place at the institution. Because the academic enterprise tends to be separated into colleges, schools, departments, and even down to the course level, communication from one academic department to another about activities which are taking place is at best only limited.

An experience that illustrates this limited communication occurred during the authors' service as consultants on one campus. During the training session, a practical exercise was assigned to assure that the participants understood the material and were able to apply the concepts. The exercise called for the group to identify existing "locally developed" means of assessment and to evaluate their use for assessment purposes. The authors witnessed what could most charitably be described as an "explosion" in one working group as a member rose to her feet and began shaking her finger excitedly at another of the participants. The institution's head librarian had just learned that the chief student services officer had been distributing an exiting student questionnaire for over ten years, which the librarian had not known existed. The survey included several questions concerning the library, and the highly critical results of that survey had never been shared with the librarian.

Figure 8 provides a format for identifying existing assessment data and activities on a campus. In the authors' opinion, usually between 30% and 35% of the assessment data ultimately needed by an institution is already available on the campus and can be identified through the early conduct of an inventory of assessment activities currently underway on the campus. Once this inventory is complete, it is important that its results be published in order for those on the campus to see examples of where assessment activities are already in place in many components of the institution.

## Figure 8

### FORMAT FOR IDENTIFYING EXISTING ASSESSMENT DATA

For each study or data set, identify the following:

| What is it (brief description)? | Who has it (office/person)? | What population does it cover (e.g., freshmen, remedial students, etc.)? | When was it done (i.e., term, year, etc.)? | Special features or limitations |
|---|---|---|---|---|
|  |  |  |  |  |
|  |  |  |  |  |

Source: Peter T. Ewell and Robert P. Lisensky, ASSESSING INSTITUTIONAL EFFECTIVENESS. (Washington: Consortium for the Advancement of Private Higher Education, 1988, p. 55).

Among those disciplines likely to report assessment activities already in place are the allied health areas — nursing, inhalation therapy, radiological technology etc., and other disciplines with professional accreditation requirements, such as the National Council for the Accreditation of Teacher Education (NCATE) and the American Association of Collegiate Schools of Business (AACSB). In addition to these areas, assessment activity will also likely be taking place in disciplines within which there are professional licensure requirements. In both of these instances, professionals practicing in the field have taken the initiative to assure the overall quality of their graduates and in so doing often establish an assessment program both to improve the performance of their programs and to ensure the public of at least minimal levels of competence by the practitioners in the field. These existing programs can continue, but their resulting documentation will need to be adapted to the institutional documentation format.

## Planning of the Assessment Process at the Departmental/Unit Level

Design or planning of the assessment processes within the institution will need to take place in direct response to identification of intended educational (student learning) outcomes and administrative objectives/outcomes as well as means of assessment within academic departments and AES units. **A clear order to this process exists. First, educational (student learning) outcomes and administrative objectives/outcomes are formulated by respective academic and administrative or educational support units. Then, means of assessment are identified.**

The natural tendency at this point in the implementation process is for faculty and staff as they begin working on the development of their program or unit assessment plans to focus upon the means of assessment first, rather than upon the educational (student learning) outcomes or administrative objectives/outcomes the achievement of which the assessment plans are intended to measure. This reversal of implementation order happened at several of the "Case Study" institutions, and the authors have experienced this on campus after campus. Why do institutions shift planning from identification of intended educational (student learning) outcomes to the means of assessment at this point? Based on the authors' experiences and those of several institutions described in *Assessment Case Studies*, there seems to be several reason for this tendency. First, the means of assessment are **tangible**, can be observed by the participants, and are the subject of much national attention. Second, by moving immediately to the means of assessment, necessary substantive discussions concerning the nature of the discipline and individual differences of opinion can be avoided or at least postponed. Third, as programs and units begin the assessment process, they are often overwhelmed at the perceived difficulty and additional time assessment will require, and they look for any short cut. Each of these reasons leads to actions which actually delay final implementation success through use of results.

In planning for assessment implementation, it is absolutely essential that planning for the means of assessment follow or flow from the identification of intended educational (student learning) outcomes and administrative objectives. If this is not the case, two events tend to transpire on campuses. First, much effort is wasted as institutions "do assessment" and then try to ascertain what they had intended to measure. This is most easily identified on campuses where literally mounds of assessment data are present, but the use of results is almost totally absent. Second, the extent of use of assessment results is greatly diminished as the faculty members have depleted their energy in developing the assessment process. Therefore, they have lost the willingness to focus their efforts before they get to the more difficult and substantive act of using the results.

The single greatest mechanism for saving money in the cost of assessment activities is to limit the amount of assessment accomplished to only enough to verify accomplishment of intended educational (student learning) outcomes and administrative objectives. The best assessment techniques in the world, not focused upon intended educational (student learning) outcomes or administrative objectives/outcomes, are a waste of precious resources and should be eliminated in the planning stage before ever taking place on the campus.

The relationship in assessment planning between selection of intended educational (student learning) outcomes and identification of the means of assessment is a sensitive one. Frequently, faculty will initially identify intended educational (student learning) outcomes which can only be described as "ideal." On the other side of the table (literally in some cases), those charged with assisting in the design or planning of the institutional assessment process are more likely to be concerned with more pragmatic issues regarding the feasibility of implementation of the means of assessment. In the long run, what most often takes place is the selection of important intended educational (student learning) outcomes and administrative objectives/outcomes which have been refined or focused into "operational terminology" and are more subject to identification of means of assessment. In this process, neither faculty "idealist" nor assessment "pragmatist" is victorious, but a working compromise between these two often extreme points of view is established.

While the emphasis in assessment planning for use to guide campus implementation is on "planning rather than the paperwork," the patterns of thought reflected in Figure 9, "Assessment Planning Conceptual Matrix," and Figure 10, "Assessment Planning Detailed Documentation," on the following pages may be useful. The Conceptual Matrix shown in Figure 9 relates a specific intended educational (student learning) outcome to the types of assessment activities to be utilized to ascertain the accomplishment of that outcome. Keeping this "one on one" relationship between intended educational (student learning) outcomes and means of assessment clear to all parties is important. Otherwise, means of assessment tend to take on a life of their own, cease to be a means, and become an end in themselves.

Figure 10, "Assessment Planning Detailed Documentation," takes the logic outlined above one step further, and for each means of assessment identified in the conceptual matrix poses a series of questions concerning its implementation. Carried to the extreme across a large and complex institution, the implementation of either of these models would create a mountain of assessment planning paper, which is unnecessary on most campuses. However, the organizational structure upon which these figures are premised should be considered by those planning and designing the assessment process on any campus.

**Figure 9**

## ASSESSMENT PLANNING CONCEPTUAL MATRIX

| Undergraduate English Program | Means of Assessment | | | | | |
| --- | --- | --- | --- | --- | --- | --- |
| | Cognitive Measures | | | | Attitudinal Measures | |
| Intended Outcomes | Local | MFAT | Licensure | | Graduating Student | Alumni |
| 1. Students completing the Baccalaureate program in English will compare very favorably in their knowledge of literature with those students completing a similar program nationally. | | √ | | | √ | |

# Figure 10

## ASSESSMENT PLANNING
## DETAILED DOCUMENTATION

Program/Department: Undergraduate English Program

Intended Outcome/Objective: Students completing the Baccalaureate program in English will compare very favorably in their knowledge of literature with those students completing a similar program nationally.

| Means of Assessment | What | When | Responsible | Type of Feedback | Use of Results |
|---|---|---|---|---|---|
| 1a. The average scores of the graduates of the Baccalaureate program in English on the "Literature in English" MFAT subject test (which they will be required to take shortly before graduation) will be at or near the 50th percentile compared to national results. | | | | | |
| 1b. Ninety percent of the graduates of the English Baccalaureate program will "agree" or "strongly agree" with the statement "In the field of literature I feel as well prepared as the majority of individuals nation wide who have completed a similar degree during the past year." | | | | | |

## Implementation Timing and Logistics

Following the necessary organizational/institutional activities and detailed design at the important departmental level, careful planning needs to take place regarding initial implementation of assessment activities. The timing of most assessment activities on campuses tends to be "spring loaded," as most institutions, including community colleges, graduate the majority of their students at the close of the second term in approximately May/June of each year. Because most assessment activity is focused around end-of-program measures, this particular time of year is one of very heavy assessment effort. Summer and fall program completing or graduation periods' data should be added to that data gathered each spring in order to present a year-round or annual picture of student accomplishments. The summer and fall periods usually have substantially fewer graduates and may also be useful in "pilot testing" means of assessment before their full implementation in the spring.

Every attempt should be made through careful planning to spread assessment activities that can be moved from the late second term into other parts of the academic year. As an example, Alumni and Employer Surveys can be conducted in the fall term without doing damage to response rates. Wherever possible, the assessment workload should be spread as evenly as possible throughout the academic year.

The sheer logistics or "person power" necessary to accomplish most institutions' assessment activities is staggering. Volunteer assistance from members of the faculty as well as from professional and clerical staff will provide some of the hands necessary to conduct assessment activities. Also, the student government can be expected to provide a modest level of assistance on some campuses. However, it may well be necessary to employ on a temporary basis additional personnel to stuff envelopes, administer examinations, collect results, etc., during the late spring semester or potentially the early summer. Unfortunately, the highest demand for assessment activities (late spring) occurs just as much of the voluntary assistance pool (faculty and students) are leaving for the summer.

Planning for initial implementation at institutions with the foresight to begin this process well in advance provides the luxury of being able to phase in campus-wide implementation over a period of several years. This phase-in can take the form of one or more components initially beginning the implementation process while others begin the next year. This approach has the advantage of allowing lessons learned from the initial components of the institution implementing the process to be put into use in the other units of the institution beginning implementation the following year. On the authors' own campus, implementation was commenced over a two-year period with one half of the academic programs and AES units (spread across all colleges or departments) beginning assessment activities during the first academic year and the balance of the university during the following year. This approach allows the luxury of easing into the assessment burden sure to follow initial departmental implementation and can facilitate an alternate year approach to assessment reporting.

The alternate year reporting sequence also eases a portion of the logistical burden of assessment implementation. With this approach (while all programs and AES units do assessment activities each year), only a pre-designated half of those programs and units submit reports each year. This alternative year reporting cycle (a) eases the paperwork on the units, (b) makes it more feasible to review and respond to each assessment plan/report, (c) helps small programs to accumulate a sufficient or meaningful number of graduates for making decisions to change, and (d) is sufficient to satisfy regional accrediting association requirements. However, this alternative reporting cycle is usually not initially possible for institutions rushing to complete a single comprehensive set of plans/reports for review as soon as possible for the regional accrediting agency.

### Preparing the Assessment Plan

While the primary purpose of this section has been to describe actual assessment planning in preparation for implementation, the authors certainly also acknowledge the need to provide, upon occasion, assessment plans to representatives of state government as well as regional accrediting associations. The outline in Figure 11 is provided as a suggestion for such an assessment plan. This outline of a plan was developed after studying several regional accrediting association guidelines concerning assessment plans as well as the actual assessment plans of numerous institutions. While not warranted to meet any regional accrediting association's expectations, it is provided as a good starting point from which the institution may develop its own assessment plan.

Assessment planning is essential to successful implementation; however, it should be acknowledged that it is impossible to cover all eventualities in any assessment planning. Therefore, the refinements to assessment planning, made annually, constitute a never-ending dynamic adjustment to institutional assessment practices. From the experiences of the case study institutions, clearly those institutions which had made the effort to establish a straightforward plan for assessment activities were among those likely to have been able to demonstrate the use of results for the improvement of academic programming and administrative and educational support services. Doubtlessly, this is now the case at the majority of institutions nationwide.

One of the first questions which will need to be addressed on each campus is the structure or means through which to best implement assessment or institutional effectiveness activities. The choices are basically two: the incorporation of institutional effectiveness and assessment activity into existing institutional procedures or the establishment of a separate institutional effectiveness or assessment cycle.

### Incorporation of Institutional Effectiveness/Assessment into Existing Institutional Procedures

A strong case can be (and usually is) made *for* incorporation of assessment activities into existing institutional procedures. Normally, one hears argumentation regarding avoidance of the "duplication of effort" and the requirement, through association with an existing institutional procedure, that assessment will actually take place each year.

**Figure 11**

# Suggested Outline for Assessment Plan

I. <u>Assessment Philosophy</u>

    A. **Formative nature of assessment activities**

    B. **Assessment as a means through which to improve student learning as well as administrative and educational support services**

    C. **Secondary importance of regional accreditation, state accountability reporting, and performance funding**

II. <u>Description of Planned Assessment Procedures</u>

    A. **Relationship to mission and goals**

    B. **Identification of programs/units (including General Education)**

    C. **Description of institutional assessment cycle (consider using paradigm)**

    D. **Common format for assessment planning and reporting (consider using Five-Column Model or ARB forms)**

    E. **Institutional level means of assessment**

        1. **Surveys - alumni, graduating student**

        2. **General Education measures**

    F. **Procedures through which to insure use of results or "closing the loop" (linkage, if any, to strategic planning/budgeting)**

III. <u>Roles in Implementation</u>

    A. **Faculty role in design and implementation of assessment procedures**

        1. **Policy level substantive guidance**

        2. **Primary leadership within instructional programs**

    B. **Administrative roll**

        1. **Responsibility of deans & departmental administrators**

        2. **Limitation of administrative role**

    C. **Leadership role**

        1. **Importance of assigning individual**

        2. **Establishment of a faculty based Assessment Committee**

IV. <u>Assessment Logistics</u>

    A. **Establishment of a realistic timeline for implementation**

    B. **Personnel supporting assessment implementation**

    C. **Funding for means of assessment**

V. <u>Implementation Evaluation</u>

    A. **Review and critique of program and unit assessment plans and reports**

    B. **Evaluation of overall implementation plan results**

VI. <u>Program and Unit Assessment Plans</u>

    A. **Example assessment plans (three-column models) from all major institutional components**

    B. **Example assessment reports (five-column models) from as many areas as possible**

VII. <u>Strong Closing Statement</u>

    A. **The ability to implement —evidence that plan is already partly implemented**

    B. **The will to implement - commitment of Chief Executive Officer to plan implementation**

Much less frequently heard (but every bit as cogent) are the arguments *against* incorporation of institutional effectiveness or assessment activities into existing institutional procedures which include:

- Acquisition by assessment of whatever "baggage" is carried by the procedure into which it is incorporated--assessment is not the most popular subject on most campuses, to further burden it, by potential association with another "loathsome" procedure is almost a certain "death warrant."
- Conflicting terminology and structure--the basic unit of analysis for assessment purposes in the academic sector of the institution is "educational (student learning) programs;" while in most other processes, it is the academic department, which may be composed of a number of educational programs.
- Timing issues--association of assessment activities with other procedures invariably leads to adoption of the timing necessary for the existing procedures, which may or may not coincide with the best time to utilize assessment results.
- Differences in purposes--the purpose of assessment activities is formative in nature, leading to improvements; while the purposes of other procedures on campus are often summative, leading to judgments concerning individuals and potentially programs.

Incorporation of institutional effectiveness or assessment activities processes into the following existing institutional procedures is often attempted:

- Annual institutional reports
- External reports
- Program review
- Budget planning
- Strategic Planning

Incorporation of assessment activities into an institution's annual report can be accomplished successfully; however, it requires a very substantial cultural change at many institutions. Annual reports from the institutions, as well as their components, are primarily public relations — a document concerning how wonderfully the unit or institution has been functioning. How many corporate, institutional, or departmental annual reports have you ever read which admitted that some aspect of their operations was not functioning the way the entity thought it ought to function? However, this is the degree of candor which assessment requires before improvements can take place. It is exceedingly unusual that an institution will change its culture to this extent.

Only if departments and programs are given no choice but to address their intended outcomes and means of assessment in their annual report will this need be addressed. Otherwise, units will avoid the subject, unless they have achieved all of their intended outcomes. In this regard, the authors are familiar with one institution that has adopted a unique aspect of this annual report approach. Each year a retreat away from the college is held for several days during which senior administrators are required to make a half-hour presentation concerning the assessment activities accomplished dur-

ing the past year and the improvements made in their programming based on this assessment. This presentation is made in front of their contemporaries and the chief
executive officer of the institution. The lack of having any assessment information to
report, not to mention program improvements, had a very salutary effect on several
deans and led to substantive assessment/improvement implementation in the following year.

Incorporation of assessment activities into external reporting requirements is a particularly attractive alternative in those states in which some type of assessment reporting is required. Such incorporation into external reporting evidences a number of
limitations. First, external assessment reporting requirements dictate which data are to
be provided and tend to discourage departmental faculty involvement. "If 'they' are going to dictate to 'us,' then why should we be involved?" Second, the external data requirements often do not match the intended outcomes established in the various
academic programs. Frequently, the measures dictated by external agencies describe
the educational *process* as opposed to the *outcomes* or results of that process and lead
to confusion regarding this important differentiation. Finally, the timing of external reporting may not coincide with the opportunity for institutional collection of the information. In one state with which the authors are acquainted, a "report card" type of
legislation requires "assessment data" to be reported by each institution as the legislature comes into session in February. Because of this timing, the data reported to the legislature is primarily taken from the end of the spring semester (almost nine months
previous to the reporting).

Without any doubt, though, the primary disadvantage of incorporation of internal assessment and program improvement procedures into external reporting requirements is
the fact that the emphasis on the campus shifts from program improvement to *pleasing
the external agency.* In essence, instead of improving programs, the institution is "playing
the game." While apparently an attractive alternative, the authors have never been associated with a successful institutional effectiveness or assessment implementation associated with an institution's external reporting.

Frequently, institutions seek to incorporate assessment activities into their program
review process. The term "program review" has a number of meanings. If the primary
purpose of the program review process on a campus is perceived by the faculty (whether
intended or not) as related to program discontinuance, then the reaction of the faculty will
be to "circle the wagons." Under these circumstances, nothing other than outcomes which
the faculty are absolutely positive of successfully accomplishing will be proposed, and
no improvement of learning, or services in the case of AES units, is likely to take place.
In addition, if the program review process occurs periodically (3-5 years), little assessment activity is likely to take place between reviews unless steps are taken to require interim measures.

It is possible to implement assessment and institutional effectiveness activities successfully within a program review process but only if great care is taken in the design of
that process. If the process is designed to include both the potential for program termination and program improvement, then the two separate components of the process should

be clearly described and data utilized for the program termination component (number of staff, number of students, number of graduates, etc.) should be clearly separated from those data, such as employment rates, standardized tests scores, locally developed assessment results, etc., associated with the program improvement components. No doubt should exist in anyone's mind regarding the distinct separation of these components, and the information from the program improvement aspect should never be utilized in relationship to program termination.

In addition to the above differentiation between functions of the program review process, it will be necessary to establish some type of interim reporting procedures between complete program reviews. The purpose of this procedure should be for programs to report their assessment activities and use of results concerning the program improvement component of the process. This should alleviate the potential problem regarding the conduct of assessment activities only every three to five years.

Earlier, in Chapter Two, incorporation of assessment activities into ongoing strategic planning and budgeting processes were discussed. Suffice it to say, that such an incorporation, while appearing attractive, is the least likely method to result in successful implementation of assessment activities. While incorporation of assessment activities into each of the potential existing institutional procedures referenced is an apparently attractive option, there exists just as strong a justification for not accomplishing this end. It is distinctly possible that incorporation of assessment activities into any of these existing procedures will be detrimental to the future of both procedures.

### The Separate Institutional Effectiveness Cycle

Rather than incorporation into any of the existing institutional processes referenced, it is the authors' suggestion that a separate process be put in place for assessment. The advantages of a separate annual institutional effectiveness cycle include: its timing to correspond with data and faculty availability, its focus on program and service improvement, and its complimentary relationship with existing procedures. The primary disadvantages of such a process are its appearance as an additional chore to be accomplished each year and the need to sustain such a cycle separately without reference to external requirements such as budgeting or reporting. Nonetheless, after working with over three hundred institutions, it is the authors' opinion that the establishment of a separate annual cycle can be accomplished with a minimum of effort and with maximum benefit.

Such an annual cycle should be established at the end of the generic implementation shown in Figure 12 (explained in greater detail below). This cycle would be applicable to administrative and educational support (AES) units, as well as academic programs, and would highlight program/service improvements. While this plan was designed only for educational programs, assessment of AES services is growing in importance for comprehensive institutional effectiveness, and the process steps fit very nicely for both. In Chapter Nine the differences between AES units and educational programs will be highlighted in greater detail.

# Figure 12

## A Generic Model for Implementation of Institutional Effectiveness and Assessment Activities in Higher Education

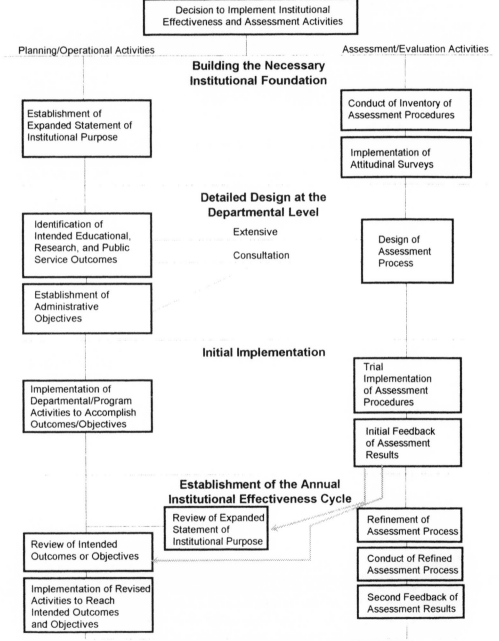

Decision to Implement Institutional Effectiveness and Assessment Activities

Planning/Operational Activities          Assessment/Evaluation Activities

**Building the Necessary Institutional Foundation**

Establishment of Expanded Statement of Institutional Purpose

Conduct of Inventory of Assessment Procedures

Implementation of Attitudinal Surveys

**Detailed Design at the Departmental Level**

Extensive

Consultation

Identification of Intended Educational, Research, and Public Service Outcomes

Design of Assessment Process

Establishment of Administrative Objectives

**Initial Implementation**

Implementation of Departmental/Program Activities to Accomplish Outcomes/Objectives

Trial Implementation of Assessment Procedures

Initial Feedback of Assessment Results

**Establishment of the Annual Institutional Effectiveness Cycle**

Review of Expanded Statement of Institutional Purpose

Review of Intended Outcomes or Objectives

Refinement of Assessment Process

Conduct of Refined Assessment Process

Implementation of Revised Activities to Reach Intended Outcomes and Objectives

Second Feedback of Assessment Results

REPEAT FOURTH-YEAR ACTIVITIES -- CONDUCT COMPREHENSIVE INSTITUTIONAL AND PROCESS EVALUATION IN EIGHTH YEAR

End of Implementation Year

*The Generic Plan for Implementation*—In 1986 as *A Practitioner's Handbook For Institutional Effectiveness and Student Outcomes Assessment Implementation* was being initially conceived, the generic model shown on page 18 of that publication and reproduced in this document as Figure 12 was developed to depict a reasonable model for implementation over a four-year period. This period of four years was based upon an assumption of absolutely "Ground Zero" implementation currently in existence on the campus and the ultimate need to be comprehensively implemented.

The phases in implementation described in Figure 12 remain as current today as they were at that time and are described below in the excerpt taken from a *Practitioner's Handbook*.

### Building the Necessary Institutional Foundation

During the first year of implementation, most activity of a planning/operational nature will be focused on "Establishment of an Expanded Institutional Statement of Purpose" as a foundation for further activities. The "Implementation of Attitudinal Surveys" and the "Conduct of an Inventory of Assessment Procedures" (as currently being employed at the institution or available to the institution) highlight the assessment/evaluation activities during the first year or period of implementation and can be described as **Building the Necessary Institutional Foundation**.

### Detailed Design at the Departmental Level

The second year of implementation is characterized as **Detailed Design at the Departmental Level**; during which time the work accomplished the previous year at the institutional level will be extended to the departmental level. Planning/operational activities during the second year or period include the "Identification of Intended Education, Research, and Public Service Outcomes" and the "Establishment of Administrative Objectives," both of which are closely linked with, and support accomplishment of, the expanded statement of purpose developed during the first year of implementation. These important statements of intended outcomes and objectives are closely coordinated with the "Design of the Assessment Process," through which accomplishment of these intentions will be evaluated.

### Initial Implementation

During the third year or period of implementation activities, the **Initial Implementation** of institutional effectiveness operations takes place. Based on its work during the previous year, the institution's components will be involved in "Implementation of Departmental/ Program Activities to Accomplish Intended Outcomes/Objectives." The primary events during this third year or period will be the "Trial Implementation of Assessment Procedures," as designed during the previous year, and the "Initial Feedback of Assessment Results."

### Establishment of the Annual Institutional Effectiveness Cycle

**Establishment of the Annual Institutional Effectiveness Cycle (AIEC)** is brought about in the fourth year of implementation activities. In that year, and each succeeding year, planning and operational activities will include a "Review of the Institutional Statement of Purpose," "Revision of Intended Outcomes or Objectives," and/or "Implementation of Revised Activities to Reach Original Intended Outcomes and Objectives." Likewise, during each year in the annual cycle, a "Refinement of the Assessment Process," "Conduct of Refined Assessment Procedures," and "Feedback of Assessment Results" will take place. It is within this AIEC that institutions will readily be able to demonstrate use of assessment results to improve programming and "Closing the Loop."

At this point in the development of the assessment movement across the country, very few campuses are literally at "Ground Zero" in their implementation efforts. While many colleges and universities have isolated pockets of implementation taking place, most campuses are in the more common situation of having had a series of failed implementation efforts on a campus-wide or individual unit basis. Often these previous efforts make current implementation more difficult because of the confusion and frustration left from their attempts in the past. Successful implementation at this stage in the assessment movement normally takes place with some combination of the first and second phases of the four-year model laid out in Figure 12 completed, coupled with a combined implementation of the third and fourth phases.

# Figure 13

*Two Year\* Sequence of Events Leading to Assessment/Institutional Effectiveness Implementation*

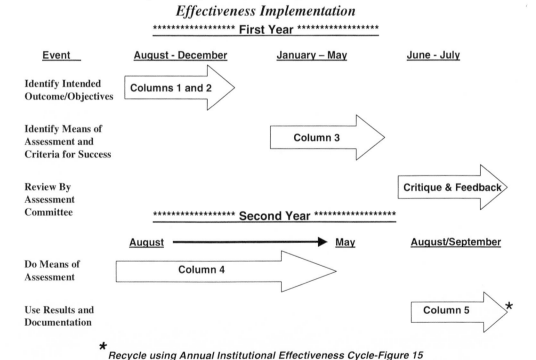

\* *Recycle using Annual Institutional Effectiveness Cycle-Figure 15*

Assuming the existence of a usable statement of purpose and the willingness to accept a relatively uneven first year use of results, assessment implementation is currently brought about on most campuses in a one- to two-year period of time. The two-year implementation model shown below in Figure 13 is the most common approach to assessment implementation and may begin anywhere between August and November of the first year. In this model, essentially during the first year, the first two phases of the four-year model or generic model shown in Figure 12 are implemented; while in the second year of the model, the third and fourth phrases of the generic implementation model are put in place. In this two-year model, the administrative and support services will probably move much faster than the academic or instructional programs will be expected to move.

Implementation of assessment activities within a single year is possible only if the process is begun at the very beginning of the academic year and if the institution is willing to endure the Herculean effort. The model shown in Figure 14 calls for detailed design at the departmental level in the early fall semester through early spring semester with initial implementation taking place at the end of the spring semester and a use of results at the beginning of the following fall semester. This is a pace which many institutions may find desirable but which few institutions are capable of sustaining with any degree of comprehensiveness.

Both the one- and two-year models outlined in Figures 13 and 14 approach implementation with the expanded statement of purpose being reviewed/refined separately and brought

## Figure 14

### *One Year (Rushed)\* Cycle for Implementation of Institutional Effectiveness*

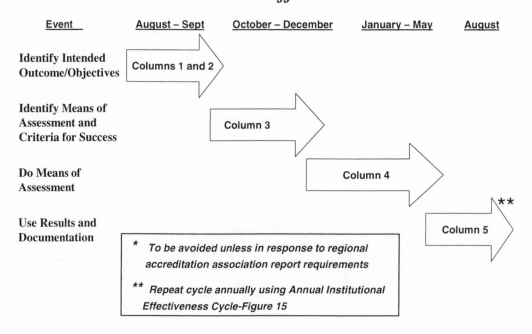

| Event | August – Sept | October – December | January – May | August |
|---|---|---|---|---|
| **Identify Intended Outcome/Objectives** | Columns 1 and 2 | | | |
| **Identify Means of Assessment and Criteria for Success** | | Column 3 | | |
| **Do Means of Assessment** | | | Column 4 | |
| **Use Results and Documentation** | | | | Column 5 ** |

\*  To be avoided unless in response to regional accreditation association report requirements

\*\*  Repeat cycle annually using Annual Institutional Effectiveness Cycle-Figure 15

into the process near the end rather than beginning of the process and result in a comprehensive, but uneven, implementation to closure of the loop. It is the authors' experience that roughly 80-90% of the programs and units will be able to "close the loop" at the end of the first assessment period, and it will be at the end of the second collection of data that implementation through closure of the loop will be relatively comprehensive across the institution.

Among the primary purposes of institutional effectiveness is the creation of a continuous program of assessment-based improvement in the campus' academic/instructional program and administrative and educational support (AES) units. That purpose is illustrated in the "Institutional Effectiveness Paradigm," Figure 12, and is applied to an institution's typical academic year calendar, shown below in Figure 15. This "Annual Institutional Effectiveness Cycle" (AIEC) is established at the end of the implementation process, described above in Figures 12 – 14, and takes place each year.

## Figure 15

### *Annual Institutional Effectiveness Cycle*\*

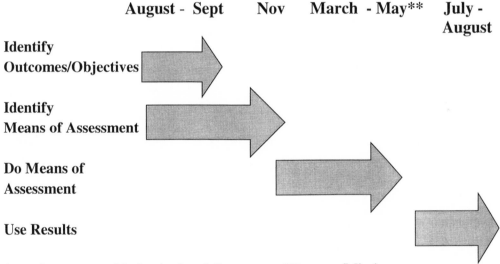

| August - Sept | Nov | March - May\*\* | July - August |

**Identify Outcomes/Objectives**

**Identify Means of Assessment**

**Do Means of Assessment**

**Use Results**

\*    Assumes usable Institutional Statement of Purpose/Mission
\*\*    Comprehensive assessment activities

*The Annual Institutional Effectiveness Cycle (AIEC)*—Just before the start of the fall term each year, each academic department revises the AIEC for each of its academic programs (five-column models), and AES units do the same for their models. This revision is based upon the closure of the previous year's plans and submission of the report concerning use of results as well as brief consideration of the fit or support of each educational program or AES unit with the Expected Institutional Statement of Purpose (ESIP). As part of this renewal process, both the short list of "Intended Educational (Student Learning) Outcomes" as well as AES unit objectives/outcomes (Column 2) and the "Means of Assessment with Criteria for Success" (Column 3) are revised.

It is very unusual for an entirely new short list of intended educational (student learning) outcomes to be identified. Rather, those outcomes not accomplished and those regarding which changes have been accomplished are normally retained for verification that the change was successful in making the improvement intended in student learning, while those accomplished are returned to the long list as an equal number are brought from the long list to the short list for assessment. However, care should be exercised that the "short list" of intended educational (student learning) outcomes never numbers more than five.

The description of the means of assessment (MOA) is annually revised for two reasons. First, revisions are made in the MOA to adjust performance and correct or improve administrative procedures. While this is technically "use of results," it does not constitute improvement of instructional programs. Second, entirely new MOA may well be required based upon the changed intended educational (student learning) outcomes established in Column 2. Adjustments to the criteria for success, while not required, are frequently made based upon participants' performance. Frequently, institutions will seek to review the revised assessment plans prior to their implementation during the balance of the academic year.

The revised assessment activities described are conducted at the close of the fall term, but the primary period of time for data gathering is just before the end of the spring semester when most institutional program completions or graduation takes place. Thus, while some assessment data are available in mid January each year, the great bulk of data concerning the institution's academic programs is not available until the June-July period each year. It may well be necessary for the institution to schedule faculty time (a summer contract) during the summer to process the data into usable and focused information for utilization by the departmental faculty members when they return for the fall term.

A separate occasion needs to be established for thoughtful consideration of the assessment information resulting from the activities concluded at the end of the immediately preceding spring semester. This type of careful consideration is not likely to occur during regular faculty meetings early in the fall term. Establishment of a day in August, while faculty are "on contract" but before the beginning of classes, for reviewing assessment results, determining their use, and completing the necessary documentation is by far the best approach to creating this separate opportunity for reflection. This time is frequently described as "Professional Development," "Fall Symposium," or "Fall Retreat" on many campuses. After such "closing of the loop" for the past academic year, requiring usually one half of a day, the faculty begins the yearly renewal of the Annual Institutional Effectiveness Cycle (AIEC) by creation of the assessment plan for the year just beginning. This step should also take approximately one-half of a day. Hence, after one and a half days at the beginning of each fall, faculty and staff will have completed assessment activities for the past academic year and will have established the assessment plan for the academic year just beginning.

The Annual Institutional Effectiveness Cycle (AIEC) for AES units is much more flexible than the cycle for academic units because of the twelve month nature of AES employees and the fact that their means of assessment are not as closely associated with the graduation cycle. While it is possible for institutions to establish a separate cycle for AES units, the components of the cycle will be similar to those shown in Figure 15. However, for many of the AES units, the period just before the beginning of the fall term is among the worst times for them to schedule an occasion for consideration of results from their means of assessment. On many campuses, mid-summer tends to be the best time for AES units to make their AIEC report and plan for the coming year. AES units often tie their assessment cycle better with the timing of the fiscal cycle used on many campuses of June 30 – July 1.

### Identifications of the Causes for Failed Previous Campus Implementation Efforts

As indicated earlier in this chapter, very few campuses across the country are completely without a history of implementation efforts. Most of these efforts can be described as partially successful, uneven, and discontinuous. As you begin the process of implementation, it will be very useful to determine why this is the case upon your own campus. Speculation as to the cause for failure to implement more fully on your campus will be easy to come by, depending upon those parties queried. A more systematic approach to identification for reasons for lack of implementation previously on your campus should be explored. This author has upon several occasions conducted such inquiry and found it extremely useful in designing the implementation plans specifically tailored to the needs of the campus.

It is best to begin this discovery with an open-ended survey of campus faculty and staff regarding the reasons for not having the desired full implementation of the Five-Column Model on the campus. As the degree of candor with which most faculty feel comfortable on a campus is remarkably limited, it is important that the responses be anonymous. The ten most typical reasons reported regarding how institutions *discourage implementation* of assessment activities include the following:

1. Considering Assessment as a *Passing Fad*
2. *Top Down* Implementation
3. Changes in Administration
4. Making Assessment *Too Much Work*
5. Procrastination until Too Late
6. Everyone's Thinking It's *Not My Job*
7. *Lack of Training f*or Those Who Must Implement
8. Considering Assessment Activities a *Meaningless Busy Work* or "Jumping through Hoops"
9. *Inadequate Funding* and Support from Administration
10. *Absence of Coordination* with Other Assessment and Reporting Requirements

Once these survey results are tabulated, a discussion of their relative importance by the assessment committee composed of primarily faculty discussed in Chapter Four will provide an interesting and fruitful topic for consideration. List on the left-hand side of a chalk or white board each of the reasons cited for failure to implement assessment activities fully on your campus. The authors suggest that this be done in priority order based upon the survey results. Then, on the right-hand side of the chalkboard, list those campus actions which can be taken to counter each of the perceived problems which have stalled implementation in the past. While the solution to some of the issues cited regarding matters such as "work load" are not readily identified, many of the issues brought forward can be initially addressed, therefore easing the way through previously identified problems and facilitating implementation. It is surprising how many of these issues once identified and fixed in plain view can be addressed in a manner which resolves issues that have heretofore stalled implementation.

### "Selling" Implementation on the Campus

The institution will need to get the attention of a number of audiences if assessment is to be implemented in a timely fashion. These audiences include: the faculty, staff, senior administrators, and those administrators responsible for implementation. By any stretch of the imagination, gaining the attention of the faculty will be the most difficult. Faculty members on most campuses perceive themselves as already heavily loaded with teaching responsibilities and, in general, loathe the introduction of what they perceive often as an additional "administrative" activity such as assessment into their already hectic lifestyles.

Staff members employed in educational support and administrative units are relatively compliant in acceptance of the requirement to do assessment. In many cases, assessment activity is already taking place in their units as part of some type of "quality enhancement" effort. In many cases all that has to be done is a change in format.

While it would seem apparent that senior administrators would be aware of assessment activities, they are another audience difficult to mobilize in support of this effort. Senior administrators tend to respond to that which they perceive as a threat to their administration of the institution. Therefore, it may be necessary to portray the negative aspects of not doing assessment based improvement to these individuals, rather than the more positive aspects of implementation, which will be referred to later.

The easiest group to mobilize in support of assessment is those administrators on campus who are the first individuals aware of the requirement and are hence most likely to be designated as responsible for seeing that assessment takes place. This awareness of assessment needs may take place through knowledge of regional accrediting association requirements, knowledge of the field of higher education and its development, or word of mouth discussions with colleagues on other campuses. For whatever reason, these individuals are normally self-motivated and will be "ready, willing, and able" to go forward with implementation.

A key to the mobilization of campus attention toward implementation will be understanding of the cause or reason for that activity. If faculty/staff members in particular see assessment activities as evaluations of themselves individually, they will likely be reluctant to take part willingly. Faculty, staff, and administrators need to understand that implementation of assessment activities is for the purpose of identification of areas for improvement and not for individual evaluation. The specific implementation activity may be *occasioned* by the forthcoming review by the regional accrediting association; however, the *reason* must always be stressed as the improvement of student learning and services.

In preparation for writing *Assessment Case Studies: Common Issues in Implementation with Various Campus Approaches to Resolution,* Agathon Press, 1995, considerable research was conducted concerning the most effective "message" in motivating faculty constituencies toward implementation. Beyond any doubt, the most effective message identified by the participant institutions was a blend of the "importance of assessment for improvement purposes" combined with the "need for continued institutional accreditation." In all cases, the punitive aspects of "assessment for accountability" proved to be a negative motivator and should be avoided in initial discussions with faculty (particularly concerning the importance of implementation). While some administrators respond very well to this message of "accountability," the majority of the campus community rebel at the notion of some outside party holding them accountable for the learning or services provided.

The most effective means for communicating "the message" concerning the importance of implementation of assessment activities on the campus was found to be a verbal as well as written follow-up communication from the chief executive officer of the institution concerning the subject. Such a verbal presentation might be made at the beginning of a fall or spring semester with a written follow-up sent immediately thereafter confirming to the campus community the importance of the subject. This communication from the highest level of the institution should be followed by similar communications from the vice presidential level. These communications should establish the responsibility for implementation and communicate a general timeline for implementation to take place. This timeline should be monitored for successful initiation to take place. Individuals simply need to understand that action is going to transpire and that it will be their responsibility to see that the required action takes place. It has been the authors' experience on the subject of assessment (as well as on other subjects) in higher education that those actions that are not "followed up" on campus generally do not take place in a comprehensive manner.

## Continuation of the Process Between Reviews

The only thing more difficult than starting assessment or institutional effectiveness operations on a campus is restarting them a number of years after they have been suspended. The "track record" across the country depicts institutions who successfully "geared up" assessment activities for accreditation and immediately following a successful conclusion of the accreditation review ceased the assessment efforts until the next time scheduled for review by their peers. The authors have actually heard the statement, "Well, those people (the accrediting association) won't be back for ten years, and I will be retired by that time."

Each time an institution starts and stops this type of process, initiation becomes progressively harder. This difficulty transpires because faculty in particular question the value of any procedure which is so quickly terminated following its use to satisfy external requirements. However, some steps can be taken to mitigate discontinuation.

The first of these actions is to design the process itself from its outset for simplicity and ease of continuation. The assessment process implemented should be as simple as possible and described on the campus from its inception as one of a continuous nature rather than episodic in nature geared only to the cycle of the regional accrediting association's review. While a sophisticated and burdensome assessment process may be initiated for a short term to satisfy the needs of an external party, it will not be continued over the longer haul. Far better to design a simple process within which the faculty and staff see long term value, than to seek to implement a short term solution "to dazzle" (hopefully) the reviewers.

In between regional accreditation efforts, professional accreditation can be utilized as a lever to continue the process of assessment in those fields taking part voluntarily in such endeavors. Almost all professional accreditation associations ask that assessment activities and improvements based thereon be included in their visitation requirements. Hence, faculty in those fields will be readily willing to continue assessment efforts between regional accrediting visits. This continued work can be publicized on campus to demonstrate to the rest of the faculty the value of continuing assessment activities.

Regardless of the occasion, successful assessment programs leading to the improvement of student learning and services need to be given high visibility by the institutional administration. Continuing positive comments by senior administrators regarding these efforts go far in stimulating other disciplines to continue assessment between regional accrediting visitations.

The continuation of the processes begun initially in order to satisfy regional accreditation requirements is among the best means through which to facilitate continuing assessment and improvement operations. On the authors' home campus in the year following the last accreditation review, 117 assessment reports were due by a given date. Over 110 reports were received on time by the university assessment committee. When asked to reflect upon why this level of continuation took place without the immediate threat of scrutiny by an external agency, many of the faculty members and department chairs stated that the *process* had become "part of our routine" and that they saw value in the use of results.

Ultimately, the continuation of assessment and improvement operations over any period of time will be contingent upon the amount of value attached to these operations by faculty and staff. If the process is accomplished in a manner that genuine improvements based upon a reasonable amount of assessment efforts can be readily identified on the campus, a high probability of continuation exists. If, on the other hand, the assessment burden has led to few improvements based upon great amounts of work, it is likely that the process will stall until called back into being by external factors of one type or another. A primary focus for those charged with assessment is to see that the former event rather than the later takes place on their campus.

The determination of the plans, structure, and strategies for the institution's assessment/institutional effectiveness implementation activities needs to be among the initial decisions reached by the institution, probably in conjunction with its assessment committee. It is important that, as the process identified is "launched," faculty and staff have a good sense of direction and the belief that those guiding implementation at the central administration level "know what they are doing" in order to inspire institutional confidence in the process.

# CHAPTER FOUR

# ROLES IN INSTITUTIONAL EFFECTIVENESS OR ASSESSMENT IMPLEMENTATION

*Road maps are utilized by individuals taking any trip. These individuals play a variety of roles during the journey—each different (driver, navigator, passengers, etc.) and all important. Just as in a "road trip," those implementing a successful program of institutional effectiveness or assessment activities must play various roles if the trip is to be characterized as "smooth and successful."*

Modern college and university administrators face one of the most complex leadership challenges in American society. This complexity is primarily due to the unique culture existing in higher education and the roles played by line administrators, as well as the faculty governance systems on campuses. While this milieu varies considerably from campus to campus and time to time, in the process of implementation of institutional effectiveness this complexity of relationships becomes quickly apparent.

Line administrators, individual faculty and staff, members of the institutional assessment committee, and a small core of individuals leading this process on each campus have distinct roles in implementation. Most of these roles call for persuasive rather than directive or coercive leadership. In every instance, working with faculty as well as staff, a collegial approach to implementation should be attempted prior to the necessity of becoming more directive.

## Institutional Level Roles and Functions

Line administrators (presidents, vice presidents, deans, department chairs/heads) are responsible for seeing that assessment activities are actually accomplished on campus. These individuals, if assessment activities are unsuccessful, will bear the brunt of criticism and must ultimately be held accountable. However, their roles in implementation of institutional effectiveness or assessment activities (particularly regarding the institution's academic programs) must be *through* persuasion, facilitation, and assistance. If line administrators become too directly involved with setting academic policy by establishment of outcomes, means of assessment, criteria for success, etc., without what is perceived as adequate input, then quickly many groups of faculty will disengage from the process and be more than happy to let the administrators take over the additional work. Unfortunately, the process can not be brought to successful conclusion by administrators alone as faculty members are necessary to make the necessary changes in the instructional program and curriculum. Thus, the role of line administrators can best be described as one of "gentle persuasion."

The most important thing that a chief executive officer (CEO) at an institution can accomplish in relationship to institutional effectiveness or assessment implementation is the persuasion of the campus community (particularly faculty) that this activity is a fundamental and important process of learning and service improvement which has his/her complete support and endorsement. The chief executive officer must stress that the **reason** for implementation of assessment activities is the improvement of student learning and educational support services and that the review by the regional accreditation association is merely the **occasion** for demonstrating this concern and continuing improvement. This acceptance is particularly important in order to facilitate institutional continuation of assessment activities following the (hopefully successful) review of the institution.

In addition to this important role of "selling" institutional effectiveness implementation, the chief executive officer should establish the structure for and funding of the project. The nature of the structure through which to guide implementation, its potential cost, and the criteria for selection of the campus leader are discussed later in this chapter. However, it is the chief executive officer who must initiate these activities and support them with his/her personal and visible commitment to the campus community.

Vice presidents and deans have a particularly difficult role to play in implementation. Administrative officers appointed to these positions normally are relatively assertive and focused on "getting things done." However, in this case, the most common advice which the authors offer to such officers is to "be constructive and encourage those you supervise in their implementation activities." Among the most dangerous of pitfalls in implementation is the creation of "layering" in which well-meaning administrative officers establish goals, objectives, outcomes, etc., at the vice presidential level, college/school level, or department level (as shown in Figure 16).

This action leads to the establishment of a series of layers of administrative bureaucracy and red tape, which tends to stifle both the creativity and interest of those within the academic departments, as well as within the administrative and educational support units. Within the academic sector of the institution, deans or department heads simply can not be put in a position of dictating the educational (student learning) outcomes of degree programs without the serious threat of appearing to violate the academic freedom of the faculty involved. Even worse, they stand a very good chance of the faculty deserting the project and leaving these administrators with a situation in which it is impossible for the institution to be successful. Administrative vice presidents may attempt to dictate administrative objectives that their administrative and educational support (AES) units should seek to achieve. If staff members perceive this to be the case, their great tendency will be to control the assessment process so as to ensure that the senior administrator's objectives are met. However, the identification of areas in which genuine service improvement can take place in the AES units will be lost.

## Figure 16

## *Layering of Institutional Mission and Goals*

| **Institutional** |
| Mission/ Goals/Objectives |

| **Divisional or Vice Presidential** |
| Mission/Goals/Objectives |

| **College** |
| Mission/Goals/Objectives |

| **Department** |
| Mission/Goals/Objectives |

What then should vice presidents and deans do to support the implementation of institutional effectiveness or assessment activities? First, see that these activities take place by serving as the ultimate last authority ("court of last resort") to see that the units reporting thereto accomplish the assessment processes planned by the institution. Second, support the process in a visible manner by taking part in their own academic department's identification of program intended outcomes, means of assessment, criteria for success etc., or choosing one of their AES units within which to take part as a peer. Third, recognize and praise those administrative or academic departments under their supervision which have accomplished substantive improvements through the institutional effectiveness process. The key concept in the role of line administrators in the assessment process is one of support with direct intervention being the very last resort.

### The Role of the Faculty and Staff in Implementation

Beyond any question, and without any doubt, a substantial portion of the faculty must be actively involved in the assessment process if successful implementation is to take place on any campus. The authors of this publication have combined over forty years of substantive experience as college and university administrators. Implementation of institutional effectiveness or assessment activities in the academic sector of the institution is the single activity most requiring a "shared approach to governance." Because of the nature of the instructional program and the role of the faculty, line administrators can not accomplish this matter by themselves. Conversely, without appropriate administrative support and encouragement, faculty will be overwhelmed by this task. The two simply must work **together** if implementation is to be successful.

What will it take for the faculty and staff to accept and support implementation of educational (student learning) assessment and service improvement activities concerning the institution's academic programs and within the AES units? The answer to this question can probably be stated most simply by saying the faculty and staff need to (a) feel secure in cooperation with this effort and understand that its results will not be utilized against their interests, (b) believe that what is being asked of them is accomplishable within a modest amount of additional effort, and (c) see the potential usefulness of the resulting information to improve student learning or AES services (Figure 17).

## Figure 17
### *Keys to Faculty and Staff Assessment Motivation*

> ## 1. A feeling of security
> ## 2. A feasible amount of effort required by assessment process
> ## 3. A belief that the process will lead to improvement

What does it take for the faculty and staff to feel secure in the assessment endeavor? The authors have found faculty and staff on most campuses to be initially paranoid regarding the subject of assessment. The only question is the degree of paranoia regarding this subject present among campus faculty and staff at a given time. The primary fear or insecurity of faculty and staff concerning assessment is that the results will be used to make a judgment concerning them individually. The institution's administrators must make certain, both in their statements and actions, that assessment results are not used in any way in relationship to individuals or the discontinuance of academic programs. On many campuses, this assurance on the part of the central administration is best conveyed in a written statement concerning "use of assessment results" signed by the chief academic officer and chief executive officer. (See Appendix C) Only after having such written assurance in hand will some faculty reach a level of comfort or security with the process.

Another way in which faculty members should feel secure about their responsibility in this process is through their visible and substantive role in the leadership of the process at the institutional level, as well as within the academic departments of the institution. Faculty members need to feel "in control" of the assessment effort on the campus in order to ensure that what they perceive as their proper role is being maintained and that assessment doesn't become "the tail that wags the academic dog." The institutional assessment committee discussed in the next section (and the dominant role played by faculty on that committee) is a good start in that direction. The faculty within each academic department (as opposed to the chair) need to assume the leadership role in this endeavor. While all faculty members can not be expected to actively participate in this (or any other) academic process, all faculty need to be invited to be active participants, and it is the authors' experience that once the department starts to make positive changes in its academic programs based upon assessment results, a large portion of those members initially reluctant to take part will come along.

One of the common complaints initially heard from faculty concerning assessment activities is that "they violate academic freedom." This simply is not true. No outside authority is dictating what the faculty should teach or supervising their instructional activities in the classroom. Quite on the contrary, faculty are being asked to work together to establish their common intended educational (student learning) outcomes and means of assessment and then to use the results of that assessment to improve their program. From the standpoint of the public, this is a reasonable expectation. If faculty are unwilling to meet this expectation and assume academic responsibility for each program, the K-12 educational system is a model of the extent to which the public will exert (through one means or another) its control over higher education to see that learning is actually taking place.

## The Assessment Committee

In seeking to make assessment activity as broad-based and faculty-involved as possible, most institutions establish an "assessment committee." This committee should be composed primarily (almost exclusively) of teaching faculty with some limited representation of educational support and administrative staff. The faculty members appointed provide evidence of faculty leadership of the process, while the administrative and educational support staff can provide input into the design of the process from the standpoint of those types of units. The committee will need to be supported by the office charged with coordinating/facilitating implementation of assessment activities.

The selection of the particular faculty members for service on the institutional assessment committee should be based upon interest and representation. Those members appointed should be faculty at the institution who are most committed to the teaching and learning process. Deans and department heads are a good source for identifying these faculty members. Such faculty are also normally easily identified on a campus by their peers and will be the most devoted to seeing that this project is completed. AES staff appointed should represent "middle level" managers with none above the director level of authority. On some campuses, nomination of committee members by faculty governance system has proven to be a useful process.

It is recommended that the assessment committee be chaired by a faculty member. If at all possible, it would be best that this party represent the liberal arts or humanities disciplines at the institution. On most campuses, the greatest skepticism regarding assessment implementation is readily expressed from these disciplines. Such an appointment will ease some of the faculty's concern about the assessment process and its relationship to the "academic integrity" of the institution.

The institutional assessment committee can serve a number of purposes, including those shown in Figure 18. The recommendation of assessment policy concerning sensitive matters, such as the use of assessment results or access to assessment information, can be made by this body based upon the representativeness of its membership from each major academic unit on the campus as well as administrative and educational support units (student services, finance, physical services, and development).

### Figure 18
#### *Purpose of the Assessment Committee*

---

• **Policy Guidance**

• **Constituent Representation**

• **Quality Assurance** – **The Most Important**

• **Leadership Training**

---

Two of the most vexing initial questions which the campus will need to face can be stated thus: "What are the institution's academic programs *for assessment purposes*?" and "To what extent are the institution's administrative and educational support units defined by its administrative departments?" The answers to both of these questions are contained later in the sections relating to establishment of educational (student learning) outcomes and assessment in administrative and educational support units. However, early on in this process of implementation, the institutional assessment committee can serve a valuable purpose by working with individual administrative and academic departments to answer these questions and thereby establishing the structure for institutional effectiveness or assessment implementation.

If not already accomplished, the establishment of a timeline or schedule for implementation of institutional effectiveness or assessment activities is a worthy project for the institutional assessment committee. This committee is also well equipped to follow up on that timeline to see that academic departments as well as administrative and educational support units are in compliance. It is always better if these departments and units respond to the request of the committee rather than the committee ultimately having to resort to the line administrative structure to see that activities on the timeline are accomplished.

Among the most valuable contributions to implementation which the institutional assessment committee can make is service as the quality assurance mechanism for the process. In this regard, the committee needs to be placed in the position of reviewing and critiquing assessment plans and then assessment reports concerning each individual academic program and administrative and educational support unit on the campus. While the committee should not be asked to "dictate chemistry to the chemistry department," there simply must be a means through which the assessment plan for each instructional program, as well as AES unit, is reviewed and critiqued relative to its *assessment merits*. This review is necessary in order that these programs and units not engage in assessment activities which are counter productive, a waste of valuable time, or frustrating to the process. Enclosed as Appendix E is a critique form which has been found useful for this purpose. It is aligned with the Five-Column Model presented in the Chapter Two and described in detail in Chapters Six to Nine. The authors' experience has been that, in most cases, a peer review process results in a far more rigorous critique by a committee of peers of program/unit assessment plans than any evaluation an administrator could tactfully accomplish.

The activities on the part of the institutional assessment committee described above do not take place without guidance. The individual selected to lead implementation on the campus should serve ex-officio on the committee, and the committee should be provided on-going training concerning the nature of its responsibilities and in particular the means through which to review and critique assessment plans and reports.

Finally, the institutional assessment committee should be connected through dual membership with a separate general education assessment committee discussed later in this publication. The assessment of general education is one of the most complex matters on any campus. The overall institutional assessment committee should not be charged therewith. However, it should be aware of the processes taking place within this separate committee; and, hence, interlocking membership is advised.

In the authors' opinion, the institutional assessment committee will be one of the most active committees ever appointed on a campus. The committee should be supported by the central administration in every way possible, with the exception of release time or pay for its members. Membership, as on other university or college committees, should be seen as part of the responsibilities of individual faculty and staff. However, in recognition of the heavy workload of this committee, the members should be cycled through on a roughly three-year rotation and appropriate recognition for their service (for example, letters of appreciation from the institution's chief executive officer) be provided.

## Leadership and Resources for Implementation

A wealth of evidence exists that among the most important characteristics associated with institutions that have been successful in implementation of institutional effectiveness is the appointment of an individual responsible to the chief executive officer and/or chief academic officer with the specific duty of implementing assessment and institutional effectiveness activities on the campus. Without such an appointment, the assessment project tends to become an "orphan" with no one willing to assume responsibility for its success and all seeking to avoid accountability for its failure.

At the initial stages of implementation, assumption of this leadership responsibility requires approximately a half-time level of commitment (work) on most modest size campuses. There is no need to establish a separate institutional effectiveness or assessment office on most campuses. Frankly, the additional overhead associated with a separate office does not justify its existence except at larger institutions. However, if an institution can not, through release time of one type or another, provide at least a half-time position for leadership of institutional effectiveness implementation, then a separate office staff is probably the best solution.

What are the characteristics which an institution should consider in the selection of its implementation leader? The following characteristics are appropriate for the leadership position in institutional effectiveness or assessment implementation.

- Respect of the faculty – the individual charged with this responsibility must have the respect of the faculty and be an acknowledged advocate of, if not an expert in, this field of assessment-based program improvement.
- Ability to work independently – the nature of this task requires a leader able to plan and execute implementation plans without substantive supervision from the chief executive or chief academic officer.
- Numeric capability – the individual chosen should not be a stranger to data. However, he/she does not need to be a "number cruncher." The data associated with most assessment activities is relatively simple and straightforward, and the leader chosen should be comfortable at least with working with descriptive statistics.

What are likely sources for such a leader within a campus community? Frequently the leadership position in assessment or institutional effectiveness activities is identified from within existing institutional faculty and staff. The assessment leader is most likely to spring from one of three sources:

- A faculty member committed to improvement of learning--This person should be provided with at least a half-time release from teaching responsibilities to lead the implementation process.
- An associate/assistant chief academic officer – On a number of occasions an individual carrying the title of assistant vice president, associate dean, assistant to the vice president, etc., is identified as having overall responsibility for implementation. Under this circumstance, the institution should provide a reduction in the individual's other duties so that he/she may commit roughly half time to this task over the first two years of implementation.
- An institutional research officer – On perhaps more occasions than advisable, the college's institutional research officer is identified for this leadership capacity based upon the mistaken assumption that the position requires a statistician. On some campuses, the institutional research officer has the respect of faculty members and the ability to work with them. This combination has led to successful implementation on many campuses. On other campuses, excellent institutional research officers whose primary skills lie in producing data, rather than in leading groups, are assigned leadership of the implementation process. Under these circumstances, substantive problems are frequently encountered.

What are the duties likely to be incumbent upon the party charged with leadership of institutional effectiveness or assessment activities? These duties can be divided into those

(a) relating to the leadership of the process and the people involved and (b) provision of technical and support services. The assessment leader should be expected to coordinate formulation of the timeline, serve ex-officio on the assessment committee, and "hold hands" with faculty and staff as they implement the procedures called for in this publication. This hand holding takes many forms but can be described as careful guidance or "walking them through" the implementation process and activities. The assessment leader should serve as a facilitator in this process and avoid the temptation to "do it for them."

The support services provided relate to both technical and general services. The technical services necessary at some institutions include the conduct of survey research and support of attitudinal assessment as well as (if called upon) the administration of standardized testing selected by the academic program. General support activities include development of a knowledge base on the campus concerning the assessment process and the presentation of seminars to groups of faculty and staff regarding their expectations. Also included in this general support role is that of monitoring implementation in accordance with the established timeline.

Technical support for assessment activities on a campus are most frequently found either in the institutional research office, a center for social science research, or within an assessment office. Wherever these services are located, they will need to be focused on the provision of the necessary services required by the institution's intended educational (student learning) outcomes as well as its administrative objectives.

What type of cost should the institution expect regarding implementation of assessment and institutional effectiveness activities? Findings from *Assessment Case Studies* (1995) indicated that an institution can expect somewhere between two and three dollars per fall head count enrollment in "out-of-pocket" cost for assessment activities. These costs should be made through a central assessment budget so the actual cost can be easily tracked and the institution can demonstrate its financial commitment to assessment readily to external agencies. This budget would cover the cost of developing attitudinal surveys, conducting standardized tests, distribution of documents, etc. A second area of expenditure for the institution is the cost of the centralized leadership function (at least a half-time position) plus the out-of-pocket costs. These costs should total in the vicinity of eight to nine dollars per fall head count student. These rough cost estimates do not take into account the largely unrecompensed and unrecognized cost of faculty and staff time in the implementation process. It is absolutely essential to successful implementation that out-of-pocket costs and centralized support be funded on the campus. These funds represent a visible commitment to implementation by the central administration. Faculty members must perceive this tangible support of implementation if they are to offer their "voluntary" (without additional remuneration) commitment of their limited time to this process. One way to kill successful implementation effort is for the faculty to perceive that they do not have the financial support to accomplish the assessment task planned. Why should faculty members freely commit their time to do assessment if the institution (central administration) will not provide them with the tools (out-of-pocket costs) with which to do the job?

## Academic and Administrative and Educational Support Unit Leadership

The academic department chair has, in this instance as well as most others, the most difficult role to play within an institution. The role of the chair in this instance is one of peer or colleague, rather than of supervisor. Chairs should be seen by their colleagues as "first among equals" in identifying intended educational (student learning) outcomes. The chair can accomplish the following actions:

- Ascertain what is to be accomplished, including the format and due date from the administration
- Determine what support to the department in the assessment process is available
- Schedule the first meeting
- Ask for input from faculty prior to the meeting
- Ultimately serve as the department secretary

However, the department chair must avoid the great temptation to procrastinate until the day before the departmental assessment plan is due to the dean, isolate himself/herself for several hours, and emerge from his/her office with the educational (student learning) outcomes for the department's program, as well as the means for their assessment and criteria for success. While this method will provide the "paper" required by the dean, its lack of involvement of faculty will come back to haunt the department chair as the conduct of assessment activities and use of results get under way.

The department chair may play a bit more directive role in actual accomplishment of assessment activities. Faculty are used to seeing the department chair ask for volunteers followed by assigning responsibility for various departmental tasks among the faculty. In addition to coordinating the conduct of the assessment activities, the department chair will also need to lead the faculty in consideration of the data resulting and its use in program improvement. Department chairs should realize that their charge is not conducting assessment activities. Their charge is *leading the faculty* in conducting assessment activities resulting in substantive program improvement. Finally, at most institutions, the academic department chair is responsible for documentation of assessment activities and the improvement of programs within his/her unit. Further information concerning this subject is developed in greater detail later in Chapter Thirteen.

Some department chairs find it useful to appoint an "assessment liaison" representative who coordinates assessment activities in the department in the name of the chair and the faculty. The advantage of this approach is that it separates this collegial process from the more directive aspects occasionally associated with being department chair and is one less job for the department chair.

As previously mentioned, the involvement of individual faculty members in this matter is absolutely essential. This role is to be considered as one of the responsibilities of faculty membership and is fiscally unrecognized by additional remuneration or release time. *Participation in assessment activities* is certainly appropriate as one of the bases for faculty evaluation. However, *consideration of assessment results* in faculty evaluation would be entirely inappropriate.

Motivation of the faculty and staff to take part in the assessment process can either be through the extrinsic structures described in the previous chapter or through the intrinsic motivation discussed earlier in this chapter. The greatest factor contributing to the willingness of faculty and staff to actively take part in assessment activity is their belief that it will lead to improved student learning and unit services. As previously stated, once faculty feel secure in this activity and believe it accomplishable with a reasonable amount of effort, the great majority will willingly take part.

From the chief executive officer through the vice presidents to the department chairs and heads, as well as individual faculty and staff, there are various roles to play in implementation of institutional effectiveness and assessment activities. These roles are all essential and none by itself is sufficient to accomplish the task at hand. Recognition of the relationships between these roles is key to implementation. Clearly, implementation of outcomes assessment and institutional effectiveness requires a more "shared governance" approach than any other administrative activity taking place on a campus.

## CHAPTER FIVE

# ESTABLISHING THE EXPANDED STATEMENT OF INSTITUTIONAL PURPOSE

*Any road trip has a starting point and a destination. The journey toward implementation of a successful institutional effectiveness or assessment plan begins and ends with the institution's Statement of Purpose. All subsequent statements of program and unit outcomes or objectives are established to support the institution's Statement of Purpose—its intended destination.*

The purpose of the expanded statement of institutional purpose (ESIP) is to provide central guidance for the institution's development and to reflect institutional level "intentions" of the college or university. The expanded statement of institutional purpose (ESIP) is one of the most important aspects in assessing institutional effectiveness and should be thought of as being composed of two separate but related parts (Figure 19): (a) the institutional mission and (b) the institutional goals.

## Figure 19
### *Components of the Expanded Statement of Institutional Purpose (ESIP)*

> **Institutional Mission—Broad statement of institutional philosophy, role, scope, etc.**
> **Institutional Goals—Institutional level action statements that implement, support, and are derived from the Mission**
> > **a . . . . . . . . . . . . . . . .**
> > **b . . . . . . . . . . . . . . . .**

The institutional mission statement is sometimes also referred to as the statement of purpose for an institution. Typically, this document is printed in the front section of the institution's catalog or bulletin. Institutional goals, supporting or developed from the mission, constitute the institutional level action plan. Collectively, these two components (mission and goals) give direction to the overall operation of the institution and clearly identify its intentions. Each of the regional accrediting agencies requires that institutions have a valid, up-to-date mission or purpose statement. As an initial part of the process of developing an institutional effectiveness program, this statement must be evaluated, updated, and in many cases expanded by the institution. The ESIP should be comprehensive and describe all primary institutional activities.

The process of assessing institutional effectiveness is based upon the degree of accomplishment of the institution's stated purpose as reflected in its mission or purpose statement (ESIP). Because the institution is encouraged to formulate program and unit statements of intentions (outcomes or objectives) consistent with the institution's purpose, great clarity and specificity are needed in the statements of institutional intentions contained in the ESIP. Although an institutional mission statement should not reach an operational level of detail, it should include substance sufficient to provide a framework for subsequent statements of institutional goals, which, in turn, provide a clear sense of direction for the program/unit statements. The ultimate determination of institutional effectiveness is in relationship to the accomplishment of the ESIP.

The expanded statement of institutional purpose (ESIP) is different from both historical statements of institutional development and statements of vision frequently identified with fund-raising efforts. "Visionary" statements depict what those at the institution would like to see in the future and are commonly found on many campuses. These statements are of immense use for fund-raising purposes but must be recognized as "want to be" statements. On the other hand, historical discussions of the development of the institution from its inception to the current time are often encountered in place of an ESIP. Neither of these documents represents a statement of purpose concerning what the institution (given roughly its existing resources) intends to accomplish at this time. That expanded statement of institutional purpose (ESIP) is the statement to which institutional effectiveness or assessment activities should be linked. Prior to the advent of institutional effectiveness requirements, frequently statements of purpose or vision were 90% aspiration and 10% reality. Given the need to provide the evidence that the institution is accomplishing its statement of purpose/ESIP, these statements have currently become more in the proportion of 90% reality and 10% aspiration.

## The Institutional Mission Statement

Institutional mission statements convey the broad scope or philosophy of the institutions and are very rarely changed. These statements were frequently established at the time of the founding of the institution and are often found in public law for state supported institutions. Statements such as those included in Appendix A constitute the essence of the institution; however, these mission statements provide little practical guidance for institutional development or operations without subsequent elaboration by institutional goals.

Mission statements are exceedingly resistant to change because, in many cases, generations of students (now alumni) are dedicated to the institution and its historical mission. Substantively changing mission statements usually takes place only when dramatic changes in the institution, such as its transformation from a two- to a four-year college, shift from private to public, reduction of identification with a particular religious denomination, or other similarly dramatic events transpire.

## Institutional Goals

Institutional goals are clearly related to and support the mission statement as described above. They provide, at the institutional level, a clearly articulated sense of current intentions on the part of the institution to achieve its mission. Appendix A provides examples of institutional goals for private, public, and two-year institutions.

While institutional mission statements rarely change, institutional goals are reviewed from year to year; and as one is accomplished or becomes inappropriate, it is discontinued, and additional goals are established. Since these institutional goals are specific and yet support the mission statement of the institution, they frequently are the point to which educational program and administrative and educational support (AES) unit outcomes and objectives are linked for the purpose of demonstrating institutional effectiveness.

The creation of additional "layers" of guidance for the institution's programs and units as described earlier (Figure 16) should be avoided. It is the authors' recommendation that even in substantially complex organizational structures, such as major research universities, linkage be maintained directly from each educational program and administrative and educational support unit to the expanded statement of institutional purpose (ESIP) (mission and goals) of the institution. This action avoids "layering," simplifies the process, and provides maximum flexibility for those actually delivering the educational programs and AES services to seek their improvement.

## Insuring that the Institution Has Evidence of Its Effectiveness

One of the tasks which each institution needs to accomplish is creation of the ability to provide the chief executive officer with evidence that all aspects described in the Mission Statement or Institutional Goals are being addressed by one program or unit of the institution. The institution needs to prepare a "back map" from each institutional level commitment to the units as well as educational programs supporting that statement. Shown in Figures 20 and 21 is an example of such a "back map." Figure 20 identifies the institutional goals from a major public research university, and Figure 21 illustrates the manner in which they were "back mapped" to the institution's instructional programs as well as administrative and educational support units.

This linkage to the institutional goals is sufficient to demonstrate support of the ESIP in that these institutional goals are derived from an elaboration of the more general statements contained in the mission.

## Figure 20

*Institutional Goals of the University of Mississippi*

| | |
|---|---|
| Goal 1 | The University will improve undergraduate education, especially in lower-division courses. |
| Goal 2 | The University will concentrate graduate education and research in areas of strength consistent with the Focus Areas. |
| Goal 3 | The University will increase employee compensation to the Southern University Group (SUG) average in order to attract and retain a highly qualified faculty and staff. |
| Goal 4 | The University will improve educational support services (library, computer networking, database availability, instructional support, etc.) to increase access to information and communication on the campus. |
| Goal 5 | The University will disseminate its expertise and knowledge to non-academic communities throughout the State of Mississippi and the Mid-south region. |
| Goal 6 | The University will continue to develop leadership and to instill in its students a sense of justice, moral courage, and tolerance for the views of others. |
| Goal 7 | The University will maintain efficient and effective administrative services to support the University's instructional, research, and public service programs. |
| Goal 8 | The University will increase faculty and staff involvement in University planning. |
| Goal 9 | The University will increase its efforts to secure support from federal, state, and private sources. |

# Figure 21
## Institutional Back Mapping

| Assessment Record | Goal 1 | Goal 2 | Goal 3 | Goal 4 | Goal 5 | Goal 6 | Goal 7 | Goal 8 | Goal 9 |
|---|---|---|---|---|---|---|---|---|---|
| **Instructional** | | | | | | | | | |
| Art, B.A | ▥ | | | | | | | | |
| Geology, B.S. | ▥ | | | | | | | | |
| Geology, M.S. | | ▥ | | | | | | | |
| Geology, Ph.D. | | ▥ | | | | | | | |
| Music, B.A. | ▥ | | | | | | | | |
| Mechanical Engineering, M.S. | | ▥ | | | | | | | |
| Chemical Engineering, B.S. | ▥ | | | | | | | | |
| Chemical Engineering, M.S. | | ▥ | | | | | | | |
| Chemical Engineering, Ph.D. | | ▥ | | | | | | | |
| Civil Engineering, B.S. | ▥ | | | | | | | | |
| Civil Engineering, M.S. | | ▥ | | | | | | | |
| Civil Engineering, Ph.D. | | ▥ | | | | | | | |
| Accountancy, B.B.A. | ▥ | | | | | | | | |
| Economics, B.B.A. | ▥ | | | | | | | | |
| Marketing, B.B.A. | ▥ | | | | | | | | |
| Business, MBA | | ▥ | | | | | | | |
| Management, B.B.A. | ▥ | | | | | | | | |
| Management, Ph.D. | | ▥ | | | | | | | |
| Biology, B.S. | ▥ | | | | | | | | |
| Biology, Ph.D | | ▥ | | | | | | | |
| English, B.A. | ▥ | | | | | | | | |
| English, M.A. | | ▥ | | | | | | | |
| English, Ph.D | | ▥ | | | | | | | |
| History, B.A. | ▥ | | | | | | | | |
| History, M.A. | | ▥ | | | | | | | |
| Psychology, B.A. | ▥ | | | | | | | | |
| Psychology, Ph.D. | | ▥ | | | | | | | |
| Mathematics, B.A. | ▥ | | | | | | | | |
| Social Work, B.A. | ▥ | | | | | | | | |
| Social Work, M.S.W. | | ▥ | | | | | | | |
| Sociology, B.A. | ▥ | | | | | | | | |
| Audiology, B.S. | ▥ | | | | | | | | |
| Speech Pathology, B.S. | ▥ | | | | | | | | |
| Elementary Education, B.Ed | ▥ | | | | | | | | |
| Secondary Education, B.Ed | ▥ | | | | | | | | |
| Elementary Education, M.Ed | | | | ▥ | | | | | |
| Educational Leadership, Ph.D. | | ▥ | | | | | | | |
| Criminal Justice, B.S. | ▥ | | | | | | | | |

| Assessment Record | Goal 1 | Goal 2 | Goal 3 | Goal 4 | Goal 5 | Goal 6 | Goal 7 | Goal 8 | Goal 9 |
|---|---|---|---|---|---|---|---|---|---|
| **Admin and Ed Support** | | | | | | | | | |
| Accounting | | | | | | | X | | |
| Admissions | | | | | | X | | | |
| Advising | | | | | | X | | | |
| Alumni Affairs | | | | | | | | | X |
| Bookstore | | | | | | | X | | |
| Bursars | | | | | | | X | | |
| Campus Recreation | | | | | | X | | | |
| Campus Security | | | | | | | X | | |
| Career Center | | | | | | X | | | |
| Center Sourthern Culture | | | | | | | X | | |
| Counseling Center | | | | | | X | | | |
| Dean of Students | | | | | | X | | | |
| Diversity Center | | | | | | | | | X |
| Financial Aid | | | | | | | X | | |
| Graduate School | | X | | | | | | | |
| Housing | | | | | | | X | | |
| Human Resources | | | X | | | | | | |
| Institute for Continuing Studies | | | | | X | | | | |
| Internal Audit | | | | | | | X | | |
| Intercollegiate Athletics | | | | | | | X | | |
| Law Library | | | | X | | | | | |
| Main Campus Library | | | | X | | | | | |
| Physical Plant | | | | | | | X | | |
| Purchasing | | | | | | | X | | |
| Registrars | | | | | | | X | | |
| Testing Services | | | | | | | X | | |
| Univ Plan & Inst Research | | | | | | | | X | |
| Wellness Center | | | | | | X | | | |

Such a "back map" should be initially designed based upon the voluntary subscription of academic programs as well as administrative and educational support units to the goals of the institution. Once this "voluntary" identification of the goals supported on the campus is accomplished, then any gaps in coverage of the institutional goals should be identified. At that time, those at the institutional level should seek to have goals not "voluntarily" supported considered by the educational programs or administrative and educational support units that would seem naturally to relate with such goals or otherwise delete the goals from the ESIP. Thus the process begins with what some would describe as "bottom-up planning" and concludes, if necessary, with somewhat "top-down planning" to cover the gaps identified.

One of the questions occasionally heard on campuses is: "Should every unit and educational program support every institutional goal?" After careful consideration, the answer should be a clear—"no." One would not expect the financial aid department to contribute toward Goal # 2 in Figure 20 (graduate level education and research). At the same time, it would be illogical for the graduate level programs referenced in Figure 21 to contribute to Goal #1 in Figure 20 (undergraduate learning). Hence, every educational program as well as administrative and educational support unit will not support all goals of the institution. In reality, what usually transpires is that each educational program as well as administrative and educational support service unit identifies the single institutional goal with which it most closely relates. Occasionally, a program or AES unit may support several goals; however, these are the exception rather than the rule and are more common in AES units than in educational programs.

### Development of the Expanded Statement of Institutional Purpose (ESIP)

The expanded statement of institutional purpose can be developed through a number of different methods, including both strategic planning and more traditional and collegially oriented processes. Strategic planning processes are described by numerous authors (Cope, 1981; Keller, 1982; Shirley, 1982, 1983) who have provided descriptions of the process that have a number of important concepts in common. All authors agree that strategic planning seeks to identify the institution's role within society. It basically asks: "What is the business of this institution, and how does this institution fit into the educational picture of the city, region, state, or country?" All concur that assessment of internal strengths and limitations is advisable and in one manner or another and suggest a SWOT (strengths, weaknesses, opportunities, threats) analysis of the institution.

A related, though somewhat more traditional and collegial, approach to the process of establishment of the statement of purpose is shown in Appendix B. This series of events, taking approximately twelve months to complete, moves in a steady and systematic process from consideration of the then existing statement of purpose through presentation on the campus of a revised ESIP. This approach is characterized by careful analysis of data from within and from sources external to the institution; participative input by faculty and staff into the formulation of the document; review by the chief executive officer; and, ultimately, approval by the institution's governing board. Either approach, strategic planning or the more traditional approach outlined in Appendix B, will lead the institution to the establishment of the foundation for its institutional effectiveness activities—the expanded statement of institutional purpose (ESIP).

Shown below in Figure 22 is the One-Column Model extracted from the previously shown Five-Column Model in Figure 7.

# Figure 22

## *Undergraduate English Program-One Column*

### Expanded Statement of Institutional Purpose

### Institutional Mission Statement:
**The principal focus of Our University's curricular program is undergraduate education in the liberal arts and science...**

### Institutional Goal:
**... all graduates of baccalaureate level will have developed a depth of understanding in their major field.**

Each educational program and AES unit at the institution will need to select that portion of the ESIP which it supports and identify that portion in the first column of the model as well as ultimately on the assessment record book forms described later in Chapter Thirteen for documentation purposes. Administrative and educational support (AES) units will need to handle such linkage to the statement of purpose in a slightly different manner, explained later in Chapter Nine.

### Problems Frequently Encountered in Preparing the Expanded Institutional Statements of Purpose (ESIP)

Both substantive and procedural problems are frequently found in preparation of the statement of purpose (ESIP) for institutions. From the standpoint of the procedures utilized to prepare the statement of purpose, timing, input, and linkage to performance measures are frequently identified as potential problems.

Revisions to the statement of purpose need to take place several years before the initiation of the self-study or reaffirmation procedures in order for the institution's educational programs and AES units to provide evidence of the statement's accomplishment.

If the institution waits until eighteen to twenty-four months before reaffirmation to begin revision of its statement of purpose (ESIP), it will probably be too late to be of substantive use in establishing institutional effectiveness.

On more occasions than certainly warranted, the ESIP for an institution is found to be the sole product of the chief executive officer or the chief executive officer and cabinet. All of the regional accrediting associations require participative input into the statement, and because of the visibility now associated with that statement as part of institutional effectiveness requirement, failure to seek such input is easily identified on the campus.

The essence of institutional effectiveness is providing evidence that the institution is either accomplishing its statement of purpose or making changes leading to the accomplishment of that statement. Unless institutional performance (through the "back map" earlier described) is linked to the institution's expanded statement of purpose, evidence of institutional effectiveness is not possible.

In addition to these procedural problems, there are a number of substantive problems apparent in the review of many institutional statements of purpose. Among the most common of these problems is what the authors describe as excess "truth and beauty." Common in many statements of purpose are terms such as "excellence," "unsurpassed," "outstanding," etc. These terms, while easily uttered, are quite difficult to operationally define and even more difficult to provide the evidence concerning their fulfillment. Some "truth and beauty" should be expected in a statement of purpose. However, institutions should guard against an *excess* of such statements, making too many statements beyond the institution's ability to provide evidence of their accomplishment.

One of the common problems with statements of purpose (ESIP), from the standpoint of administrative and educational support units, is the lack of a point for their connection to the institutional level. Many traditional statements of purpose simply ignore the role of the majority of employees on the campus (those in administrative and educational support units) and focus only upon instruction, research, and public service. At least one point in each statement of purpose should be included (such as Goal 8 in Figure 20) to which administrative and educational support units can "hook" their assessment initiatives.

In many cases, statements of purpose for the institution are either too general or too specific. If too general in nature, while failing to provide sufficient guidance, they succeed in offending no constituency. If too specific, they become operational in nature, restricting units within the institution and, in many cases, establishing unreasonable expectations. This is particularly true when statements regarding general education are incorporated into college statements of purpose.

None of the problems discussed above are insurmountable. Careful planning and participative execution of a plan to revise the institution's traditional statement of purpose into an expanded statement of purpose (ESIP) that provides genuine guidance for the institution can be among the most positive aspects of institutional effectiveness implementation.

The necessary support, structure, and leadership at the institutional level as described in Part One of this book is essential. Once the campus comprehensively has developed a clear understanding of the institutional effectiveness concept and has developed a support structure for the process (which includes the necessary leadership and resources), then it can begin to extend the overall structure to its programs and units for successful implementation.

Part Two of the book will describe a basic structure for building and operating institutional effectiveness in educational programs as well as the administrative and educational support units. Assessment activities in particular educational contexts (general education, two-year college, and graduate/professional education) will be covered in Part Three. While there exists a degree of uniqueness in each of these specialized context, the framework developed in Chapters Six to Nine concerning overall implementation within instructional programs also pertain to implementation in the special contexts described in Part Three.

## Works Cited

Cope, Robert. *Strategic Planning, Management and Decision Making*. Washington, DC: American Association for Higher Education, 1981.

Keller, George. *Academic Strategy: The Management Revolution in American Higher Education*. Baltimore, MD: John Hopkins University Press, 1983.

Shirley, Robert C. Limiting the Scope of Strategy: A Decision Based Approach. *Academy of Management Review*, 7(2), 37-46, 1982.

Shirley, Robert C. Identifying the Levels of Strategy for a College or University. *Long Range Planning, 16*(3), 92-98, 1983.

# Part Two

# IMPLEMENTATION OF INSTITUTIONAL EFFECTIVENESS WITHIN INSTRUCTIONAL PROGRAMS AND ADMINISTRATIVE AND EDUCATIONAL SUPPORT UNITS

# CHAPTER SIX

# PREPARING STATEMENTS OF INTENDED EDUCATIONAL (STUDENT LEARNING) OUTCOMES IN EDUCATIONAL PROGRAMS

*All road trips ultimately "get the show on the road" or begin movement toward their destinations. Based upon careful preparation at the institutional level, described in Chapters Three to Five, the journey toward successful implementation of an institutional effectiveness or assessment effort regarding instructional programs begins within the institution's academic departments through the establishment of educational (student learning) outcomes for each instructional program. At most institutions, during this activity is when faculty members become directly involved with assessment.*

For each educational program (major), general education and developmental education, identifying the educational (student learning) outcomes expected of those completing the instructional program is necessary.

## What Is an Instructional Program?

While each campus has the authority to identify instructional programs as it deems appropriate, most public colleges and universities begin this process by identification of the "degree programs" normally maintained in an inventory of such programs with their governing board or state coordinating agency. Private colleges normally begin the identification of instructional programs by a review of their catalogs to determine the use of the term "major."

It is not unusual to find instructional programs identified which have a number of tracks, emphases, options, etc., fitting under a single umbrella of an overall major or degree program at either public or private colleges. This "umbrella factor" is common at public institutions required by their states to maintain a certain number of degree completions per program or be faced with review or potential discontinuation of those programs. The primary question in these circumstances becomes: "When does a track, emphasis, option, etc., become sufficiently different from the others to constitute (for assessment purposes) a separate instructional program?" The decision is certainly for each program's faculty to make. However, if dissimilar instructional programs remain aggregated together under an umbrella title for one reason or another (e.g., a history degree program with concentrations in European, American, Asian, and South American history), then only the material in courses shared in common by all tracks will be subject to assessment. As a general benchmark, if more than half of the courses in a concentration, track, option, etc., are different from the core of courses shared by all students in the degree program, then the option probably should be treated for assessment purposes as a separate degree program requiring a unique Five-Column Model.

### Why Do We Really Need to Establish Statements of Educational or Student Learning Outcomes?

Regional accrediting associations explicitly require using one term or another (expected results, intended student academic achievement, student learning outcomes, etc.) for the establishment of statements regarding what the faculty intend for students to be able to think, know, or do when they have completed their educational programs. While the terminology in the various regions may vary, all share this requirement that educational outcomes be identified.

Even without an explicit requirement to establish intended educational (student learning) outcomes, the authors strongly recommend this step for two other important reasons. The establishment of educational (student learning) outcomes assists the institution in focusing its assessment effort only upon assessment of the outcomes under consideration at one time. This limits the amount of assessment effort taking place to only that which is essential at the time and may actually result in the discontinuation of assessment activities that are not providing substantive information concerning intended educational (student learning) outcomes in programs. Assessment activities should not be considered as a shotgun blast, attempting to hit something that may be of use, but as a rifle shot, targeted specifically on the intended educational (student learning) outcomes identified.

In addition to narrowing the assessment effort to only those areas necessary, the identification of intended educational (student learning) outcomes provides a ready market for assessment results. On many campuses, institutional research staffs have conducted surveys of graduates and alumni, as well as other potentially useful assessment activities, which have been relatively little used in the past. Focusing these studies on answering the questions posed by identification of what we intend for students to think, know, or do creates a ready market for such long neglected assessment results.

### Describing Educational (Student Learning) Outcomes as Opposed to the Educational Process

Stated as simply as possible, statements of intended educational (student learning) outcomes describe what students will *think* (affective), *know* (cognitive), or *do* (behavioral/ performance) when they have completed a degree program. As faculty work to develop assessment plans, the recognition of the definition of educational (student learning) outcomes is easily accomplished, but putting that definition into practice is more difficult.

The first real opportunity in the implementation process to take the "wrong turn" on the road to successful implementation is in the identification of educational (student learning) outcomes. In roughly half the cases which the authors have encountered, unless other wise guided, faculty in identification of student academic achievement, outcomes, expected results, etc., tend to describe instead, what they (faculty) intend to do (teach better, add courses, acquire resources, etc.) rather than what the students/graduates will be able to do upon completion of the program.

The authors have repeatedly reviewed statements *concerning what the faculty intended to accomplish* mislabeled as educational (student learning) outcomes. The authors have noted that this is particularly likely when any type of resource request process is tied to institutional effectiveness. This is the case because the faculty activities described have a direct influence and relationship to requests for funding, whereas student educational (student learning) outcomes do not. Unless statements describing the educational process (what faculty intend to do) are corrected and turned into student learning outcome statements, then all assessment actions will necessarily relate to faculty activities rather than student accomplishments.

## Outcomes Concerning Growth, Change, or Value Added

The classical research model requiring a pre-test to establish a baseline and after treatment a post-test, necessary to measure growth or change, is rarely utilized in outcomes assessment research and is not required. The term *outcomes* itself describes what a group of students will think, know, or do *at the time they have completed* a program of instruction. Only if the faculty desire, and have the ability to do so, is the concept of growth or change from a pre-test to a post-test situation necessary.

At some institutions, the ability to show "value added" through a pre-test and later a post-test model is an attractive alternative frequently suggested by the central administration (particularly at community colleges). While theoretically possible, this approach is practically very difficult and fails to take into account the many intervening variables which take place during a student's educational process.

As statements of intended educational (student learning) outcomes are identified in a department, it will be necessary to insure that those statements describe what students will be able to think, know, or do and that these statement identify whether they will be accomplished in absolute terms or in relationship to student growth during their enrollment in the instructional program.

## Desirable Characteristics of Statements of Intended Educational (Student Learning) Outcomes

The only absolute requirement regarding educational (student learning) outcomes is that they be stated in terms of what the student will be able to think, know, or do upon completion of the program. However, a number of desirable characteristics of such intended outcomes statements are shown in Figure 23, and the institution may wish to evaluate the initial statements of intended educational (student learning) outcomes formulated by the faculty.

# Figure 23

## *Suggestions for Evaluating Statements of Intended Educational Outcomes*

1. Consistent with expanded statement of purpose
2. Reasonable given the ability of students
3. Reflect key concepts
4. Clear and accomplishment is ascertainable
5. Singular
6. Rotate when validated

The outcomes for instructional programs (taken as a whole) should be *consistent with the statement of purpose* (ESIP) for the institution as described in Chapter Five. It is not unusual to find circumstances in which the outcomes stated for a program are inappropriate to the institutional purpose. As an example, the ESIP concerning an undergraduate liberal arts college included in the mission that it desired to "become one of the outstanding undergraduate liberal arts colleges in . . ." and identified a related institutional goal "to strengthen the core curriculum in light of changes in society." The addition of "graduate programs" as an intended outcome would be inappropriate for two reasons. *First*, it identified what the institution intended to do (process) rather than its students; *second*, the institution identified itself as an undergraduate institution. On the other hand, identification of an outcome for general education stating that "graduates would be able to identify current societal problems" is the type of linkage and support that should exist between the ESIP and outcomes within the various academic programs or general education.

In addition to consistency with the expanded statement of institutional purpose, educational (student learning) outcomes should be *reasonable given the ability of the students enrolled* within the program. On numerous occasions, the authors have reviewed statements of intended educational (student learning) outcomes which are obviously far beyond the ability of the group of students enrolled in the program or at the institution. In many cases, elevated outcomes appear to be the result of the mistaken assumption on the part of the faculty that the students enrolled in their programs are "just like we were" when the faculty were students. Faculty members are a bright group of professionals and in almost all cases are clearly more capable than the group of students enrolled in their program. Hence, one of the first questions which program faculty will want to ask is, "What are the students enrolling in our program like in terms of entrance examination scores or academic capabilities?"

Having identified the ability of the entering students in its program, faculty next need to consider how far it is reasonable for these students to develop over the period of time they are enrolled in the program. "How far can we 'stretch' these students reasonably during their matriculation through our program?" In reality, the actual question is, "How far can the program (the unit of analysis) go in developing its students during their enrollment?"

Unfortunately, on some campuses statements of intended educational (student learning) outcomes can be described as accomplishable by any "warm breathing body" that has traversed the campus in the last 100 years. Statements such as "students will identify biology as being among the natural sciences" are occasionally found in a list of intended outcomes for programs. This type of statement of outcome most frequently occurs when the institution has failed to separate outcomes assessment for program improvement purposes (formative assessment of the program) from individual faculty evaluation for rank, tenure, promotion, etc., (summative evaluation of the individual). Both processes leading to program improvement and faculty evaluation are necessary on every campus. However, they simply must be described, maintained, and acted upon *separately*. Otherwise, the faculty will set outcomes for their instructional programs which are unreasonably low in order to protect themselves from potentially adverse actions. The faculty need to feel free to set outcomes for their educational programs which are challenging and stretch the students (and, in so doing, the program) without fear that failure to accomplish these outcomes will cause an adverse personnel action concerning the faculty individually. Only through this means will programs actually seek to improve to that level which is possible, given the time and resources available.

Once faculty have started identifying program level outcomes, statements of student learning usually start to flow in torrents. In many cases, the outcomes identified by faculty will be concerning their individual courses rather than the program overall. In some cases, it may be necessary to identify similar outcomes put forward (representing several courses) and generalize them to the program level. Faculty must *choose carefully the most important or key* educational (student learning) outcomes for initial assessment.

Faculty should seek to conduct assessment activities on *no more than three to five intended educational (student learning) outcomes at any one time* for any individual program. Fortunately, regional accrediting associations do not indicate that institutions need to "measure everything all the time." They require an institution to have a *systematic program* of outcome assessment activities. Unless the faculty members limits the number of outcomes being assessed at one time to between three and five per program (in order to reduce the assessment effort necessary and ease the potential paperwork), they will "choke and die" doing assessment. It is far better to select three to five outcomes for assessment activities and use the results to improve programs, than to attempt to assess fifteen different outcomes and never complete "closure of the loop" on any of them because of the effort required in implementing the assessment plan.

How does a department go about selecting three to five intended educational (student learning) outcomes for each program? Figure 24, the "Short-List/Long-List Concept", illustrates the procedure suggested for this purpose.

**Figure 24**

# *SHORT LIST/LONG LIST CONCEPT*

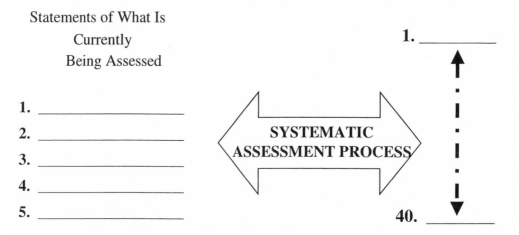

To begin with, the chair should ask each of the faculty (including part-time and adjunct) to anonymously forward up to five intended educational (student learning) outcomes which graduates of the program should achieve. Following discussion among the faculty and with some "word smithing," the chair should be able to identify several outcomes for which a consensus among the faculty exists. These outcomes constitute the beginning of the short list. The selection of the outcomes for assessment from the longer list of program outcomes can be among the most difficult issues encountered in implementation. Faculty have invested their lives in the particular field for which outcomes are being identified. They can be expected to argue strongly that the importance of their portion of the field warrants its inclusion on the initial short outcomes list. Ultimately, through one means or another, the department will need to limit the number of outcomes for assessment to three to five.

The original long list resulting from faculty submissions should not be discarded. The long list will be referred to as the faculty develop their systematic process. Assuming that assessment has taken place regarding outcome number three on the short list and that there is clearly demonstrable evidence that those completing the program are able to achieve this outcome, then the original third outcome on the short list should be returned to the long list and the assessment activities regarding it ceased. At that time, another outcome (not originally assessed) should be moved from the long list to the short list and assessment activities begun. It is this alternation from the long to the short list that demonstrates to regional accrediting association representatives the dynamic nature of the systematic process for ultimately assessing all educational program outcomes for a given degree program. In reality (and in no way compromising this systematic nature of this process), what transpires is that a change in technology, new technique, or fresh discovery about the instructional program often takes place, and a resulting outcome is considered vital so that its mastery must be assessed before other suggested outcomes of much longer standing on the long list. Hence, the outcome regarding the new mastery is moved to the short list ahead of those longer standing outcomes on the long list.

Educational (student learning) outcomes should be *clear in their meanings to faculty in the department*. This requirement sounds awfully simple; however, it will need to be verified by departmental discussions concerning the exact meanings of the outcomes identified. In that regard, faculty should feel free to use the jargon in the field if that helps them specify exactly what they intend for students to achieve as a result of their matriculation through the program. However, faculty may need to explain their jargon in supplemental notes for clear understanding during the reaffirmation process.

Should all outcomes be *measurable*? Undoubtedly, on your campus there exist one or more faculty members who will argue until their last breath that the educational process which they conduct is not measurable, ascertainable, or in any way quantifiable. Frequently, these folks will also accuse you of profaning their profession and/or demeaning them personally and, upon some occasions, may question the nature of your parentage. While the authors can not agree with most of this type of rhetoric, we do agree that not everything we attempt as educators is "measurable to three decimal places." However, as educators, we have frequently extended this position to say, "Everything we do is not measurable; just trust us and send the money." Unfortunately, public trust in higher education (as well as in a number of other social enterprises) is running at or near an all time low, and the public (through one means or another) expects to see hard evidence that educators are worthy of their continued support.

Statements of intended educational (student learning) outcomes should relate to only a single expectation on the part of faculty for students and, hence, should be *singular in nature*. Statements of intended educational (student learning) outcomes which contain commas, semi-colons, or conjunctions are immediately suspect of being "bundled" together or composed of numerous expectations expressed into a single outcome. Earlier in this chapter, practitioners were advised not to try to assess more than three to five outcomes during any one period. If care is not exercised, outcomes listed in three to five sentences may in reality contain many more expectations, each of which is subject to assessment. The authors have reviewed "bundled" outcomes containing twenty-four outcomes in one incredibly complex sentence. The program had taken on enough assessment work for the next six to eight years. Every separate expectation punctuated with a comma, semi-colon, or conjunction requires a separate assessment data point. The goal is to have each statement of intended educational (student learning) outcomes relating to only one expectation.

Formulation of educational (student learning) outcomes that are singular in nature is similar to the process of hypothesis simplification utilized in more traditional research. In this process, the faculty is asked to state the educational (student learning) outcome as a single idea. In such a manner, a single test (means of assessment) can be applied to each hypothesis in turn and, if possible, without interaction with other variables. In the process of learning outcomes assessment, limitation to a single expectation is also important to restrict the amount of assessment taking place at one time.

Once an outcome has been assessed and found to have been met, it should be *rotated back to the long list* and another intended educational (student learning) outcome moved to the short list. This rotation of outcomes demonstrates the systematic nature of the assessment process and justifies the selection for assessment of a limited portion of the long list at any one time. However, there are occasions when an outcome is vital to an educational program (for example, employment for an occupational technical program), and it is retained on the short list even after demonstration of it having been met.

### Examples of Intended Educational (Student Learning) Outcomes

Between three and five intended educational (student learning) outcomes should be identified for each educational program by the faculty (full-time, part-time, and adjunct) who actively participate in teaching within the program. Figures 25 and 26 provide specific examples at a four-year institution of undergraduate or baccalaureate programs in English and Accounting. In each of these examples (for the purpose of graphic representation), the number of outcomes has been limited to three. These models illustrate linkage to the statement of purpose (ESIP) of the institution as well as the program intended educational (student learning) outcomes for each of the programs. Additional models concerning general education, graduate education, and programs typically found in two-year institutions are developed in later chapters in this book.

### Potential Problems in the Preparation of Statements of Intended Educational (Student Learning) Outcomes

Figure 27 highlights problems often encountered in the establishment of intended educational (student learning) outcomes.

Achieving initial *faculty participation in and ownership of* intended educational (student learning) outcomes is an often identified problem. It is more important that all faculty be *invited* to take part in identification of intended educational (student learning) outcomes than it is that all faculty take part. The majority of the faculty who are willing to take part should be encouraged and their input utilized. It has been the authors' experience that after the process begins and faculty can start to see improvements made in their programs, many of the faculty who had initially decided not to take part in this process.

# Figure 25

## *Undergraduate English Program-Two Columns*

<u>Expanded Statement of<br>Institutional Purpose</u>

<u>Institutional Mission<br>Statement:</u>
The principal focus of Our
University's curricular program
is undergraduate education in
the liberal arts and science…

↓

<u>Institutional Goal:</u>
… all graduates of
baccalaureate level
will have developed a
depth of understanding in
their major field.

<u>Program Intended Educational Outcomes:</u>

1. Students completing the baccalaureate
program in English will compare very
favorably in their knowledge of literature
with those students completing a similar
program nationally.

2. Graduates will be able to critique a
brief draft essay.

3. Students completing the baccalaureate
program will be capable of writing an
acceptable journal article.

# Figure 26

## *Accounting Degree Program – Two Columns*

<u>Expanded Statement of<br>Institutional Purpose</u>

<u>Institutional Mission<br>Statement:</u>
The principal focus of Our
University's curricular program
is undergraduate education in the
liberal arts and sciences…

↓

<u>Institutional Goal:</u>
All graduates of baccalaureate
programs will have been
afforded the opportunity to
prepare for a career.

<u>Program Intended Educational<br>Outcomes:</u>

1. Students completing the
baccalaureate program in accounting
will be well prepared for their first
position in the field.

2. Baccalaureate graduates of the
accounting program will readily find
employment in the field.

3. Graduates will be skilled in the use of
personal computers for accounting
procedures.

A major problem is narrowing the number of intended educational (student learning) outcomes being assessed at one time to *between three and five per program*. Often faculty (particularly if they are untenured) seek to be non-confrontational and interested in creating as broad a base of participation as possible. While this is a good and noble intention, it frequently results in expansion of the number of outcomes to be assessed to more than three to five. As stated earlier, three to five educational (student learning) outcomes is all that a department can hope to assess at any one time and continue with their teaching loads and/or research activities.

## Figure 27
### *Problems in Preparation of Statements of Educational (Student Learning) Outcomes*

- **Achieving faculty ownership**
- **Limiting the number of statements**
- **"Backing into" educational (student learning) outcomes from means of assessment**
- **Revising statements of intended educational (student learning) outcomes**

As described earlier in this section, departmental faculty should review the draft statements of intended educational (student learning) outcomes proposed to ascertain if commas, semi-colons, or conjunctions are contained in them. If so, there is a substantial chance that the fifth, fifteenth, and twenty-fifth proposed educational (student learning) outcomes from the long list have been *bundled into a single educational (student learning) outcome* in order to meet the suggested number of three to five outcomes per program. This bundling results in a minimum of nine to fifteen assessment activities to be conducted for each educational program and virtually insures that assessment activities, while appearing to have been thoroughly planned, will "crash and burn" as the faculty are unwilling (for good reason) to conduct that much assessment. Departmental faculty need to select from the long list the most important three to five intended outcomes, avoiding the temptation to aggregate into single outcomes those concepts that are totally unrelated.

One of the great temptations early in the implementation process will be for faculty to *back into intended educational (student learning) outcomes from assessment activities already taking place* on other campuses, or immediately available through standardized testing. The danger in so doing is that by thoughtlessly adopting one of these means of assessment, the faculty have implicitly adopted the intended educational (student learning) outcomes of the test maker or other campus faculty rather than asserting control over the curriculum at their own campus. Additionally, these readily available means of assessment may not measure the outcomes that the faculty on the campus find important and, therefore, potentially useful. Backing into intended educational (student learning) outcomes from some other source is a tempting way to make progress quickly through the first three columns of the model, but this process usually encounters substantial difficulty when faculty are actually asked to utilize the results to improve programs.

Finally, faculty tend to believe that once they have established the first set of statements of intended educational (student learning) outcomes for their program, these outcomes are "written in stone." Faculty need to understand that statements of educational (student learning) outcomes are *subject to change* frequently as the results of their assessment indicate that the outcome is being accomplished. If statements of intended educational (student learning) outcomes remain constant year after year, then representatives of the regional accrediting association reviewing the materials recognize that the assessment process is only episodic and not systematically being utilized to improve student learning but only to satisfy the regional accrediting association.

The identification of intended educational (student learning) outcomes is a very important first step in the assessment process. In many cases, it is abbreviated in nature so that "we can get on with assessment." To shorten this step seriously undermines the use of results from the assessment activities described in the next chapter.

# CHAPTER SEVEN

# IDENTIFICATION OF MEANS OF ASSESSMENT AND CRITERIA FOR SUCCESS

*Once the "road trip" has begun, those making any journey are curious regarding progress toward their destination (outcome). The means of assessment described in this chapter can be considered the "unit of measure" selected by the travelers to indicate their progress toward the planned destination. The "criteria for success" described later in the chapter serve the purpose of benchmarks/mile markers along the road, which are utilized to gauge satisfaction with the progress toward achieving the destination (outcome) intended.*

Assuming that intended educational (student learning) outcomes for the program have been formulated, then the next logical step is identification of the means through which to ascertain accomplishment of their achievement. These means of assessment or approaches can be described utilizing several sets of characteristics.

## Approaches to Assessment

One of the first things which will need to be done on a campus is to dispel the common misunderstanding that assessment requires standardized testing. Faculty need to understand that they may choose to utilize standardized testing; however, it is only one among many choices available to them.

*Criterion vs. Normative Based Assessment*—In most cases, the intended educational (student learning) outcomes identified will point clearly toward the appropriate type of assessment. As an example, "Program completers will exhibit an average level of performance of 2.4"; this calls for a simple average of program completer performance compared to the criterion set. Some outcomes describe the performance of groups of students in comparison to a national or other normative group. Such outcomes lead naturally to the requirement for standardized testing. On other occasions, outcomes will identify a particular level of achievement that may be measured either by locally developed or standardized means of assessment. Both of these approaches, normative and criterion (locally) based assessment, are readily acceptable by all regional accrediting associations.

*Direct vs. Indirect Means of Assessment*—**Direct** means of assessment provide evidence of outcome accomplishment that is observed without the possibility of influence by another source of student achievement. A test including math questions would be direct evidence or assessment of knowledge regarding mathematics; the sound of a musical performance would be direct evidence of musical skills; a design project at the end of their program is direct evidence of engineering ability, etc.

On the other hand, **indirect** evidence of assessment is based upon the perception that because an event transpired that it was based upon another event. For example, if graduates are employed after graduation, employment is an indirect measure of their attainment of skills. A person's assertion or perception that she has improved her writing skills "very much" is not a direct measure of those skills but simply her perception or belief (some would say uninformed belief) regarding her improvement in writing skills.

This differentiation between direct and indirect assessment means has taken on added importance as regional accrediting associations seek to increase the level of rigor associated with what they consider as primary evidence. Indirect means of assessment should only be used as supporting evidence and not the only or primary evidence of outcome accomplishment. Caution should be exercised when using any form of indirect means of assessment, and indirect assessment should be considered no longer as a sufficient means of assessment for the accomplishment of intended educational (student learning) outcomes.

In the authors' opinion, three issues still need to be addressed regarding regional accrediting associations' positions on indirect means of assessment. First, the exact definition of indirect means of assessment needs to be consistently applied and understood. In one of the associations, it was observed that any information resulting from questionnaires was considered "indirect." However, a distinction can be drawn between opinions of the respondents (indirect) and reports of events, such as reading patterns or church attendance (direct). Second, many important value-laden educational outcomes intended by private institutions (spiritualism, commitment, formation, etc.) are best, if not exclusively, assessable through attitudinal or indirect means of assessment. (Value assessment is handled in greater detail in Chapter Ten). Third, some regional accrediting association reports describe feedback from employers, supervising teachers, and practicum/internship supervisors as indirect or supporting evidence. This narrowly applied definition of indirect assessment disallows some of the most important information regarding students' abilities to demonstrate the skills learned during their classroom experience. The expert opinion of employers or those independent observers trained in a field should be considered as direct evidence of the accomplishment of student learning outcomes.

*Qualitative vs. Quantitative Means of Assessment*—Qualitative means of assessment are characterized by faculty judgments regarding the entirety of a student's work as a whole and are typified by non-numerical reports. Examples of such qualitative assessment are normally found in the fine and performing arts departments at an institution as well as in a limited number of other instances. Examples of qualitative assessment include portfolio review, public performances, juried competition, and oral examinations.

An excellent example of qualitative assessment, and the inappropriateness of quantitative assessment, is that of sculpture. Assume for a moment that your institution has an art department which includes a degree program in sculpture. The final product of the sculpture degree program is the culminating piece of sculpture prepared by each student.

How will that sculpture be assessed? It is possible to get several quantitative measures concerning the sculpture. One could weigh the sculpture and assumed that "heavier sculpture is better sculpture," or it could be measured and assume that "bigger sculpture is better sculpture." However, neither of these quantitative measurements truly captures the nature of the sculpture. Rather, the faculty will need to make an overall judgment concerning the extent to which the sculpture meets their standards for the program's completers.

Qualitative assessment offers the advantages of being able to view a piece of work (such as the piece of sculpture described above) within the context of a student's development and other factors. Qualitative assessment is truly open to a great deal of flexibility in its findings; and, on many occasions, qualitative assessment will yield important results not necessarily identified in the program standards.

The primary disadvantages of qualitative assessment include the identification of standards, objectivity of evaluators, and consistency or reliability in judgment between evaluators over time. The identification of standards for qualitative assessment is the most difficult aspect of this assessment methodology. As you can imagine from the example cited, the discussion among faculty in the department of art concerning the standards which should be met for the sculpture program is indeed a rich blend of strongly held opinions. One of the techniques which the authors have used to deal with this difficult task is to ask the departmental faculty to identify the best three to five pieces of student/graduate work which have been produced under their direction in the last several years. The faculty are then asked to write a brief description of why they have identified these pieces of student work as exceptional. Often from such *descriptions,* faculty find common themes that they can weave together into *standards* for activities such as sculpture, painting, dramatic performances, etc., when it is seemingly impossible to move directly to standards.

Another potential disadvantage of qualitative assessment relates to objectivity. When faculty members have established a truly close working relationship with students, how objective can they be in evaluating the students' final works? If the sculpture faculty member in the department of art has worked with a student through Sculpture I, Sculpture II, Sculpture III, Sculpture IV, knows the student/graduate's spouse, has met the student/graduate's children, and perhaps even the graduate's parents, to what extent can he/she be an unbiased evaluator? Many schools deal with this issue by asking contemporaries in identical disciplines at comparable institutions to make the final qualitative judgment regarding student works based upon the standards set for the program by the initiating institution. Utilization of the student presentation or show juried by external evaluators is a version of this type of more objective evaluation described above. In a different field, evaluation of the student's final recital or performance by the faculty overall provides a measure of objectivity as well. Finally, substantial difficulties often develop regarding consistency or reliability in judgment between groups of evaluators. Improvement in reliability or consistency in evaluations is best accomplished by the evaluators conducting trial reviews of various works and then discussing their critiques in an effort to move toward greater inter-rater reliability. Creation of detailed rubrics regarding assessment of individual works will also improve this reliability.

Most of the disadvantages cited concerning qualitative assessment can be dealt with by establishment of a detailed set of guidelines within which professional judgment is rendered and reported. The process described for development of such guidelines or rubrics is described further in this chapter. This procedure requires such judgments to be made in a systematic manner and results in useful information when combined with the "Column and Row Matrix" concept shown later in Figure 33.

Portfolio assessment is the type of qualitative activity most likely to be adopted outside the fine and performing arts. It is not an uncommon approach in relationship to writing and occasionally in professional schools such as that of education. Portfolio assessment is a legitimate form of assessment. However, in order to be used for assessment purposes, similar material should be contained within each portfolio (third paper in first course, fourth project in fifth course, second examination in third course, etc.), and before an overall judgment is made concerning the portfolio, some description of the expected performance to be demonstrated on each item in the portfolio must be arrived at in discussions with the faculty. If these activities are accomplished, then portfolio assessment can be successful in these fields, though not without considerable expense.

The primary limitation regarding portfolio assessment is the amount of time involved in carefully reviewing the contents of each portfolio and making a judgment concerning its adequacy. On many campuses, this review is found to be an overwhelming task when attempted with even a moderate number of student portfolios. Additionally, decisions regarding maintenance and storage of portfolios will be required if this form of assessment is utilized.

Qualitative assessment is extremely important to the fine and performing arts, and faculty in these areas should not be "forced" into using quantitative means of assessment. On the other hand, faculty in the fine and performing arts need to justify the faith put in their qualitative assessment techniques by documenting the use of results of those techniques to improve instructional programming in their area. This documentation often calls for clarification of the reasons for qualitative judgments and the maintenance of at least minimal records of these justifications.

Without any doubt, most assessment activities in higher education are quantitative in nature. That is to say they result in discrete numbers representing the total evaluation conducted and, in many cases, separate numerical data concerning each of the components evaluated as a part of the whole. Quantitative assessment may be subdivided into the components shown in Figure 28 and is composed of cognitive assessment, attitudinal assessment, and behavioral/performance types of assessment. Each of these types of assessment is discussed in some detail in the following subsections.

## Figure 28
### *Types of Quantitative Assessment*

> • **Cognitive – Knowledge**
> • **Attitudinal – Beliefs or Opinions**
> • **Behavioral/Performance – Ability and Use**
>   **of Knowledge**

Cognitive assessment has to do with a student's mastery of the knowledge covered in a particular field. Such cognitive assessment is called for in assessing outcomes using the terms know, understand, explain, etc. It is differentiated from the ability to use such knowledge for purposes intended which will be discussed later in performance and behavioral means of assessment. While these differences may seem trivial, they have a substantive bearing on the means of assessment ultimately selected for their ascertainment.

### Locally Developed vs. Standardized Means of Cognitive Assessment

One of the first issues facing most educational programs is the choice of either standardized or locally developed cognitive means of assessment. In virtually every educational program, at least one of the intended outcomes chosen for assessment relates to mastery of a body of knowledge, thus calling for cognitive assessment. If the outcome identified relates to comparison of the institution's students/graduates with those of other institutions, then standardized tests will be required. On the other hand, in many instances, the intended outcome leaves open the choice of either standardized or locally developed means of assessment.

The advantages of standardized means of assessment are shown in Figure 29. They include a perceived objectivity in their origination by a national panel of experts, the ability to use them to make normative comparisons, ease of administration, as well as completely documented validity and reliability.

## Figure 29
### *Advantages of Standardized Means of Assessment*

> • Reduction of charges of subjectivity or bias because of origination by national "panel of experts"
> • Availability of normative data from other institutions
> • Ease of administration
> • Establishment of validity and reliability

The disadvantages of standardized testing are reflected in Figure 30 and are certainly not difficult to identify.

The primary disadvantage is the frequent failure of standardized tests to reflect the educational program's intended educational (student learning) outcomes. Roughly seven out of ten times, faculty reviewing standardized tests available in their field conclude that the test reviewed does not sufficiently cover the material included in their degree program and/or that it also includes a considerable amount of material not covered in their degree program. Nonetheless, we recommend that if a standardized test is available in a discipline offered by your institution that it at least be reviewed by the faculty to ascertain what a national panel of experts believes is the essential body of knowledge in the field before use of the test is rejected.

# Figure 30
## *Disadvantages of Standardized Means of Assessment*

- Contents may not reflect institution's intended educational (student learning) outcomes.
- Scores may not be reported in manner meaningful for assessment.
- Normative comparisons may be inappropriate.
- Tests are expensive to purchase and to score.

The failure of some standardized tests to report data in a meaningful manner for assessment activities is another of the limitations encountered. Standardized tests originally designed for evaluation of individuals for admission to graduate school are concerned with an overall score for entrance examination purposes. Such a single score is not very useful for assessment purposes as it fails to identify areas in which the students have done well and those in which improvement is needed. For example, in the reaffirmation process, one institution sought to highlight to its regional accrediting association the improvements in placement results for the purpose of improving its developmental courses. The institution learned (too late to avoid embarrassment) that the test chosen did not provide diagnostic sub-scores and was hence useless for the purpose proposed.

One of the significant challenges in dealing with standardized tests for assessment purposes is identification of a normative group. Comparing the normative test scores from private highly selective institutions to that of open admission community colleges is entirely inappropriate. Likewise, difficulties may arise in the comparison of test scores from full-time traditional students to part-time non-traditional or adult students. Simply stated, the institution needs to identify a normative group of institutions that enroll students of roughly a comparable level of academic achievement with whom to compare its data. In many cases, test makers are willing to work with institutions to establish such a representative peer group.

Finally, standardized tests can be relatively expensive to purchase and to score. Who should pay for standardized testing taken by students/graduates of an institution? If the student is the primary beneficiary of taking the standardized test, such as NCLEX (nursing licensure), CPA exam, cosmetology licensure examination, etc., then certainly the student should pay for the examination, and the institution should utilize the score for assessment purposes. On the other hand, if the institution is the primary or (in most cases) the exclusive beneficiary of students/graduates taking an examination, then the institution should pay for the examination.

Within the institution, who should pay for standardized testing taking place regarding academic programs? The institution should establish a central assessment account which can be drawn on by academic departments to fund standardized testing should they select that type of assessment instrumentation. Funding for this purpose should not be allocated to the academic department because other priorities within the department will, in many cases, "siphon off" these funds; and, should there be budget reductions, necessary assessment funding will be the first departmental victim.

The advantages and disadvantages of standardized tests often lead to their rejection by faculty and to serious consideration of a locally developed cognitive means of assessment as an alternative. The advantages of locally developed cognitive measures or tests are depicted in Figure 31.

## Figure 31
### *Advantages of Locally Developed Means of Assessment*

- Contents can be tailored to exactly match intended educational (student learning) outcomes
- Detailed analysis is possible.
- Results are more likely to be used by faculty.
- Faculty "ownership" of tests is assured.

The ability to tailor locally developed means of assessment to match exactly the intended student outcome and curriculum developed by the faculty contributes greatly to the credibility of the assessment results. Faculty members do not question whether the test measures what they taught because they made the test and have confidence in their own work.

The ability to accomplish detailed analysis of results, including item analysis, provides the faculty with a level of information normally not available in standardized test results due to issues of security. Within a given context area, faculty can determine exactly what information was not learned by the students.

These two characteristics, confidence in means of assessment and ability to do detailed analysis of the results, lead to increased use of results from locally developed means of assessment. Often standardized means of assessment are utilized as a preliminary screen to identify possible academic areas in which improvement is needed, and locally developed means are devised to make final judgments prior to initiation of change.

"Faculty ownership" of locally developed tests is absolutely assured based upon their construction by faculty members in the department. However, the amount of faculty involvement necessary to prepare locally developed means of assessment also relates to the disadvantages of such instruments (as shown in Figure 32).

# Figure 32
## *Disadvantages of Locally Developed Means of Assessment*

- Commitment of great amounts of faculty time over an extended period of time to develop, score and maintain
- Lack of normative data for comparison
- Little external credibility for accountability purposes
- Absence of validity and reliability records

The greatest disadvantage of locally developed means of assessment is the commitment of great amounts of faculty time over an extended period of time to develop, score, and maintain these instruments. The time spent on the task is, on the vast majority of campuses, unrecompensed and unrecognized. The construction of locally developed means of assessment is seen as part of the faculty's traditional responsibilities, much in the same light that committee service is expected. This disadvantage, in many cases, has a chilling effect on faculty as they consider their options regarding standardized or locally developed testing.

By definition, locally developed testing lacks normative data for comparison purposes. While this deficiency is not a substantive disadvantage from the standpoint of regional or professional accreditation, this lack of normative comparison contributes to the loss of external credibility of these measures for accountability purposes by state governing agencies. Validity or reliability research concerning locally developed testing is in the main part absent. While such statistical constructs would be welcomed, in most cases there is insufficient time or energy to conduct such studies prior to utilization of the instruments.

Despite the limitations cited above, the movement seems to be toward utilization of more locally developed tests and fewer standardized tests on campuses. The sole exception to this general movement is those increasing number of states requiring standardized testing for public accountability purposes.

## Use of Class Grades as a Means of Cognitive Assessment

Class grades represent individual faculty members' evaluations of students and are not generally accepted as a means of assessment. The authors are not aware of any regional or professional accrediting association that accepts class grades as a primary means of cognitive assessment. Most associations do not explicitly exclude them as means of assessment but do so implicitly in their requirements and most assuredly in the practices of their reaffirmation committees.

Why are individual class grades rejected as a means of assessment for educational programs? As faculty, we are the only profession that (through class grades) certifies its own success. A physician's success is evaluated by patient wellness or mortality. A lawyer's performance is judged by juries. We *individually* provide instruction and certify that it has been successful in stimulating student learning through the grading practice. The fact of both providing and certifying obviously differs from the other professions and leads naturally to questions regarding potential objectivity of the evaluation. For this reason, any time (such as in class grading) that the individual instructor responsible for instruction in a field is the *only* party evaluating or assessing the results of that instruction, its utilization as a means of assessment is severely compromised and of little practical assessment value. The citation of grades or a summary of grades, such as a grade point average (GPA), as a means of assessment by an institution is akin to "running a lightning rod up in the middle of a thunderstorm." It is sure to draw fire from the reaffirmation team and should be avoided.

There are only two circumstances under which class grades are usually accepted as a means of assessment—the assessment of developmental programs by grades in college courses and the assessment of two-year colleges by grades of transfer students in four-year colleges. In the case of developmental program assessment, the grades of developmental program completers in their first college level classes are often found acceptable based upon the passage from the pre-collegiate to collegiate level and the fact that frequently different groups of faculty at the institution present the instruction. Use of the grades from four-year colleges as an assessment of work at the two-year college is likewise found acceptable based upon the transition or passage from one type of institution to another and the presumed objectivity of faculty at the four-year institution. Both of these exceptions are further explored in greater depth in Chapter Eleven.

The inability to use class grades as a means of assessment is often not well received by many faculty members who feel that they individually are the sole authority for evaluation of student learning. No one is challenging the primacy of faculty authority to evaluate student learning. Faculty will continue to award student grades just as always. However, in order to assure greater objectivity, the assessment of learning at the degree program level has been elevated to the corporate level of the departmental faculty or its representative group. Either the entire departmental faculty, or a panel of the faculty, can provide the desired distance from that individual faculty member directly responsible for class grades and be readily accepted as objective evaluation of student learning in a degree program.

In many instances, activities will take place within a class that are potentially usable as a means of program assessment. Under these circumstances, the individual faculty member should continue to award the grade for the student in the class. However, the product (project, paper, examination, etc.) should be retained and then reviewed a *second time* by the faculty in the department, or a panel thereof, for the purpose of program assessment.

Another useful way to deal with faculty members' frustration regarding their inability to use individual student and class grades as a means of assessment is shown in Figure 33, the "Column and Row Model."

# Figure 33
## *Relationship Between Individual Student Scores and Educational Outcomes Assessment —*
### *The "Column and Row Model"*

| Individual Students Scored by Various Faculty | | | | | Criteria/Intended Educational Outcomes Average |
|---|---|---|---|---|---|
| **Criteria** Student1 | **Student 2** | Student 3 | Student 4 | Student 5 | |
| **Spelling**    3 | **4** | 1 | 2 | 3 | **2.6** |
| **Grammar**    2 | **5** | 3 | 2 | 5 | **3.4** |
| **Punctuation**  4 | **5** | 2 | 3 | 4 | **3.6** |
| **Structure**    4 | **3** | 4 | 5 | 3 | **3.8** |
| TOTAL    13 | **17** | 10 | 12 | 15 | |
| Individual | | | | | |
| Student Grade   C | **A** | D | C | B | |

*Total "Down the Columns" for Individual Student Grading*
*Analyze "Across the Rows" for Assessment of Intended Educational Outcomes Accomplishment*

Often faculty in a department have agreed for grading purposes to common criteria for evaluation of projects, papers, performances, etc. These common criteria, as depicted in the field of writing in Figure 33, are applied to individual students by various faculty. Traditionally, faculty "look down the columns" at each student's performance to determine (in the example on a five-point scale) how well the student achieved these commonly agreed upon criteria, and this review ultimately results in a student grade being awarded at the bottom of the column. As indicated previously, the utilization of student grades as a means of program assessment is sure to be rejected by regional accreditors. However, analysis of the individual criteria scores "across the rows" to identify areas of common student weakness is readily accepted as a means of assessment. In the example cited, an outcome could be stated thus: "Graduates of the program will be able to spell satisfactorily (an average score of 3.0 or more) in the field as judged by the commonly applied rubrics developed by the English Department as applied to a writing sample chosen. . . . " When analyzing the data in Figure 33, it is obvious that the average score is only 2.6 on the spelling criteria of this requirement, thus leading the faculty to conclude that on spelling students were not performing at the desired level in the program. From that finding, they would seek to identify means through which to improve the program completers' performance in spelling.

The "Column and Row" model is one of the most powerful means through which to move from little assessment information to a wealth of useful assessment information quickly. Whenever a student has completed or will complete a project, internship, practicum, or cooperative education experience near the end of the course of study, the potential for its utilization as a means of assessment is created. On many occasions, institutions have accomplished such activities in the past. If adequate records have been maintained and the observation procedure meets the objectivity and representiveness criteria regarding performance assessment described later in this chapter, rapid progress can be made by analysis of the existing observations utilizing the "Column and Row Model" shown in Figure 33.

### Standardized Cognitive Examinations

Most standardized cognitive assessment at four-year colleges is accomplished through (a) instruments specifically designed for assessment purposes, (b) licensure examinations, and (c) graduate school admissions tests of one sort or another.

Graduate school admissions tests can be divided into those relating specifically to graduate level fields of study or discipline (GMAT, LSAT, MCAT, etc.) and the overall Graduate Record Examinations (GRE) from the Educational Testing Services (ETS). Neither of these types of examinations is of much practical use in assessment. In most cases, the GMAT, LSAT, and MCAT type of specialized professional school admissions test does not measure the achievement or learning of students in an undergraduate program but is highly correlated with the student's ability to learn as measured in undergraduate admissions tests. Prior to considering use of such examinations as a measure of baccalaureate program achievement, institutions should carefully examine the characteristics of these examinations.

The Graduate Record Examination (GRE) from ETS is also of little help assessment wise. The verbal and quantitative portions of the examination are pure aptitude in nature and do not measure student achievement. The GRE field tests are a measure of student achievement at the undergraduate level. However, they suffer from two significant shortcomings as assessment instruments. First, they are not available for faculty review and confirmation of content. Second, the normative group for these GRE field tests consists of students voluntarily selecting to take the test as a prelude to graduate school enrollment. Hence, if the GRE field tests are administered to all graduates of the program (a necessary requirement in order to demonstrate representativeness of the sample for assessment purposes), then the normative group to which those graduates will be compared is a selective group that had previously taken the examination voluntarily.

On the other hand, instruments designed specifically for assessment purposes, such as the Major Field Tests (MFAT) from the Educational Testing Service and the Area

Concentration Achievement Tests (ACAT) are potentially of considerable use. The Major Field Tests from ETS (Figure 34) were, early in their history, somewhat dated GRE field tests. Since that time, all of the Major Field Tests shown in Figure 34 have been revisited and updated.

## Figure 34
### *Means of Assessment in the Major from Educational Testing Service (ETS)*

| Graduate Record Examination (GRE) | | |
| --- | --- | --- |
| Major Field Achievement Texts (MFAT) | | |
| Political Science | Chemistry | Biology |
| Computer Science | Economics | Physics |
| Education | History | Psychology |
| Literature in | Mathematics | Sociology |
| English | Criminal Justice | Business |
| Music | | |
| Master of Business Administration | | |
| www.ets.org | | |

The primary advantages of these tests (compared to the GRE field tests) are (a) the willingness of ETS to forward these test to the campus for faculty review and (b) the normative group for the test, which is composed of all students completing degree programs, as opposed to the GRE field tests, which only those students seeking admission to graduate school take.

During the last several years, two significant developments have taken place regarding ETS testing. *First*, both the GRE and MFAT are now available on-line. This availability greatly facilitates turn-around time for test results and insures that MFAT scores can be available for utilization as part of class grades (a major motivation technique in encouraging students to take the test seriously). *Second*, ETS has expanded its MFAT testing to the graduate level. The MFAT is the first such instrument to offer a test covering the Masters in Business Administration. ETS is currently in the early developmental stages of a similar instrument concerning the graduate field of educational administration.

The Area Concentration Achievement Tests (ACAT), originally housed at Austin Peay State University, were initially funded by a Fund for the Improvement of Post-Secondary Education (FIPSE) grant, which expired a number of years ago. Since that time, the ACAT tests have proven to be both durable and worthwhile. The ACAT approach to standardized testing in the fields, shown in Figure 35, is to establish an item bank regarding the subfields of each discipline shown. An institution may then shop among the subfields within each discipline to create a "standardized" test based upon only the subfields covered in the institution's degree program. Hence, the result is a standardized test that has been customized to institutional needs. The primary disadvantages of the ACAT tests rest in the relatively limited number of fields in which these examinations are offered and the number of institutions that have utilized this service.

## Figure 35
### *Area Concentration Achievement Test (ACAT)*

- **Standardized Item Bank**

- **Selection of scales based upon institutional curriculum**

- **Fields available:**

| | |
|---|---|
| **Agriculture** | **History** |
| **Art** | **Literature** |
| **Biology** | **Political Science** |
| **Criminal Justice** | **Psychology** |
| **Geology** | **Social Work** |

*www.collegeoutcomes.com*

Institutions choosing instruments from either ETS or ACAT will need to address issues concerning normative groups and small numbers of annual graduates in some fields. Each institution will need to consider the normative group of institutions to which their participants' scores will be compared. If, for some reason, the institution composing the national normative group offered by the vendor is substantially dissimilar from the institution utilizing the test, the additional expense of selecting a more appropriate sub-set of the national normative group for comparative purposes may be warranted.

Problems relating to small numbers of graduates taking the exam annually (less than five) are frequently encountered. In these instances, the vendors are, for statistical reasons, very unwilling to release the subscale scores. For the educational program, the sub-scale information is the most useful assessment information. In such instances, in order to get data, institutions will need to accumulate over several years a sufficient number of participants to meet the vendor's minimum number for sub-scale information. Programs may need to petition the vendor for the opportunity to combine participants from the several identified testing years in order to receive the full subscale information. This request may entail additional cost to the institution. In the intervening period, this delayed action should be reported in Column Four, and no action for improvement can be taken regarding changes in the program until data is available.

Licensure examinations, such as those shown in Figure 36, are also frequently utilized as standardized tests of student cognitive development through baccalaureate programs. Students are well-motivated to take these examinations; many of our curricula are constructed intentionally to prepare students to pass licensure examinations; and the results are widely accepted by the public and other institutions as a barometer of student achievement.

## Figure 36
### *Licensure Examinations Commonly Found at 4-Year Colleges*

## <u>Examples:</u>

- **Bar Examination**

- **Medical Examination**

- **Certified Public Accountant Examination**

- **National Teacher Examination**

- **Nursing**

- **Counseling**

- **Social Work**

The primary issue concerning licensure examinations is the amount and type of information that can be obtained from the licensure examination. If the only information available to an institution is the extent to which its graduates "pass" the overall licensure examination, this information is of marginal use for assessment purposes. On the other hand, if the institution can get sub scores by various components of the licensure exam, then it has identified a powerful means of assessment. Access to licensure exam results varies considerably from the NCLEX nursing examination, which has in the past provided almost item analysis, to several other licensure examinations, from which it is difficult to obtain even pass/fail rates for an institution. Clearly, if the licensing agency wishes to improve the preparation of practitioners in its field, then the maximum amount of information concerning participant performance possible (without compromising the examination) should be provided to the institutions from which practitioners graduate.

On countless occasions, departmental faculty members have reported to the authors that only "pass/fail" information from the licensure examination is available, later to find otherwise. Often, unless the institution asks, only "pass/fail" results are provided by the licensure agency. Once the agency is questioned, institutions have often found that more detailed sub-score information is available, though frequently at a small price. A further problem encountered on some campuses is the failure to distribute sub-score data to interested programs throughout the campus. On one major research campus visited by the authors, the liberal arts departments wanted to use sub-scale scores regarding teacher-licensure examinations. However, the School of Education professed strongly that no sub-scale scores were available. The following day, a staff member came forward with five years' worth of sub-score information that was "liberated" from the file cabinet of the teacher certification officer in the School of Education where the scores had been secured (unopened) from the time when they first started giving the exam. In both of the cases described, it took an active need for meaningful data from these licensure exams before the sub-scale information was made available and utilized by the programs.

Near the end of this publication is a "Resource Section" which briefly reviews the standardized means of assessment commonly utilized in two- and four-year colleges. This Resource Section provides preliminary descriptions and contact information regarding these and other standardized tests.

## Locally Developed Cognitive Measures

It has been the authors' observation that locally developed cognitive measures of student learning, commonly known as comprehensive examinations, are increasingly utilized for assessment at all program levels. The principal means for administration of these examinations is through embedding them in a "capstone" course near the end of the students' matriculation. As stated earlier in this chapter, the primary factor limiting even greater utilization of locally developed means of cognitive assessment is the large time commitment necessary to develop, administer, maintain, and score such instrumentation. Only on a very few campuses is "release time" (or additional compensation) provided for this substantial increase in work load.

Capstone courses are designed to draw together students' knowledge from across a wide variety of classes in the major, many of the classes taken in previous years. The capstone course itself is not a means of assessment: however, it provides a vehicle for motivating students to take comprehensive examinations or complete projects, as well as a number of other assessment activities designed to be administered at the end of the program. A comprehensive examination is often administered within the class and evaluated once by the faculty member in charge of the class for grading purposes and then reviewed a second time by a panel of faculty for assessment purposes. Often this review is conducted using the "Column and Row Model" shown earlier as Figure 33.

Cognitive assessment in the major is the most common form of assessment activity regarding those students completing baccalaureate, graduate, or professional level degree programs. It is accomplished through either standardized or locally developed means, and its analysis is one of the most important pieces of information concerning the manner in which the degree program is functioning. However, the ability of the students to use the knowledge gained at the time they complete the program and, to a lesser extent, their attitudes then and later in life are also subject to assessment.

## Attitudinal Means of Assessment

While cognitive assessment provides "hard" or "direct" information concerning the acquisition of knowledge, attitudinal assessment is frequently described as among the "warm and fuzzy" types of information available. Attitudinal assessment information consists primarily of affirmation of program accomplishments by students, graduates, or alumni. As discussed earlier in this chapter, these types of attitudinal assessments are characterized as "indirect measures" and are primarily of use for supporting information for the educational programs as institutions are asked by their regional accrediting associations to provide more than one means of assessment for most intended educational (student learning) outcomes. Regional accrediting associations consider such assessment information as insufficient in itself to provide an indication of student academic achievement. It is important to note that such attitudinal assessment remains entirely appropriate and completely accepted in relationship to clients in educational support and administrative units.

The four basic types of attitudinal assessments are the enrolled student survey, the graduating student survey, alumni survey, and employer survey. The attitudes of newly enrolled students are in the authors' opinion of minimal value in assessing the major as many of these students will have seen only a portion of the curriculum. The graduating student survey, on the other hand, is among the most cost effective means of attitudinal assessment in the major. Quite high (95% plus) response rates may be realized by integration, distribution, and intake of graduating student surveys into the students' process for applying for degrees. Studies at the University of Mississippi have indicated that responses regarding program satisfaction by students as they graduate differ very little from responses on alumni surveys one year after graduation. If they loved you when they graduated, they will still love you on the alumni survey. On the other hand, if they hated you when they graduated, they find little reason to change those beliefs based upon experiences later in life. The saying "they don't understand now, but they will later in life" doesn't seem to hold up in reality in this regard.

Information from such graduating student survey results needs to be sorted by major to be of use in educational program. The graduating student survey should include a place for the educational departments to provide items relevant to the intended educational (student learning) outcomes for their program. (See Figure 37.)

# Figure 37

Mark Reflex® by NCS EM-161209-2:65432     ED06     Printed in U.S.A.

## THE UNIVERSITY OF MISSISSIPPI
## GRADUATING STUDENT SURVEY

**OFFICE USE ONLY**

CONGRATULATIONS UPON COMPLETION OF YOUR DEGREE REQUIREMENTS AT OLE MISS! As an alumna or alumnus of our institution, I know that you take pride in your accomplishment and want to help further improve the educational experiences enjoyed by those who follow you at Ole Miss. To gather information concerning your Ole Miss experience, this brief questionnaire is provided for your completion. It asks for information about yourself and your plans after graduation, as well as the extent to which you are satisfied with Ole Miss in general, University services, and your specific degree program. Your answers will remain confidential and will be used to improve your alma mater's academic programs and administrative services. Please return this questionnaire when you file your Application for Diploma in the Office of the Registrar.

*Robert C. Khayat*
Robert C. Khayat, Chancellor

**DEGREE PROGRAM CODE**

USE NO. 2 PENCIL ONLY     CORRECT MARK     INCORRECT MARKS

**BIOGRAPHICAL/ENROLLMENT DATA**   Indicate only one response for each item by marking the appropriate circle.

**1. GENDER**
- Male
- Female

**2. RACE**
- White
- Black
- Other

**3. CITIZENSHIP**
- U.S.
- Other

**4. RESIDENCY AT TIME OF ADMISSION**
- Resident of Mississippi
- Non-resident of Mississippi

**5. CURRENT AGE**
- 22 or under
- 23–25
- 26–28
- 29–31
- 32–34
- 35 or older

**6. CURRENT STATUS**
- Undergraduate
- Graduate

**7A. (UNDERGRADUATE STUDENTS ONLY) WHILE PURSUING THIS DEGREE, DID YOU:**
- Originally enroll (and remain) at Ole Miss
- Transfer from a 2-year institution
- Transfer from a 4-year institution

**8. NUMBER OF YEARS IN ATTENDANCE AT OLE MISS**
- One
- Two
- Three
- Four
- Five
- Six+

**9. PLEASE ESTIMATE YOUR CUMULATIVE GPA (including only Ole Miss courses) UPON COMPLETION OF THIS DEGREE.**
- 3.75+
- 3.50–3.74
- 3.25–3.49
- 3.00–3.24
- 2.75–2.99
- 2.50–2.74
- 2.25–2.49
- 2.00–2.24
- Below 2.00

**10. NUMBER OF SEMESTERS YOU HAVE LIVED IN AN OLE MISS RESIDENCE HALL**
- None
- One
- Two
- Three
- Four
- Five+

**11. ARE YOU ACTIVE IN AN OLE MISS SOCIAL FRATERNITY OR SORORITY?**
- Yes
- No

**7B. (GRADUATE & LAW STUDENTS ONLY) UNDERGRADUATE DEGREE FROM:**
- Ole Miss
- Other institution

**12. AVERAGE NUMBER OF HOURS EMPLOYED (ON/OFF CAMPUS) PER WEEK DURING THE PAST YEAR**
- None
- 1–10
- 11–20
- 21–30
- 31–40
- 40+

**PLANS FOLLOWING GRADUATION**   Indicate only one response for each item by marking the appropriate circle.

**13. What are your immediate employment plans?**
- (a) I plan to continue working in the same job I had prior to completing this educational program.
- (b) I plan to work in a job I recently obtained.
- (c) I am currently looking for a job.
- (d) I do not plan to work outside the home.
- (e) I plan to continue my education before working.
- (f) I have not yet formulated my employment plans.

**14. If you indicated in #13 that you currently have or will be starting a new job, to what extent is it related to your major or area of study at Ole Miss?**
- (a) Directly related.
- (b) Somewhat related.
- (c) Not related.

**Is the job in Mississippi?**
- (a) Yes.
- (b) No.

**15. Do you currently have plans for additional education?**
- (a) No, not at this time.
- (b) Yes, I plan to reenroll at this institution.
- (c) Yes, I plan to enroll at another institution. *
- (d) Yes, I have been accepted for enrollment at another institution. *
- (e) I am currently undecided about additional education.

*If you chose responses "c" or "d" above, please indicate name of institution you will attend.

**16. If you indicated in #15 that you plan to continue your education, what is the highest degree you plan to earn?**
- (a) Master's degree
- (b) Specialist degree (e.g., Ed.S.)
- (c) Professional degree (e.g., medicine, law, theology)
- (d) Doctoral degree (e.g., Ph.D., Ed.D., D.B.A.)

**GENERAL LEVEL OF SATISFACTION WITH ATTENDANCE AT THE UNIVERSITY (Undergraduate Students Only)**

For each of the following items which apply, please indicate the extent of your agreement with the statement as it describes your experience at Ole Miss.

| Within my degree program or because of my experiences at Ole Miss, I: | NOT APPLICABLE | STRONGLY AGREE | AGREE | NEUTRAL | DISAGREE | STRONGLY DISAGREE |
|---|---|---|---|---|---|---|
| 17. Acquired a basic knowledge in the liberal arts (humanities, social sciences, and natural sciences). | NA | SA | A | N | D | SD |
| 18. Felt academically challenged. | NA | SA | A | N | D | SD |
| 19. Developed the ability to write effectively. | NA | SA | A | N | D | SD |
| 20. Felt adequately prepared for graduate study in my major field. | NA | SA | A | N | D | SD |
| 21. Was prepared to assume the responsibilities of my chosen profession. | NA | SA | A | N | D | SD |
| 22. Developed the ability to express myself effectively through speaking. | NA | SA | A | N | D | SD |
| 23. Developed multicultural and global perspectives. | NA | SA | A | N | D | SD |
| 24. Would recommend to others that they study within the same program at Ole Miss. | NA | SA | A | N | D | SD |
| 25. Would recommend Ole Miss to prospective students. | NA | SA | A | N | D | SD |

**OVER**

## OPINIONS CONCERNING UNIVERSITY ENVIRONMENT AND SERVICES (Graduate and Undergraduate Students)

Please indicate your level of satisfaction with each of the following University environmental conditions and services which you have used or directly experienced.

| Environment and Services | NOT APPLICABLE OR DID NOT USE | VERY SATISFIED | SATISFIED | NEUTRAL | UN-SATISFIED | VERY UN-SATISFIED |
|---|---|---|---|---|---|---|
| 26. Admissions | NA | VS | S | N | U | VU |
| 27. Telephone Registration | NA | VS | S | N | U | VU |
| 28. Regular Registration | NA | VS | S | N | U | VU |
| 29. Fee Payment Process | NA | VS | S | N | U | VU |
| 30. Bursar Office Services | NA | VS | S | N | U | VU |
| 31. Academic Advising in School or College | NA | VS | S | N | U | VU |
| 32. University Counseling Center | NA | VS | S | N | U | VU |
| 33. Teaching and Learning Center Services/Disability Services | NA | VS | S | N | U | VU |
| 34. Recognition and Promotion of Cultural Diversity | NA | VS | S | N | U | VU |
| 35. Student Housing and Residence Life Services and Programs | NA | VS | S | N | U | VU |
| 36. Student Programming Board Programs and Activities | NA | VS | S | N | U | VU |
| 37. Department of Campus Recreation | NA | VS | S | N | U | VU |
| 38. International Student Advisory Services | NA | VS | S | N | U | VU |
| 39. Dean of Students Office | NA | VS | S | N | U | VU |
| 40. Student Media/Newspaper, Yearbook, Radio, and Television | NA | VS | S | N | U | VU |
| 41. Financial Aid Processed in Timely Manner | NA | VS | S | N | U | VU |
| 42. University Police Department Public Safety Services | NA | VS | S | N | U | VU |
| 43. Student Health Service | NA | VS | S | N | U | VU |
| 44. Student Health Education Presentations/Programs/Counseling | NA | VS | S | N | U | VU |
| 45. Student Health Center Pharmacy | NA | VS | S | N | U | VU |
| 46. Career Services Center Information | NA | VS | S | N | U | VU |
| 47. Financial Aid Services | NA | VS | S | N | U | VU |
| 48. Food Services | NA | VS | S | N | U | VU |
| 49. Overall Classroom Conditions | NA | VS | S | N | U | VU |
| 50. Condition and Maintenance of University Grounds | NA | VS | S | N | U | VU |
| 51. J.D. Williams Library and its Music and Science Branch Libraries | NA | VS | S | N | U | VU |
| 52. Law Library | NA | VS | S | N | U | VU |
| 53. Computer Center Services | NA | VS | S | N | U | VU |
| 54. Bookstore | NA | VS | S | N | U | VU |
| 55. Graduate School Office | NA | VS | S | N | U | VU |

## ITEMS RELATED TO YOUR DEGREE PROGRAM

While the opinions you expressed above concerning the University in general are important, your thoughts about your specific degree program are most important. When you received this form, you were also provided a separate sheet of colored paper with items (numbered 56–75) that relate directly to your degree program. Please indicate below the extent of your agreement with each statement contained on the colored paper.

| | NOT APPLICABLE | STRONGLY AGREE | AGREE | NEUTRAL | DISAGREE | STRONGLY DISAGREE | | | NOT APPLICABLE | STRONGLY AGREE | AGREE | NEUTRAL | DISAGREE | STRONGLY DISAGREE |
|---|---|---|---|---|---|---|---|---|---|---|---|---|---|---|
| 56. | NA | SA | A | N | D | SD | | 66. | NA | SA | A | N | D | SD |
| 57. | NA | SA | A | N | D | SD | | 67. | NA | SA | A | N | D | SD |
| 58. | NA | SA | A | N | D | SD | | 68. | NA | SA | A | N | D | SD |
| 59. | NA | SA | A | N | D | SD | | 69. | NA | SA | A | N | D | SD |
| 60. | NA | SA | A | N | D | SD | | 70. | NA | SA | A | N | D | SD |
| 61. | NA | SA | A | N | D | SD | | 71. | NA | SA | A | N | D | SD |
| 62. | NA | SA | A | N | D | SD | | 72. | NA | SA | A | N | D | SD |
| 63. | NA | SA | A | N | D | SD | | 73. | NA | SA | A | N | D | SD |
| 64. | NA | SA | A | N | D | SD | | 74. | NA | SA | A | N | D | SD |
| 65. | NA | SA | A | N | D | SD | | 75. | NA | SA | A | N | D | SD |

## COMMENTS

Please feel free to add your written comments in the space provided at the right and return this form to the Office of the Registrar at the time you file your Application for Diploma.

Your completion of this survey is greatly appreciated and will help to improve your alma mater. Again, Congratulations!

# Figure 38

## The University of Mississippi
## Undergraduate Alumni Survey

This survey concerns the degree and major indicated below which you recently received from The University of Mississippi. Even if you have received an additional degree, please focus your responses for the degree indicated. List any corrections for degree and major in the blanks provided. The number code on the label below is designed only for office follow-up on nonreturned surveys to ensure a representative response for all majors of the University.

| Degree (e.g., B.A.) | Field of Study (e.g., English) | Year Degree Conferred |
| --- | --- | --- |

For Office Use Only
① ②

In which type of degree program have you enrolled since receiving the degree indicated on the label?

① I have not enrolled in a degree program.
② I have enrolled in another undergraduate degree program.
③ I have enrolled in a master's degree program
④ I have enrolled in a professional degree program (e.g., J.D., Pharm.D., M.D.)
⑤ I have enrolled in a doctoral degree program.

Please provide information about the institution in which you are enrolled for this degree.

Institution Name _____ City _____ State _____

Have you taken a professional examination related to your major since graduating from The University of Mississippi?  ① Yes  ② No    Did you pass the examination?  ① Yes  ② No

*Please enter the name of the examination.* _____

Have you become licensed or certified since graduating from The University of Mississippi?  ① Yes  ② No

*In what area have you become licensed or certified?* _____ *When?* _____

Please darken the oval indicating the extent to which you agree or disagree with each of the following statements.

| | strongly agree | agree | neutral | disagree | strongly disagree | not applicable |
| --- | --- | --- | --- | --- | --- | --- |
| The curriculum for my degree was relevant to the position I now hold. | ⑤ | ④ | ③ | ② | ① | ✸ |
| I would recommend Ole Miss to other students. | ⑤ | ④ | ③ | ② | ① | ✸ |
| I would recommend my undergraduate degree program to other students. | ⑤ | ④ | ③ | ② | ① | ✸ |
| My undergraduate experience at The University of Mississippi… | | | | | | |
| prepared me for graduate study in my major field. | ⑤ | ④ | ③ | ② | ① | ✸ |
| prepared me for professional employment in my field. | ⑤ | ④ | ③ | ② | ① | ✸ |
| enabled me to compete effectively with colleagues educated elsewhere. | ⑤ | ④ | ③ | ② | ① | ✸ |
| | | | | | | |
| While attending The University of Mississippi… | | | | | | |
| I acquired the skills necessary for success in my field. | ⑤ | ④ | ③ | ② | ① | ✸ |
| I obtained the knowledge necessary for success in my field. | ⑤ | ④ | ③ | ② | ① | ✸ |
| I received good career advising from my department. | ⑤ | ④ | ③ | ② | ① | ✸ |
| I gained the ability to understand issues of general social and political interest. | ⑤ | ④ | ③ | ② | ① | ✸ |
| I learned to analyze and evaluate competing or contradictory information or points of view on topics. | ⑤ | ④ | ③ | ② | ① | ✸ |
| I developed the ability to write effectively. | ⑤ | ④ | ③ | ② | ① | ✸ |
| I developed the ability to express myself effectively through speaking. | ⑤ | ④ | ③ | ② | ① | ✸ |
| I developed good listening skills. | ⑤ | ④ | ③ | ② | ① | ✸ |
| I developed the ability to understand the relationship between skill/knowledge and the obligation to use that skill/knowledge ethically. | ⑤ | ④ | ③ | ② | ① | ✸ |

For Office Use Only

When were you offered the first full-time position you held after graduation?

① I have not yet obtained a full-time position.
② I secured employment before graduation.
③ 1-3 months after graduation.
④ 4-6 months after graduation.
⑤ 7-9 months after graduation.
⑥ 10-12 months after graduation.

How many job offers did you receive before accepting your first position after graduation?

① 0 - 3
② 4 - 6
③ 7 - 9
④ more than 10

| ① | ① ① ① |
| ② | ① ① ① |
| ③ | ② ② ② |
| ④ | ③ ③ ③ |
| ⑤ | ④ ④ ④ |
| ⑥ | ⑤ ⑤ ⑤ |
| ⑦ | ⑥ ⑥ ⑥ |
| | ⑦ ⑦ ⑦ |
| | ⑧ ⑧ ⑧ |
| | ⑨ ⑨ ⑨ |

**Current Employment Questions:**

**How did you learn of your present position?**

① I worked with the employer before graduation.
② The University of Mississippi Career Center
③ Employment agency
④ Newspaper advertisement
⑤ Faculty contact or reference
⑥ Personal contact
⑦ I am currently not employed.
⑧ Other _____

**What are you currently doing?**
**(Mark all that apply.)**

① I am working full-time for pay.
② I am working part-time for pay.
③ I am working without compensation.
④ I am pursuing further education.
⑤ I am unemployed and looking for a position.
⑥ I am unemployed and not looking for a position.

**If you are currently not working for pay, why not?**

① I chose not to enter the workforce at this time.
② It has been difficult to find a position in my field.
③ It has been difficult to find a position paying an appropriate salary.

**Indicate the range of your beginning salary (Optional)**

① Under $25,000
② $25,000 - $35,000
③ $35,000 - $45,000
④ $45,000 - $55,000
⑤ Over $55,000

What is the company name of your current employer? _____ What is your job title? _____

What is your employment address? _____ City _____ State _____

**While attending The University of Mississippi, did you...**

**Yes  No**
Ⓨ  Ⓝ  register with the Career Center?
Ⓨ  Ⓝ  receive assistance with writing your resume from the Career Center?
Ⓨ  Ⓝ  develop a job search plan with the assistance from the Career Center staff?
Ⓨ  Ⓝ  receive information on interview techniques from the Career Center?
Ⓨ  Ⓝ  interview for employment through the Career Center?

**Please darken the oval indicating your response to the questions concerning the Alumni Association.**

**Yes  No**
Ⓨ  Ⓝ  Did you receive your free membership in the Alumni Association when you graduated?
Ⓨ  Ⓝ  Did you accept the $10 special alumni membership offered for your second year following graduation?
Ⓨ  Ⓝ  Have you attended your local alumni club meeting?
Ⓨ  Ⓝ  Have you visited the Alumni Association's webpage: www.alum.olemiss.edu?
Ⓨ  Ⓝ  Do you plan to become involved in alumni activities?

**What is your gender?**

① Female
② Male

**What is your ethnicity?**
① African American
② Asian/Pacific Islander
③ Caucasian
④ Hispanic American
⑤ Native American
⑥ Other_____

**What was your approximate final G.P.A.?**

① 2.00 - 2.50
② 2.51 - 3.00
③ 3.01 - 3.50
④ 3.51 - 4.00

Please use the space below to write comments regarding your University of Mississippi undergraduate experience.

_____

_____

**THANK YOU for your response!!! Please return survey in envelope provided by January 17, 2000.**

Alumni Survey, The University of Mississippi, 217 Martindale Center, University, MS 38655

Surveys of alumni allow the institution to ask questions concerning their experiences since leaving the institution and can be very helpful in determining continuation of important institutional values, such as continuous learning, citizenship, or service to others. Unfortunately, the greatest problem with such surveys is the relatively modest (25-35%) response rates realized from such surveys. This problem is compounded by the need to use alumni association records for addresses in most instances. Such a source is hardly unbiased, as those individuals with the most positive feelings concerning the institution are most likely to maintain their institutional relationship through membership in the alumni association. When conducting an alumni survey, such as that shown in Figure 38, two items need to be carefully considered in order not to reduce already modest rates of response. First, the survey should be seen by the respondent as part of the educational enterprise of the institution and not part of its alumni/fundraising effort. Otherwise, the response rate will suffer substantially. Second, the survey should avoid asking information concerning earned income. At most, alumni should be asked to identify their income by general brackets. Asking for specific information concerning one's salary has always led to reduced response rates.

Commercially developed surveys are available from a number of sources, such as those shown in Figure 39. They are further identified and described in the Resource Section entitled "Attitudinal Assessment Surveys" by Daniel Weinstein near the end of this publication. The advantages of using such commercially developed surveys are their ready availability and normative comparisons. Each of the companies identified in Figure 39 and in the Resource Section can provide survey services on very short notice. Many of them include in that service distribution and processing of the results. Only through such commercially developed surveys can normative comparisons of respondents be accomplished. In many cases (parking, food services, financial aid, etc.) without normative response comparisons, locally developed information is of marginal use. These types of surveys provide little more than public relations information.

## Figure 39
### *Sources of Commercially Developed Surveys*

- American College Test
- National Center for Higher Education Management Systems
- Educational Testing Service
- Noel-Levitz
- Cooperative Institutional Research Program

The primary disadvantages of the use of commercially developed surveys are their relative expense and appearance. Survey research from a commercially developed source may easily range from $3 to $4 per survey instrument, depending upon the exact service required. Additionally, there is little institutional identification (a major factor influencing response rates) from such commercial surveys. Institutions choosing a commercially developed survey will need to do everything possible to make the questionnaire appear to be from the institution rather than from the vendor.

Locally developed surveys, on the other hand, can be custom tailored to the institution and evidence great institutional identity. Locally developed questionnaires can use the names of familiar structures, majors, and, upon rare occasion, even individuals so that the survey best fits the experience and recognition of the respondent. In addition, great institutional identification can be brought about through the use of the institutional logo, symbols, colors, etc., thus serving a public relations as well as research function. The primary disadvantages of locally developed instruments include the time involved in preparation and the lack of normative data. Design through production, distribution, and data processing of locally developed surveys takes approximately six to twelve months per instrument. Further, no normative comparison with participants' responses is possible. However, the extent to which some survey items found on locally developed instruments resemble those on commercially available ones is not surprising.

Employer/supervisor surveys, in the authors' opinion, are a very different type of attitudinal survey. These surveys constitute the attitude of the consumers toward our product (the educated student). While employer/supervisor surveys are, upon occasion, listed among the indirect measures that an institution may utilize, this type of survey research for those educational programs directly concerned with preparing students for employment is among the most important indicators of a program's success. Because the opinions of regional accrediting associations vary and are changing regarding whether this measure is a direct or indirect assessment of intended educational (student learning) outcomes, the institution should ascertain the direct or indirect status of employer feedback at the beginning of the reaffirmation process from its regional accrediting association contact. If this is not possible, the authors suggest you consider employer feedback as direct evidence and proceed.

The nature of the employer survey should be as specific and directly related to the field as possible. Very general terms such as "ability to work in groups" should be succinctly defined on the survey instrument so as to control the feedback received from the employer. Employers should respond to the institution's definition of "ability to work in groups" rather than their own definition of that term.

Response rates from employer surveys can be found to be very low (10 – 15%) on some occasions. The reason for such a low response seems to come about because of the effort required to complete such surveys and the employer's concern for potential litigation. As a general rule, no survey placed in the mail should be more than one page in length (front and back) with printing of sufficient size to be easily read. Due to the fear of litigation, employers will also want to be assured that any information regarding an individual employee has been cleared for release by that individual. Group questions (such as, "On the average, how well can graduates of our Business Management Program communicate orally with clerical employees?") are entirely acceptable. However, on any occasion upon which the opinion of an employer concerning a specific graduate is sought, the permission of that graduate to ask for such information is required by the Family Rights and Privacy Act. Some institutions seek to achieve this end by distribution of employer surveys through alumni. This method usually results in only those alumni who believe they are doing well with their employer forwarding the survey for completion. A better manner for distribution of the employer survey is to gather permission at the time of the student's graduation for a survey asking individual specific information and then to make the distribution directly to the employer with a copy of the permission enclosed. An alternative, and reportedly just as reliable, form of feedback concerning individual or groups of graduates is often found by asking recruiters who are representing employers. These recruiters, who visit the campus to interview and attend career fairs or similar events, are very knowledgeable concerning the performance of recent hires by their companies. They also can provide a comparison between your graduates and those of other campuses. The primary advantage of asking recruiters vs. the administration of an employer survey is that the recruiters are a captive audience and are actually on your campus. They have a vested interest in the improvement of the learning on the part of your students.

The legal restrictions regarding permission to contact employers outlined previously do not apply within the internship or co-op education situation. In these circumstances, the students have provided implicit permission to contact their supervisors through enrollment in the educational process, freeing the institution from further Family Rights and Privacy Act requirements. The primary concern in this circumstance is that the internship or co-op responses are representative of the population of students completing the program. Because often the best students self-select internship and co-op options when these are offered, the result is that a representativeness is not always possible unless *required of* all graduates.

The two primary logistical issues in survey research are means of distribution and control from over-surveying the population. The survey response rate in any circumstance in which distribution and return is made by means other than mail will be better than if the same survey is placed in the mail. Whenever possible, surveys should be integrated into another process (such as graduation) to obtain results from a captive audience.

Whether locally developed or commercially available, when attitudinal surveys are utilized, some "tricks of the trade" will increase the response rate to any survey administered through the mail. First, use commemorative stamps on both the outgoing and return envelopes. While business reply envelopes are cheaper, as are bulk mail rates, both are seen by respondents as indicative of a lack of personal interest and tend to lead toward a lowered response rate. Second, particularly concerning alumni surveys, mail surveys during the Christmas holidays. Respondents are more likely to have time to complete surveys and generally are in a more positive and often reflective frame of mind at that time. Include a personal note from a party at the institution to whom the respondent can relate. Often this person will be a senior professor in a department or the chief executive officer of the institution. Each of these techniques is known to increase response rates slightly; however, the receipt of responses past 35% is exceedingly unusual.

Among the greatest survey research problems which a unit or the institution needs to guard against is the over-surveying of the student population. The authors can recall one experience when they were visiting an institution where the campus hotel was operated as part of the Hotel Management instructional program. A point-of-contact survey was distributed as part of the hotel registration process to ascertain guest satisfaction with the registration procedures. In the room, another point-of-contact survey was present to ascertain satisfaction with the facility and its cleanliness. In the restaurant operated by the hotel, another point-of-contact survey was found under the dinner plate soliciting the customer's satisfaction with the meal and service. Frankly, the authors expected point-of-contact surveys in the hotel's public restrooms. The point is simple. If the population is over-surveyed, the response rate will decline; and, more importantly, the sincerity of the responses will diminish significantly as respondents begin to mark all of one response (for example, all of #3 or "satisfied"). Institutional coordination (possibly through the institutional research component) should limit the number of point-of-contact surveys that are conducted each semester or quarter so the student population will not be over-surveyed.

Both exit interviews and focus groups provide the advantage of two-way oral communication through which attitudinal assessment may be ascertained. In both instances, the great advantage of this technique is that follow-up questions can be identified in areas of concern expressed by the participants. The interview process should be conducted initially in a rather structured manner so that a common and often limited group of questions is posed to all respondents. Based on these responses, the interviewer can go into depth regarding specific areas of concern on the part of the interviewee and become more flexible. Additionally, either means provides an ideal "open end" for participants to bring forward concerns not initially anticipated.

In the case of exit interviews, one of the greatest dangers is that the nature of the interviewer (potentially the department head) may bias the response of the participants. Exit interviews are best conducted by parties perceived by the interviewee as risk free. Examples of these types of individuals are graduate students, departmental staff, and counseling center personnel.

Focus groups also should conduct initially a rather structured process concerning the topics identified. These groups are best conducted by trained professionals, and the primary issue regarding these groups is the composition of the participants and the extent to which that composition reflects the population. Focus groups should contain no more than eight (8) representative members. These groups are given four to five issues for discussion. When an outside professional is not available to conduct the focus group, a leader can be selected from the group. The group leader is instructed to report back on a specific day as to the findings.

Attitudinal assessment is a viable and, in many cases, less expensive form of gaining valuable information. However, educational programs should understand that if their assessment process is based solely upon attitudinal affirmation, it will, in most cases, be found insufficient by reviewing teams.

**Performance Type Means of Assessment**

Performance type assessment measures include those shown in Figure 40. In such instances,students are placed in an environment similar to that in which they will be functioning after graduation and are asked to <u>perform</u> the task or skill for which they are being educated. Performance type assessment is based upon cognition (knowledge); however, it also includes an action component in which that knowledge is put into practical use. Performance assessment is, upon some occasions, described as "authentic" assessment due to its engagement of the student/graduate in real world environments.

## Figure 40
### *Performance Type Assessment Opportunities*

- Case Studies
- Internships
- Simulations
- Projects

The performance observed may take place at the institution in the presence of trained evaluators or panels of faculty with knowledge in the field, such as in an art show or the review of design projects at the close of an engineering program, or it may be observed by independent experts off the campus, as in student teaching, internship, or co-operative education. This latter circumstance blurs the distinction between this type of performance assessment, which is clearly viewed as direct in nature, and employer survey results, which are occasionally viewed as indirect by some regional accreditors.

The advantages of performance assessment are many and include its popularity among students and acceptance by employers. For most of their collegiate lives, students have taken one cognitive examination following another. Generally, they react very well to opportunities to use the knowledge which they have gained through performance type assessment activities. Employers and others outside of higher education also react favorably to performance types of assessment measures. These measures, in the jargon of the public, go past "book learning" and into skills that make a clear contribution to society.

The primary disadvantages of performance assessment include the amount of time necessary to logistically prepare for such assessment and the need to control to the maximum extent possible extraneous variables. It is certainly easier to prepare a cognitive written examination than for the evaluation of the performances in a three-act play. In this latter circumstance, the expectations of each role must be established; the evaluators taking part in the evaluation must be trained; and the overall production staged. While this type performance assessment will certainly evaluate the ability of graduates of a theater arts program to put on a production more thoroughly than a pencil and paper test, the difference in the amount of work to prepare for the performance assessment described is probably many fold over that for a written examination.

Because of the complexity of performance assessment, any number of extraneous variables may impact the performance at one time. Continuing the example previously described, suppose the orchestra supporting the theater presentation described above is inadequate. What impact will that have on the overall production and the evaluation thereof? What impact does the fact that a company is in the process of downsizing have on its evaluation of its co-op or internship students? To what extent does the nature of the supervising teacher's own teaching skills impact his or her evaluation of student teachers? These and a host of other questions need to be borne in mind as institutions prepare to conduct performance assessments.

Any time that students in a degree program take part in a case study, simulation, project, internship, or cooperative education experience near the end of their program, the opportunity is ripe for performance assessment. On countless occasions, the authors have worked with academic departments to ascertain existing assessment activities, only to find that students already take part in these types of evaluative activities for the purpose of individual grading. In most cases, it takes no more than insuring that one of the evaluators of the performance is other than the faculty member teaching the course and the application of the "Column and Row Model" described in Figure 33 to establish "instant and creditable assessment data" that can be used to improve the programming within a very short period of time. To accomplish this purpose it is necessary to establish a detailed "check list or rubric" through procedures similar to those next described.

## Developing Rubrics as a Means for Assessment

### *Eliot Elfner*

A rubric is a predefined scoring scheme to guide the analysis of student performance or artifacts. It is applied as a set of rules for evaluating student performance. Rubrics are used when a *judgment* of the **extent** to which a criterion has been met is necessary. They provide detailed descriptions of each level of performance as to what is expected.

Rubrics set a common understanding among multiple judges about what represents success in student learning. They provide a process for gathering and aggregating reliable judgments from multiple judges about student learning, and they define levels of performance by describing various degrees of success when judging student learning.

Rubrics answer questions like the following about what criteria the work will be judged by: "What is the difference between good work and weaker work? How can we make sure our judgments (or scores) are valid and reliable? How can both performers and judges focus their preparation on excellence?"

Rubrics yield benefits both from the development process and their application. When preparing a rubric for a particular student assignment or performance, the need for a group of faculty to carefully determine the important success criteria and define carefully different levels of performance a respondent can manifest results in a common understanding among the developers about desired student performance. When applied to student work, they provide support for the extent to which the specified criteria have been met, and they provide feedback as to what can be done to help students improve learning. Sharing the criteria and performance descriptions with students previews expectations with them as well. But developing rubrics requires an extensive effort for development from a number of interested parties involving several steps, testing, and revisions before the rubric can be applied with confidence.

*Types of Rubrics*—Rubrics can be classified in several ways. A *holistic scoring rubric* considers the several performance criteria in aggregate on a single descriptive scale. It yields a single judgment about the performance level of the student effort and allows for a more open-ended comprehension of the unique properties of student work. It has the advantage of requiring less work to develop and implement and minimizes the amount of student work that needs to be evaluated, thereby making it more efficient. Its disadvantage is that it lacks specificity; therefore, it is best used for benchmark assessments. An *analytic scoring rubric* recognizes the several factors of performance for any assigned task or process and allows for the separate evaluation of each. There is an option of assigning variable weights to each of the several performance factors. It also has the advantage of being able to analyze each component, identifying needs and strengths in student performance, but its disadvantage is the time needed for its development and implementation.

A rubric can also be categorized as a general scoring rubric or a task specific scoring rubric. A *general scoring rubric* is used to evaluate a particular activity or process without concern for the specific context or subject matter assigned (such as oral presentations). A *task specific scoring rubric* is used to evaluate student performance on a single, particular, context specific assignment (such as an oral presentation on a specific topic). Figure 41 illustrates the four types of rubrics.

## Figure 41
### *Four Types of Rubrics*

| Holistic – General Scoring Rubric | Analytic – General Scoring Rubric |
|---|---|
| -a single scoring scale, used to evaluate a particular activity or process without concern for specific context or the subject matter assigned<br>i.e. – oral presentations, writing samples, or lab reports all rated on a single dimension | -multiple scoring scales based on several relevant criteria used to evaluate a particular activity or process without concern for specific context or the subject matter assigned<br>i.e. – several scales relevant to writing (grammar, organization, clarity, etc.) applied to general writing samples from several sources |
| **Holistic – Task Specific Rubric**<br>-a single scoring scale used to evaluate student performance on a single, particular, context specific assignment<br>i.e. - oral presentation of an assigned topic, written essay on a specific topic, or a lab reports on a particular experiment, all rated on single dimension | **Analytic – Task Specific Rubric**<br>-multiple scoring scales based on several relevant criteria used to evaluate a particular activity or process on a single, particular, context specific assignment<br>i.e. – several scales relevant to a specific topic applied to a writing sample from a student assignment |

Whatever the type of rubric selected, rubrics can be applied in several different educational settings. Often, teachers will use a rubric to grade a student on a given assignment, giving precise feedback about the student's performance on the criteria defined in the rubric. This allows for a learning opportunity for the student, who can identify the areas in the assignment that need improvement. Another application of rubrics is for monitoring classroom progress. By aggregating scoring results from a rubric applied across all the students in a specific class, an instructor will be able to determine the general level of achievement for which the students can be held responsible. A third application of rubrics is at the program level, where scores earned on rubrics applied to program completers give an indication of program success. Finally, institutional level outcomes can be addressed by appropriately designed rubrics. The assessment process we are discussing is concerned primarily with the development of rubrics for application at the program level of assessment.

*Steps in Developing a Scoring Rubric*—First, decide on the purpose of the rubric (analytic vs. holistic and general vs. specific task). At the program level of assessment it is usually preferable to develop an analytic rubric so that results can indicate where improved learning might be best accomplished when using the assessment results. Holistic rubrics are best used to gather general benchmark information about student performance. Should the performance be below expectations, a further assessment using a more analytical approach can be implemented for subsequent assessments.

Next, determine the performance artifact by which students will demonstrate capability. The appropriate artifact to which a rubric is to be applied is one that was developed in response to a course assignment. Students will take the assignment seriously if they know that the work will contribute to their class grades. The course instructor can use this imbedded assignment to provide input to the students' grades determined on any basis relevant to the instructor's objectives, but the assignment should then be reassessed based on the program learning objectives and evaluated by the program assessment rubric. Artifacts can be any number of different assignments. Figure 42, opposite, lists some artifacts that can be used to assess student learning.

The third step in developing a rubric is to clearly identify several criteria by which a student's work or performance could demonstrate successful performance (for each criterion in analytic rubrics or by aggregating the factors into a single dimension in holistic rubrics). These criteria make up the key performance factors that a student should be expected to exhibit when faced with the given assignment. Each assignment will have unique criteria, and those that are relevant to the program learning outcomes should be incorporated into the rubric. As examples, Figure 43 presents several ideas regarding the different factors that could be relevant to various student assignments.

Next, define how many levels of performance need to be judged for each criterion. Each level of performance should use descriptors that are clearly presented. There could be as few as two levels (has criterion or does not have criterion) or as many as perhaps five different levels of performance defined in the rubric. These different levels can be

## Figure 42
### *Example Student Artifacts for Assessment*

| | |
|---|---|
| – Assignments (in or out of class) | – Debates |
| – Feedback or practice (choral, instrumental, drawing, etc.) | – Essay exam questions |
| | – Lab notes |
| – Self evaluation | – Letters |
| – Peer evaluation | – Journals |
| – Role plays | – Topic outline |
| – Pre- and post-tests | – Research paper |
| – Simulation | – Literature review |
| – Case studies | – Role Play |
| | – Etc. |

characterized in many different ways, such as "exemplary, "proficient," "adequate," or "needs improvement" for a four-point scale. (See Figure 44 for an illustrative list of performance level characterizations.) It is probably best to have three or four levels of performance defined for each criterion. More than that will require extensive effort to reach consensus about the descriptions, and fewer than three will likely not result in sufficient information to use when "closing the loop," that is using the results of assessment to improve the learning process.

## Figure 43
### *Exemplary Performance Criteria*

| | |
|---|---|
| • **Organization and structure** | • **Voice** |
| • **Level of understanding** | • **Comprehension** |
| • **Complexity of ideas presented** | • **Acceptance of responsibility** |
| • **Support for ideas presented** | • **Initiative, motivation** |
| • **Coherence of presentation** | • **Creativity** |
| • **Knowledge of material demonstrated** | • **Degree of task completion** |
| | • **Collaboration** |
| • **Awareness of audience** | • **Attitude** |
| • **Mechanics: writing, language, style, etc.** | • **Enthusiasm** |
| | • **Empathy for others** |

## Figure 44
### *An Illustrative List of Performance Levels*

| | |
|---|---|
| • Missing-Included<br>• Inappropriate-Appropriate<br>• Incomplete-Complete<br>• Incorrect-Partially Correct-Correct<br>• Vague-Emergent-Clear<br>• Marginal-Acceptable-Exemplary<br>• Distracting-Neutral-Enhancing | • Usual-Unexpected-Imaginative<br>• Ordinary-Interesting-Challenging<br>• Simple-Complex<br>• Reports-Interprets-Analyzes<br>• Few-Some-Several-Many<br>• Never-Infrequently-Usually-Always<br>• Unsatisfactory-Satisfactory-Outstanding |

Once you have agreed upon the desired number of performance levels, these several levels of performance must be described in sufficient detail that raters can reliably judge the student performance on the various criteria. This definitional activity can be addressed in two basic ways. First the end points of the continua can be described: precisely describe the lowest level of performance on each criterion and then describe the highest level of performance on each criterion. Then describe each of the remaining levels of performance in such a way as to distinguish them from the end points and from each other. The result of this effort will be a narrative description of each level of performance for each of the several criteria that can be judged by a rater to reflect the performance of the student artifact.

Another way to undertake the step of definitional activity is to define first the **proficient** level. This is the level that a rater would judge to be the desired level of performance for students to demonstrate who were exhibiting the student outcome at an acceptable level. Descriptors of each of the other points on the scale should represent a smooth continuum. Write descriptors for each of the performance levels in terms of behaviors. Use the concept words presented in Figure 44 above and convey various degrees of performance such as Depth, Breadth, Quality, Scope, Extent, Complexity, Degrees, or Accuracy.

*Tips for Developing Rubrics*—At each of the previous steps, involve two or more groups of people familiar with the process to classify and rate the critical incident descriptions. Have each group check the others' classifications and ratings to insure reliability. Conduct a pilot test applying the rubric by several scorers to insure reliability. Work with peers. It is always helpful to have someone react to and critique your assessments. It is especially helpful if the peers teach in the same area. Start with a project or activity you have used before. When you start with something familiar, you already have a pretty good idea of what you are looking for and what students' work will look like. Examine sample rubrics. Look at well-written examples in your subject area, if available. If someone else's statements are clear, you can adapt or modify some of the language. Don't expect perfection. View each rubric as a draft that you will improve upon after you have used it with students. Don't try to assess everything in one task. Choose the three areas you are most concerned about for that performance task and assess them well. Focusing raters' attention on a few criteria will result in higher quality work. Train an independent group of raters on the scoring criteria and critical incident descriptions. Conduct pilot test, scoring sample artifacts with the independent group of trained raters. Assess the reliability of the ratings by the several members of the trained rater group. Finally, make adjustments and implement the rubric with cadre of trained raters.

As an example of a general education outcome often addressed, an approach toward assessing "Critical Thinking" with a rubric is shown in Figure 45 (Kelly-Riley, 2003). Any rubric used to assess such an outcome needs to be developed thoroughly, following the steps outlined above. As an example of the type of outcome measure suitable for gathering evidence about student learning, this example rubric illustrates the key concepts appropriate for assessing the ineffable outcomes of general education programs, including those addressing student values.

## Behavioral Means of Assessment

Behavioral means of assessment take place when the "behavior" of students is noted or observed without any attempt to create a hypothetical circumstance. Examples of such behavioral assessment include job placement, admission to graduate school, acceptance to four-year institutions, receipt of academic awards or distinctions, grades at the four-year college to which two-year college graduates transfer, church attendance patterns, service in leadership capacity, etc. The sources for this type of information include graduating student and alumni surveys, as well as other public sources of information (including other institutions), and, in some states, statewide employment security records.

The advantages of behavioral means of assessment are that they take relatively little additional effort to accomplish and often extend past the students' direct association with the institution. On many graduating student and certainly alumni surveys, the addition of items asking students to *report* various activities such as employment, promotions, continuing education, reading patterns, church attendance rates, etc., takes little further effort on the part of the institution. The ability to gain much of this information after students' matriculation and completion of degree programs provides an additional dimension of assessment information to that commonly collected near graduation.

The primary disadvantage of such behavioral assessment is the often limited ability to gather such information from external sources. The circumstances concerning the provision of feedback to two-year colleges by four-year colleges is covered in detail in Chapter Eleven. However, the ability to obtain employment, licensure, salary, etc., information from public agencies is often severely restricted by state law and certainly by state boundaries.

# Figure 45

Student Name or Id. _____

Scoring Rubric for General Education – Critical Thinking

Intended Learning Outcome: Students will demonstrate the ability to apply critical thinking competencies.

(Assignment guideline: written essay in which students present an argument on an issue of relevance to capstone General Ed course)

| Rating | Problem Identification | Recognize Alternative Perspectives | Identify & Incorporate Relevant Evidence | Recognize and Critique Key Assumptions | Draw Logical and Rational Conclusions from Analysis |
|---|---|---|---|---|---|
| Level 4 Exemplary | 4. Identifies main problem and subsidiary issues, describes them clearly | 4. Identifies one's own perspective and contrasts it with several others | 4. Examines multiple sources of evidence critiquing, its accuracy, relevance, and completeness, recognizes cause and effect relationships | 4. Identifies key assumptions and ethical dimensions that underlie the issue and critiques their validity. | 4. Using the preliminary analysis draws rational conclusions, and contrasts the chosen perspective to alternative approaches. |
| Level 3 Proficient | 3. Identifies main problem and some subsidiary issues, describes them adequately | 3. Identifies one's own perspective and describes several others | 3. Examines two or three sources of evidence, critiquing its accuracy, relevance, and completeness, recognizes cause and effect relationships | 3. Identifies some of the key assumptions and ethical dimensions that underlie the issue and critiques their validity. | 3. Using the preliminary analysis draws rational conclusions, and presents justification for the chosen perspective. |
| Level 2 Adequate | 2. Identifies main problem and describes it adequately | 2. Identifies one's own perspective describes an alternative approach | 2. Examines multiple sources of evidence critiquing its accuracy, relevance, and completeness, recognizes cause and effect relationships | 2. Identifies one or two of the key assumptions and ethical dimensions that underlie the issue and discusses their validity. | 2. Using the preliminary analysis draws a rational conclusion, relevant to the evidence presented. |
| Level 1 Insufficient | 1. Does not identify and summarize issues or problem | 1. Addresses single point of view, fails to acknowledge alternative perspectives | 1. Describes evidence without critiquing its accuracy, relevance, and completeness, does not distinguish cause and effect relationships from correlation | 1. Merely describes one or two, or does not even discuss any, of the basic assumptions or ethical issues that underlie the issue or does so superficially | 1. Does not draw a conclusion or presents one that is not related to the evidence presented. |
| TOTAL Score = | Factor Score = | Factor Score = | Factor Score = | Factor Score = | Factor Score = |

**DIRECTIONS:** Assess the quality of the student's response for each factor and enter the appropriate number in the bottom cell. Then enter the total score in the left total score cell.

*Adapted from Kelly-Riley, Diane, "Washington State University Critical Thinking Project: Improving Student Learning Outcomes Through Faculty Practice," **Assessment Update**, July-August, 2003, Vol. 15, No. 4, pp. 5-7+*

Behavioral means of assessment are exceedingly valuable to programs preparing students for direct employment or graduate school. In addition, and ironically, it is also highly valued as a means of assessment information by those institutions seeking to pass on a set of values to guide the lives of their graduates. However, whether this assessment information is direct or indirect (as discussed earlier in this chapter) should be considered.

Cognitive, attitudinal, and behavioral/performance means of assessment are only the simplest of typologies regarding this field. They are often combined and their definitions blurred on campuses. The nature of assessment activities is truly limited only by the imagination of practitioners.

Each of the regional accrediting associations stresses that multiple means of assessment for each outcome should be utilized whenever possible. In many cases, that will mean two different types of assessment activities regarding an outcome. However, some outcomes lend themselves only to one particular means of assessment, and practitioners should not be reluctant to identify only one means of assessment, assuming that most other outcomes utilize multiple means of assessment activities.

Assessment activities, however, must be emphasized as only the means to the end of improving programming and student learning within the institution's educational programs. Establishment of the "criteria for success" discussed in the next section is the single greatest means toward that end.

## Establishing the Criteria for Success

Each educational program and administrative and educational support (AES) service, after identifying their appropriate means of assessment, should identify the level of performance or benchmark on each means of assessment which is expected if the program/ service is performing as the faculty/staff think it "ought" to work. The purpose of establishing this level or "Criteria for Success" is to engage the faculty/staff in a meaningful discussion regarding how well their program/ services should perform. It is not sufficient for faculty/staff to identify outcomes and means of assessment without some indication of the qualitative aspect of student or unit performance they expect.

Criteria for success are expressed in a number of ways. A locally developed group criterion such as "an average score of ___" or individually related criterion "no score less than___" is common. A normative related criterion such as "the average score will be at the ___ percentile" is common when utilizing normative means of assessment. In these cases the faculty/staff are establishing their own target for group performance.

This establishment of a commonly accepted target for group performance or *criteria for success* is essential for assessment efforts to progress to the important point of use of results. In order for such use to take place, faculty/staff must identify the need for change. Stating "Criteria for Success" allows the faculty/staff members to identify jointly what they believe to be the *ideal* state or what "ought" to be the result of their instructional or service efforts. When the actual data is collected from assessment, it represents the *reality* of what "is" the case. Only when a disparity exists between what "ought" to be and, in reality, what "is" are most human beings (including faculty/staff) willing to entertain the notion that change is needed. The creation of this potential difference between what "ought" to be and what "is" is the single greatest force leading to program and service improvement.

Once faculty/staff have identified criteria for program/service success and reviewed the actual results of the assessment process, they may take several actions. If the actual assessment results exceed the criteria for success, certainly there should be a "celebration" as the program/service is functioning as desired and all concerned should be satisfied with their achievement. On the other hand, if the actual assessment results indicate a shortfall in performance of the students or services compared to the criteria for success, several options for action exist. *First*, the faculty/staff are welcome to change (lower) the benchmark or criteria for success if they believe it to have been set unreasonably high. *Second*, and occurring more frequently, faculty/staff may go about identifying the reasons for the shortfall and take action to change (improve) the program/service so that the students or services in the future may perform better. It is this latter course of action (changing the program/service) that constitutes the use of assessment results completing the institutional effectiveness paradigm and "closing the loop."

The criteria for success established should be reasonable given the nature of the students enrolled in the program, the resources available to conduct the instructional process, and the time (usually expressed in number of credit hours) which the faculty have with the students. The criteria for success should be established before the first assessment takes place. Otherwise, faculty/staff in reviewing the initial data tend to accept the first assessment results as the benchmark and thereby accept the current "status quo" or what "is" the performance of students or services, *rather than what ought to be the performance*. It is important that the faculty be asked to address the question, "How well should the group of students perform? "or the staff, "How well should the unit be providing service?" if improvement of performance is to take place.

# Figure 46
## *Criteria for Success*

Overall—Minimum total score, rating, response
      expected if program/unit functioning at an
      acceptable level.
Component—More detailed minimum sub-scale
      or item score below which faculty/staff need
      to review.

Criteria for success should be set at both the "Overall" and "Component" levels as reference points or benchmarks for program performance (Figure 46.) The "Overall" (primary) criteria for success establish the general target for student performance, such as an "Average rating of 85 or higher." (Figure 47.) The potential use of results for program improvement can be greatly enhanced by setting the "Component" (secondary) criteria for success, which require more detailed analysis, such as "On no component will the average score be less than seven." (See also Figure 47.) While overall performance may meet or exceed the "Overall" criteria for success, faculty/staff are informed of opportunities for improvement through consideration of the "Component" or secondary analysis of those more specific areas, scales, or individual items falling short of their expectations. Whenever feasible, faculty/staff should set both an overall and more detailed (or component) criteria for success and conduct detailed analysis of assessment information to the level necessary for it to be of use.

It has been the authors' experience that the clear majority of "use of results" is brought about by the establishment of component criteria for success. While faculty/staff may be assured that the results of assessment will not be used adversely against them, many remain skeptical the first time they complete their assessment plan and set the overall criteria for success at what they consider to be a "safe" level. However, the identification of component level criteria along with overall level allows the faculty/staff to realistically identify areas for improvement, while at the same time allowing them to feel secure in having met the overall criteria for success. This dual level of criteria (overall and component) is particularly useful early in implementation or in a threatening institutional environment.

## Figure 47

# *Criteria for Success Example*

## Oral Communication Evaluation Sheet Example:

| Material Organization | Points |
|---|---|
| Subject | 1-10 |
| Logical Organization | 1-10 |
| Content | 1-10 |
| Supporting Material | 1-10 |
| **Delivery and Presentation** | |
| Voice and Enunciation | 1-10 |
| Language | 1-10 |
| Gestures | 1-10 |
| Eye Contact | 1-10 |
| **Overall Effectiveness** | |
| Audience Appeal | 1-10 |
| Speaker Attitude | 1-10 |
| Total | 10-100 |

### *Criteria for Success*

**Overall Criteria**

Average Rating 85 or Higher

**Component Criteria**

On No Item will Average Score be Less Than Seven (7)

Whether the criteria established are higher than might otherwise be considered reasonable or lower makes little difference. Those faculty/staff groups setting their criteria higher than is actually realistic are free to change them once they have reviewed the actual assessment data. Those faculty groups setting an unreasonably low criteria for success usually raise them once they actually see the results of their students' performance and come to accept the fact that the results will not be used against the faculty.

There are several approaches to establishing criteria for program success, any of which may work on your campus. In general, the more realistic the approach to setting criteria for success the more successful it will be. However, asking, "How well ought our students to be able to perform (or services function) on this means of assessment if our program is working as we think it ought?" is relatively abstract, and some faculty/staff groups find it difficult to consider. A more specific, and often useful, approach is that of describing alternative scenarios in which a number of sets of possible results of program/ service assessment results are described, and the faculty/staff are asked to discuss their feelings should each set of results of assessment activities actually take place. This approach usually leads quickly, but meaningfully, to identification of one set of results as most desirable and feasible. This set becomes the program's/unit's initial criteria for success.

The criteria for program/unit success (both overall and component) are among the most important aspects of assessment leading toward its ultimate use by faculty/staff members to improve instructional programming and unit services. An example of the importance of the establishment of criteria for success to both the faculty and staff can be demonstrated in this experience encountered at a major research university. Professor Smith, Chair of the Philosophy Department and faculty leader of long standing, described as a "curmudgeon" and vocal skeptic regarding the value of assessment and outspoken critic of the administration, was in the audience during a recent presentation regarding assessment and the establishment of criteria for success by one of the authors. After rising slowly, Professor Smith addressed the author, "I just want to get a few things straight. This 'assessment thing' then is not about self-justifications. We can set our own targets for student learning, correct? It is about self-improvement, and the administration is not going to dictate our standards, correct?" After being answered in the affirmative, Professor Smith said "thanks" and sat down. That next day, Professor Smith sent out an email to all the department chairs at the institution, which was one of the strongest endorsements concerning assessment for improvement the authors have ever encountered.

## The Program Assessment Plan

All of the information in this and the previous chapter has been focused on the necessary information to prepare an assessment plan for each academic or educational program and indirectly in administrative and educational support (AES) units at the institution. This plan, or Three-Column Model, is the basis for subsequent actual accomplishment of assessment tasks and use of results. It is a *necessary, but insufficient,* component of complete assessment implementation, which requires the use of results from assessment activities to improve student learning and programming as well as AES services.

While the assessment plans shown in Figures 48 & 49 are of primary importance to the individual instructional departments in guiding their assessment activities, they also provide credibility to institutional level assessment planning. The plans (three –column models) for as many educational programs as possible should be appended to the overall institutional assessment plan to provide *evidence* that assessment planning within the institution has penetrated past the upper echelons and has become substantive in nature within each educational program at the institution. Without such plans at the educational program level, regional accrediting associations often characterize institutional assessment plans as "plans to plan" rather than genuine assessment planning.

The Three-Column Models (provided in Figures 48 & 49) combine the first two columns previously depicted in Figures 25 & 26 with a third column, which describes in some detail the actual means of assessment to be utilized and the overall criteria for success and, where practical, component criteria for success.

Examples of assessment plans of other types of educational programs are included in their respective chapters:

Chapter Ten – Assessment in General Education

Chapter Eleven – Assessment in Two-Year Colleges

Associate Degree Technical Programs

    Associate Degree Transfer Programs

    Developmental Education

Chapter Twelve – Assessment in Graduate and Professional Schools

    Graduate Level Programs

    Professional Degrees

Assessment plans using the same structure for administrative and educational support (AES) service units are provided in Chapter Nine.

The following are publications in this series which include additional examples of assessment plans developed using the structure described:

- *The Departmental Guide and Record Book for Student Outcomes Assessment and Institutional Effectiveness* (Agathon Press, 2000)
- *General Education Assessment for Improvement of Student Academic Achievement* (Agathon Press, 2001)
- *Assessment Case Studies: Common Issues in Implementation with Various Approaches to Resolution* (Agathon Press, 1995), Appendix B
- *The Department Head's Guide to Assessment Implementation in Administrative and Educational Support Units* (Agathon Press, 2000)

It is important to keep the relationship between the intended outcomes (educational programs) and objectives (AES service units) apparent if faculty and staff are ultimately to use the results of their assessment efforts to improve student learning and unit services.

# Figure 48

## Undergraduate English Program – Three Columns

### Expanded Statement of Institutional Purpose

### Institutional Mission Statement:
The principal focus of Our University's curricular program is undergraduate education in the liberal arts and science....

### Institutional Goal:
... all graduates of baccalaureate level will have developed a depth of understanding in their major field.

### Program Intended Educational Outcomes:

1. Students completing the baccalaureate program in English will compare very favorably in their knowledge of literature with those students completing a similar program nationally.

2. Graduates will be able to critique a brief draft essay.

3. Students completing the baccalaureate program will be capable of writing an acceptable journal article.

### Means of Program Assessment and Criteria for Success:

1a. The average score of the graduates of the BA program in English on the MFAT "Literature in English" will be at or near the 50th percentile compared to national results and no subscale score will be below the 30th percentile.

1b. On the Graduating Student Questionnaire, 90% of the English BA program graduates will "agree" or "strongly agree" with the statement "In the field of literature, I feel as well prepared as the majority of individuals nation wide who have completed a similar degree during the past year".

2. As part of a "capstone course" during the final semester, students will critique a short draft essay. 80% of the program's graduates will identify 90% of the errors in the draft essay. Additionally, none of the 14 rubrics utilized to evaluate the student's critique will appear to be consistently unmet.

3a. A jury of English dept. faculty from an institution comparable to Our University will judge 80% of those journal articles submitted acceptable for publication based on commonly accepted standards.

3b. 20% of journal articles submitted will be published in student or other publications.

## Figure 49

# *Accounting Degree Program – Three Columns*

| Expanded Statement of Institutional Purpose | Program Intended Educational Outcomes: | Means of Program Assessment and Criteria for Success: |
|---|---|---|
| **Institutional Mission Statement:** The principal focus of Our University's curricular program is undergraduate education in the liberal arts and sciences… | 1. Students completing the baccalaureate program in accounting will be well prepared for their first position in the field. | **1a. 80% of accounting majors taking the CPA exam will pass at least three of four parts on the exam. Further, the rate of passage on any single part will not be less than 80%.** **1b. Responding employers of accounting program graduates hired through Our University Placement Service will indicate on a survey forwarded to them by the Placement Service one year after employment of the graduate no less than a 7.5 overall average (on a scale of 1-10) on their evaluation of the ten critical accounting skills exhibited by the graduate. No individual skill rating will be less than an average of 5.0.** |
| | 2. Baccalaureate graduates of the accounting program will readily find employment in the field. | **2a. Career Center will report 90% of accounting graduates registered each fall received a job offer by the close of spring semester.** **2b. 60% of students completing the accounting degree program will indicate that they are currently employed or have accepted a job offer in their response to Our University's Graduating Student Survey.** |
| **Institutional Goal:** All graduates of baccalaureate programs will have been afforded the opportunity to prepare for a career. | 3. Graduates will be skilled in the use of personal computers for accounting procedures. | **3. Graduates will be required during their last semester to complete successfully (as judged by a jury of faculty from the department), a major accounting project utilizing personal computer applications. 80% of the projects will be judged acceptable on first review. This judgment will be based upon utilization of a twenty-five item rubric provided by software vender (Quick Books VII). On no individual item will the yearly average be less than a 4.0 on 1.0-5.0 scale.** |

# CHAPTER EIGHT

# DOING ASSESSMENT AND USING RESULTS IN EDUCATIONAL PROGRAMS

*Certain events or decisions are sure to be encountered in all journeys (making turns, "refilling" the vehicle with fuel, locating rest stops, identifying places along the way to eat or spend the night, etc.),and each trip ultimately results, if successful, in reaching the desired destination. In the case of implementation of institutional effectiveness or assessment implementation, "use of results" to improve learning or services is our journey's destination, and the choices and events described in this chapter should be considered as likely events or decisions to be encountered during the trip.*

## Issues Concerning Assessment Activities

*Responsibility for Assessment*—Actually accomplishing assessment activities is a shared responsibility between the institutional level and educational program faculty or staff in an administrative and educational support (AES) unit. A number of assessment activities, such as standardized testing, survey research of graduates and alumni, and gathering information from other higher education institutions are best accomplished at the institutional level by some type of assessment support unit such as institutional research. However, there are a number of other assessment activities, such as preparation and administration of locally developed comprehensive testing, performance assessment in the major, employer surveys, etc., which can be conducted only by the faculty in instructional departments. This apparent subdivision of effort is frequently blurred by services offered from the institutional level to support instructional department assessment activities and conversely by faculty within instructional departments taking part in institutional level support activities.

It is essential that departmental faculty/staff perceive that administrators at the institutional level are providing their share of support for the effort required. Faculty/staff are asked to contribute (without additional compensation) their services to this activity. They justifiably believe that the least the central administration can do is to support their work. This support should be evidenced by:

- Provision of direct support (centralized surveys, data exchange, testing, etc.)
- Funding of "out-of-pocket" expenses for assessment activities at the departmental level (standardized tests, locally developed surveys, employer surveys, etc.)

- Making available professional level expertise or guidance in assessment procedures to advise and assist those within the departments
- Recognition in the reward structure (promotion, salary increase justification, tenure qualification, etc.) of the services rendered by faculty/staff in assessment implementation.

Successful and continuing assessment implementation on a campus is an activity requiring shared effort and responsibility. The central administration itself cannot accomplish implementation of changes in educational programs because of the curricular implications. The faculty/staff cannot accomplish implementation without the fiscal and logistical support of the administration. For implementation to be successful, cooperation in this endeavor is a matter of necessity and often takes place where cooperation in other matters is relatively absent.

*Sample or Population*—Since the focus of the assessment effort is on improvement of the instructional programs based upon assessment results from *groups* of students, as opposed to each individual student, there is no requirement that all students take part in all assessment activities. The program or unit needs to obtain a representative sample of student work or performance by which it can gauge the overall performance of the program.

The notion of representativeness (as opposed to randomness) means that those in the sample should "represent" or "resemble" the students completing the program overall. Programs or AES units will need to insure that their sample is not biased by entrance examinations scores, race, sex, enrollment status (full- or part-time, day or night), or other characteristics that might indeed distort the group's results. The program/unit needs to be in a position of defending, should it be necessary, the representativeness of the sample chosen or resulting from the assessment activities conducted. If the resulting or chosen sample is not found to be representative of the overall group of students completing the program/service, then alternative means of assessment, student motivation, logistics, etc., should be considered.

One of the frequently asked questions regarding sampling for assessment is, "How many are enough?" It is important to recognize that unlike dissertation quality work, research being conducted for assessment purposes needs result in only the identification of general patterns or trends rather than significance of the .001 level. Therefore, assuming a substantial (50-100) overall population, a representative sample of 25-30% should be sufficient for making most general judgments regarding assessment. The lower the actual number in the population of students completing a program, the higher the proportion of the sample which should be chosen. In some cases, you may even need to collect the sample for more than one year to achieve a minimum of ten observations upon which to base your change.

In many cases, the nature of the sample will not be "chosen" so much as "result" from the number of graduates that voluntarily take part in the assessment activities. Under those circumstances, departmental faculty will need to carefully review the educational and biographical characteristics of those students voluntarily taking part in assessment activities. The issue again is one of "representativeness," and in many cases only the best students will voluntarily take part in such assessment activities. If this is the case, the resulting data may be severely questioned by a reaffirmation review committee.

*Student Motivation*—The authors do not recommend requiring certain scores on means of assessment in order for students to graduate or continue their education unless your institution employs a very good attorney with little else to accomplish. The means of assessment available at this time are, frankly, not sufficiently precise to warrant potentially vocational/life changing decisions regarding individual students based exclusively on the instrumentation available. Additionally, if the institution has provided passing grades for the students in their courses and yet refuses to grant a degree based on students' failure to "pass" a means of assessment, then a reasonable assumption is that the majority of such students will sue the institution. Under these circumstances, the institution is guaranteed to lose the case in the court of public opinion. The case will make the front page of the local or state newspaper, and the institution will be accused of depriving the student of his/her rightful recognition after having certified his/her achievement through the awarding of grades. Should the institution happen to win the case, such may be noted under the obituaries or, at the very most, be relegated to an obscure reference. However, in the more likely event that the institution loses the case, it will be dragged back through the media again on the front page in celebration of the student's (David's) victory over the institution (Goliath). This is certainly a circumstance that the institution can not "win."

How then do institutions go about motivating students to meaningfully or seriously take part in assessment activities? The key terms here are "*meaningfully* or *seriously.*" The institution in its catalog can require that students take part in assessment activities for a degree to be granted, and the courts will sustain that position. However, the institution can not require that the students take part meaningfully or seriously in assessment activities.

Only the uninitiated, naive, or foolishly optimistic will assume that by merely asking students to commit part of their already busy schedules to assessment activities will there be sufficient participation. On one campus, a frustrated department chair stated that his department had decided to utilize the MFAT as its means of assessment. The faculty informed the fifteen students completing the program that year that the exam would be in the department secretary's office and that it would take three hours to complete. The students were told, "Come by anytime that is convenient for you to take it." In addition, the department informed the students of the importance of the exam, asked for the students' cooperation, and was then "shocked" that only three voluntarily took the test. It was most difficult for the authors to maintain a straight face when the department chair provided that information.

Experiences such as the one described above indicate that such requests for voluntary participation will result in approximately 20% of the students taking part and perhaps half of that proportion taking the assessment activity seriously. Simply appealing to the intrinsic motivation of students to "do what is right" will not work.

Beyond much doubt, the most effective means for student motivation to seriously take part in assessment activities is to embed these activities within ongoing classes. Students are told, truthfully, that their performance on the means of assessment presented will be one component of their overall grade for the class. This is normally sufficient motivation both to get students there and to have them take the means of assessment seriously. The exact mechanics of how this affects the class grade ranges from a percent of each students' overall grade to "bonus points" or the ability to use the score on the means of assessment to "block out" another grade. Obviously, this requires cooperation on the part of the faculty members responsible for the classes and must be followed through in the grading if students are to continue to take part in the assessment activities during the next iteration. Such integration into the ongoing class activities can take place in either a regular class that students normally take near the end of their program or within a capstone course.

A capstone course, far from a new pedagogical technique, is a course occurring at or near the end of a student's program which is designed to pull together information from across all the student's earlier courses and result in a culminating educational experience. The capstone course itself is not a viable means of assessment; however, what can be done within the capstone course, through embedding means of assessment, is certainly important. Capstone courses can be utilized to motivate students' participation in comprehensive testing, projects, simulations, etc. It is an ideal forum for assessment activities and provides a ready logistical means for conducting them and motivating the students to take part seriously.

Unless the means of assessment is course embedded, departments and institutions have to become considerably more creative in motivating students to take part seriously. Each campus needs to analyze its own culture to determine what "turns students on" at the institution. The following are among the techniques which the authors have seen used for motivation of students to take part seriously in assessment activities:

- Modification of the registration system priorities so that students who have scored well on a general education measure at the close of their second year receive preferential course scheduling consideration during their junior and senior years
- Use of assessment results to establish "honors" or other distinctions at the time of graduation or on transcripts
- Presentation of highly visible awards to fraternities and sororities for the highest assessment scores on a given instrument
- Establishment of an honors parking lot in the center of the campus (access to which is limited to students achieving a certain level on a standardized test)
- Provision of T-shirts, cold drinks, pizza, concert tickets, etc.

While some of the mechanisms cited may seem demeaning or verging upon bribery, the issue of student motivation must be taken very seriously by each campus. The authors suggest that those conducting assessment activities meet with campus student leaders to discuss the means through which to motivate their contemporaries to actively take part in assessment procedures.

*Timing of Assessment Activities* — Assessment activities can be conducted across several periods of time or concentrated on one day. The conducting of a number of assessment activities across a period of time is probably the more common of the assessment timing techniques. This period of time is typically the last semester of students' matriculation through a degree program. The primary advantage of this approach is that it facilitates integration of assessment activities into ongoing periods or blocks of time, particularly course periods. Even standardized examinations running three to five hours in duration can often be broken into segments of approximately a class period in duration, which are more easily adapted to student availability.

The other approach, an extended period for assessment activities during one period of time, is typified by those institutions holding an "assessment day." Some institutions have chosen a particular day to suspend classes and, in lieu thereof, direct students to various assessment activities. Such "assessment days" have met with mixed results, depending upon the type of campus and the culture present. It should be borne in mind that while students may be required to take part in assessment day activities, there is no assurance that they will *meaningfully* or *seriously* take part in these activities.

*Distribution of Assessment Results* — The primary market for assessment results is not at the institutional level but rather the faculty and staff members responsible for individual educational programs and AES services. Hence, while data such as survey results, standardized testing information, performance assessment results, etc., may be forwarded to a central clearinghouse for assessment information, it must be distributed to the academic departments, programs, and AES service units before its ultimate usefulness takes place. To accomplish this, it will be necessary to identify participants by program area so that their responses can be sorted to a useful level.

On countless occasions, the authors have found examples wherein assessment results have been received on a campus at the institutional level and, for one reason or another, not been distributed to those who could potentially make use thereof. The inventory of means of assessment currently conducted by an institution, and referred to earlier in Figure 8, should identify such lapses. It will also allow faculty members to know what assessment is being done and where to look for the information that they need or from whom to request the information.

## The Nature of Assessment Results

The Four-Column Model shown in Figures 50 & 51 illustrates extension of the academic assessment *plan* into actually *doing* assessment. The assessment findings resulting from conducting of the activities described in Column Three should meet the criteria shown in Figure 52.

It is not necessary to describe in excruciating detail all of the findings of assessment activities. The results cited should focus upon the extent to which the outcomes identified in Column Two have been accomplished.

**Figure 50**

## *Undergraduate English Program – Four Columns*

| Expanded Statement of Institutional Purpose | Program Intended Educational Outcomes: | Means of Program Assessment and Criteria for Success: | Summary of Data Collected: |
|---|---|---|---|
| **Institutional Mission Statement:** The principal focus of Our University's curricular program is undergraduate education in the liberal arts and science… | 1. Students completing the baccalaureate program in English will compare very favorably in their knowledge of literature with those students completing a similar program nationally. | **1a.** The average score of the graduates of the BA program in English on the MFAT "Literature in English" will be at or near the 50th percentile compared to national results and no subscale score will be below the 30th percentile. **1b.** On the Graduating Student Questionnaire, 90% of the English BA program graduates will "agree" or "strongly agree" with the statement "In the field of literature, I feel as well prepared as the majority of individuals nation wide who have completed a similar degree during the past year." | **1a.** MFAT score for year's graduates (18) found to be at the 37th percentile. This was due to a 23rd percentile score on the "American Literature" subscale. **1b.** 93% responded "agree" or "strongly agree." |
| **Institutional Goal:** … all graduates of baccalaureate level will have developed a depth of understanding in their major field. | 2. Graduates will be able to critique a brief draft essay. | **2.** As part of a "capstone course" during the final semester, students will critique a short draft essay. 80% of the program's graduates will identify 90% of the errors in the draft essay. Additionally, none of the 14 rubrics utilized to evaluate the student's critique will appear to be consistently unmet. | **2.** 92% of graduates identified 87% of errors. However, grammatical conventions regarding capitalization were not consistently applied. |
| | 3. Students completing the baccalaureate program will be capable of writing an acceptable journal article. | **3a.** A jury of English dept. faculty from an institution comparable to Our University will judge 80% of those journal articles submitted acceptable for publication based on commonly accepted standards. **3b.** 20% of journal articles submitted will be published in student or other publications. | **3a.** 55% of articles reviewed were found acceptable for publication. **3b.** 10% of articles were published. |

# Figure 51

# *Accounting Degree Program – Four Columns*

| Expanded Statement of Institutional Purpose | Program Intended Educational Outcomes: | Means of Program Assessment and Criteria for Success: | Summary of Data Collected: |
|---|---|---|---|
| **Institutional Mission Statement:** The principal focus of Our University's curricular program is undergraduate education in the liberal arts and sciences… | 1. Students completing the baccalaureate program in accounting will be well prepared for their first position in the field. | 1a. 80% of accounting majors taking the CPA exam will pass at least three of four parts on the exam. Further, the rate of passage on any single part will not be less than 80%. | 1a. 72% of those taking the CPA exam passed all four parts. 97% passed three of four parts. Only 74% passed the auditing portion. |
| | | 1b. Responding employers of accounting program graduates hired through Our University Placement Service will indicate on a survey forwarded to them by the Placement Service one year after employment of the graduate, no less than a 7.5 overall average (on a scale of 1-10) on their evaluation of the ten critical accounting skills exhibited by the graduate. No individual skill rating will be less than an average of 5.0. | 1b. Average rating of 8.3 was recorded. However, the critical skill "ability to work with clients" received an average evaluation of 4.2. |
| | 2. Baccalaureate graduates of the accounting program will readily find employment in the field. | 2a. Career Center will report 90% of accounting graduates registered each fall received a job offer by the close of spring semester. | 2a. 73% received a job offer or current employment. |
| | | 2b. 60% of students completing the accounting degree program will indicate that they are currently employed or have accepted a job offer in their response to Our University's Graduating Student Survey. | 2b. 80 % indicated receipt of job offer. |
| **Institutional Goal:** All graduates of baccalaureate programs will have been afforded the opportunity to prepare for a career. | 3. Graduates will be skilled in the use of personal computers for accounting procedures. | 3. Graduates will be required during their last semester to complete successfully (as judged by a jury of faculty from the department), a major accounting project utilizing personal computer applications. 80% of the projects will be judged acceptable on first review. This judgment will be based upon utilization of a twenty-five item rubric provided by software vender, (Quick Books VII). On no individual item will the yearly average be less than a 4.0 on 1.0-5.0 scale. | 3. 63% of graduates' computer applications were judged acceptable on first review by faculty panel. 47 student projects reviewed, averaged 3.87 on the "fully utilized software capabilities" rubric. |

## Figure 52
## Asssessment Results <u>Should</u>:

> * Highlight the extent to which outcomes were accomplished
> * Appear to have resulted from the means of assessment earlier described
> * Be in sufficient detail to convince the reader that assessment actually took place
> * Justify the "use of results" later identified

The assessment results cited should appear to have resulted from the means of assessment earlier described. On more than one occasion, the authors have reviewed assessment reports in which the actual assessment data cited was, at best, only distantly related to the means of assessment described. If the means of assessment originally provided in the assessment plan has changed, the description of the means of assessment shown in Column Three should be updated.

The data provided should be presented in a thorough enough manner to convince the reader, often the representative of a regional accrediting association, that assessment actually took place. The reviewer should not be left asking, "Where's the beef?" after consideration of the information contained in Column Four. Comments such as "met criteria for success," "all passed," or "as anticipated," simply do not provide sufficient detail to convince a reader that assessment actually took place. While in each of the cases cited, assessment may have actually taken place, results such as these do not create the type of credibility needed. Quite the contrary, they are an open invitation for a reviewer to ask to see each of the examinations, surveys, performance assessment reports, etc., and a detailed data analysis concerning results of the means of assessment. Assuming a reasonably complete summary of data is provided, it should be necessary to maintain the actual assessment artifacts (tests, surveys, rubrics, etc.) for the year immediately before the anticipated review by the regional accrediting agency.

The now Four-Column and soon to be Five-Column Models represent hypothesis testing or application of the scientific method. They should flow logically across the page. The results cited in Column Four should justify and lead naturally to the use of results identified subsequently in Column Five.

Assessment results presented in Column Four certainly should not (Figure 53) exactly match the criteria for success, be reported in convenient numbers, or be statistically impossible or unlikely. Assessment results which exactly match the criteria for success identified in Column Three are suspicious at best and, at worst, could lead to the assumption that the assessment cited actually did not take place. With a number of observations of any substantive size, what are the odds that the average, proportion, frequency distribution etc., cited in the criteria for success will be met exactly when the assessment is conducted? When this transpires, the institution appears to have first conducted the means of assessment and then, wishing to make no changes, identified the criteria for success.

# Figure 53
## Assessment Results <u>Should Not</u>:

- Exactly match criteria for success cited
- Be reported in "convenient numbers"
- Be statistically impossible or unlikely

Those in the research community realize that studies seldom result in convenient numbers such as 50%, 75%, and 100%. Only if a very small number of observations are involved should convenient numbers such as those cited above be found in the assessment results column. If so, for the credibility of the institution and the program, please cite 100% (5 of 5), 75% (3 of 4), 50% (3 of 6),etc., to provide some measure of "face validity."

Finally, assessment results cited should not be statistically impossible or unlikely. The authors remember quite well reviewing one assessment report indicating that "80% of the seven respondents. . ." Incidentally, 80% happened to be exactly the criterion for success established for the particular means of assessment. Impossible or unlikely data only provide further doubt concerning the assessment results presented and the institution's credibility.

## Using Assessment Results for Improvement

*Characteristics of Use of Results*—Everything previously described in this "road map" has led to the next subject to be discussed, the use of assessment results to improve learning/services. Assessment plans and the conduct of assessment activities are merely preludes to the final act—using results to improve programs and services.

The Five-Column Models concerning the Undergraduate English Program, depicted in Figure 54, as well as the Accounting Program, in Figure 55, complete development of the model begun earlier in this book. Note that for each outcome, there have been one or more means of assessment and criteria for success, each of which has yielded a separate set of data and regarding which now a use of results has been described.

This Five Column Model is the linear representation of the Institutional Effectiveness Paradigm, show in Figure 2 (page 12), and is a structural representation of the "state-of-the-art" model in outcomes assessment based learning/service improvement. The final column added should exhibit the characteristics outlined in Figure 56.

# Figure 54

## *Undergraduate English Program – Five Columns*

| Expanded Statement of Institutional Purpose | Program Intended Educational Outcomes: | Means of Program Assessment and Criteria for Success: | Summary of Data Collected: | Use of Results: |
|---|---|---|---|---|
| **Institutional Mission Statement:** <br><br> The principal focus of Our University's curricular program is undergraduate education in the liberal arts and science… <br><br> **Institutional Goal:** <br><br> … all graduates of baccalaureate level will have developed a depth of understanding in their major field. | 1. Students completing the baccalaureate program in English will compare very favorably in their knowledge of literature with those students completing a similar program nationally. <br><br> 2. Graduates will be able to critique a brief draft essay. <br><br> 3. Students completing the baccalaureate program will be capable of writing an acceptable journal article. | 1a. The average score of the graduates of the BA program in English on the MFAT "Literature in English" will be at or near the 50th percentile compared to national results and no subscale score will be below the 30th percentile. <br> 1b. On the Graduating Student Questionnaire, 90% of the English BA program graduates will "agree" or "strongly agree" with the statement "In the field of literature, I feel as well prepared as the majority of individuals nation wide who have completed a similar degree during the past year." <br> 2. As part of a "capstone course" during the final semester, students will critique a short draft essay. 80% of the program's graduates will identify 90% of the errors in the draft essay. Additionally, none of the 14 rubrics utilized to evaluate the student's critique will appear to be consistently unmet. <br> 3a. A jury of English dept. faculty from an institution comparable to Our University will judge 80% of those journal articles submitted acceptable for publication based on commonly accepted standards. <br> 3b. 20% of journal articles submitted will be published in student or other publications. | 1a. MFAT score for year's graduates (18) found to be at the 37th percentile. This was due to a 23rd percentile score on the "American Literature" subscale. <br> 1b. 93% responded "agree" or "strongly agree." <br> 2. 92% of graduates identified 87% of errors. However, grammatical conventions regarding capitalization were not consistently applied. <br> 3a. 55% of articles reviewed were found acceptable for publication. <br> 3b. 10% of articles were published. | 1a. Course offerings in "American Literature" were reviewed to ascertain degree of match with MFAT "American Literature" subscale. Added additional course LIT 317 (Survey of American Lit) as requirement. <br> 1b. Criteria met. At this time no action required. Question is deleted from next year's questionnaire. Faculty has added question relating to electronic reviews of literature. <br> 2. Faculty use of commonly accepted conventions regarding capitalization in reviewing upper division papers has been emphasized. <br> 3a. English 407 (advanced writing) modified to include journal article exercise. <br> 3b. Additional outlets for student publishing have been identified. |

**Figure 55**

## *Accounting Degree Program – Five Columns*

| Expanded Statement of Institutional Purpose | Program Intended Educational Outcomes: | Means of Program Assessment and Criteria for Success: | Summary of Data Collected: | Use of Results: |
|---|---|---|---|---|
| **Institutional Mission Statement:** The principal focus of Our University's curricular program is undergraduate education in the liberal arts and sciences… | 1. Students completing the baccalaureate program in accounting will be well prepared for their first position in the field. | 1a. 80% of accounting majors taking the CPA exam will pass at least three of four parts on the exam. Further, the rate of passage on any single part will not be less than 80%. 1b. Responding employers of accounting program graduates hired through Our University Placement Service will indicate on a survey forwarded to them by the Placement Service one year after employment of the graduate, no less than a 7.5 overall average (on a scale of 1-10) on their evaluation of the ten critical accounting skills exhibited by the graduate. No individual skill rating will be less than an average of 5.0. | 1a. 72% of those taking the CPA exam passed all four parts. 97% passed three of four parts. Only 74% passed the auditing portion. 1b. Average rating of 8.3 was recorded. However, the critical skill "ability to work with clients" received an average evaluation of 4.2. | 1a. **Methods of teaching auditing revised by faculty to provide more case studies.** 1b. **Accountant/Client relations practicum integrated into Accounting 428.** |
| | 2. Baccalaureate graduates of the accounting program will readily find employment in the field. | 2a. Career Center will report 90% of accounting graduates registered each fall received a job offer by the close of spring semester. 2b. 60% of students completing the accounting degree program will indicate that they are currently employed or have accepted a job offer in their response to Our University's Graduating Student Survey. | 2a. 73% received a job offer or current employment. 2b. 80 % indicated receipt of job offer. | 2a. **Accounting "Job Fair" has been scheduled mid-spring semester to boost early employment.** 2b. **Criterion on Graduating Student Survey raised to 80%.** |
| **Institutional Goal:** All graduates of baccalaureate programs will have been afforded the opportunity to prepare for a career. | 3. Graduates will be skilled in the use of personal computers for accounting procedures. | 3. Graduates will be required during their last semester to complete successfully (as judged by a jury of faculty from the department), a major accounting project utilizing personal computer applications. 80% of the projects will be judged acceptable on first review. This judgment will be based upon utilization of a twenty-five item rubric provided by software vender, (Quick Books VII). On no individual item will the yearly average be less than a 4.0 on 1.0-5.0 scale. | 3. 63% of graduates' computer applications were judged acceptable on first review by faculty panel. 47 student project reviewed, averaged 3.87 on the "fully utilized software capabilities" rubric. | 3. **More personal computer applications were integrated into core accounting classes (101, 103, etc.). In each class, 2 additional applications of Quick Book VII have been implemented.** |

## Figure 56
## Use of Assessment Results <u>Should Be</u>:

- **Responsive to shortcomings revealed in the assessment results reported**
- **Substantive in nature**
- **Detailed enough (course number and nature of change) to convince the reader that the change actually took place**
- **<u>Stated in the past tense</u>**

The use of results presented in the fifth column should be responsive to the shortcomings or data described in the previous column. As stated earlier, moving across the Five-Column Model from outcomes to use of results is very much like application of the scientific method. The outcomes cited represent the hypothesis postulated by the faculty regarding a program's accomplishments as reflected by students. The means of assessment and criteria for success describe the research to be conducted, while the summary of data collected represents the findings. The use of results is the ultimate end of this experimental model and in addition to leading toward clear improvements in the program or services in AES units may suggest other areas for inquiry. As foolish as it seems, this last connection between the data presented under "Summary of Data Collected" and the actions described under "Use of Results" needs to be ensured. In some cases, the authors have reviewed apparently worthwhile changes in programs for which no assessment data could be found. This was the case because the changes had been brought about based on the collective judgment of the faculty/staff concerning the development of the field rather than any assessment activities.

Further, the uses of results described should indeed be substantive in nature. The field of assessment implementation is far beyond the time at which "studying the problem" was an acceptable means for utilizing assessment results. Clear and unequivocal steps should be outlined through which improvements of the programs (responsive to the assessment data collected) or services have been made.

The description of the use of results should be detailed enough to convince the reader that the change actually took place. In most cases, a description of the course number in which the change took place and the nature of the change itself will suffice. Statements regarding "global" remedies (e.g., "increased homework in all sections") should be avoided.

Where necessary or advisable, changes described, such as those referenced above by course number, may be supported by evidence of either change in the course syllabus or evidence of committee action. This is particularly true if changes require governance system action. Reaffirmation review committee members are by their very nature and charge a suspicious lot, and satisfying that suspicion as early in the process as possible is certainly in the interest of the institution.

Finally, such descriptions should be stated in the past tense to indicate what changes the faculty/staff *have accomplished, rather than promises to accomplish* in the future. The word "will" should be treated as a "four-letter-word" when describing use of results. *The times for promises in this field have indeed passed*, and reaffirmation committees look for *actions that have already taken place*, based upon assessment results that have *already been provided*.

Curricular or service change need not take place on every occasion upon which assessment results are considered. On the other hand, no program is so perfect or sacrosanct that in *all* Column Five entries words similar to "no change needed or necessary" appear. The utilization of component criteria for success described in Chapter Seven should provide the type of information through which at least one improvement can be cited in each assessment period for each degree program or service unit.

When program and institutional assessment activities fail to result in improvements, programs and/or institutions are often cited by regional accrediting agencies as failing to conscientiously take part in these activities. The utilization of component criteria for success, as well as the "short list" vs. "long list" approach described in Chapter Six should generate for the programs and units the type of dynamic and responsive assessment implementation desired.

*Common Types of Use* — It is impossible to forecast what use will be made of the assessment results until assessment activities are conducted and the results are considered and discussed by the faculty/staff. Programs should therefore refrain from speculatively completing Column Five. However, once assessment data are presented, the most common types of changes made in educational programs as a result of assessment activities relate to adjustments in what is taught and how it is taught. (See Figure 57.) Changes in instructional material often relate to the currency of the materials and the extent to which it meets external needs. Additionally, changes in what we teach are also reflected in the identification of those courses required and the sequence thereof. Most of these changes are of such a nature that they do not require governance system consideration.

Changes also take place regarding how that material is conveyed to the student (teaching methodology). In general, the movement is toward more active participation in the learning process by students through laboratories, practicum, homework, etc., which normally results in less reliance upon the more traditional means of the lecture. In many cases, changes in instructional methodology are implemented through computer-aided projects, case studies, simulations etc. The use of assessment results in regard to educational programs, as well as administrative and educational support (AES) services, supports the *evolutionary* improvement of learning and services, as opposed to *revolutionary* or drastic change. Improvements resulting from this process are usually gradual and subtle rather than sudden and obvious to all. For this reason, great care must be exercised in documentation of the changes or adjustments brought about through continuous assessment of student learning and services. Evidence of these processes' contribution to improvement in learning and services is more likely to resemble the cumulative effect of a slow rain rather than a dramatic downpour. Those expecting assessment for improvement to be evidenced by institutional upheaval will be disappointed; they must be satisfied with gradual changes, which over time will result in substantially improved student learning and services.

## Figure 57
## Types of Assessment Results with Academic Programs

• <u>**What We Teach**</u>
  - **Relationship to external needs**
  - **Currency of instructional material**
  - **Sequence and requirements**

• <u>**How We Teach**</u>
  - **Methodology and technology**
  - **Active participation in learning**

*Encouraging Use of Assessment Results*—In the movie *Field of Dreams*, a baseball diamond is constructed in the middle of a Midwestern cornfield. The builder has a vision of bringing to the present the joy experienced by great baseball players of the past. His neighbors can not understand the farmer's vision or purpose in building the baseball diamond and ridicule him continually regarding his dream. However, from the beginning, the farmer is encouraged to continue working toward his goal through the message he hears repeatedly from the cornfield: "If you build it, they will come."

In much the same manner, early endeavors in the assessment movement were built on what some would describe as a vision or "blind faith"—that if data or information were available suggesting change was needed to improve student learning, then faculty would naturally make those changes. Unfortunately, just because you have assessment data, doesn't mean faculty/staff will use it. Just as in the movie *Field of Dreams,* most people are naturally reluctant to accept anything that would suggest that they change. Hence, on many campuses, assessment data have been produced for some period of time; however, relatively little or no use of the data to bring about change has resulted. While the separate "Annual Institutional Effectiveness Cycle," illustrated in Figure 15, sets the stage for "closing the loop," actions *within* educational departments and AES units must be taken to provide the primary motivation for faculty and staff to use results.

Within the instructional department and AES unit, faculty and staff can be motivated to utilize the results by accomplishment of a number of activities, such as those described in Figure 58.

All of these activities are based upon the faculty and staff's comfort with the assessment process and the belief that it is "ok" to acknowledge a shortfall in expectations for graduates or services without that shortcoming having an adverse impact upon individual faculty/staff members. Without such a level of comfort with the process, faculty and staff are extremely reluctant to acknowledge any weaknesses or make any changes that would apparently imply that there were shortcomings in the educational program or AES services.

## Figure 58
## Intrinsic Motivation of Faculty and Staff Toward Utilization of Assessment Results

> • **Direct involvement of faculty and staff in selection of student learning outcomes or administrative objectives/outcomes**
> • **Active participation in review of means of assessment by faculty and staff to build confidence in results**
> • **Maintenance of clear linkage between intended outcomes and means of assessment**

Early in the design of the assessment plan, faculty and staff must be actively involved if later they are to use the results to improve student learning and AES services. Educational and administrative department chairs simply must resist the temptation, as overwhelming as it may be sometimes, to simply prepare the assessment plans themselves and not bother the faculty or staff. While such a short-term remedy would make many faculty and staff happy and provide the chief academic officer or other administrator with the assessment plan necessary, the absence of meaningful input by the faculty and staff early in this process almost always assures their lack of involvement in making changes once the results are received.

The issues addressed in the educational (student learning) outcomes and administrative objectives/outcomes identified for assessment should be substantive in nature and of importance to the faculty and staff in the department. If only relatively simple outcomes that are easily measured are identified, the interest of the faculty and staff in making changes based thereon is substantially reduced. If "trivial" outcomes are set, then "trivial," as opposed to "substantive," use will probably result.

Confidence in the means of assessment is essential if the data resulting therefrom are to be used as the basis for change. The foundation for establishing this confidence takes place when the faculty and staff are actively involved early in the process in reviewing and selecting the means of assessment. While assessment results will not themselves dictate changes in curriculum, such results, if they come from means of assessment in which the faculty and staff have confidence, can provide clear direction for improvement in student learning and AES services. It is important to realize that the collection of data does not bring about change. If credible, the data presented will begin *discussion* among the faculty and staff. It is from the discussions that change emerges.

The assessment results provided should focus clearly upon the outcomes identified. They should be stated in a concise and relatively easy to understand manner so that the faculty and staff might take action thereon. Most assessment data are descriptive in nature and seldom require the use of inferential technique.

Finally, faculty and staff need to have a reflective occasion upon which they may consider the assessment data received. It is recommended that a one- or two-day working period be established for faculty/staff to review the assessment results from the previous year and to make or design the changes to take place as a result thereof. Without the opportunity for this occasion for use of results, faculty and staff will not have the time in their normal meetings to conduct the necessary in-depth discussions regarding the issues often revealed in assessment information.

Chapters Six, Seven and Eight have primarily described a method for successful implementation of institutional effectiveness for an institution. In these chapters, the baccalaureate level educational programs in English and Accounting were used as examples for the development of the Five Column Model. For an institution to comprehensively apply this systematic process for all of the campus, the administrative and educational support (AES) units need to be included. In Chapter Nine, the Five Column Model is developed for these units. Following the basic steps outlined in Chapters Six, Seven, and Eight, Chapter Nine highlights the differences between implementation for educational units and administrative and educational support units. These four chapters combined (Six, Seven, Eight and Nine) describe a comprehensive implementation process for all aspects of the campus, as illustrated in the "Institutional Effectiveness Paradigm" shown in Figure 2 (page 12).

# CHAPTER NINE

# ASSESSMENT IN ADMINISTRATIVE AND EDUCATIONAL SUPPORT (AES) UNITS

*As the institution follows its "road map" towards improvement, it is important to notice that there are two itineraries outlined on the map. Both itineraries begin with the Expanded Statement of Institutional Purpose (ESIP) and follow a similar route, which ends in improvement. However, a closer examination reveals that there are differences. Each of these itineraries includes "side trips" making them significantly different. The itinerary for the administrative and educational support (AES) units clearly shares the final destination with the educational programs—to make improvement based upon assessment results. The following chapter highlights the many similarities between these itineraries and explains the few side trips that are particular to assessment in administrative and educational support units.*

## Introduction

Assessment is more natural for the administrative and educational support (AES) units for than for educational programs for several reasons:

1. AES units are used to dealing with the improvement process and are used to terminology and processes, such as Continuous Quality Improvement (CQI).
2. The process is very much like what is done on a weekly basis during their staff meetings. A problem is identified by the unit personnel, who then brainstorm a possible solution to that problem, test the solution, bring results back to the staff meeting, and make further changes if necessary or move on to a new problem.

Putting together an assessment plan for administrative and educational support (AES) units follows much the same pattern as the pattern for the educational programs covered in earlier chapters. The same processes identified on the outside of the paradigm shown earlier in Chapter Two are followed. Beginning with the institutional level mission statement, the units then formulate administrative objectives and outcomes; do assessment on those objectives; and, based on the results of assessment, make improvements in **services** offered by the administrative and educational support units (Figure 2) as opposed to the focus on the educational programs in the improvement of student learning. As in the educational programs, the administrative and educational support (AES) units also build a Five-Column Model. The AES Five-Column Model follows much the same structure described in earlier chapters; however, the authors believe the differences in assessment for the AES units and the instructional programs are significant enough to be highlighted in this chapter.

For the campus to develop a successful culture for the assessment of administrative and educational support (AES) units the following are needed:

1. An understanding of regional accrediting association requirements in regards to service and educational support units
2. A list of what is considered on any given campus to be an administrative and educational support unit
3. A structure for the assessment process
4. Simple step by step directions to follow

### Developing an Understanding

As the process begins, each administrative and educational support unit needs to be aware of what its own regional accrediting association requirements are as they relate to assessment of administrative and educational support (AES) units. In some accrediting associations, the requirements for AES units are clearly defined, while others focus on educational support services or student services only. The regional accrediting associations' recognition of the *important role played by AES units* in the overall effectiveness of an institution has been steadily growing since 1992. More and more teams who examine campus assessment practices expect to see comprehensive involvement of AES units in assessment on the campus. "If assessment is important enough for the campus' educational programs, why isn't it important enough for its administrative units?" is a question frequently voiced by faculty members. The best answer is, "If you are indeed seeking to improve the quality of your institution, then you will need the information gained from a systematic assessment process of *all the campus components*."

### What Is Considered an Administrative and Educational Support (AES) Unit?

As an institution begins the process of building a comprehensive assessment plan for the institution and is considering how to bring its AES components into the process, it is important to keep in mind that the goal of AES assessment is to examine *how well the unit is providing* **services** *to its individuals/groups of clients*. As AES units are identified for developing an assessment plan and report, they are often identified as a sub-set of more complex organizational areas found on a campus. Two-year colleges and small campuses often combine administrative and educational support areas under large organizational umbrellas, such as Student Services, Financial Services, or Physical Plant. For assessment purposes, these large organizational areas need to identify the individual AES units that provide unique services within such an organization.

For example, often an umbrella organizational unit, such as Student Services, is found on a campus' organizational chart. However, within that large umbrella area, numerous unique **services** are being provided: counseling, academic advising, tutoring, testing, housing, orientation, events planning, career services, disabled student services, etc. Each one of those areas providing a unique **service** is considered a "unit" for assessment purposes under the organizational structure of Student Services. On campuses with a more defined organizational structure, an examination of the organizational charts will identify AES units by a separate box or dash on the organizational chart. A further means an institution can use to identify an AES unit is to find units that receive a separate budget to accomplish their **services**. Once the AES units are identified, the assessment of the services offered can begin.

## A Six-Step Assessment Process for Administrative and Educational Support Units

Seven years ago the authors visited a large state university. The purpose of the visit was to evaluate the status of the university's current assessment and build an assessment process that would *first* help satisfy its regional accrediting association requirements and *secondly* be an assessment process that would continue providing information for future improvements. During one of the informational meetings with department heads, the author was describing the importance of assessment and laying out a series of things that needed to be accomplished when the department head politely said: "Look, I am an administrator; I do what I am asked to do; just tell me the simplest way to do it and give me a form to record it on." Reflecting on the author's own experience as an administrator, the truth of that statement was very profound. As an administrator, when asked to complete a project, the first order of business was to specify what needed to be accomplished. Then outline the actions necessary to complete the assigned task. Next, explore whether someone else has accomplished the task before so the process could be "cloned" and adjusted to fit the particular request. If no cloning was possible, then look for the easiest and fastest way to complete the assigned task. The final step was to assign the resources (time and personnel) and go about completing the task assigned.

It took the author several unsuccessful years of trying "cloning" from educational programs before it became evident that the most effective and easiest way to accomplish assessment of **services** is for the unit to work through the process in a systematic fashion by following a simple step-by-step process. This simple and easy to follow step-by-step process is described in Figure 59.

*Step 1 – Establish a Linkage to the Institution's Statement of Purpose* — Assessment in AES units begins, as it does in the educational programs, with demonstrating support of the institutional Statement of Purpose. Each of the AES units needs to review regularly the institution's mission and goals to assure that the **service** provided by the unit supports the direction and purpose of the institution. Unfortunately, few campuses provide a statement or goal to which the AES units can point as the place where they can demonstrate their support to the institution. On those campuses where there is a clear link, it is as simple as using a highlighter. The director of the AES unit reads the institutional Mission Statement as described in the campus catalogue and using a highlighter underlines that portion of the Mission Statement that is supported by the **services** provided by the unit.

However, if the administrative and educational support (AES) unit cannot find a place to show how it supports the mission of the institution, often a review of the institutional goals can provide a location where the AES unit can demonstrate how the **services** they provide support the overall Expanded Statement of Institutional Purpose (ESIP) of the institution. You will note in the example of Column One of the Career Center (Figure 60 later in this chapter) the Career Center had to use Institutional Goal #6 to find its linkage to the overall purpose of the institution.

## Figure 59

# *Suggested Steps for Administrative Assessment Process*

### Formulating Unit Assessment Plan:

*First -*    Establish a linkage to the institution's statement of purpose. Identify which portion of the Expanded Statement of Institutional Purpose the Administrative Unit Supports

*Second -*    Establish Administrative Unit Mission Statement

*Third -*    Formulate Unit Administrative Objectives

*Fourth -*    Identify Unit Means of Assessment and Criteria for Success

### Moving from Planning to Implementation and Use of Results

*Fifth -*    Conduct Assessment Activities

*Sixth -*    Demonstrate and Document Use of Results for Service Improvements

The question will often arise as the AES unit attempts to complete Step 1, "What do I do if there is no 'hook' for my administrative and educational support unit in either the mission statement or the goals?" At this point the best thing to do is to bring this oversight to the attention of the institution's senior administrators. They are the ones who will have to rectify the situation. The author has seen two paths taken depending on the time available: (1) begin the long process of changing the mission statement of the institution (which often takes several years) or (2) add a statement to the institutional goals stating, "_____ institution will provide administrative and educational support services to support the educational endeavors of the campus." (This statement has been modified most successfully in many different fashions.) Until one of these actions has taken place, the administrative and educational support (AES) unit has no choice but to use, as best it can, what is currently available.

*Step Two – Establishing an Administrative Unit Mission Statement*—In most cases, the AES unit already has a Mission Statement. Such mission statements were created either when the unit was first formulated, as part of a grant requirement, or have been developed as part of the strategic planning process. For the most part, they are good philosophical statements relating to the purpose of the AES unit.

Whether a unit currently has a Mission Statement or not, *for assessment purposes*, the unit will need to establish a listing of the **services** it provides. These **services** should be included in the Mission Statement. Often the unit has to group its **services** if the list is longer than ten. Expressing this list of **services** as a statement could suffice very nicely as the unit's mission statement. More likely, the unit will be add a sentence to its philosophical Mission Statement indicating the **services** provided. The Career Center Model, highlighted in Figure 60, shows the combination of a philosophical statement and a service statement.

# Figure 60
## *Career Center-One Column*

### Institutional Reference and Unit Mission:

### Institution Mission/Goal:
(Goal 6) … The University will continue to develop leadership and to instill in its students a sense of justice, moral courage, and tolerance for the views of others …improve admissions, academic, *career and placement counseling.*

$$\downarrow$$

### Unit Mission Statement:
… to assist students in transition from academia to the world of work by preparing students for life after graduation …. Career Center offers services which include: career counseling; three classes for academic credit; workshops and seminars on career-related subjects; assistance with resume writing and interviewing; and opportunities for part-time jobs, internships, and full-time jobs.

First presented is the philosophical statement— "to assist students in transition from academia to the world of work by preparing student for life after graduation…." Sounds good, but this statement can be used in any Career Center in the country. The uniqueness of this specific Career Center is described as it lists the **services** provided: "the Career Center offers **services** which include: career counseling; *three classes for academic credit;* workshops and seminars on career-related subjects; assistance with resume writing and interviewing; and opportunities for part-time jobs, internships, and full time jobs."

Developing a **service** related Mission Statement is important because it is those **services** that the AES unit is responsible for providing. It is assessment of those **services** that will provide the data that will give the unit information concerning the unit's level of effectiveness and provide direction for making improvements. It is important to revisit this Mission Statement at least once a year to determine if any **services** have been added or are no longer provided by the unit. The first column of the model (Figure 60), the linkage column, is now completed.

*Step Three – Formulating Intended Administrative Objective/Outcomes* — In the second column of the model, the administrative and educational support (AES) unit seeks to formulate statements that will provide answers regarding the level or nature of the **service** provided. AES units are seeking to answer the question: "How will the unit know it is accomplishing its purpose and is providing the described **services** to its clients?" To answer the question, the unit will formulate its administrative objectives relating to its **services**.

For the AES units the administrative objectives/outcomes need to refer to *currently* existing **services** as described in the unit mission statement rather than administrative planning activities that are *future* focused. The task of focusing on current **services** instead of planning activities is the most difficult concept most AES units face. The confusion is natural as the main task for AES units is to analyze problems and seek to gather the necessary resources for correcting the problems. As a result, AES units spend the majority of their time on the "future focused" side of the triangle. (See Chapter Two, Figure 3.) If the unit is focusing on the left side of the triangle, it is evaluating what resources are *needed to improve* the institution/unit and the **service** provided to its clients. A unit needs to do both—evaluate its planning (future focused) activities and at the same time assess the current **services** it is providing. These are parallel but separate types of planning. It is important to recognize the differences between these two types of planning that need to exist on a campus. Often when a campus tries to combine the two processes, the result is confusion in terminology. The establishment of a Glossary of Assessment (Appendix G) will help reduce this confusion.

The process of creating administrative objectives/outcomes begins with the unit staff reviewing the **services** as described in their Mission Statement. They create a long list of objectives/outcomes relating to those **services**. From that list the AES staff members select the objectives/outcomes to be assessed during the up-coming assessment cycle. The author is often asked how many objectives/outcomes a unit should work on per assessment cycle. The simplest answer is *no fewer than two* and *no more than three* per assessment cycle. The regional accrediting associations do not dictate how many objectives/outcomes a unit should have. However, if only one, the question is raised; "Is the unit taking the assessment of its **services** seriously?" On the other hand, if the unit assesses more than three objectives/outcomes per cycle, the staff will have very little time for anything else. For those **service** areas administered by only one or two individuals, it is suggested that *only two* objectives/outcomes per assessment cycle be chosen. Remember the unit is developing a systematic process. This process involves the selection of a few objectives/ outcomes at a time. Assess their effectiveness, put improvements in place, and then move on to assess another aspect of the **service**s the unit provides. Once improvements have been made to that **service**, the unit chooses the next aspect of its **service** to be assessed. As described in Chapter Six, an effective and systematic process for choosing **service**s for assessment is the "long list"–"short list" concept. This continual cyclical movement from the long list of objectives/outcomes to the short list of objectives/outcomes for as- sessment creates a manageable process that leads to improvement of the AES unit offer- ing the **service**s.

Constructing these administrative objective/outcomes begins by looking at the **ser- vice**s listed in the Mission Statement for the unit. The unit's assessment objective is to find answers to the following questions:

- How well do our current administrative **service**s function?
- What is the skill/knowledge we want our clients to receive from the current **service**s offered?
- Are the students we serve learning from the current **service**s offered?
- What is the level of satisfaction of our clients with current **service**s offered?

The information gained from doing assessment of the questions above provides data that are then used to determine which aspect of the AES **service**s needs improvement.

There are four simple guidelines to use when formulating unit administrative objec- tives. First, make sure the objective is related to something that is under the control of the unit. For example, the registrar's office wishes to improve the time for posting grades to the final transcripts—a good objective. They can influence, but they *do not control* when the instructor gets the grades to them for posting. A better objective would be stated: "Once grades are received, the registrar's office will improve the time for posting of grades."

Second, the objective/outcomes should be worded in terms of what the unit will ac- complish or what its clients should think, know, or do following the provision of **service**s. Following this guide will help units focus on assessment of *current* **service**s instead of assessment of planning activities future focused. (See Figure 61.)

Third, the objective/outcome should lead to improved **service**. This means that when objectives/outcomes are assessed, the results should provide information/data the unit can use to determine what aspects of its **service**s need improvement. A helpful guide when thinking through the objective is if the potential answer to the question is either "yes we did" or "no we didn't," then chances are a future planning objective instead of assessment of current **service**s is taking place. For example, the Library will develop an electronic bibliographic file of all books in the library. When assessment is attempted of that objective, the only information that can be gathered is either "*no* the library didn't develop the file" or "*yes* it did develop the file." Assessment of current **service**s will generate information/data that can be used to guide the unit's decisions concerning improvement.

# Figure 61

## *Examples of AES Objectives/Outcomes*

*Administrative Objectives Based on **Currently** Existing Services*

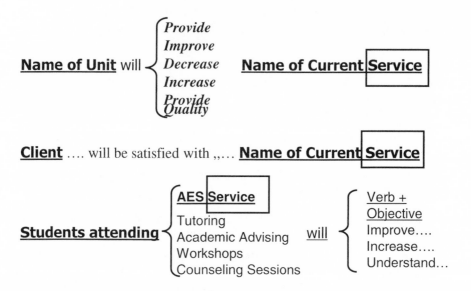

The fourth guideline is to make sure the objective/outcome is linked to a **service** described in the unit Mission Statement—If the **service** described is not in the Mission Statement, the unit should consider first whether the **service** needs to be added to the Mission Statement or second whether some other unit of the campus needs to provide this **service**. The Two-Column Career Center Model presented in Figure 62 provides an example of the development of AES objectives/outcomes. Figure 63 shows the connection of the AES objectives/outcomes to the unit's Mission Statement. Not all of the **services** provided by the unit need be assessed every assessment cycle.

Note that the unit objectives/outcomes stated are rather general. Greater detail will occur in the Third-Column ("Means of Assessment"). Not all of the **services** provided by the Career Center are being assessed at this time. The staff rationale for choosing these three **service** areas first were the following:

Objective #1 – *Student Learning Outcomes*—A preliminary staff review of senior resumes submitted to recruiters indicated that resumes were lacking in quality. Staff wanted to make sure students attending resume workshops were able to produce interview winning resumes.

# Figure 62

## *Career Center-Two Columns*

**Institutional Reference and Unit Mission:**

**Administrative Objectives/ Outcomes:**

**Institution Mission/Goal:**
(Goal 6) … The University will continue to develop leadership and to instill in its students a sense of justice, moral courage, and tolerance for the views of others …improve admissions, academic, *career and placement counseling.*

**1. Students attending Career Center resume workshops will produce quality resumes.**

**Unit Mission Statement:**
… to assist students in transition from academia to the world of work by preparing students for life after graduation …. Career Center offers services which include: career counseling; three classes for academic credit; workshops and seminars on career-related subjects; assistance with resume writing and interviewing; and opportunities for part-time jobs, internships, and full-time jobs.

**2. Career Center will provide job search assistance.**

**3. Graduates will be satisfied with services provided by the Career Center.**

# Figure 63

## *Career Center Objectives/Outcomes*
## *Linkage to Mission Statement*

**Institutional Reference and Unit Mission:**

**Administrative Objectives/ Outcomes:**

**Institution Mission/Goal:**
(Goal 6) … The University will continue to develop leadership and to instill in its students a sense of justice, moral courage, and tolerance for the views of others …improve admissions, academic, *career and placement counseling.*

**1. Students attending Career Center resume workshops will produce quality resumes.**

**Unit Mission Statement:**
… to assist students in transition from academia to the world of work by preparing students for life after graduation …. Career Center offers services which include:

… career counseling;
… three classes for academic credit;
… workshops and seminars on career-related subjects;
… assistance with resume writing and interviewing;
… opportunities for part-time jobs, internships, and full-time jobs.

**2. Career Center will provide job search assistance.**

**3. Graduates will be satisfied with services provided by the Career Center.**

All Services

Objective #2 – *Current Service Assessment*—This **service** in the eyes of the staff was the most important **service** they provided, and they wanted information that the unit was meeting the needs of the students.

Objective #3 – *Client Satisfaction*—The staff was not happy with its original satisfaction rating of 1.9 four years earlier on the institutional level graduating student survey. (They were below food services.) During the last four years, great efforts were made to improve this rating,

The objectives/outcomes in administrative and educational support services change more frequently than those in the educational programs. A change in personnel will often result in some aspect of the unit's **service** no longer being available. New **service**s are added to the list of **service**s. One only needs to look at the Library on any campus to understand the constantly changing **service**s offered by AES units. The **service**s offered by the Library now are entirely different from the **service**s offered by the Library five years ago.

*Step 4 – Means of Assessment and Criteria for Success*—The process for completing Step 4 (third column of the model) requires the AES units to ask, "What will provide us with the information as to whether we are accomplishing this objective/outcome, and what level of accomplishment will we hope to see?"

The selection of the "what will provide the information," or the identification of the "Means of Assessment," is a much easier process for AES units than it is for the educational programs. First, it is easier for an AES unit because the answer to the question above is often found from the records maintained on a regular basis in its office. Second, AES units do not have to wait until the students complete the programs before conducting their assessment. Third, they do not have to search through a variety of instruments to select a match to their programs. Whereas educational programs have a variety of methods available for assessment, the AES units are limited in the types of assessment available to them (Figure 64).

# Figure 64
## Types of Assessment for Administrative and Educational Support Units

| |
|---|
| • **Attitudinal assessment—measuring the levels of client satisfaction** |
| • **Direct measures—counting the degree/volume of** *service* |
| • **External validation—offered by agencies or peers not associated with the institution** |
| • **Observation or performance of clients** |

*Attitudinal assessment* is the most common form of assessment for AES unit. This is rightfully so, as the opinions of those who receive **service**s rendered are very important. Proper use of attitudinal assessment can provide the unit with much needed information regarding **service**s rendered. From attitudinal assessment, the AES units can determine what aspects of their **service**s are least satisfactory to the clients.

Two types of attitudinal assessment can be used on a campus. First are standardized assessments, such as Noel Levitz, ACT, NCHEMS, and others referenced in the Resource Section regarding Attitudinal Assessment Surveys by Daniel Weinstein. These instruments are machine readable, generally easy to administer, and often required by state boards/legislators. Public Relations offices love the comparisons available from standardized assessment as they can take full advantage of good comparative scores for generating a strong public imagine, at the same time ignoring or downplaying lower scores. The down side of standardized attitudinal assessments is that they are expensive for the institution to administer, and the overall score provided often does not give the AES unit information as to what specific area of **service**s needs improvement. (Read Chapter Seven for more information concerning attitudinal assessment.)

The second type of attitudinal assessment used on campuses is locally developed attitudinal assessment. These assessments include graduating student, alumni, employer, and point of contact surveys. For the institution, these locally developed attitudinal surveys are less costly to administer and can be customized to best fit the institutions and its **service**s. (Examples of these surveys can be found in the monograph *The Department Head's Guide to Assessment Implementation in Administrative and Educational Support Units*, Agathon Press, 2000). The graduating student and alumni surveys are institutional level surveys as described earlier in Chapter Seven. These surveys provide the institution and the AES units with general information as to the *overall level* of student/client satisfaction. If the level of **service** is unsatisfactory in an AES unit, a more detailed point of contact survey is administered. It is from the more detailed point of contact survey that specific information for improvement of **service**s can be obtained. The point of contact survey goes beyond asking an overall satisfaction question (an "atta boy") to asking specific questions concerning **service**s. (See Figure 65.)

## Figure 65

### *Overall and Component  Criteria for Success*

#### *Library Satisfaction Survey Example*

| | Very Dissatisfied | | | | Very Satisfied | *Criteria for Success* |
|---|---|---|---|---|---|---|
| **Course Reserves** | 1 | 2 | 3 | 4 | 5 | **Overall Criteria** |
| **On-line Library Catalog** | 1 | 2 | 3 | 4 | 5 | Students will report  an average of  3.4 or higher score as to Overall Satisfaction with the Library |
| **Electronic Database** | 1 | 2 | 3 | 4 | 5 | |
| **Media Equipment** | 1 | 2 | 3 | 4 | 5 | |
| **Staff Assistance** | 1 | 2 | 3 | 4 | 5 | **Component Criteria** |
| **Overall Satisfaction** | 1 | 2 | 3 | 4 | 5 | On no component of the survey will the average rating be less that 3.0 |

Notice that the Library has selected five specific **service**s about which it is soliciting feedback from its users concerning their satisfaction. (Yes, the Library has more than five **service**s that it offers, but during this assessment cycle, these specific **service**s relate to the objectives chosen.) The *overall satisfaction* question is still present to make the Library staff feel good, but it is from the responses to the more detailed questions that the Library staff will get an indication as to satisfaction with that current **service**. If the level of satisfaction does not meet the staff's opinion of what it should be, the Library now has information as to what areas of **service** need attention. The responses to specific questions related to current **service**s provided give the AES units information concerning the level of satisfaction with those specific **service**s. For example: If the responses to one **service** is rated lower than the staff feels it should be, the Library staff will begin the discussions as to how to bring that **service** to the level of satisfaction that would be acceptable. These discussions often lead the AES unit into setting plans/actions for the improvement of that specific **service**.

Point of contact surveys can be a very effective means of assessment for the AES unit if they avoid the tendency to over-survey the students. Two effective ways can be used to avoid over-surveying: (a) Have a central administration office, such as Institutional Research/Effectiveness office, provide guidance in developing and scoring the point of contact surveys. They are also responsible for monitoring to whom and when the point of contact surveys are being given. (b) Those units whose scores on the general institutional attitudinal assessment measure were not at the desired level would be encouraged to develop and administer point of contact surveys. Whichever way is chosen, it is important not to *over-survey* the population. First ask, *"Can we obtain this information any way other than with a survey?"*

When deciding to use attitudinal assessment or not, several points need to be considered:

1) Historically, in the early days of assessment when regional accrediting associations were happy to see any assessment taking place, attitudinal assessment was extremely popular in educational programs as well. For the AES units, attitudinal assessment was viewed as an easy way to get credit for doing assessment. Some states still strongly encourage the use of standardized attitudinal assessment for campuses' administrative and educational support (AES) units. However, after years of reviewing the use of attitudinal assessment in instructional and AES units, several of the regional accrediting associations have questioned the value of the information obtained from most attitudinal assessment.

2) Several of the regional accrediting associations now consider attitudinal assessment as an indirect or secondary means of assessment. The best suggestion concerning attitudinal assessment is to use it sparingly. However, it is important to recognize that it is good assessment practice for AES units to ask the groups/clients they serve the level of satisfaction with the **service**s provided.

3) Do not overlook other assessment measures from which a unit can get the same and often better satisfaction information than from surveys. Be creative when attempting to answer, "What will provide us with the information as to whether

we are accomplishing this objective/outcome?" Consider attitudinal assessment as an indirect means of assessment, unless you are getting specific information you can use for **service** improvement, as demonstrated in the Library point of contact survey provided in Figure 65.

*Direct measures of assessment* can be an informative means of assessment for many AES units. AES units like the Accounting Department, Development Office, and Physical Plant are able to collect very useful information from the assessment of the processes/**service**s provided. This is simply done by counting:

- Volume of activity, such as number of persons served
- Levels of efficiency, such as the average time for response
- Measures of quality, such as average errors per audit

When examining the Three-Column Model of the Career Center (Figure 67 later in the chapter), Administrative Objective/Outcome #2 ("Career Center will provide job search assistance.") has as its "Means of Assessment" a "direct measure." Objective #2 is assessed by measuring the volume of activity and usage.

*External validation* is a third means of assessment available for AES units. This is an often overlooked means of assessment by AES units. This assessment is the validation of the department/unit's efforts as representing "good and acceptable practices" by "neutral" persons who are knowledgeable in the field, such as auditors, public health inspectors, or fire marshals. Because this is often a process that is already required due to the nature of the **service**s provided, validation is an easy and time efficient way of obtaining some very valuable data that can be used for making improvements in the unit. Consultants, visitors from units at similar institutions as yours, and peers from your professional organization can also be useful as external evaluators.

*Observation or client performance* is the last means of assessment available for AES units. This type of assessment begins as an informal means of assessment which may include: phone complaints, suggestions from clients or peers, information acquired at a professional meeting, or observation by a member of the staff regarding some aspect of **service** not working the way the unit had hoped it would. Whatever the observation, the issue is generally introduced during a staff meeting. In the meeting, the staff will discuss the informal observation and brainstorm ways in which a "fix" can be put in place, or they develop plans to use a different approach. This informal means of assessment can easily be turned into a formal means of assessment.

After the staff members formulate an objective/outcome ("Students will enjoy the night activities planned by Campus Events."), the staff begins to develop its means of assessment. "What will give us information as to the fulfillment of this objective?" In the case of Campus Events, it is decided the best method would be to observe students who attend the events. Now the staff members begin to develop a formal means of assessment:

Step 1. The staff as a group will list several factors expected to be seen if students are enjoying an event. For example, students enjoying an event will probably do the following: show an interest in what is going on, be smiling, attend the event, show appreciation after the event, and provide positive comments to the staff concerning the event.

Step 2. The staff develops a common set of facts they believe are important in providing a quality Campus Event for students. This becomes the checklist/rubric for evaluating the Campus Event. (Refer to Chapter Seven for suggestions on developing a checklist or rubric.)

Step 3. The staff sets up a timetable which requires more than one staff member to attend future events and use the checklist/rubric for recording observation of student enjoyment of the event.

The staff has turned informal assessment to formal assessment by first establishing a checklist/rubric and then making sure more than one person is doing the observing. Figure 66 describe what should be covered when writing the "Means of Assessment" for each objective.

# Figure 66
# Means of Assessment Should Include the Following:

| |
|---|
| • **Specificity when naming the instrument/report to be used** |
| • **A description of "to whom" and "when" the assessment will be administered** |
| • **A statement referencing "by whom" and "based upon what" the results will be judged** |
| • **An indication as to what level of success is desired** |

Following the guidelines laid out in Figure 66, the "Means of Assessment and Criteria for Success" for events objective/outcome would be stated as follows:

The staff will use the "enjoyment checklist and rating sheet" to assess the level of student enjoyment of events. After each evening event held during the regular school year, at least two staff members attending the event will individually rate his/her observation of student enjoyment of the event. An overall average score of 3.6 on level of enjoyment will be received by all events, with no individual event receiving less that 2.5 enjoyment rate.

In this example and in the examples in the Three-Column Career Center Model, it is important to note that each "Means of Assessment" has a level of accomplishment (criteria/benchmark) chosen following the guidelines discussed in Chapter Seven.

Examining the model of the Career Center found in Figure 67 reveals that several "Means of Assessment" have been chosen by the AES unit staff. Objective #1 is a "student learning outcome" that will be measured using a checklist/rubric developed by the staff for determining quality resumes. Objective #2 is assessment of the current **service**s offered; the Career Center will use a direct means of assessment and count the volume of **service**. For assessment of client satisfaction, Objective # 3, the staff selected to use two

# Figure 67

## *Career Center-Three Columns*

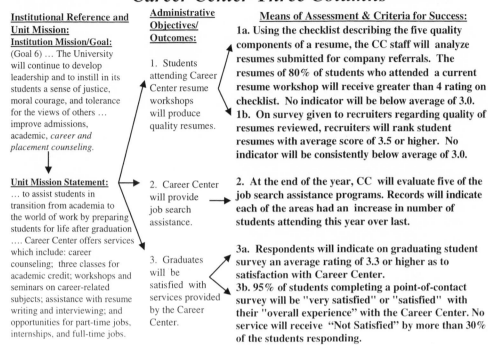

**Institutional Reference and Unit Mission:**

**Institution Mission/Goal:**
(Goal 6) … The University will continue to develop leadership and to instill in its students a sense of justice, moral courage, and tolerance for the views of others … improve admissions, academic, *career and placement counseling.*

**Unit Mission Statement:**
… to assist students in transition from academia to the world of work by preparing students for life after graduation …. Career Center offers services which include: career counseling; three classes for academic credit; workshops and seminars on career-related subjects; assistance with resume writing and interviewing; and opportunities for part-time jobs, internships, and full-time jobs.

**Administrative Objectives/ Outcomes:**

1. Students attending Career Center resume workshops will produce quality resumes.

2. Career Center will provide job search assistance.

3. Graduates will be satisfied with services provided by the Career Center.

**Means of Assessment & Criteria for Success:**

1a. Using the checklist describing the five quality components of a resume, the CC staff will analyze resumes submitted for company referrals. The resumes of 80% of students who attended a current resume workshop will receive greater than 4 rating on checklist. No indicator will be below average of 3.0.

1b. On survey given to recruiters regarding quality of resumes reviewed, recruiters will rank student resumes with average score of 3.5 or higher. No indicator will be consistently below average of 3.0.

2. At the end of the year, CC will evaluate five of the job search assistance programs. Records will indicate each of the areas had an increase in number of students attending this year over last.

3a. Respondents will indicate on graduating student survey an average rating of 3.3 or higher as to satisfaction with Career Center.

3b. 95% of students completing a point-of-contact survey will be "very satisfied" or "satisfied" with their "overall experience" with the Career Center. No service will receive "Not Satisfied" by more than 30% of the students responding.

locally developed attitudinal means of assessment. The first is an institutional level *general* survey administered to all students at the time they graduate from the institution. On that survey, using a scale of 1-5, students are asked, "How satisfied are you with the **ser-vice**s provided by the Career Center?" A second attitudinal assessment instrument used is a "point of contact" survey similar to the Library example, Figure 65. This survey serves as a supporting piece of documentation. From the "point of contact" survey, the Career Center determines information concerning usage and satisfaction with specific **service**s (computer/internet job search sources, SIGI Plus Software Program, Resume Writing Assistance). There is also a question relating to the knowledge of the counselors as well as a section that measures students' perceived growth as a result of the **service**s offered.

With the completion of the Third Column of the Career Center Model (Figure 67), the "assessment plan" has been completed. Steps Five and Six are the implementation portion of our process. Though they are very similar to those described for the educational programs in Chapter Eight, there are some significant differences.

*Step Five – Conduct Assessment Activities* - Different from the educational programs, whose assessment primarily occurs in the spring semester when most students complete their educational program, AES units' data collection varies according to the type of **service**s offered by the AES unit. For example: The New Student Orientation unit collects most of its data before classes have even met.

The Fourth Column of the model is reserved for recording the data/information collected from the assessment conducted by the AES unit. The question that often arises is, "How much data is enough?" A summary of the unit's findings is usually enough. There must be enough data available that the reader is convinced that the assessment actually took place.

In recording the data, the overall findings are presented first. If available, a comparison is made of those findings with previous years findings. (It is not realistic for most AES units to do a comparison of more than one assessment cycle's information, mainly because of the rapid changes that take place in AES units after a very short time.) Next, and where appropriate, the unit reports the assessment findings of the subsets. This detailed information or subsets is where the units are best able to distinguish what specific area of their **service** is not working the way the unit thinks it "ought to." (See Chapter Eight for more detailed descriptions regarding the reporting of the data.)

A summary of the results of the assessment is recorded in Column Four of the Career Center model (Figure 68).

The purpose of doing assessment is to gain data/information that the AES unit can use to indicate where a change in **service**s needs to be made and to use that information as a guide in making improvements. Once the assessment has been completed, it is important to record the data. This data should be recorded in a concise and readable way so whoever is reading the "Summary of Data Collected" is convinced that assessment actually was conducted and can see how the data collected led logically to the use of results.

*Step Six - Demonstrate and Document Use of Results for* **Service** *Improvements*—The final step in the assessment process is the most important. The five steps presented previously all lead to the point where the AES unit describes improvements it has made in its **services** based on the information gathered from assessment (data-based decision making). The guidelines reported in Chapter Eight for the educational programs are the same for the AES units. There are, however, two major areas where completing the fifth column of the model is different for the AES units.

First, because of the nature of the **services** AES units offer, the data collected from doing assessment often will lead to informing the future planning (Strategic Planning) side of the triangle (Figure 69).

For example, the result of assessment conducted by the Library has indicated that the students believe the lighting in the study area is inadequate. The first thing the Library does is to rearrange some bookcases providing more natural light to the study area. Having tried numerous ways to improve lighting without additional resources, it is obvious that new lighting is needed in the study section of the library. The next step is to inform Physical Services of the need for new lights for the library. Once the request for new lights for the library is received, facilities adds the request to its list of priorities. Following institutional protocol, when the library's request is at the top of the priority list, the lights are replaced. As this is an institutional decision as to how best to use resources, this process often takes several assessment cycles to complete (Figure 70).

# Figure 68

## *Career Center-Four Columns*

| Institutional Reference and Unit Mission: | Administrative Objectives/ Outcomes: | Means of Assessment & Criteria for Success: | Summary of Data Collected: |
|---|---|---|---|
| **Institution Mission/Goal:** (Goal 6) … The University will continue to develop leadership and to instill in its students a sense of justice, moral courage, and tolerance for the views of others …improve admissions, *academic, career and placement counseling.* | 1. Students attending Career Center resume workshops will produce quality resumes. | 1a. Using the checklist describing the five quality components of a resume, the CC staff will analyze resumes submitted for company referrals. The resumes of 80% of students who attended a current resume workshop will receive greater than 4 rating on checklist. No indicator will be below average of 3.0. | 1a. 536 resumes were reviewed. 316 resumes were from students who attended workshops. 213 resumes received quality score of 5 (67%); 89 scored 4 (28%); 14 received a 3. The quality indicator consistently missed by students was "use of action verbs". |
| | | 1b. On survey given to recruiters regarding quality of resumes reviewed, recruiters will rank student resumes with average score of 3.5 or higher. No indicator will be consistently below average of 3.0. | 1b. Recruiters rated the average quality of the resumes at 3.1. No indicator was consistently below average of 3.0. |
| **Unit Mission Statement:** … to assist students in transition from academia to the world of work by preparing students for life after graduation ..… Career Center offers services which include: career counseling; three classes for academic credit; workshops and seminars on career-related subjects; assistance with resume writing and interviewing; and opportunities for part-time jobs, internships, and full-time jobs. | 2. Career Center will provide job search assistance. | 2. At the end of the year, CC will evaluate five of the job search assistance programs. Records will indicate each of the areas had an increase in number of students attending this year over last. | 2. Overall, there was an increase in attendance at job search programs of 43. Resume workshops + 27; Interview workshops +21; Mock Interviews + 8; Job Search Techniques + 6; and On-Campus Recruiting (– 19). |
| | 3. Graduates will be satisfied with services provided by the Career Center. | 3a. Respondents will indicate on graduating student survey an average rating of 3.3 or higher as to satisfaction with Career Center. | 3a. Graduates rated satisfaction with Career Center at an average of 3.4  However, the international students only indicated a 1.4 average satisfaction rating. |
| | | 3b. 95% of students completing a point-of-contact survey will be "very satisfied" or "satisfied" with their "overall experience" with the Career Center. No service will receive "Not Satisfied" by more than 30% of the students responding. | 3b. 91% of students completing a point-of-contact survey indicated "very satisfied" or "satisfied" with "overall experience" with Career Center. However, 47% of the students indicated "Not Satisfied" rating with Computer/ Internet Job Search Sources. |

**Figure 69**

*Sharing Assessment Information for AES Units*

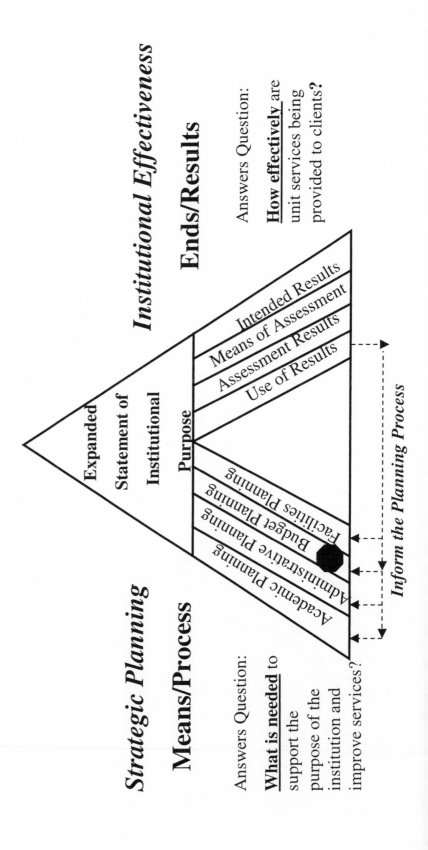

**Figure 70**

## *AES Units Planning To Service Cycle*

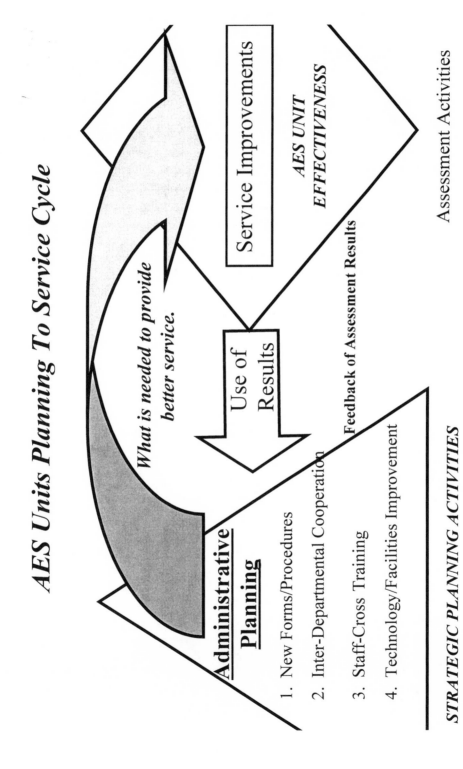

As a result, the information the Library would record in its fifth column would include what it did immediately (rearranged the book cases) as well as the information it provided to Physical Services and the status of its request. Once the lights are replaced, the Library goes back to the assessment cycle where the problem was first discovered and records in the use of results (Column Five) when the lights were replaced. It is important that the Library not assess the lighting of the study area again until the improvement has taken place. Once a problem has been identified, there is no need to continue assessing the same problem over and over. The unit simply records the action it has taken to make improvements and moves on to do assessment of other aspects of its **services**.

Second, due to the nature of AES units, the fifth column of the model ("Use of Results") is where the AES unit describes the actions it has decided to take as a result of the data that were collected. This description will include planning activities or new **services** that the staff decided need to take place prior to improvement in **service**. A review of the completed Five Column Model (Figure 71) for the Career Center indicates in the "Use of Results" column for the three objectives a level of planning activities. For example, look at "Administrative Objective/Outcome" #1a of the model (Figure 71). In the "Use of Results" column, it is stated that the "CC staff decided all students who submit resumes for referrals should be required to attend a workshop. The idea has been submitted to Vice Chancellor for consideration." Also listed in the "Use of Results" column #1a are immediate actions taken by the Career Center staff to help students further improve resume writing. Any planning activities for the creation a new/better **service** are recorded in Column Five. Once these planning activities are complete, then the new/better **service** can be assessed. Figure 70 shows this delay in improvement based on the need for doing administrative planning activities.

Having recorded the "Use of Results" from its assessment activities, the AES unit begins the process over for the next designated assessment cycle. The unit reviews its Mission Statement for changes, examines the long list from last assessment period, makes modifications to that list as it sees fit, and selects the outcomes/objectives for the up-coming cycle. Following the "Six Step Process" outlined above creates for AES units a systematic process which involves making small adjustments in the big picture to generate cumulative improvements in the **service**s offered.

Examples of Five Column Models from other AES units, greater detailed development of administrative and educational support Units, and a chapter devoted to assessment in organized research, external services, and continuing education units can be found in the monograph *The Department Head's Guide to Assessment Implementation in Administrative and Educational Support Units*, Agathon Press, 2000.

The Five Column Model presented is the basis for implementation of assessment procedures on any campus. Part II (Chapter's Six to Nine) has described the "heart" and most essential portion regarding assessment concepts during the development of the Five Column Model for educational as well as AES units. The Five Column Model can be applied to other aspects of the educational process such as the issues regarding distance learning, discussed in Appendix F. These assessment concepts lay the foundation and guidance for

# Figure 71

## *Career Center-Five Columns*

| Institutional Reference and Unit Mission: | Administrative Objectives/ Outcomes: | Means of Assessment & Criteria for Success: | Summary of Data Collected: | Use of Results: |
|---|---|---|---|---|
| **Institution Mission/Goal:** (Goal 6) … The University will continue to develop leadership and to instill in its students a sense of justice, moral courage, and tolerance for the views of others …improve admissions *academic, career and placement counseling.* | 1. Students attending Career Center resume workshops will produce quality resumes. | 1a. Using the checklist describing the five quality components of a resume, the CC staff will analyze resumes submitted for company referrals. The resumes of 80% of students who attended a current resume workshop will receive greater than 4 rating on checklist. No indicator will be below average of 3.0. | 1a. 536 resumes were reviewed. 316 resumes were from students who attended workshops. 213 resumes received quality score of 5 (67%); 89 scored 4 (28%): 14 received a 3. The quality indicator consistently missed by students was "use of action verbs". | 1a. While quality resumes were produced by students who attended the workshops, CC staff decided all students who submit resumes for referrals should be required to attend a workshop. The idea has been submitted to Vice Chancellor for consideration. The CC staff developed a skit for the workshops stressing the importance of using action verbs. Decided to use checklist again next year to compare results. Focus groups scheduled to further evaluate content of workshops. |
| **Unit Mission Statement:** … to assist students in transition from academia to the world of work by preparing students for life after graduation …. Career Center offers services which include: career counseling; three classes for academic credit; workshops and seminars on career-related subjects; assistance with resume writing and interviewing; and opportunities for part-time jobs, internships, and full-time jobs. | | 1b. On survey given to recruiters regarding quality of resumes reviewed, recruiters will rank student resumes with average score of 3.5 or higher. No indicator will be consistently below average of 3.0. | 1b. Recruiters rated the average quality of the resumes at 3.1. No indicator was consistently below average of 3.0. | 1b. Although the criteria was met, the CC staff examined the survey given to recruiters and decided the information from it gave nothing that could be used to help students with resume writing. Decided to redesign survey. |
| | 2. Career Center will provide job search assistance. | 2. At the end of the year, CC will evaluate five of the job search assistance programs. Records will indicate each of the areas had an increase in number of students attending this year over last. | 2. Overall there was an increase in attendance at job search programs of 43. Resume workshops + 27; Interview workshops +21; Mock Interviews + 8, Job Search Techniques + 6; and On-Campus Recruiting (– 19). | 2. Career Center staff is satisfied with three of the five job search programs offered. Staff decided to offer additional Job Search Techniques program each semester. Staff is concerned with On-Campus Recruiting as this is second year for a decline in student interest. Staff scheduled a focus group of recent graduates to meet in the Fall. Topic is: "Determining effective ways of increasing interest in On-Campus Recruiting." |
| | 3. Graduates will be satisfied with services provided by the Career Center. | 3a. Respondents will indicate on graduating student survey an average rating of 3.3 or higher as to satisfaction with Career Center. | 3a. Graduates rated satisfaction with Career Center at an average of 3.4 However, the international students only indicated a 1.4 average satisfaction rating. | 3a. While criteria for success was met workshops have been held by Career Center staff in conjunction with International Services to provide direct services to international students. Collecting material from nationally know programs. |
| | | 3b. 95% of students completing a point-of-contact survey will be "very satisfied" or "satisfied" with their "overall experience" with the Career Center. No service will receive "Not Satisfied" by more than 30% of the students responding. | 3b. 91% of students completing a point-of-contact survey indicated "very satisfied" or "satisfied" with "overall experience" with Career Center. However, 47% of the students indicated "Not Satisfied" rating with Computer/ Internet Job Search Sources. | 3b. Career Center staff have located several new internet sources of career information. Six additional work stations were established using computer hardware donated by Kroger and International Paper |

the final portion of this publication. The next section (Part III) explores different contexts where these concepts are applied and refined. Chapters Ten, Eleven, and Twelve describe and provide examples of implementation of assessment procedures in general education, at two-year colleges (including developmental programs), and in graduate and professional programs. Aspects of how implementation in these unique contexts differs from that described in Part II are highlighted. Additionally, contained in Part III is Chapter Thirteen, which includes a simple description of necessary procedures for documenting the assessment activities and improvements implemented on campus.

# Part Three

# ASSESSMENT ACTIVITIES REGARDING

# SPECIFIC TYPES OF EDUCATIONAL

# PROGRAMS (GENERAL EDUCATION,

# TWO-YEAR, AND GRADUATE LEVEL)

# AND DOCUMENTATION

# CHAPTER TEN

# IMPLEMENTING ASSESSMENT ACTIVITIES IN GENERAL EDUCATION

## Eliot Elfner, Contributing Author

*General Education Assessment, like assessment of administrative and educational support (AES) services, is one travel experience that virtually all institutions completing the journey toward successful implementation of institutional effectiveness must face. It is the single most challenging assessment task undertaken on most campuses due to the nature of the subject (often value related) and disciplines of the faculty involved (normally liberal arts). However, it is required by all regional accrediting associations and is the area most likely to see attention from representatives of the public, such as legislators.*

In Chapters Six to Eight, the implementation of institutional effectiveness or assessment activities in educational programs, the foundation regarding assessment activities was established. Comments contained in this chapter amplify those previously made and point out differences from those concepts as they relate to general education assessment. In addition, the monograph titled *General Education Assessment for Improvement of Student Academic Achievement: Guidance for Academic Departments and Committees,* 2001, was published by Agathon Press for the use of those constituencies, and portions of this chapter are closely related to and intertwined with the comments made in that publication. In this chapter, an important discussion of the alternative means through which to coordinate assessment of general education as well as basic approaches to the subject precedes coverage of general education student learning outcomes and means of assessment, while sample models complete implementation.

### Coordination of General Education Assessment

Coordination, administration, direction, or responsibility for general education curriculum development frequently is an orphan. Though this component of undergraduate education constitutes, in most cases, nearly half of a student's undergraduate curriculum, institutions seldom effectively oversee their general education or core curriculum programs.

At one time in the mid-twentieth century, the notion of a "general college," which was responsible for offering the courses taken in general education or the core curriculum, became somewhat popular. Among the most noted examples of this was the General College at the University of Minnesota. Under this structure, the dean of the "general college" had the overall responsibility for coordination or administration of the program of general education. However, a number of factors, including difficulty in recruiting and retaining faculty (who primarily relate to their discipline rather than general education), brought about a decline of this organizational structure throughout the balance of the century.

Following the decline of the general college model, coordination of general education has taken on a number of forms. On some campuses, there exists a general education curriculum committee responsible for the coordination of these offerings. However, more frequently general education is assigned to the institutional "curriculum committee" as its responsibility. In either case, general education or core curriculum responsibility is exercised primarily through the individual academic departments responsible for providing the service courses. Under this structure, frequently weak general education or curriculum committees are left to the tender mercies of more organized and committed faculties in the individual academic departments. Many of these departments are, in the author's opinion, intent primarily on seeing that the maximum amount of their discipline is included within the general education program required of all students.

In many cases, an individual responsible for coordination or administration of the general education program is also difficult to identify. While ultimate responsibility must lie with the institution's chief academic officer, that individual frequently passes authority (though not responsibility) for general education administration to an associate or assistant chief academic officer or to one of the committees referenced above. The most common answer the authors receive when asking the question on campuses, "Who is responsible for general education?" is (after a pause and some thought on the part of the respondent), "Well, I guess no one."

Given the fact that the individual or group responsible for general education curriculum development is difficult to identify, the question is, "What body then should be responsible for *assessment* of general education?" The answer is (a) the group identified as being responsible for coordination of general education curriculum development, (b) the institutional assessment committee, or (c) a separate committee established for the purpose of assessing general education. The advantages of utilizing the *same* group identified as responsible for general education curriculum development for its assessment include its familiarity with the subject of general education, probable representativeness of the stakeholders involved, and existing responsibility for identification of intended outcomes for the general education program.

The main disadvantage of having the *same committee responsible for development of the general education curriculum* serve the purpose of coordinating general education assessment lies in its existing level of commitment or work and its general lack of knowledge of assessment procedures. In most instances, groups or individuals who have born the responsibility for general education curriculum development consider themselves already over-committed by that act and have little interest in also dealing with assessment of the general education program. In addition, many of these committee members have little interest or expertise in assessment procedures.

Utilization of the *institutional assessment committee* to coordinate general education assessment also exhibits a number of advantages and disadvantages. The chief advantages of this approach are in the current existence of the committee (thereby avoiding the appointment of another committee) and the committee's relative expertise in assessment procedures being developed by its members. However, these advantages are more than offset by the disadvantages of this approach, which include the potential lack of representativeness of the primary stakeholders in general education as well as the fact that the institutional assessment committee is already heavily committed to other assessment activities. Assessment of general education is, in many ways, a subject unto itself.

The establishment of a *separate general education assessment committee* is probably the best approach to coordination of this important activity. One or more members of the institutional assessment committee can become the core of this committee and be augmented by the stakeholders from the primary service departments as well as "campus experts" in fields such as reading, mathematics, and writing. While this approach requires appointment of another committee, the committee's work can be linked through joint memberships to that of the institutional assessment committee. Its establishment allows the general education assessment committee to focus its attention solely on this important subject.

## Approaches to the Assessment of General Education

From the authors' experiences, there appear to exist two basic approaches to the organization and assessment of general education. These are the *departmental/course* approach and the *programmatic* approach. The departmental/course approach sees general education as a loose collection of courses from each discipline with a wide selection of distribution requirements. The programmatic approach conceptualizes general education as a coordinated whole leading to the development of the *overall* student as a member of society. This approach leads to program level outcomes and assessment. The departmental/course level approach may flow from some overreaching programmatic outcomes but focuses on course level objectives and assessment thereof. (See Figure 72.)

This departmental/course approach to general education organization and assessment is, in the experience of the authors, the more commonly chosen approach. It offers a familiar structure for faculty members (their own department), and course level assessment is initially seen as apparently easier to work with "one course at a time."

The disadvantages which lead to the failure (in most cases) of the departmental or course level approach to assessment are numerous. First, this approach fails to consider the development of the individual "as a whole" (often after describing a general education program focused upon development of the "well rounded" or "whole" student in its mission statement, catalog, and/or recruiting material). Second, this approach leads to the need to establish a relationship between course objectives and program outcomes and requires assessment of the achievement of course objectives by more than the individual faculty member teaching the course. Third, this approach generally does not fit well with regional accreditation requirements which deal with the overall concept of a general education pro-

**Figure 72**

## *The Course Level Approach*
## *to Assessment of General Education*

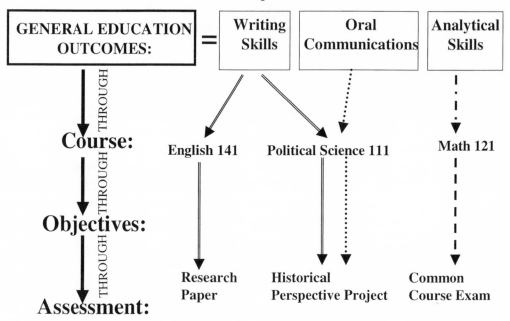

gram. Finally, it has been the author's observation that institutions that have begun this type of assessment have found that it generates a level of assessment work at the course level which is so resource and labor intensive that it can not be sustained for any meaningful period of time. The result of an institution's choosing this approach of action is most often exhaustion and disappointment on the part of the faculty involved with little meaningful change or improvement in learning. On many campuses, the department/course approach to assessment of general education often becomes "the ditch assessment died in."

Limited success for a short period of time is possible with the department/course approach to assessment of general education. The author has visited campuses where it has been possible to conduct assessment of writing and mathematical skills at the close of courses in these subjects. That ability combined with indifference toward and lack of identification with the discipline of general education has led faculty to limit assessment in general education to the department/course level approach in only math and writing. This decision results in failure to ever consider assessment beyond the most basic skills and thereby trivializes this important subject. Such limited success is normally not viewed as sufficiently comprehensive enough by regional accrediting association reviewers.

On the other hand, the programmatic approach to general education assessment considers general education as a whole with identifiable outcomes in different disciplines contributing to the overall program. The principal advantages of this approach are (a) its comprehensive treatment of the subject, (b) its facilitation of assessment "beyond the individual section and instructor level," (c) its feasibility for implementation within an achievable and sustainable level of effort, and (d) the extent to which this approach "fits" most regional accrediting association expectations.

The primary disadvantage of the program level approach to general education assessment is the need to work across departmental (and college/school) lines, which many campuses lack experience in doing. Without the existence of a previous track record or history of working cooperatively on general education, the likelihood of choosing this programmatic approach to assessment of general education is substantially reduced. The programmatic approach to assessment of general education is, regretfully, "the road less taken" due to the lack of a campus effective coordinating structure and the inability of many faculty members to see beyond their discipline to the success of the student as a whole.

The discussion above concerning approaches to assessment of general education addresses the issue of these activities at either the *program* or *departmental/course* level. There are few things which can be promised in assessment activities of any type. However, one that can be promised is that faculty at most institutions will not implement comprehensive *course* level assessment activities over a sustained period of time. Numerous institutions profess to be doing departmental/course level assessment. However, when questioned or examined in detail, these institutions are found to have only a few departments doing an outstanding job of department/course level assessment (usually for a very limited period of time). The vast majority of the departments are found not doing assessment of any type but are counting on the limited number of departments doing department/course level assessment to make up for their lack of progress. An administration simply can not apply enough "coercive finesse" to successfully implement course level assessment comprehensively. While theoretically attractive, course level assessment requirements lead institutions to "choke and die" on the assessment efforts which they have created for themselves. On the other hand, program level assessment of general education is distinctly accomplishable and sustainable year in and year out. Why "die in the ditch" of course level assessment when the road map provided in this publication and the monograph referenced can lead to success on your institution's journey to successful general education assessment?

It is the author's recommendation (based upon almost twenty years' experience and visits to over 300 institutions) that campuses accept the programmatic approach to assessment of general education and the challenge of working together toward a unified and improved curriculum in the important area of general education. The balance of this chapter is based upon this assumption of a programmatic approach to general education and its assessment.

## General Education Outcomes

*Sources of General Education Outcomes*—Before undertaking the arduous task of identifying a set of general educations outcomes from scratch, institutions should consider a number of sources which may already provide guidance in the matter. First, a review of the institution's statement of purpose (ESIP) should be conducted to ascertain if the statement of institutional level intentions contains a description of what characteristics program completers should exhibit. Often, a well-intentioned lay governing board obligates faculty to provide evidence through assessment of general education regarding matters (commitment to lifelong learning, leadership ability, ethical behavior, etc.) which the faculty had never intended to address. Second, the existence of external directives concerning general education from higher level governing or coordinating bodies should be determined. With increasing frequently, such agencies provide this type of curricular guidance. Third, the possible/probable current existence of a long list of general education outcomes should be determined. The lack of such a list playing an important role in general education curriculum development should not be considered as evidence of its lack of existence. The subject of general education outcomes is not new to most campuses and the odds are that such a long list of general education outcomes exists on the campus. Finally, justification or explanation of the rationale upon which the existing general education curriculum exist may provide useful information concerning the institution's general education expectations for its students.

*Typical General Education Outcomes*—When viewed as the outcomes or results of general education, a taxonomy of general education outcomes might include those indicated in Figure 73.

**Figure 73**

# Taxonomy of General Education Outcomes

| |
|---|
| • Basic skills |
| • Knowledge/Understanding |
| • High order thinking skills |
| • Values development |

The *basic skills* cited in most general education programs include: reading, writing, speaking, listening, performing mathematical calculations, and demonstration of basic computer skills.

There is general agreement on most campuses concerning the need for graduates to have the ability to read, write, and take part in oral communication. However, even in these most basic areas, the specific operational definitions of these terms and the answer to the question: "How well should our graduates be expected to read, write, or speak?" is often not addressed nor are the precise definitions of what are implied by these common terms.

The ability to perform fundamental mathematical calculations also is commonly accepted as a basic general education outcome, though the meaning of this term is often not described until identification of the "Means of Assessment." The emphasis here is not on knowledge concerning the meaning of the mathematical calculations or their appropriateness for a particular end but on the ability to conduct the calculations themselves.

Computer literacy is clearly emerging as a commonly accepted skill on campuses and in society. As in the cases above, it is in the "definition" of the term that most work remains to be accomplished. Computer literacy at a highly technical institution emphasizing engineering is quite a different concept from computer literacy at a liberal arts college.

Less likely, but occasionally encountered, as general education outcomes are the "life skills" espoused in the writings of authors such as John Dewey in the 1930's and 1940's. These skills include interpersonal relations, communications, self-knowledge, etc. The inclusion of these skills in general education was a more common phenomenon in the past than at the present time; however, their existence is certainly worthy of note.

In addition to the basic skills, it is often anticipated that degree recipients, or program completers, will have a *knowledge/understanding* of common themes in the culture in which they will function. Often the outcomes in this arena relate to students' knowledge of the past, which enable them to view events in historical perspective. This historical perspective may be amplified by students' familiarity with the literature and literary styles encountered in each historical period. The joint impact of the students' historical perspective and knowledge of literary styles and the culture therein often are reflected in outcomes which seek to identify different philosophical approaches to life within the current society.

Among the more recent emphases in general education outcomes noted by the authors in their visits to campuses have been the prominence of knowledge or understanding of the meaning of numerical data and existence of a global perspective on the part of the students. As quantitative reasoning has increased as a basis for decision making, colleges are tending to place more emphasis upon not only the ability to conduct calculations but also on the ability to understand the meaning of the resulting data or statistics. Also, an increasing number of institutions include in their general education outcomes the students' knowledge of their culture's place within the global village. The impact of technology and communications are often also emphasized in these type outcomes.

In addition to the "basic skills" and "knowledge or understanding of the culture," many institutions include in their general education outcomes skills commonly described as *higher order thinking skills*. These skills include terms such as critical thinking, logical reasoning, scientific/abstract inquiry, and concept integration. Each of these terms, while having specific and often different meanings in the jargon of various fields, share a great deal in common. They relate to an individual's ability to use the scientific or other methodology to discern between alternatives through the use of either inductive or deductive reasoning. These abilities are characterized as "skills of the mind" and cut across the curricular patterns described earlier. The skills can be utilized to integrate what otherwise appear to be disparate approaches to general education in the various disciplines.

*Values* are the type of outcome referenced in Figure 73 that are most difficult to measure and are unquestionably the most controversial. In public institutions, these outcomes frequently relate to a student's development of a commitment to the democratic ideal or citizenship. Acceptance on the part of students of the desirability of cultural diversity or a pluralistic society is also common among such outcomes at public institutions.

Public and private institutions share some value-related educational (student learning) outcomes. There are very few institutions that do not espouse the development of "aesthetic appreciation" by their graduates. However, the meaning of that term often remains a mystery on the campus. Likewise, the development of an ethical perspective leading to the graduation of students with high moral or ethical standards is a common general education outcome at both public and private institutions. It is often in the specification of what "ethics" or whose moral standards are expected of students that public and private institutions differ.

The single value whose development is restricted to denominationally related institutions is that of religious orientation. While some institutions with denominational relations seek only to encourage their students toward belief in a "supreme being," others are committed to their students' adoption of a particular religious doctrine. Either approach is entirely appropriate in a free society where students are able to choose the nature of their higher education.

General education outcomes should, in many ways, be similar to those described in Chapter Six. With one exception, they follow the same characteristics and patterns as do those student learning outcomes identified for the major. This sole exception relates to the institutional options concerning types of the general education outcomes to be assessed at any one time. In the assessment of general education, there are basically two approaches to the identification of the three to five outcomes to be assessed. The institution may take the approach of selecting one theme for assessment in a given year and go into considerable depth regarding the outcomes associated with that theme or concept. As an example, an institution could pick a theme such as "communications" for a given year and identify a number of general education outcomes concerning topics such as writing, oral communications, listening, etc., for assessment during that period of time. In such an instance, a portion of those faculty (such as those in the Departments of English and Speech) engaged in the general education process will be exceptionally busy with assessment activities during that period, while those in mathematics and the natural sciences would not be taking part in general education assessment activities at that time. However, they would continue to be part of the assessment activities regarding their majors.

The other (and more commonly taken) approach to selection of general education outcomes for assessment is characterized by the selection of one outcome from each of a wide variety of disciplines. This approach would include an outcome concerning perhaps communications, one concerning mathematical abilities, another concerning scientific reasoning, and others broadly representative of additional disciplines. This approach assures that most curricular areas will be doing some assessment in any given year but precludes any discipline's assessment in depth. In selecting this approach, it is particularly important to remember to limit the number of outcomes being *assessed* in any year to five, as the *tendency* will be to involve *all* disciplines every year.

Just as in assessment in the major, described in Chapters Six to Eight, identification of student learning outcomes in general education is followed by identification of the "Means for Assessment" of these outcomes. Using the "short-list" vs. "long-list" concept, it will take several years to move through an institution's repertoire of general education outcomes. However, this is to be expected and is entirely acceptable.

## Cognitive Means of Assessment in General Education

Both standardized and locally developed cognitive means of assessment in general education are widely utilized on college and university campuses. In general, these means of assessment exhibit the same strengths and limitations as that of these types of assessment in the major (previously cited in Figure 29 through Figure 32 in Chapter Seven). However, there are some unique aspects of cognitive means of assessment worthy of note. The ready availability of instrumentation and comprehensive coverage of the subject are advantages to the utilization of standardized test in assessment of general education. In many cases, assessment in general education (due to its extreme difficulty) is postponed until far too late to begin the process before reaffirmation review. In this case, the ready availability of instruments for this purpose takes on considerably greater importance. Additionally, only through the utilization of standardized instrumentation have the authors witnessed assessment of student learning outcomes that involve the higher order thinking skills.

The primary disadvantage of utilizing standardized instruments in general education assessment is the open hostility of some faculty toward these instruments and their unwillingness therefore to use the results. Because many of the faculty involved with general education are housed within the liberal arts disciplines, which in general have little sympathy for standardized testing philosophically, the hostility toward standardized testing is considerably greater than for assessment in the major. This leads, understandably, to even less likelihood of the faculty's willingness to use the results of general education's standardized testing to improve that program. The authors *have never witnessed* a substantive change in general education based solely upon the results of the standardized tests. In most cases, the results of the standardized tests in general education are questioned by the faculty, who then devise a locally developed cognitive means of assessment, and it is from that locally developed means of assessment that faculty are willing to entertain the notion of making changes in this important field. However, these locally developed means of assessment would not have been established without the original focus and motivation created by the standardized instrument.

There are three comprehensive general education means of assessment recommended for consideration as a means of assessment on your campus. These are the Collegiate Assessment of Academic Proficiency (CAAP) from ACT, College Basic Academic Subjects Examination (CBASE) from the Assessment Research Center at the University of Missouri, Columbia, as well as Academic Profile from Educational Testing Services (ETS). (At the time of this writing, Academic Profile remained available from ETS but was to be withdrawn on June 25, 2005.) A new and substantially revised general education instrument utilizing an on-line essay input with automated writing analysis was in the advanced stages of development.) Each of these instruments is based upon a slightly different set of general education expectations and assessment procedures. The remaining two instruments are described in the Resource Section concerning this subject by Paul Cunningham included at the conclusion of this book and in Figures 19 through 21 in the monograph *General Education Assessment for Improvement of Student Academic Achievement, Agathon Press, 2001*. The primary advantage of using such comprehensive measures is that they cover most of the fields normally associated with general education (reading, writing, mathematics, as well as some form of critical thinking) in one sitting and are readily available. Faculty will want to bring these instruments onto the campus to review them carefully to determine their particular appropriateness for use on each campus.

In addition to these instruments, there are two assessment instruments specifically regarding the subject of critical thinking. These instruments are the Watson-Glaser Critical Thinking Appraisal and The California Critical Thinking Skills Tests, both of which are also reviewed in the Resource Section by Paul Cunningham.

None of the standardized tests referenced above (or probably any that will ever be designed) will find ready acceptance by faculty in the disciplines which contribute most of the courses to the general education program. However, the liabilities exhibited by each of these examinations must be considered in the light of the fact that in very few instances is comprehensive locally developed assessment of general education spanning most of the basic skills or any of the likely general education outcomes beyond the most basic level achieved.

On most campuses seeking to accomplish locally developed assessment of general education, this action is successful in regards to the students' ability to write (most often by capturing a writing sample) and, in some cases, their ability to conduct (though not necessarily understand) basic mathematical calculations. Why is this the case? In the authors' opinion, the primary reasons relate to exhaustion and logistics.

The amount of exhaustion encountered on the part of faculty in developing, conducting, scoring, and analyzing the results of locally developed measures of general education exceeds even that of assessment in the major. Usually there are sufficient faculty members and energy in the English and Mathematics Departments to see that assessment gets done regarding those outcomes; however, the will to tackle such a substantial task is frequently not present outside these two major departments on college and university campuses.

The logistics of moving students from one location to another to take what are normally separate examinations in writing and mathematics fairly well exhaust the students' patience with this endeavor. This lack of patience by the students, plus the faculty's exhaustion of energy, usually leads to no meaningful assessment beyond these two very basic skills.

It is very rare (the authors know of only two institutions among the over 300 with whom they have worked) that an institution has prepared a locally developed comprehensive cognitive examination regarding general education. However, two other "locally developed" approaches to comprehensive cognitive assessment show limited promise.

On some campuses, faculty in the different disciplines servicing general education have agreed to administer, either completely or partially, common course examinations for all sections through which students completing general education pass. These examinations are administered and analyzed by a group of faculty in each department. This analysis is then combined with similar analyses from other departments, resulting in a cumulative analysis composed of the components contributed by each discipline.

Several other institutions have taken an approach involving the careful selection of the texts for their general education disciplines/courses. Texts selected all contain publisher provided cognitive examinations based upon the material covered in the text. These examinations are administered and the results combined from across several disciplines to again result in a cumulative assessment of general education. The obvious advantage of this approach is the ability to compare individual discipline responses at the institution to the criteria established in the textbook. The primary disadvantage of this approach is the limitation of assessment to only the material presented in the textbooks.

General education cognitive assessment is among the most daunting challenges on college and university campuses. There clearly is no one "correct" means of assessment, and most colleges field a mix of standardized and locally developed methods. The key in selection of those methods is to focus upon the means of assessment which is responsive to the outcome stated and will result in data that faculty are likely to use for program improvement.

### Attitudinal Assessment of General Education

Attitudinal assessment of general education exhibits the same characteristics as that regarding attitudinal assessment regarding the major (covered in Chapter Seven). In addition, supplemental information regarding attitudinal assessment in general education is amply covered in the monograph *General Education Assessment for Improvement of Student Academic Achievement,* Agathon Press, 2001. However, several points concerning these means of assessment should be highlighted. First, graduating student as well as alumni surveys routinely collect attitudinal affirmation information from students regarding the extent of their development in general education during matriculation of the institution. Second, the College Student Experience Questionnaire (CSEQ), as well as the College Student Report (CSR), provides potentially valuable standardized attitudinal means of assessment regarding general education. These are described in the Resource Section by Daniel Weinstein contained in this publication. Third, any attitudinal affirmation (because it is regarded by regional accrediting associations as an indirect measure) is insufficient on its own to verify accomplishment of the outcomes identified.

### Performance Assessment in General Education

Performance assessment takes place when a situation is contrived requiring the student to demonstrate a skill or value identified in general education outcomes while the student remains enrolled at the institution. There is no better vehicle for conducting assessment of verbal communications than the videotaping of student presentations and subsequent review of a sample of these tapes based on commonly agreed upon faculty scored rubrics or checklists. In many instances, institutions identify values such as ethics, globalism, commitment to cultural diversity, Judeo-Christian commitment, etc., which they expect students to take forward into their adult lives. An excellent means through which to assess the impact of the institution's general education program on students is to place students in a case study while still in attendance at the institution requiring them to demonstrate those values or skills. Finally, analysis of written prose collected towards the end of the student's educational experience is the most common type of performance assessment regarding writing. Students are not being tested regarding their knowledge of grammar or spelling but rather on their ability to actually write using correct grammar, sentence structure, verb tense, etc.

The strength of performance or "authentic" assessment lies in the fact that it offers *direct evidence* of the students' abilities or values. There is no implication or inference which needs be drawn, and the tendency to report or demonstrate socially acceptable responses is minimized. However, performance assessment requires a considerable period of time and effort to logistically prepare and conduct. On balance, an institution should clearly consider at least a limited number of performance assessment measures regarding general education.

### Behavioral Observation as a Means of Assessment in General Education

Behavioral observation type assessment takes place when the actions of students are "observed" or "reported" and these actions are linked to intended educational (student learning) outcomes. However, in some cases in general education, the students' reported or observed actions, either while in attendance or after leaving the institution, must be assumed to *imply* a certain set of values. In most cases in the major, this linkage is very direct through reports of employment, admission to graduate school, achievement of licensure, etc. In the case of general education, this linkage is considerably less direct.

If it is the institution's intention, as stated in its general education program educational (student learning) outcomes, that students become committed to taking part in the democratic process, then observation of voting patterns in student elections would seem like a logical behavioral indicator. If appreciation of the fine and performing arts represents a general education outcome listed by the institution, *voluntary* attendance at fine arts presentations by students would be one type of observation measure. Participation in public service activities as alumni could easily be an indicator or measure of the development of social consciousness as a part of general education. Finally, church or temple attendance following graduation is an often cited behavioral measure of a commitment to Judeo-Christian beliefs.

### Assessing Values as Part of General Education

Most institutional mission statements describe their general sense of identity, the type of students served, the geographic region from which students are drawn, and the type of programs offered. Additionally, many institutions of higher learning address in their

Expanded Statements of Institutional Purpose (ESIP) a variety of desired student learning outcomes that they deem to be most important. Included in these statements are often learning outcomes focused on an in-depth level of understanding of a particular field of study and the more general learning outcomes the institution views as necessary for a well-educated graduate. It is in this last category of statements in the institutional mission that the general education component of the academic program is validated. For institutions, statements relating to ethical and values oriented learning outcomes are included in this component of an institution's mission statement. In addition to academic outcomes, general education programs often promote student learning in the ethical and values arena. Such values statements reflect another dimension of learning for which the institution is responsible. To the extent the institution's mission statement addresses values oriented student learning, the assessment process also must consider these student learning outcomes as well.

*The Complexity of Assessing Values and Ethics Learning Outcomes*—Why is it so difficult to assess the development of values in students? Values statements in some institutions' missions may be based on religious dogma, and values are recognized as a sensitive matter of privacy for individuals. But a more general approach to the definition of values and ethics would enable an approach to assessing student learning in the values context. The dictionary defines values to be a principle or quality that is intrinsically desirable or important to an individual (noun). Alternatively, a value is described as a principle or quality in which one believes (noun). As a verb, to value something is to regard it highly or in high esteem. Assessment of values and ethical outcomes can take the form of existence of, or change in, values. This can be expressed in the context of "Educating the Whole Person," "Preparing Graduates to be 'Good Citizens,' " or "Working for the Global Common Good."

A values context is relevant in both private and public institutions. Public institutions need to avoid imposing religiously oriented values but can still assess the degree to which students hold and advocate a set of secular values. Some examples of values oriented student learning statements that are appropriate at public institutions include appreciation for diversity, practice of good citizenship, positive attitude toward lifelong learning, understanding of the ethical reasoning processes, and aesthetic appreciation of art, literature, and music. Examples of desired student learning outcome statements that illustrate the values and ethical outcomes that may be of interest to an institution include: "Make **ethical** decisions" or "Apply **ethical principles** for the good of humanity"; "Recognize the importance of **service** to others"; "Tolerate **differences of opinion** among people"; "Participate in public **elections**" or "Participate in **citizenship responsibilities** with others."

*Means of Assessing Values and Ethics Outcomes*—There are several means of assessing value/belief outcomes. A body of evidence that contributes to the assessment of values can be acquired by *asking* students about their experiences, by *testing* them for values oriented outcomes, or *reporting* on their behavior through observation or by self-report. *Asking* about values/beliefs poses the danger of respondents offering socially acceptable responses. This can be dealt with by disguising the question so that the acceptable answer is less obvious. One can also ask longitudinally about the things students value and assess the changes in values that occur in a group of students. (For examples of this approach, see the ongoing research from the UCLA Higher Education Research Institute - Cooperative Institutional Research Project – HERI-CIRP.)

*Testing* for values/beliefs can be accomplished through the use of various standard or locally developed devices. Individuals will more accurately demonstrate values/beliefs through analysis of case studies in capstone courses or by preparing papers or oral reports on values oriented topics (an imbedded measure using rubrics). Voluntary actions during enrollment also can be used to demonstrate values oriented outcomes, such as service volunteering or participation in various values oriented activities.

*Reporting* value and belief-based activities during enrollment or after graduation may also provide evidence about values oriented outcomes. Graduating Student Surveys and Alumni Surveys are often used to elicit self-reports from currently enrolled students and from graduates several years after college. Examples of such values oriented activities would be church attendance, voting experience, adult or graduate education enrollment, reading patterns, and organizational memberships/offices held.

Evidence about learning outcomes can be of differing levels of rigor. Some evidence is designated as DIRECT evidence and consists of objective indicators, such as actual measurements of data. Others kinds of evidence are considered less precise and are generally gathered by self-reported surveys of opinion, aspirations, or perceptions. These types of indicators are generally thought of as INDIRECT evidence. The table on page 180 (Figure 74) demonstrates several examples of DIRECT and INDIRECT indicators in the cognitive (KNOW), affective (THINK), and behavioral (DO) domains of evidence.

Institutions with mission statements that address values oriented outcomes must find ways in which to assess the level of success they experience in achieving these desired outcomes. General education and values assessment can and should be considered when Institutional Mission and Purpose Statements include values, and beliefs in their definition of desired student learning outcomes.

### The General Education Component of Occupational Oriented Associate Degree, Diploma, and Certificate Programs

While most discussion of General Education relates to the liberal arts, material normally taken by all baccalaureate level students primarily during their first two years of study, a similar type of general education programming is also required (through to a lesser amount) in the occupational level offerings of the community and technical college. This programming is often closely related to the major, such as technical writing, and normally does not extend past the basic skills level of the general education taxonomy. An example of this type model is provided in Figure 75.

### Concluding Comments Regarding Assessment in General Education

Figures 76 through 78 depict completed general education assessment models (through five-columns) for two-year and four-year private and public institutions. While these models seem deceptively simple and straightforward, readers must bear in mind that assessment in this area is the most complex issue on most campuses. In planning for its implementation, roughly twice the amount of time will be necessary for assessment implementation in general education through use of results as will be required for assessment in the major.

**Figure 74**

*Outcomes Assessment Matrix for Values and Ethics*

| Type of Indicator | | KNOW | FEEL | DO |
|---|---|---|---|---|
| **DIRECT** | | - describe one's own set of values with a rationale<br><br>- describe the value characteristics of one's own culture<br><br>- present and discuss the value characteristics of a foreign culture | - present arguments in favor or against particular values statements | - participate in a service learning project<br><br>- volunteer for work in a political campaign<br><br>- participate in preparing and/or presenting church services |
| **INDIRECT** | | - report agreement with survey statements regarding respondents' perceptions about what they know about values<br><br>- rate their understanding of values<br><br>- rate a set of values for respondents' personal preferences | - report commitment to certain issues<br><br>- rate the relative worth of various values | - report participating in a service learning project<br><br>- report participating in preparing and/or presenting church services<br><br>- report volunteering for work in a political campaign |

# Figure 75

## City Technical College
## *General Education Program – Career Degrees*

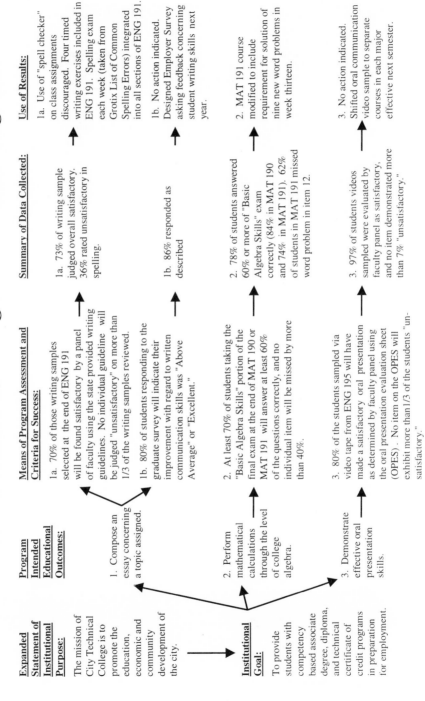

**Expanded Statement of Institutional Purpose:**

The mission of City Technical College is to promote the education, economic and community development of the city.

**Institutional Goal:**

To provide students with competency based associate degree, diploma, and technical certificate of credit programs in preparation for employment.

**Program Intended Educational Outcomes:**

1. Compose an essay concerning a topic assigned.

2. Perform mathematical calculations through the level of college algebra.

3. Demonstrate effective oral presentation skills.

**Means of Program Assessment and Criteria for Success:**

1a. 70% of those writing samples selected at the end of ENG 191 will be found satisfactory by a panel of faculty using the state provided writing guidelines. No individual guideline will be judged "unsatisfactory" on more than 1/3 of the writing samples reviewed.

1b. 80% of students responding to the graduate survey will indicate their improvement with regard to written communication skills was "Above Average" or "Excellent."

2. At least 70% of students taking the "Basic Algebra Skills" portion of the final exam at the end of MAT 190 or MAT 191 will answer at least 60% of the questions correctly, and no individual item will be missed by more than 40%.

3. 80% of the students sampled via video tape from ENG 195 will have made a satisfactory oral presentation as determined by faculty panel using the oral presentation evaluation sheet (OPES). No item on the OPES will exhibit more than 1/3 of the students "unsatisfactory."

**Summary of Data Collected:**

1a. 73% of writing sample judged overall satisfactory. 36% rated unsatisfactory in spelling.

1b. 86% responded as described

2. 78% of students answered 60% or more of "Basic Algebra Skills" exam correctly (84% in MAT 190 and 74% in MAT 191). 62% of students in MAT 191 missed word problem in item 12.

3. 97% of students videos sampled were evaluated by faculty panel as satisfactory, and no item demonstrated more than 7% "unsatisfactory."

**Use of Results:**

1a. Use of "spell checker" on class assignments discouraged. Four timed writing exercises included in ENG 191. Spelling exam each week (taken from Grotix List of Common Spelling Errors) integrated into all sections of ENG 191.

1b. No action indicated. Designed Employer Survey asking feedback concerning student writing skills next year.

2. MAT 191 course modified to include requirement for solution of nine new word problems in week thirteen.

3. No action indicated. Shifted oral communication video sample to separate courses in each major effective next semester.

# Figure 76

## *Community College - College Parallel General Education Program*

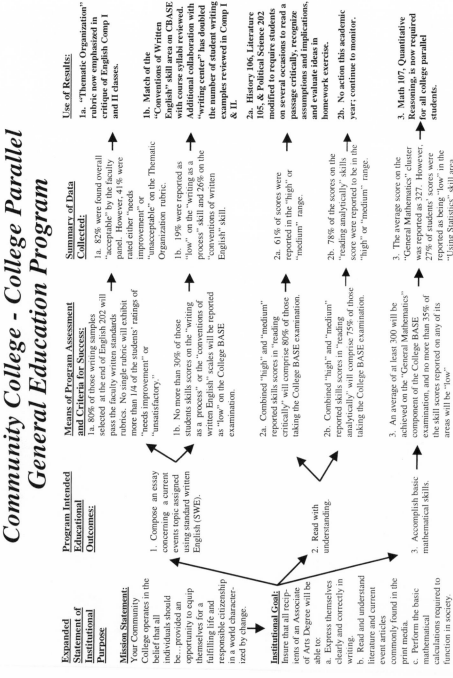

**Expanded Statement of Institutional Purpose**

**Mission Statement:** Your Community College operates in the belief that all individuals should be...provided an opportunity to equip themselves for a fulfilling life and responsible citizenship in a world characterized by change.

**Institutional Goal:** Insure that all recipients of an Associate of Arts Degree will be able to:
a. Express themselves clearly and correctly in writing.
b. Read and understand literature and current event articles commonly found in the print media.
c. Perform the basic mathematical calculations required to function in society.

**Program Intended Educational Outcomes:**

1. Compose an essay concerning a current events topic assigned using standard written English (SWE).

2. Read with understanding.

3. Accomplish basic mathematical skills.

**Means of Program Assessment and Criteria for Success:**

1a. 80% of those writing samples selected at the end of English 202 will pass the faculty written standards rubrics. No single rubric will exhibit more than 1/4 of the students' ratings of "needs improvement" or "unsatisfactory."

1b. No more than 30% of those students skills scores on the "writing as a process" or the "conventions of written English" scales will be reported as "low" on the College BASE examination.

2a. Combined "high" and "medium" reported skills scores in "reading critically" will comprise 80% of those taking the College BASE examination.

2b. Combined "high" and "medium" reported skills scores in "reading analytically" will comprise 75% of those taking the College BASE examination.

3. An average of at least 300 will be achieved on the "General Mathematics" component of the College BASE examination, and no more than 35% of the skill scores reported on any of its areas will be "low"

**Summary of Data Collected:**

1a. 82% were found overall "acceptable" by the faculty panel. However, 41% were rated either "needs improvement" or "unacceptable" on the Thematic Organization rubric.

1b. 19% were reported as "low" on the "writing as a process" skill and 26% on the "conventions of written English" skill.

2a. 61% of scores were reported in the "high" or "medium" range.

2b. 78% of the scores on the "reading analytically" skills score were reported to be in the "high" or "medium" range.

3. The average score on the "General Mathematics" cluster was reported as 327. However, 27% of students' scores were reported as being "low" in the "Using Statistics" skill area.

**Use of Results:**

1a. "Thematic Organization" rubric now emphasized in critique of English Comp I and II classes.

1b. Match of the "Conventions of Written English" skill area on CBASE with course syllabi reviewed. Additional collaboration with "writing center" has doubled the number of student writing examples reviewed in Comp I & II.

2a. History 106, Literature 105, & Political Science 202 modified to require students on several occasions to read a passage critically, recognize assumptions and implications, and evaluate ideas in homework exercise.

2b. No action this academic year; continue to monitor.

3. Math 107, Quantitative Reasoning, is now required for all college parallel students.

# Figure 77

# *Private University - General Education Program*

| Expanded Statement of Institutional Purpose | Program Intended Educational Outcomes: | Means of Program Assessment and Criteria for Success: | Summary of Data Collected: | Use of Results: |
|---|---|---|---|---|
| **Mission Statement:** Students can realize the full potential of their abilities and come to understand their responsibilities for service in the human community. | 1. Demonstrate their mastery of basic computer skills. | 1a. The performance of 85% of students taking the locally developed standardized performance test for the first time at the end of CS 208 (a required course) will be judged as acceptable, and on no individual one of the thirty rubrics will the institutional average score be less than 3.5 on a 5.0 scale. | 1a. 93% of student performances were found "acceptable" by the review panel, and no individual item scored an average of less than 3.5. | 1a. No action required at this time, will continue to monitor. |
| | | 1b. All majors will be required to complete a senior project during their required capstone course. The projects will be sampled, and 70% will be judged by computer science faculty to exhibit "a substantial portion" of the skills earlier identified in the institution's thirty item "computer skills rubrics." | 1b. The Computer Science faculty found 79% of the projects to demonstrate a "substantial portion" of the skills intended. Word processing skills were found to be best retained, and file management skills most likely to be marginal in their demonstration. | 1b. CS 208 modified to add file management exercise in student's anticipated major. |
| **Institutional Goal:** Graduates will be able to: a. Express themselves clearly, correctly and succinctly in writing. b. Make an effective verbal presentation of their ideas concerning a topic. c. Read and offer an analysis of periodical literature concerning a topic of interest. d. Complete accurately basic mathematical calculations. e. Demonstrate a sufficient level of computer literacy. f. Act in accordance with commonly accepted Judeo-Christian values. | 2. Be able to make effective verbal presentations. | 2a. An average score of 85 will result when student presentations at the close of Speech 175 (a required course) are sampled by video tape and evaluated by a panel of faculty using the Oral Communication Evaluation Sheet, and on no component will the average score be less than 7.0 on the 1-10 rubric utilized. | 2a. An average score of 88 was reported for last year's students with the "supporting material" component score of 6.2 on a ten point scale. | 2a. Importance of "supporting material" now pointed out in examples of exemplary presentations shown in Introductory Speech 175 class meetings. Critiques of student presentations during class revised to emphasize importance of supporting materials. |
| | | 2b. 90% of those responding to the Graduating Student survey will indicate "agreement" or "strong agreement" with the statement "I am confident in my ability to speak in front of an audience." | 2b. 61% reported "agreement" or "strong agreement." | 2b. Graduating student survey item modified to read "I am able to make effective verbal presentations." |
| | 3. Act in such a way as to demonstrate their commitment to commonly accepted Judeo-Christian values. | 3a. When faced with a moral dilemma as part of the case study required in each major's capstone course, 80% of the graduating class will choose the solution identified by the faculty as that demonstrating a commitment to Judeo-Christian beliefs. | 3a. 78% of students chose the appropriate solution to the moral dilemma posed. However, those majoring in Business and Pre-Med scored significantly less. | 3a. Business and Pre-Med have revised curricula to integrate material linking their field with the institutional commitment to Judeo-Christian beliefs through case studies. |
| | | 3b. The average monthly attendance at church reported on the recent alumni survey will exceed 2.5 times per month each academic year. | 3b. Average church attendance reported on the last three surveys has fallen to 1.73 days per month. | 3b. Student Life has integrated more denominationally related activities into dormitory programming and social functions. |

# Figure 78

# *State University - General Education Program*

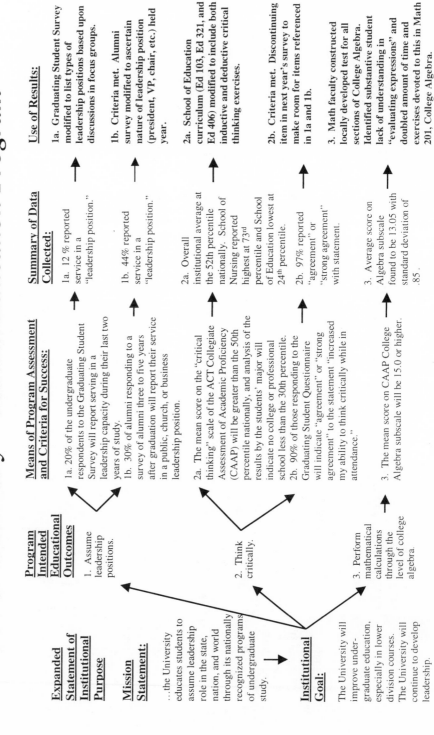

**Expanded Statement of Institutional Purpose**

...the University educates students to assume leadership role in the state, nation, and world through its nationally recognized programs of undergraduate study.

**Mission Statement:**

**Institutional Goal:**

The University will improve under-graduate education, especially in lower division courses. The University will continue to develop leadership.

**Program Intended Educational Outcomes**

1. Assume leadership positions.

2. Think critically.

3. Perform mathematical calculations through the level of college algebra.

**Means of Program Assessment and Criteria for Success:**

1a. 20% of the undergraduate respondents to the Graduating Student Survey will report serving in a leadership capacity during their last two years of study.

1b. 30% of alumni responding to a survey of alumni three to five years after graduation will report their service in a public, church, or business leadership position.

2a. The mean score on the "critical thinking" scale of the ACT Collegiate Assessment of Academic Proficiency (CAAP) will be greater than the 50th percentile nationally, and analysis of the results by the students' major will indicate no college or professional school less than the 30th percentile.

2b. 90% of those responding to the Graduating Student Questionnaire will indicate "agreement" or "strong agreement" to the statement "increased my ability to think critically while in attendance."

3. The mean score on CAAP College Algebra subscale will be 15.0 or higher.

**Summary of Data Collected:**

1a. 12 % reported service in a "leadership position."

1b. 44% reported service in a "leadership position."

2a. Overall institutional average at the 52th percentile nationally. School of Nursing reported highest at 73rd percentile and School of Education lowest at 24th percentile.

2b. 97% reported "agreement" or "strong agreement" with statement.

3. Average score on Algebra subscale found to be 13.05 with standard deviation of .85 .

**Use of Results:**

1a. Graduating Student Survey modified to list types of leadership positions based upon discussions in focus groups.

1b. Criteria met. Alumni survey modified to ascertain nature of leadership position (president, VP, chair, etc.) held year.

2a. School of Education curriculum (Ed 103, Ed 321, and Ed 406) modified to include both inductive and deductive critical thinking exercises.

2b. Criteria met. Discontinuing item in next year's survey to make room for items referenced in 1a and 1b.

3. Math faculty constructed locally developed test for all sections of College Algebra. Identified substantive student lack of understanding in "evaluating expressions" and doubled amount of time and exercises devoted to this in Math 201, College Algebra.

# CHAPTER ELEVEN

# ASSESSMENT ISSUES IN TWO-YEAR COLLEGES

Fred Trapp, Author
Cheryl Cleaves, Contributing Author

*Often a single road map may be utilized for journeys to nearby though not identical destinations. The "road map" presented to this point has related to the journey taken by institutions toward comprehensive implementation of institutional effectiveness assessment procedures. In the previous sections the four-year institution is used as the example; however, the activities outlined hold true for any type of institution of higher learning. This chapter's intent is to guide the reader through the same journey at two-year colleges. The route is similar, but to complete the journey successfully there needs to be an awareness of the different characteristics, challenges, and specific issues that are part of a two-year college. The following chapter presents specific examples and the unique elements of implementation at two-year colleges as it follows the same basics and procedures outlined earlier in this publication.*

## Introduction

Over the last two decades, as national interest in institutional effectiveness has matured, a distinction has emerged between institutional performance as expressed in terms of efficient and effective processes, including educational program performance couched in terms of student achievement vs. student learning outcomes. The former (efficiency) represents the efforts of the organization to evaluate its processes and goal accomplishments in general, including the performance of students in a program as measured by standard outcomes that are commonly a part of an accountability system, e.g., numbers of degrees awarded; success rates in courses; flow of students through a program such as an attrition rate; persistence or re-enrollment from term to term; retention as expressed in the numbers of students who complete classes they start within a single term, or counts of transfers to a second institution for advanced study in the field of concentration. It is sometimes also tempting to include counts of students placed into employment circumstances within the field for which they studied or to count the numbers of courses covered by formal articulation agreements that assure the acceptance of the course credits at senior institutions. The consideration of what students actually learned and can do with that learning (effectiveness) compels a focus upon the unique raison d'etre of a higher learning institution. Learning outcomes assessment goes to the core of the "product" or the learning experience offered by the college.

Program support considerations influence program performance in terms of student achievement and learning outcomes but should not be confused with the assessment of learning outcomes per se. Support considerations include faculty and staff efforts to locate internships and/or entry level employment placements for students, institutional efforts to consummate course to course or program level articulation agreements, student satisfaction with the services of the institution, or perception of campus climate or institutional environment. Although important considerations, none of these aforementioned considerations are direct measures of student learning.

The practice of assessment of student learning in the community colleges is influenced by four considerations that make the community colleges a distinct segment of higher education: (1) governance and stakeholders, (2) students, (3) programs, and (4) process and people.

### Stakeholders and Governance—Implications for Assessment of Student Learning

As is the case with almost all institutions of higher education, community colleges have an array of stakeholders, but unlike other postsecondary institutions, the community colleges tend to serve students in a more immediate geographic locale. They are usually not institutions with a regional or national audience. Public two-year colleges have a state governing board which sets broad policies and often also have a local board of trustees either appointed or elected by the citizens in the service area. The community college local board is another stakeholder somewhat akin to the governing board of a private college or university, as it represents the more local interests as opposed to the state interests articulated by the state governing board.

A somewhat unique stakeholder for many two-year schools is the local governing board. Most two-year institutions have an appointed or a locally elected board of trustees composed of community leaders interested in public service. The Association of Community College Trustees (ACCT) has encouraged board members to monitor the performance of the institution in order to hold the college leaders accountable for serving current and future community learning needs. The board is first asked to adopt a vision for the institution, then set goals in the form of policy statements, and finally to monitor the progress made toward the accomplishment of those goals. The American Association of Community Colleges (AACC) is the primary national organization for two-year institutions. Its publication *Core Indicators of Effectiveness for Community Colleges* details six core indicators intended to evaluate effectiveness in terms of mission achievement and student performance and progress. The authors astutely observe that "successful institutions will seek to document performance using a blend of traditional and nontraditional indicators reflecting the expectations of multiple stakeholders" (Alfred et. al., 1999). Materials from the ACCT and AACC on the topic of institutional effectiveness tend to foster an interest in process, procedure, and accountability systems that emphasize student achievement, but they do not close the door on evidence of actual learning accomplishments (Smith, 2000). A few local boards, like the Community College of Denver, Colorado, and Sinclair Community College in Dayton, Ohio, have elected to offer a learning guarantee to students who complete programs at the institutions, offering limited re-education for free if graduates can not perform essential competencies on the job. The guarantees have stimulated assessment of learning outcomes (CCD, 2004; Bodary, 2004, personal consultation).

Some state policy boards have been proactive in stimulating assessment of student learning. The State Board for Community and Technical Colleges (SBCTC) in Washington has had a plan in place, with funding, since 1989 to stimulate student learning outcomes assessment among the faculty at the 32 schools in that system. The recent emphasis of the program is to stimulate faculty and administrators at each campus to engage in discussions about student learning and to make judgments about assessment findings. Examples of good practice in assessment and key priority areas, developed by the colleges, are disseminated. The Illinois Board of Higher Education (IBHE) articulated an expectation in its 1999 plan, *The Illinois Commitment,* that "all academic programs will systematically assess student learning outcomes and use assessment results to improve programs" and asked public institutions to have assessment plans in place by 2004. Subsequent IBHE Reports indicate that the 41 community colleges in that system are making some progress in work to assess student learning outcomes; albeit the experiences are uneven. Illinois was one of five states to participate in a national pilot effort to assess graduates of two-year institutions in terms of writing, reading, quantitative skills, and locating information (Callan, 2004). The Board of Trustees for the State University of New York (SUNY), which oversees six technical colleges and 30 community colleges, formed a General Education Assessment Review (GEAR) group in 2001 to oversee the implementation of campus-based plans for assessment of student learning. The group also sponsored a best practices conference in the fall of 2003. The State Council for Higher Education in Virginia (SCHEV) was tasked in 2000 by the Governor and General Assembly to design a public reporting system that would provide information about academic quality and the efficient operation of public education in the state. The annual Reports on Institutional Effectiveness now include core competencies in general education of graduates for public institutions in the state. The reports contain specific measures of written communication and technology/information literacy, scientific reasoning, and quantitative reasoning, the measurement of which was negotiated with the Virginia Community College System through open task force groups seeking to include the 23 community colleges. These system-wide outcome measures are supplemented by locally developed assessment work. The efforts in these states are a complement to the traditional performance accountability models that focus upon resources, processes, and those outputs that can be readily counted and seen as a return on investment of public money. They are also a tentative response to the public policy discussions regarding the results of higher education which awarded low marks to the public higher education systems that are unable to monitor what students actually know and can do with that knowledge (Callan, 2002). Progress in developing approaches to the assessment of student learning in Illinois, Kentucky, Nevada, Oklahoma, and South Carolina was recognized by the National Center in its 2004 report (Callan, 2004).

Community colleges have a transfer function, unlike that of four-year schools. Therefore, they enter into stakeholder relationships with the local four-year colleges and universities that commonly receive students from the community college. The transfer program of the two-year school is likely evaluated in terms of the numbers of students who transfer, how well prepared they are to engage in the four-year school, how they perform in the upper division work, and how well they persist to complete a degree. (See Figure 81 later in this chapter.) In this relationship there is an opportunity for cooperative work through the use of administrative data from the four-year institution as an external validation of the learning experience at the two-year college.

One common relationship between the four-year and two-year institutions is illustrated in the articulation agreements that cover the transfer of credits from one school to the next. Some twenty-two states have created statewide core curricula to facilitate transfer, and most of these states specify the number of credit hours required by subject area. Another thirteen states have agreements that apply within a particular segment of higher education, such as from the community colleges to the four-year public universities, but not across the entire state, such as between different public university systems. Only fifteen states have no segmental or statewide agreements in place, but local articulation agreements often exist (Shoenberg, 2001). In all of these cases, the emphasis tends to be upon the proposed body of instruction, as represented in the official course outline of record, or the presumed learning.

One kind of reporting that four-year institutions can provide to facilitate assessment work is an aggregate summary of data which reveals the extent of transfer student success at the four-year institutions. The University of Mississippi has annually reported to the community colleges a summarized comparative GPA report that allows the community college faculty to make inferences about the extent to which their graduates are prepared to compete in upper division curriculum. As illustrated in Figure 79, the report states the GPA of seniors at the University with a distinction drawn between the community college transfer vs. native student.

A variation of this reporting is found in the California State University reporting (Figure 80) that indicates the GPA earned by transfer students after one year in the university system and provides comparisons between students who transfer from any selected community college to all community college transfers. The community college faculty of one institution can use this report to evaluate the experience of the students they prepare to the experience of students coming to the same university system from other community colleges. The comparison is not available on a campus-specific basis for the university; rather it is for the system as a whole, which includes all 23 CSU locations.

**Figure 79**

*Ole Miss Seniors Cumulative GPA at End of Five Recent Fall Semesters*

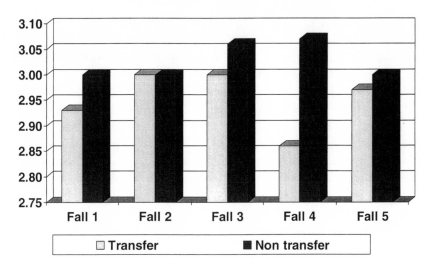

**Figure 80**

*GPA for Community College Transfers After One Year at California State University*

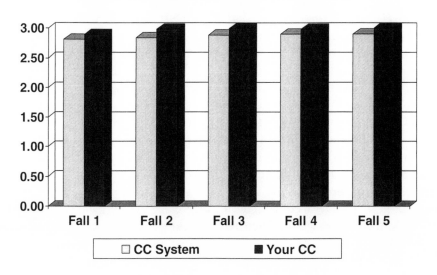

While it is a single factor analysis, the report of overall GPA at the four-year school provides some general indirect assessment of learning which may be sufficient for those institutions where there are few transfers to the four-year schools and therefore insufficient numbers of students who have genuinely majored in a field of study at the community college. Figure 81 (General Transfer Program) illustrates how the Five-Column Model might be used to organize learning outcomes assessment for an institution that sends a limited number of students to a four-year institution. Please note the multiple kinds of administrative data used as means of assessment.

Administrative data of this sort can be of assistance in a community college assessment program when the transfer program is seen as a general program due to the limited number of students who complete pre-major programs established at the two-year school or the limited number of students who transfer. Therefore, an assessment program in the two-year college might wish to seek assistance from the receiving institutions to provide an open-ended questionnaire to the transfer students in which questions like the following are posed: (1) "Do you feel as prepared for the upper division work you are doing as other students in your classes?" (2) "What did the community college do well to help you be ready for upper division curriculum?" and (3) "What does the community college need to do to improve its efforts to prepare transfer students well for their subsequent upper division experiences?" This indirect opinion evidence may be a supplement to direct evidence but should not supplant direct evidence of actual learning.

While this type of data may provide an affirmation of the general preparation offered to the transfer student, it must be balanced by some consideration of the extent to which the student actually completed the courses at the two-year institution. In many states it is possible to transfer as a lower division student without completing two years of study at the community college. Nationally, community college students with bachelor's degree intentions are not likely to earn an associate degree before transferring. Among transfers, roughly one-fifth of bachelor's degree seekers had completed the associate degree before transferring (U.S. Department of Education, NCES, 2003b). The increasing complexity of student attendance patterns is a major confound to work on academic quality assurance (Adelman, 1999). Many transfer students may have completed the units for the degree but not applied or received the award. Some 40% of the students throughout the nation who receive the baccalaureate degree attend more than one college. No comparable figure is available for community colleges, but a study in Los Angeles revealed that within the large Los Angeles Community College District, up to 25% of the students who completed 60 semester credits attended two or more colleges in that district (Dillon, 2000). Among the students who completed the required general education pattern for transfer, just over 30% attended two or more of the nine colleges in that district (Dillon, 2000). It may be the case to a greater degree in urban areas than in rural areas, but the behavior of students enrolling in several colleges during their career, enrollment swirl, confounds the ability of the faculty to ascertain the strengths and weaknesses of their programs based upon performance data provided by the receiving four-year colleges. It behooves the community college faculty to ascertain the extent to which the transferred student actually completed classes at a specific two-year institution.

**Figure 81**

# *Two-Year College General Transfer Program*

| Expanded Statement of Institutional Purpose | Program Intended Educational Outcomes: | Means of Program Assessment and Criteria for Success: | Summary of Data Collected: | Use of Results: |
|---|---|---|---|---|
| **Mission Statement:**<br><br>YCC is an open-admission, community-based, comprehensive college designed to provide inexpensive, quality educational opportunities (college transfer, career/technical, and continuing education) ... | 1. After one year of adjustment to the four-year college, the grades of students transferring will be similar to those of students who initially enrolled at four-year colleges | 1. Analysis of data concerning the grades of students transferring to four-year colleges will indicate that the differences between the average of transfer students' GPAs and that of original students are statistically insignificant one year after enrollment at the four-year college. | 1. Overall GPA of transfers found to be slightly (not significant) less than original students but significantly less in math classes. | **1. Math 107 (College Algebra) strengthened to better relate with calculus at four-year institutions.** |
| | 2. Graduates transferring to a four-year college as full-time students will complete their baccalaureate degrees at almost the same rate as those students originally enrolling at the four-year college. | 2. Analysis of data received from each of YCC three primary transfer student destinations will indicate that the difference in the average number of semesters to baccalaureate degree completion of full-time transfer students from YCC and students originally enrolling in four-year college is statistically insignificant. | 2. Degree completing time of YCC transfer students found to be virtually identical to original students. | **2. No change. Expanded number of reporting institutions for next year.** |
| **Institutional Goal:**<br><br>Serve traditional students seeking the first two years of instruction leading to a bachelor's degree.<br>a. Recipients of ...degree will be readily accepted ...<br>b. Graduates will complete their bachelor's degrees at same rate as original students.<br>c. Graduates will be as well prepared for their junior and senior years as original students. | 3. The general education learning/ skills developed in the college parallel program at YCC will be roughly comparable to that of original students. | 3. Where available from four year colleges, the average scores of YCC transfer students (when adjusted for entrance/placement examination differences) on standardized and locally developed means of assessment in general education will be roughly comparable to original four-year college students. | 3. Only Major State University reported comparative general education data. YCC graduates compared favorably (less than one SD difference from MSU original students) except in the area of science reasoning where scores were almost 1.5 SD below mean of original students. | **3. Comparison of natural science syllabus at YCC vs MSU indicated that "scientific reasoning methodology" rather than specific knowledge regarding science subjects was emphasized at MSU. After serious consideration, YCC science faculty have decided not to change courses at YCC due to content emphasis of other institutions to which YCC students transfer.** |

The community colleges need to be responsive to the local current and future employers of their career and technical graduates in particular and the larger network of business and industry interests in their service area. In many respects the two-year institutions also directly serve the citizens in the community; some of whom enroll in career and technical classes for their own personal reasons. These are stakeholders who want some general reassurance as to the learning that has been accomplished through the educational programs. In this regard the two- and four-year institutions serve similar masters who have an interest in quality assurance efforts.

### Processes and People—Implications for Assessment

A national study reports two-year schools developing a variety of strategies to support assessment efforts by building upon internal processes at the institution (Peterson, 1999). These efforts include placing student assessment in the academic mission statement, sponsoring institution-wide activities to promote involvement in and support for assessment, adopting a plan or policy for student assessment, establishing processes and structures for planning and coordinating assessment, and evaluating the assessment process itself. Associate Degree institutions are somewhat distinct from four-year schools in at least two common processes that can facilitate assessment of student learning outcomes work. To a greater degree than is the case in the four-year institutions, two-year schools engage in faculty professional development activities that are less likely to affect classroom time and are less costly than four-year practices of paid leaves or class load reductions (Peterson, 1999). Two-year schools also tend to document their curriculum and engage in broader peer reviews of that documentation to a greater degree than four-year institutions. This review is perhaps the case due to long-standing roots in the public school systems from which the community colleges evolved, but it is a practice that is certainly necessitated to support the articulation of curriculum with four-year receiving institutions.

Faculty professional development experiences and days dedicated for that purpose are often utilized to accomplish assessment work as faculty at two-year schools commonly carry heavy teaching loads, leaving little time for assessment work in addition to teaching. Sinclair Community College has utilized all-college days to discuss general education outcomes, develop means of assessment and standards of performance, and then to complete assessment activities (Zakel, 1997). The faculty members at Modesto Junior College have utilized summer retreats, supported by local college Foundation grants, to develop expertise in articulating and assessing student learning outcomes (Scroggins, 2004). The campus culture at Shoreline Community College has been reported as prizing the gathering and using of assessment data. The Shoreline culture is sustained, in part, due to the faculty development strategies employed to develop faculty leadership and foster effective peer interaction to collaborate in discussions of teaching and learning improvement (Henderson, 2002).

The faculty members at Parkland Community College have engaged in classroom assessment efforts sustained by mini-courses in the techniques of assessment sponsored by the campus Center for Excellence in Teaching and Learning (Rouseff-Baker, 2004). The nurturing of interest in assessment at Parkland has fostered campus discussions about the instructional process as stimulus to learning outcomes. Campus leaders at Joliet Junior College provide a testimonial to the role of professional development, a three-day seminar, in building campus support for assessment "one brick at a time" (D'Allegro, 2003). A small college in Ohio, Raymond Walters College, dedicated a full year to professional development for the purpose of mastering the process of primary trait analysis that the faculty used to devise assignments and build assessment rubrics (Baughin, 2002). Another small college in North Carolina has reported that faculty leadership emerged as a by-product of the series of workshops and systematic professional development discussions they have organized to foster work on the articulation of learning outcomes and the assessment of student work (Womack, 2003).

A second distinctive process at community colleges is the habit of documenting curriculum and subjecting it to peer review. The official course outline of record or the master syllabus becomes the venue for faculty to articulate their intended learning outcomes for the course and to indicate the assignments and activities to promote that learning as well as to frame the means of assessment for student work. While this habit lays the groundwork for actual assessment activities, it does not get that work accomplished. However, within a single course and across the courses required to complete a program, the documentation allows the faculty to discover where instructional experiences align to intended outcomes, and it facilitates discussions about the best ways and means to promote effective learning.

One of the helpful tasks in preparing to do assessment work is to appreciate the linkages between the articulated outcomes at the college (general education), program, and course level. Whether for general education or program assessment purposes, faculty have found it useful to trace where key bodies of knowledge or competencies are addressed. Often it is illuminating to see where material is introduced as opposed to being reinforced. The Community College of Denver has adopted a system of course curriculum guides, master course template or syllabus, and review and approval procedures to ensure that core learning outcome skills and assessment strategies are built into the curriculum as it is being approved (CCD, 2003). The faculties at Long Beach City College in California and at Grand Rapids Community College in Michigan have approached doing this audit by working through their curriculum committees and the curriculum review process (Anderson, 2004; Chesla, 2003). The faculty members at Anne Arundel Community College in Maryland have invented a charting system that illustrates the flow of intended college outcomes to those advanced by a program and then down to the course goals and assignment activities (Iyengar, 2002).

Assessment leaders at Tacoma Community College created a series of grids to portray the commonly agreed upon general education learning outcomes and then asked colleagues to fill in the grids to illustrate ways in which teaching/learning methods, embedded assessment methods, and evaluation criteria were implemented in the course and portrayed in the course syllabus. The concrete process helps faculty put a learning outcomes approach into practice (Sonandre, 2002). Faculty at Bellevue Community College in Washington elected to develop a comprehensive matrix in which they asked faculty to evaluate each course in terms of the contribution it made to the core general education outcomes (Jeffers, 2004). The Bellevue group used a rating scale in which outcome behaviors were described and scored using a range of marks from 0 to 3 describing the extent to which the outcome behaviors were taught and assessed in the course. These comprehensive approaches help the faculty groups identify areas of strength and weakness with respect to coverage and effort to promote the common learning outcomes desired.

### Students—Implications for Assessment of Student Learning

The typical student at a two-year institution is 29 years old, attends the college part-time by being enrolled in fewer than 12 credit hours a semester, and holds down a full-time job. Around 63% of the 11.3 million students who attend community colleges annually are enrolled part-time, while 37% attend full-time. Of those who do attend full-time, 30% of them also hold a full-time job. Most community college students (58%) are women. Many of these students have substantial family responsibilities that include challenges in finding child care while the student is attending class or engaging in preparation for classroom activities. Some 55% of Latino and Native American undergraduates and 46% of all Black undergraduates attend a community college (AACC, 2000). These characteristics are different from the profile of students attending the public and private four-year institutions.

Community colleges are typically open-door admission institutions intended to provide post-secondary educational opportunity to all who wish to attend. Commonly, the students enroll and depart as they see fit. As one long-time observer of higher education observed, we use community colleges for utilitarian purposes, and our relationships with them are more occasional than otherwise. We recognize the value of education, but once schooling ceases to be compulsory, we tend to go to school only on our own terms (Adleman, 1994).

Students commonly drop, stop, or job out of community colleges and then may return. National data suggest that over a three-year period only 15% of the students complete an associate degree, and in four years only 35% complete the degree. A recent national study of community college cohorts documented that twice as many community college students transfer as receive associate degrees (Berkner, Horn, and Clune, 2000). Of course, many community college students do not come to the institution intending to complete the associate degree, and many others who hold that goal alter their intentions along the way. Some enter with short-term educational aspirations, while others elect to transfer without the formal degree being awarded. Recent research has explored different kinds of enrollment swirl or multi-institutional attendance patterns, including reverse transfers from the four to two-year institutions (McCormick, 2003).

In doing assessment work, the faculty needs to balance the learning stimulated by the planned interventions or systematic instruction in a program with the learning stimulated through the natural maturation processes. The faculty must also devise ways to determine which students are "done" with the educational experience and when they are completed. Regional accrediting bodies generally do not require institutions to demonstrate a value added to the student who attends. Accrediting groups are usually asking that the faculty respond to the question of the extent to which the college is accomplishing its purposes. Therefore, assessment of students at the time they are completing the prescribed program of study is the logical place to concentrate assessment work. However, for those interested in the value added question, some form of pre- and post-test design needs to be devised. Frequently, that will require the faculty to distinguish freshman from sophomore students in terms of units accomplished and perhaps also locate classes in which most students are in their first term or year vs. the curriculum into which more advanced students enroll in large numbers. To some extent, where prerequisites are enforced, that system can be used to make those distinctions. Where they are named but not systematically enforced, inquiries of the student information system can be used to determine the courses in which most students enrolled have achieved sophomore level standing. Those students or classes can be targeted for assessment efforts.

Students come to the community college with a wide range of goals, and those goals change over time as they engage in the college experience. It is important for faculty to note that while they as faculty have defined a program of study consisting of named courses and a suggested or required sequence of enrollments, the students have their own intentions, which may not coincide with the faculty perspective. Faculty may want to consider their mental model of each program and categorize it for purposes of considering the opportune point to acquire assessment data. One common model might be called a "progressive" program model in which faculty expect students to complete courses in a sequence, obtain the degree, and find a job. A contrasting model might be characterized as the "interrupted" program model in which students do not complete but instead leave early as they see themselves as early leavers with marketable skills (ELMS). Exploring course taking behavior and determining the points at which students appear to depart from the program (when there is significant attrition) will help the faculty think about the extent to which program learning outcomes are accomplished and where natural points for assessment work may reside.

Because most community college students are commuters and often involved with employment or family responsibilities, they are not commonly at the institution for large periods of time as is the case for residential institutions or those institutions where most students are enrolled full-time. Determining when and where to "catch" the students for assessment activities is also influenced by the extent of their engagement with the institution as well as the assessment strategy being employed. A few institutions are using formal assessment days when a locally developed or standardized exam is administered. A few colleges have endeavored to pull students out of class or ask them to participate in assessment at non-peak class times. In those strategies considerable campus publicity is required to achieve student participation, and some institutions have elected to make the event required as part of the graduation criteria. The Blue Ridge Community College in Virginia mandates participation in an assessment day of all students who apply for a degree, requiring them to attend a morning, afternoon, or evening session for general education assessment consistent with the state-mandated core competencies (Anderson, 2004). The Wor-Wic Community College in Maryland requires graduates to select from a variety of days and times to complete a locally developed assessment as part of the graduation requirements (Capelli, 2004 personal consultation). Other institutions using dedicated assessment days have found it more effective to use the classroom as the venue for assessment and to randomly select classes for participation in the campus general education assessment activity (Watson, 2000; Bers, 2003; and Mee, 2004). With either approach students are very much aware of the assessment effort and are sometimes included in the planning, as the institutions see the process as an opportunity for students and faculty alike to "test" the teaching-learning process.

Other faculty have elected to solve the problem of where and when to "catch" students for assessment by using the classroom and instructional period as the venue for assessment activity by using normal assignments embedded in the courses as the artifact for assessment work, thus taking a "stealth" approach. In this approach, the students are usually unaware of the campus assessment effort. A common example of sampling student work is found at Johnson County Community College in Kansas where a sample of student work is selected before the instructor grades the work and is preserved for subsequent assessment by a faculty committee (Seybert, 1997). In other cases, students may be more acutely aware of the assessment activity as the faculty has elected to stress assessment as a means of learning. They have implemented a classroom assessment program with an emphasis upon formative evaluation providing instant feedback on particular assignments with an evaluation rubric published in advance (Fukes, 2004; Rosseff-Baker, 2004). In these cases, samples of student work are not drawn as all student work on an assignment is graded with the common rubric, and some conclusions about areas of weakness in the group are drawn by the instructor as part of the feedback process. In this second approach, faculty will need to find ways to link the classroom assessment of particular lessons to larger themes and outcomes of the institution and also find ways to sustain the effort over time.

## Programs—Implications for Assessment of Student Learning

What is a program? This is a simple question with a variety of answers which structure the assessment of student learning outcomes for faculty at two-year institutions. Most commonly, an educational program is the pattern of required courses and listed electives that faculty specify as being necessary for students to complete in order to qualify for a degree or certificate. In the case of the degree program, the pattern of required courses includes both a field of concentration in a discipline area and a general education package. The certificate more often specifies very few, if any, general education courses and is primarily focused on curriculum in the discipline field. It is not uncommon for an institution to offer several types of degrees with different configurations in the general education area. In all cases, the program that culminates in an official award from the institution is formally approved by the Governing Board and used as the basis to provide counts of awards provided to state and federal authorities. The most popular degree fields of study in two-year institutions include Liberal Arts, Health Professions, Business, Engineering-related Technologies, and Protective Services. Of these, the Liberal Arts category is by far the most popular (U.S. Department of Education, 2003a). The nature of the program effort within the college begins to answer the question we raise in Column 1 of our Five-Column Model. Namely, what is the role of the program in accomplishing the mission of the institution and helping to further the goals of the school? In answering that question the expanded statement of purpose is put in place.

One kind of "program" that two-year institutions offer consists of curriculum completed in preparation for transfer. As previously noted, many community college students make the leap to the four-year school without completing the associate degree or else complete a formal associate degree program in the community college called by such titles as University or General Studies or Liberal Arts. For two-year schools with few numbers of students who transfer in specific majors, it may be advisable to treat the entire collection of courses taken as a single program and rely upon the transfer institutions for general performance data as a way to assess the preparation for upper division work. An illustration of this single program approach to assessment of learning outcomes is described in the graphic entitled "Two-Year General Transfer Program" (Figure 81).

In other two-year schools with large numbers of transfer students, it may be possible to isolate clusters of specific discipline (major) preparation that is taken in addition to the general education experience. In these two-year institutions, the faculty provide recommendations as to which lower division courses should be completed in preparation for a major in that field at a four-year school in addition to providing the general education experience. These recommended patterns of courses for major preparation are not always formalized as a program in which an associate degree can be award but nevertheless could represent an informally defined program. In these cases, the community college faculty has an opportunity to garner assessment data about the major preparation as well as the general education preparation.

Whether a few or a great many students transfer from the two-year institution and without regard to whether those transferring students are awarded the associate degree, the community college faculty have an obligation to engage in an assessment of the learning outcomes they intend to foster from their general education requirements. As a general rule, students preparing for transfer to a four-year institution are required to take more credit hours of general education than are students pursuing career and technical programs intended for transfer to the world of work in entry-level positions. Community college faculty may chose to describe the learning outcomes that arise from those various required general education course patterns as core skills or general education competencies, but collectively they constitute a program worthy of assessment activity.

A second type of "program" is that which is intended for career and technical education leading to initial employment or career advancement. Some award a degree and certificate, others award only a certificate, and others also facilitate transfer. An Automobile Technology program will be used to illustrate how the five-column model can be applied to assessment work in this sort of program.

A third type of "program" commonly found at two-year institutions is a pattern of courses intended to develop the basic academic skills that students will need to successfully engage collegiate instruction. Commonly referred to as developmental instruction, these programs usually do not culminate in a formal award. Based upon placement examination processes, this curriculum may be required of students or may be merely highly recommended. The developmental offerings may be required of students before being allowed to enter into the degree-applicable courses offered at the institution, or students may be allowed to take them concurrently (Roeuche, 1993). Among two-year institutions, developmental instruction is not uniformly characterized as credit bearing and therefore eligible for financial aid awards. It is sometimes categorized as noncredit or zero unit courses that are not eligible for financial aid. Large numbers of community college students are identified as needing developmental instruction, but some states restrict the number of courses of this nature that can be offered or cap the number of units a student may accumulate in this kind of curriculum. The effectiveness of programs that deliver these courses is essential to the successful learning experiences of these students.

A type of "program" related to developmental instruction that is found at community colleges is the collection of instructional activities and services that are designed to support students in the process of learning how to be college students. These do not instruct in a traditional discipline field. These academic support service activities and courses, such as tutoring, career planning, orientation to college, supplemental instruction, study skills, etc., do not culminate in the award of a degree or certificate. They are organized within the academic or instructional portion of the institution and are within the student services. For purposes of this monograph, these activities are addressed as an academic and educational support service, and their assessment is focused on the efficiency, economy, and effectiveness of the services provided and the student satisfaction with those services.

The final perspective on an educational program found at community colleges is the collection of short-term training experiences that constitute the workforce preparation or economic development activities of the college. Commonly, these programs ask for student achievement, placement, and persistence information as a way to assess the efficacy of the effort. It may behoove community college providers to obtain self-reported information from the graduates upon completion of the training and also pursue employer surveys as a strategy to obtain third party judgments about student performance and, by implication, educational program quality.

## Articulating Learning Outcomes

Each of these kinds of educational programs plays a different role as an expression of the mission of the two-year institution and is therefore described with slightly different language in Column One of the Five-Column Models used in this monograph. The educational outcomes of an instructional program, illustrated in Column Two in our model (Figure 82), resulted from addressing these commonly asked questions:

**Figure 82**

# *Automotive Technology Program-Two Column*

**Expanded Statement of Institutional Purpose**

**Program Intended Educational Outcomes:**

**Mission Statement:**
Your Community College is an open-admission, community-based, comprehensive college.

**Institutional Goal:**
Serve persons of all ages in preparing for job entry and careers in a variety of fields.

1.  Graduates of the Automotive Technology Program will be successfully employed in the field.

2.  Graduates of the Automotive Technology Program will be technically proficient.

3.  Employers of the Automotive Technology Program graduates, in the five-county service area, will be pleased with the education received by their employees.

1. What roles do we see our program graduates taking in society or the next segment of the higher education experience?
2. What skills and knowledge are necessary for those roles (outcomes)?
3. What has to be taught or mastered now, while they are enrolled in a specific course or program?

If asked in that order, the faculty engages in a process to plan its educational program and the assessment thereof "backwards," as compared with the way in which students "consume" or participate in the program. The backwards planning process may assist faculty to develop broader statements of the learning outcomes from the program and to see the interrelationships among the learning experiences.

Several techniques can be used to articulate the program outcomes or to reach consensus about them. The first approach was pioneered at Ohio State University and is known as the Day of Curriculum (DACUM) process. The technique brings together six to a dozen experts in a field to analyze job skills and knowledge. With a facilitator who leads a brainstorming process, the group pinpoints tasks, duties, and responsibilities of new hire employees. The group then sequences the tasks. A second group validates the task list in terms of affirming that they represent entry level work. This strategy is useful when the career and technical program is tightly coupled with an occupation or a set of related occupations. However, the process can be equally useful for transfer oriented programs when the assembled experts are faculty from four-year institutions to which large numbers of community college students transfer. The discussion is focused upon the knowledge, skills, and abilities essential for successful upper division study in the major or a set of related majors. Such a process is being undertaken in California through the Intersegmental Major Preparation Articulated Curriculum (IMPAC) project and in Illinois through the work of the Illinois Articulation Initiative (IAI) major panels, to name but two collaborative efforts of this sort.

The second technique is an application of the Delphi Process to the articulation of program learning outcomes. Rather than assembling the experts in one place, nominations are requested to identify a large number of experts in the career and technical field. The experts are asked to complete a survey intended to elicit their opinions as to the tasks, duties, and responsibilities of entry-level positions in their occupational area. Several rounds of surveys are administered. Each survey is analyzed for agreements and disagreements so that some consensus can be developed through informed judgments about the importance of specific skills essential to the entry-level employee.

Reports of desired entry level competencies by industry or occupational cluster have been accomplished under the auspices of the National Skills Standards Board and have been sometimes mirrored by state employment departments such as Washington, Colorado, and Oklahoma.

### Exploring Means of Assessment

*Immediate Job Entry Programs - Student Learning Outcomes Assessment*—In planning an assessment for any educational program, several questions need to be considered:

When in the program should the assessment be completed? To whom should the assessment be administered? By whom should the assessment be conducted? How should assessment be accomplished? What standards of performance should be expected? The answers to these questions depend in part upon the nature of the program and the nature of student engagement in the program. In an ideal sense, it is best to introduce program level assessment toward the end of the student's experiences and focus the context in which learning is demonstrated upon integrated learning opportunities. In a perfect setting, only those students reaching this plateau of accomplishment should participate in the assessment activities. Student learning assessment in career and technical programs intended for immediate job entry is commonly pursued in terms of three domains: (1) didactic or theory, (2) manipulative or skills, and (3) attitudes and social interactions. The example of the Automotive Technology Program offers illustrations of all three domains. (See Figure 83.) The venues and techniques used as means of assessment in Column Three of our model are quite varied for career and technical programs. They often include an examination for licensing or certification, a capstone course or project in which the student integrates the learning accomplished through the required courses in the program, or perhaps a series of internships or field placements.

One popular way to accomplish assessment is provided outside the program, such as by means of licensing or certification exams. In other cases, faculty may provide a simulated licensing or certification exam experience to be completed in a final course in the program in the form of a capstone project or set of examination experiences. In some fields, major corporations, such as Microsoft, Novell, or Cisco in the computing field, provide certification for the industry, but they can be costly. External examinations are common place among the allied health occupational programs. For example, registered and vocational nursing programs, radiological technology, dietetic technicians, emergency medical technician, and respiratory care programs are accredited by separate reviews apart from the regional accrediting body and commonly require licensing examinations that provide opportunities for students to demonstrate their learning and for faculties to monitor the results for the purpose of discovering potential shortcomings in the management of the program. For some programs, the numbers of students who pass these exams are important criteria for success or continued accreditation of the program.

The National Council of State Boards of Nursing has sponsored computer-based examinations to test for candidates' entry-level competencies for licensure as Registered Nurses or Practical/Vocational Nurses. The National Council Licensing Examination (NCLEX) process is administered by a third party with the results provided to the state licensing board. The candidate who is unsuccessful receives a Candidate Performance Report (CPR) from the state licensing board to identify his or her strengths and weaknesses so that he or she may use that information when he or she prepares to retake the examination. Aggregated exam results for the cohort of students taking the licensing exam can be purchased from NCLEX, and they do provide a comparison of one school to national averages. Some state boards report quarterly on the success and failure results of students by date of graduation. The results reported as an overall pass rate provide only a general

**Figure 83**

# *Automotive Technology Program-Three Columns*

| Expanded Statement of Institutional Purpose | Program Intended Educational Outcomes: | Means of Program Assessment and Criteria for Success: |
|---|---|---|
| **Mission Statement:** … Community College is an open-admission, community-based, comprehensive college. | **1.** Graduates of the Automotive Technology Program will be successfully employed in the field. | **1a.** 50% of the responding graduates of the Automotive Technology Program will report employment in the field on the Graduating Student Survey administered at the time of program completion.<br>**1b.** 80% of the responding graduates of the Automotive Technology Program will report employment in the field on the recent Alumni Survey administered one year after graduation. |
| | **2.** Graduates of the Automotive Technology Program will be technically proficient. | **2a.** At the close of their final term, 90% of the graduates will be able to identify and correct within a given period of time all of the mechanical problems in five test cars that have been "prepared" for the students by Automotive Technology Program faculty. No single automotive malfunction will fail to be identified and corrected by more than 20% of students.<br>**2b.** 80% of Automotive Technology Program graduates will pass the National Automotive Test. On no subscale will participants average missing 30% or more of the items. |
| **Institutional Goal:** Serve persons of all ages in preparing for job entry and careers in a variety of fields. | **3.** Employers of the Automotive Technology Program graduates, in the five-county service area, will be pleased with the education received by their employees. | **3.** 80% of the respondents to an Employer Survey conducted every 3 years by the college will respond that they would be pleased to employ future graduates. |

guide to the effectiveness of the instructional effort but if reported by broad areas of the discipline may be helpful to pinpoint areas of curriculum weakness.

Radiological Technologist programs are another example of external certification in combination with state licensing that yields valuable information for program assessment purposes. The computer-based entry-level examination process is also administered by a third party with results reported to the licensing boards in approximately two-thirds of the states that contract for such services with the American Registry of Radiologic Technologists (ARRT), under whose auspices the entry-level competency exams are developed and administered. The ARRT reports pass/fail results publicly for cohorts of candidates seeking certification and provides each approved school summary reports of the results for their candidates taking the exams.

However, a single exam score or data about success rates of a cohort of program graduates taking the exam, captured in Column Four of our the five-column Automotive Technology model (Figure 84), will not provide adequate information to guide instructional improvement. Data about the performance of students on sub-areas of the occupational field are essential for faculty who intend to make instructional improvements, which might be described in the fifth and final column of our model. Rather than acting upon a single set of results, the faculty leadership may plot the results for each sub-area of the examining process for several cohorts of candidates so that over time a portrait is drawn of the *consistent* experience of program completers participating in the examination process.

There are organizations which provide points of contact for additional information about examining processes that may be used for assessment of learning outcomes. The National Organization for Competency Assurance (NOCA) was established in 1997 as a not-for-profit membership organization for the purpose of setting quality standards for credentialing organizations in the United States. NOCA is a clearinghouse for information on the latest trends and issues of concern to practitioners and organizations focused on certification, licensure, and human resource development. The National Commission for Certifying Agencies (NCCA) is the accreditation body of NOCA that reviews the certification program and processes used to measure competency. The Council on Licensure, Enforcement, and Regulation (CLEAR) is an international clearinghouse for agencies or organizations involved in the licensing or non-voluntary certification or registration of regulated occupations or professions.

One provider of job-ready standardized exams is the National Occupational Competency Testing Institute (NOTCI). (See Resource Section by Paul Cunningham regarding standardized tests.) These tests are designed to measure knowledge of basic occupational processes, including the identification and use of terminology and tools expected in entry-level position. The experienced worker exams provided by NOTCI are intended to measure knowledge of higher-level concepts, theories, and applications in the occupation for those who have three or more years of work experience and education. Reports of scores which are returned to the participating colleges as well as to the individual candi-

# Figure 84

## *Automotive Technology Program-Five Columns*

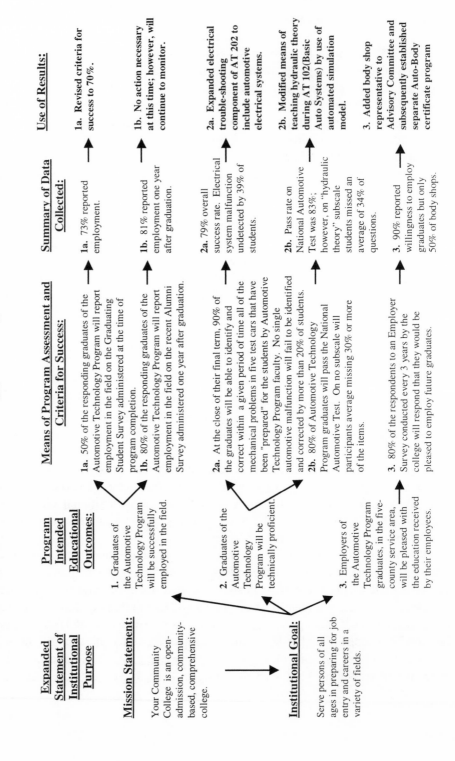

**Expanded Statement of Institutional Purpose**

**Mission Statement:**

Your Community College is an open-admission, community-based, comprehensive college.

**Institutional Goal:**

Serve persons of all ages in preparing for job entry and careers in a variety of fields.

**Program Intended Educational Outcomes:**

1. Graduates of the Automotive Technology Program will be successfully employed in the field.

2. Graduates of the Automotive Technology Program will be technically proficient.

3. Employers of the Automotive Technology Program graduates, in the five-county service area, will be pleased with the education received by their employees.

**Means of Program Assessment and Criteria for Success:**

**1a.** 50% of the responding graduates of the Automotive Technology Program will report employment in the field on the Graduating Student Survey administered at the time of program completion.
**1b.** 80% of the responding graduates of the Automotive Technology Program will report employment in the field on the recent Alumni Survey administered one year after graduation.

**2a.** At the close of their final term, 90% of the graduates will be able to identify and correct within a given period of time all of the mechanical problems in five test cars that have been "prepared" for the students by Automotive Technology Program faculty. No single automotive malfunction will fail to be identified and corrected by more than 20% of students.
**2b.** 80% of Automotive Technology Program graduates will pass the National Automotive Test. On no subscale will participants average missing 30% or more of the items.

**3.** 80% of the respondents to an Employer Survey conducted every 3 years by the college will respond that they would be pleased to employ future graduates.

**Summary of Data Collected:**

**1a.** 73% reported employment.

**1b.** 81% reported employment one year after graduation.

**2a.** 79% overall success rate. Electrical system malfunction undetected by 39% of students.

**2b.** Pass rate on National Automotive Test was 83%; however, on "hydraulic theory" subscale students missed an average of 34% of questions.

**3.** 90% reported willingness to employ graduates but only 50% of body shops.

**Use of Results:**

**1a.** Revised criteria for success to 70%.

**1b.** No action necessary at this time; however, will continue to monitor.

**2a.** Expanded electrical trouble-shooting component of AT 202 to include automotive electrical systems.

**2b.** Modified means of teaching hydraulic theory during AT 102(Basic Auto Systems) by use of automated simulation model.

**3.** Added body shop representative to Advisory Committee and subsequently established separate Auto-Body certificate program

dates allow analysis by sub-area of the testing topics and comparisons across cohorts taking the same exam.

The National Institute for Certification in Engineering Technologies (NICET) is another source for engineering technician programs. The NICET certification process involves a multiple- choice written exam, a work history, recommendations, and a supervisor's verification of the experience. Exam results can be shared if authorized by the examinee or if the college pays for group testing. Where certification and licensing are not available, a career and technical program can use a capstone or end-of-sequence examination as an indicator of student learning. These might be locally developed assignments that prompt students to integrate their learning across several courses, examination procedures, or commercially produced standardized exams. Fashion Design and Computer Graphics program faculty at Mesa College in San Diego have collaborated to use the annual fashion show as a venue for authentic assessment activities in both programs (Lee, 2003). Instructors teaching English as a Second Language and Emergency Medical Technology at Capital Community College in Hartford, CT, have both used capstone projects as venues for assessment where students were asked to integrate their program learning (DeVito and Schuyler, 2003).

Another way in which career and technical programs can conduct assessment of student learning is through partnerships with corporations and agencies where students are able to extend their classroom learning in the real world while still enrolled in the college. One example is the corporate partnership formed with major employers in the Findlay, OH, area and the Owens Community College Industrial and Engineering Technologies Division faculty (Devier, 2002). Some of the partnerships are part of national programs sponsored by Ford, General Motors, or John Deere, while others are tailored to local needs. In each case, the college is utilizing technical field experience of corporate supervisors to assist in the assessment of student learning.

To obtain information about the effectiveness of their vocational educational programs many community college faculty survey former students and employers. (See Resource Section by Daniel Weinstein regarding attitudinal surveys.) These surveys are commonly mailed to graduates several months after they have completed their program with the intent of learning how well the program prepared students for employment or advancement in their occupation. Separate surveys are mailed to employers when the student has provided permission to do so. Examples of these survey instruments are available at a web site hosted by the Peralta Community College District (Oakland, CA) on behalf of the National Council for Research and Planning (NCRP). The NCRP recently changed names to the National Community College Council for Research and Planning (NCCRP), but the web address has not changed http://www.peralta.cc.ca.us/indev/ncrp/ncrp.htm#srvbank.

One example of a locally developed assessment process was designed to improve instruction in clinical decision making among nursing students while they are still moving through the two-year program (Goldman, 1999). The program faculty had paper-and-pencil examination results and clinical evaluations of student work available to them and continue to use those. However, the faculty wanted to strengthen the ways in which students would be able to apply or use the knowledge they had learned. Because the clinical setting for nursing students may not always provide the range of circumstances desired for optimal teaching and assessment of program learning, the faculty at Sinclair Community College developed a Structured Simulated Clinical Examination (SSCE) as a performance assessment to augment both the paper-and-pencil and clinical evaluations. The faculty wrote scripts to describe medical problems as case studies, recruited drama students as patient-actors, developed grading rubrics, and trained raters. The student nurse is expected to seek additional information and act as if she were in the actual clinical setting engaged in a problem solving/decision making process. Attention was given to the validity of the rating scales by involving professional experts from the area hospitals and by using professional standards. Faculty raters were trained as a group to help promote inter-rater reliability, while short practice sessions were conducted with the student actors. The results of the assessment efforts pointed to ways in which the curriculum could be enhanced to promote active decision making and critical thinking in courses throughout the program leading to the clinical or field experience.

### Liberal Arts/Major Preparation/Transfer Programs—Learning Outcomes Assessment

Assessment approaches for the liberal arts or general education experience of the community college student follow the model that has been detailed elsewhere in this work. However, the kinds of general education outcomes that are commonly pursued in a two-year program tend to fall into two broad areas. The freshman and sophomore curriculum usually emphasizes the core skills of general education, such as numeric literacy, communications competence, perhaps talent in using a personal computer and/or information literacy. A second typical area is a series of knowledge and understanding outcomes across the traditional domains of historical perspective, literary styles, culture and society, global perspective, meaning of numeric data, and scientific inquiry. While the experience may broach values development or higher order thinking skills, those outcomes are more aggressively pursued through advanced curriculum.

Far and away the most heavily enrolled curriculum at many two-year institutions is the collection of courses in the general education pattern(s) intended to support transfer to a four-year school or to support the associate degrees awarded for immediate job entry. At the same time, this "program" is challenging to assess. Figure 76 in Chapter Ten illustrates the use of our Five-Column Model for those general education packages that are intended to be a College Parallel General Education Program where transfer to the four-year institution is the role of the general education experience, while Figure 75 in Chapter Ten illustrates a General Education program for Career and Technical fields of study where immediate job entry is the purpose of the program.

Supported by grant funding, the League for Innovation in the Community Colleges launched a national project to stimulate thinking about learning outcomes for the 21st century. This work generally encourages participating institutions to articulate their intended outcomes, then operationalize the general statements, and eventually map those operational statements into the curriculum offerings to explore where the skills and knowledge are initially taught or reinforced. It has been much harder, however, to approach ways to actually assess the accomplishment of the intended learning. What follows is a set of examples describing how several colleges have approached the work of Column Three in our model, specific strategies and tactics to assess student learning in general education.

One approach to general education assessment is to devise assessment experiences that do not depend upon the assignments or learning experiences of any one course. Illustrative of this approach are the efforts at Mesa Community College in the Maricopa Community College District that services Phoenix, Arizona, (Mee, 2002); Oakton Community College at Des Plaines, Illinois, (Bers, 2000); or the work at College of Du Page in Glen Ellyn, Illinois, (Geesamann, Klassen, and Watson, 2000). The faculties at these colleges are treating general education as a program by examining direct evidence of learning produced while the students are enrolled on the campus. For the most part, all three faculties have decided to provide students with an assessment experience outside the normal course-based assignments. In each of these cases, the faculties have articulated several general education learning outcomes after extensive campus discussion and several revisions. They have then explored the cumulative impact of the general education curriculum by comparing the assessment performance with expected standards the faculty developed and by comparing the performance of beginning students to students who are toward the conclusion of their lower division work or by considering student demographic and academic characteristics in combination with the assessment performance.

For most general education outcomes at Mesa Community College and Oakton College, the faculties have created prompts of their own to stimulate student responses that rely upon the skills and knowledge to be nurtured through the general education experience. The faculty at Mesa Community College uses only one standardized examination, while the faculty at College of Du Page has selected a well-known standardized exam that is published in multiple parts and designed for two-year institutions. In their last round of assessment, the Oakton faculty elected to use regular classroom assignments rather than non-course based prompts they had been using because that strategy was a better fit to the intended learning outcome. In the one case in which the Mesa Community College faculty members are using a standardized exam, it is supplemented with other assessment means to evaluate the learning outcome. In their case as well as that of the College of Du Page, the faculty made these selections after considerable discussion as to the fit of the intended general education outcomes with the coverage of the exams. The locally created prompts that the Oakton and Mesa Community College faculty have generally used were developed from the agreed upon learning outcomes. Some prompts come with questions to which the students provide a written response, while other prompts are more structured multiple- choice exam items. In the case of the College of Du Page, the assessment experience is a multi-part exam of mostly multiple-choice questions focused on skills, not knowledge, in reading, writing, critical thinking, science reasoning, and mathematics.

All three institutions randomly select classes, after stratifying the scheduled offerings to distinguish those classes in which most students are in their beginning phase of the college experience from those classes in which students typically have completed much of their lower-division work. Instructors are asked to provide a class period to facilitate voluntary student participation. Not all students in the selected classes at College of Du Page are responding to the same prompts, as typically the segments of the standardized exams are divided among the students. As general education assessment is practiced at Mesa Community College and Oakton community colleges, all students in the class are responding to the same general education prompts. Armed with a student identifier, the college research office can link the information about the student, including units completed, to the responses provided as an aid to data interpretation. Not all general education outcomes are assessed each year.

In the case of Mesa Community College and Oakton Community College, interdisciplinary teams of faculty grade the student responses using rubrics they developed, compare those results against their expectations, note the extent of growth and change between the "freshmen" and "sophomore" student groups, and then prepare a report of their findings. Copies of the summary reports are posted to the web pages of those institutions. Faculty committees at the colleges then study the results. Oakton has structured faculty meetings to discuss the results and provide feedback to guide future assessment work.

A significant accomplishment occurred at Mesa Community College in the academic year 2002-03 that provides a clear example of how the assessment program has begun to "close the loop" by formalizing the use of assessment results. A Results Outreach Committee (ROC) was formed as a sub-committee of Student Outcomes Committee (SOC). The ROC was charged with exploring avenues for strengthening and formalizing the use of assessment results throughout the college community. With support from the Dean of Instruction, the committee defined its purpose and initiated discussions with the SOC concerning possible avenues for promoting the use of assessment results. A faculty survey was conducted to gather feedback about what types of activities would be meaningful, and faculty events were held to share examples of classroom-based use of assessment results. In the spring of 2004, ROC established a process for using assessment results which was approved by SOC, the Faculty Senate, and the Dean of Instruction. Budget was allocated and a pilot "call for proposals" was disseminated to all faculty members to submit proposals for projects specifically targeted to improving student learning based upon assessment results. Several proposals were submitted, and two were funded for projects to be completed in the summer and fall of 2004. One project involved sponsoring activities to raise awareness of assessment results; the other focused on developing workshops to improve student writing skills across the disciplines (Green, 2005).

At College of Du Page, the exam booklets are sent to the commercial firm for scoring and, where they are available, results of the general education exam are compared with the placement exam results of the same students and to national norms for community college students. Students directly receive their results along with comparisons with peers at Du Page and with students in similar institutions using the same exam. A faculty committee shares the findings with the faculty at large to stimulate campus discussion of the areas for possible change in curriculum. Presentations are made to division-level meetings of faculty. Asynchronous discussions and focus groups have been used to further explore the implications for the future action. At least one Academic Quality Improvement Program (AQIP) project has been spawned from the preliminary findings. Armed with a student identifier, the research office can add information about the student and explore relationships between the outcome data and the experiences of the student at the community college. This general education assessment effort is complemented by a vigorous classroom assessment techniques program that helps the learning of current students while they are still enrolled in the course.

An equally valid approach to assessment of general education has been conducted using class-embedded assessment that arises from the normal classroom or homework tasks and assignments given to students. Representative of this approach is the work at Johnson County Community College in Overland Park, Kansas, and Raymond Walters College in Blue Ash, Ohio. In the case of Johnson County, interdisciplinary teams of faculty framed learning outcomes for the general education experience, suggested representative kinds of assignments or performances, framed a grading rubric, and established minimum performance standards. The faculty as a whole determined which of the established courses were contributing to each of the general education outcomes and essentially made the commitment that general education was the responsibility of the entire faculty (Seybert and O'Hara, 1997). Each term a random selection of classes is made by the research office from among the courses designated as supporting a particular general education outcome. Faculty are then asked to select an assignment of student work for the assessment committees. The research office arranges to make copies of pre-graded student work submitted to the instructor. In the following term, interdisciplinary teams of faculty assemble to review samples of the duplicated work and apply the agreed upon grading rubrics. The findings are then shared with the faculty for further discussion and possible change in the educational program.

In contrast to these examples, in which the focus of assessment work is upon the cumulative effect of the general education experience, some faculties have elected to focus upon a theme in general education and use a course and work required therein as a unit of analysis. At Raymond Walters College, the faculty engaged in a full-year of faculty development activities to consider the ways in which assignments might be designed to foster critical thinking, a general education ability the faculty wanted to concentrate upon assessing. The faculty acquired experience in using a technique called primary trait analysis to clarify expectations for academic performance and to evaluate student work. The focus of assessment was located in each course and used assignments embedded in the normal course work for both grading and then later for assessing the teaching-learning process as faculty shared their materials and experiences with one another (Walvoord and Anderson, 1998). The Raymond Walters approach illustrates a thematic emphasis throughout the campus focusing upon one general education competency for a period of time and developing course portfolios to be shared among faculty colleagues. Butler

# Figure 85

# *Business Transfer Program-Five Columns*

| Expanded Statement of Institutional Purpose | Program Intended Educational Outcomes: | Means of Program Assessment and Criteria for Success: | Summary of Data Collected: | Use of Results: |
|---|---|---|---|---|

**Mission Statement:**

YCC is an open-admission, community-based, comprehensive college designed to provide inexpensive, quality educational opportunities (college transfer, career/technical and continuing education) ...

**Institutional Goal:**

Serve traditional students seeking the first two years of instruction leading to a bachelor's degree.

a. Recipients of ...degree will be readily accepted ...

b. Graduates will complete their bachelor's degrees at same rate as native students.

c. Graduates will be as well prepared for their junior and senior year as original students.

---

**Program Intended Educational Outcomes:**

Students transferring from YCC after completing the Business Transfer Program will:

1. After one year of adjustment, exhibit grades similar to those of students originally enrolled at the four year institution.

2. If pursuing a degree as a full-time student, complete their BA degree in Business at almost the same rate as business students originally enrolled at the four-year college.

3. Possess roughly the same level of knowledge/skills in basic business fundamentals as those native business students enrolled at the four-year college.

---

**Means of Program Assessment and Criteria for Success:**

1. Analysis of data concerning the grades of business transfer students from YCC at four-year colleges will indicate no substantial difference in grades in business courses from business student originally enrolled at the four-year college.

2. Analysis of data received from each of YCC's three primary transfer destination institutions will indicate that the difference in the average number of semesters to BA degree completion of full-time business transfer students and students originally enrolling in business at the four-year college is statistically insignificant.

3. The scores of YCC business transfer students on the ETS Major Field Test in Business Administration (designed to assess the "common body of knowledge") administered by two out of three of YCC's primary transfer destination institutions' four-year college business schools will be similar by field to those business students originally enrolled at the four-year college.

---

**Summary of Data Collected:**

1. Business GPA of business transfer students not statistically different (-.07) than native business students. However, grades in junior level accounting courses substantially lower (almost .74) than native students. Students from YCC found to be inexperienced in use of PC's.

2. Degree completion by YCC full-time business transfer students found to be very similar to native students.

3. MFAT in Business Administration scores of YCC's business transfer students received for 327 students (72%) of those transferring. Overall, YCC's scores quite similar to native students except in accounting where YCC's student's scores were substantially less.

---

**Use of Results:**

1. Use of PC's in YCC Accounting 201 greatly expanded to include four entirely computer based major accounting projects.

2. No change necessary. Comparison by fields within business possible next year.

3. Accounting 101-102 and 201-202 sequences have been completely overhauled and brought into compliance with AACSB and AICPA guidelines. See extensively revised syllabus for each course.

Community College in Kansas used a similar thematic approach to assessing general education learning but selected a different theme each year. They asked the faculty to select work students had completed in a general education course and subsequently provided it to faculty groups for a review using an assessment rubric (Speary, 2001).

Some faculties have elected to offer a capstone course or seminar experience as a venue to assess student learning in general education. One college elected to help students develop a portfolio which provided a venue to showcase the accomplishment of general education outcomes. In asking students to respond to scenarios, the faculty obtained a work product that at least two faculty members could score using a simple grading rubric (Hunt, 2000). Another institution created a seminar in which a series of assignments were made to students in an effort to afford them an opportunity to apply the general education competencies they had learned (Jensen and Wenzel, 2001).

An illustration of assessment in the major field of study preparation for transfer, which draws upon data shared by the receiving four-year schools, is found in Figure 85, entitled "Business Transfer Program." Where sufficient numbers of students are preparing to transfer to the four-year school in a specific field of study, assessment work is furthered by the availability of actual data about the performance of transferred students in the field of concentration (major) at the four-year institution. While this is indirect evidence of student learning outcomes from the two-year school experience, it is a reflection of student learning. At least two kinds of reporting back to the two-year schools from the receiving institutions are potentially helpful for assessment purposes. One form of this reporting has been practiced by the University of Mississippi for many years in the form of a unitary level report on the performance of students who had transferred from a community college. (See Figure 86.) Student success in general, and in the major field of

## Figure 86

### *Student Performance Report*

**Student** ___(SSN)___

| Crs Abv | Crs No. | Crs Title | Cr. Hr. | Grade |
|---------|---------|-----------|---------|-------|
| ACCY | 301 | Admin Accounting | 3 | C |
| ECON | 230 | Economic Statistics I | 3 | C |
| FIN | 353 | Real Estate Valuation | 3 | C |
| FIN | 451 | Real Estate Law | 3 | B |
| MGMT | 372 | Operations Mgmt I | 3 | B |
| MGMT | 491 | Organization Behavior | 3 | C |

study in particular, can be explored by listing the university courses taken along with the grades earned. When the student began the major field of study at the two-year school, this feedback can be particularly helpful information to the community college faculty teaching the lower division curriculum in that major.

However, it does not provide the focused feedback which results from the transcript analysis. A variation of this grading report also results from focused transcript analyses in which a comparison is made between grades earned by transfer students and those of native students, groups enrolled in upper division courses for which there are prerequisites taught at the community college. Comparisons of grade point averages earned can be used to stimulate discussion about the alignment of the curriculum in terms of the expected learning outcomes at various stages in the program of study and the effectiveness of the instructional strategies. These comparisons substantially assist the community college faculty in evaluating effectiveness. Work of this sort has been undertaken in California and New Jersey (Quandry, 1998).

In this reporting strategy the rights of students under the Family Educational Rights and Privacy Act (FERPA) must be safeguarded. The purpose of the federal legislation is to protect student educational records and to allow for the correction of those records, as well as to regulate the release of information from the private record. A provision of the law, however, does permit the disclosure of individual student academic records for the purpose of research that will improve instruction. Creation of a binding inter-agency agreement may be helpful for this purpose. Federal law stipulates that the personal identity of students must be suppressed when a research study is reported. Also, data must be destroyed when the study is completed.

The transfer program where pre-major work is started at the two-year institution and completed at the four-year college represents a special case for the purposes of assessing student learning. One course-based approach has been pioneered in Virginia (Quantry, Dixon, and Ridley, 1998). Initially, faculty at Thomas Nelson Community College and Christopher Nelson University collaborated. Subsequently, these two institutions shared the process with other institutions in Virginia. Their course-based model to evaluate transfer success pairs the lower division prerequisite course in a major field with the corresponding upper division class offered in that discipline by the four-year school. Enrollment records for the two-year and four-year institution are examined to explore the success of those students taking the follow-on course who had completed the prerequisite at the two-year institution with those who had completed the prerequisite at the four-year school. The analysis provides a grade distribution in the follow-on course plus a flag indicating at which institution the student completed the prerequisite offering. A summary for the course grade distributions over several terms was prepared as well as a summary for that discipline. Finally a chi-square analysis was used to determine if any observed differences were statistically significant. The resulting data were shared with faculty at both the two-year and four-year institutions so that the faculty could review the curriculum when the data suggested that students who had successfully completed the prerequisite course were not prepared for subsequent coursework (Quantry, Dixon, and Ridley, 1998).

# Developmental Studies Programs—Student Learning Outcomes Assessment

## *Cheryl Cleaves*

Over the past few decades, developmental education has become a significant part of the two-year college curricula. The developmental studies program in a college may be centralized in one academic or student support unit, or it may be decentralized into two or more academic and support units. As with general education, no matter how the developmental studies component is structured, for institutional effectiveness purposes it should be considered as a separate academic unit. The institutional effectiveness plan will have many parallels to the general education plan, but there will also be some significant differences.

The scope of the developmental education program varies from institution to institution. Many programs align with the definition of developmental education given by the National Association of Developmental Education (NADE).

> Developmental education is a field of practice and research within higher education with a theoretical foundation in developmental psychology and learning theory. It promotes the cognitive and affective growth of all postsecondary learners, at all levels of the learning continuum. Developmental education is sensitive and responsive to individual differences and special needs among learners.

> Developmental education programs and services commonly address: (1) academic preparedness, (2) diagnostic assessment and placement, (3) development of general and discipline-specific learning strategies, and (4) affective barriers to learning.

> Developmental education includes, but is not limited to:

> • All forms of learning assistance, such as tutoring, mentoring, and supplemental instruction

> • Personal, academic, and career counseling

> • Academic advisement

> • Course work

Additional details are available at the NADE website (www.nade.net).

The developmental studies program of an institution can be linked in Column One of our model (Figure 87) to the portion of the college's mission statement that addresses the providing of quality education to its students. In some instances, a specific goal statement addresses the goal to provide developmental education for students who need basic academic skills. To identify some appropriate goals for linking the developmental studies program, the goals of developmental education as presented by NADE may be useful.

> • Developmental education, as an umbrella term for a wide range of learning-centered activities, has several key goals:

> • To preserve and make possible educational opportunity for each postsecondary learner

> • To develop in each learner the skills and attitudes necessary for the attainment of aca-

demic, career, and life goals

• To ensure proper placement by assessing each learner's level of preparedness for college coursework

• To maintain academic standards by enabling learners to acquire competencies needed for success in mainstream college courses

• To enhance the retention of students

• To promote the continued development and application of cognitive and affective learning theory

As with other academic units, the institutional effectiveness of developmental studies program focuses on intended educational (student learning) outcomes and describes them in the second column of our model. (See Figure 88.) These outcomes often address the traditional subject areas of developmental studies programs—the ability to write, the ability to perform mathematical processes, the ability to read with comprehension, and the ability to use appropriate study skills. The sample Two-Column Model (Figure 88) illustrates some appropriate intended educational outcomes. As with other academic units, the educational outcomes should be limited to three to five outcomes per cycle. In establishing the means of assessment and criteria for success of the education outcomes for the developmental studies program, it is important to consider the needs of the students, the expectations of the institution, and best practices of other institutions as ideas are fashioned for the third column of our model. A source for information from other institutions is *What Works: Research-Based Best Practices in Developmental Education* (Byland, 2002).

Since students exiting a developmental studies program at an institution ordinarily continue in an academic program at the institution, it is often possible to obtain valuable assessment information from data already collected by the college. For example, completing developmental studies students can be tracked through their first college level course in the appropriate subject areas. An analysis can be made comparing the success rate of former developmental studies students and students not requiring developmental studies courses. Another source of useful information is the persistence to graduation of developmental studies students. If the developmental studies program is sufficiently large, a representative sampling can be used.

Some typical primary means of assessment are standardized exit tests, locally prepared exit tests, pre-tests in entry-level college courses, portfolios and writing samples, and success in entry-level course grades. To be able to use the results of assessment data for program improvement, a comparative analysis using the "Column and Row Model" (Figure 33 in Chapter Seven) can be helpful. A secondary means of assessment is the use of a satisfaction survey. Information from both students and faculty who teach the students who have completed the developmental studies programs can be useful. The identification of the means of assessment and criteria for success completes the assessment plan for the developmental studies program (Figure 89).

# Figure 87

## *Two-Year College Developmental Studies Program –One Column*

### Expanded Statement of Institutional Purpose:

### Institutional Mission Statement:

The purpose of …. Community College is to provide low-cost technical education…, college transfer, and … that meet the needs of its students and community.

### Institutional Goal:

To provide developmental education for students who need basic academic skills.

# Figure 88

## *Two-Year College Developmental Studies Program – Two Columns*

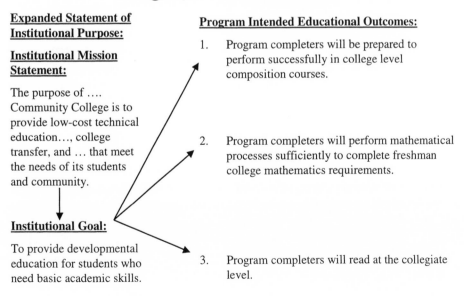

**Expanded Statement of Institutional Purpose:**

**Institutional Mission Statement:**

The purpose of …. Community College is to provide low-cost technical education…, college transfer, and … that meet the needs of its students and community.

**Institutional Goal:**

To provide developmental education for students who need basic academic skills.

**Program Intended Educational Outcomes:**

1. Program completers will be prepared to perform successfully in college level composition courses.

2. Program completers will perform mathematical processes sufficiently to complete freshman college mathematics requirements.

3. Program completers will read at the collegiate level.

The summary and analysis of the data collected and the use of the results of the assessment to make program improvement follow the same model as all other academic units with respect to how entries might be made in the fourth and fifth columns of our model. Figure 90 illustrates a completed Five-Column Model.

The developmental studies program at an institution is rarely an academic unit that operates in isolation. It is important for the development and implementation of the institutional effectiveness plan for all stakeholders to be included. The structure of the program may or may not include a learning support unit, but the institutional effectiveness plan should address all the needs of the students. Another issue that may be prevalent is that courses are taught predominately by inexperienced or adjunct faculty. Faculty development is very important for all faculty teaching in the developmental studies program. The content of the courses should include the "soft skills" (study habits, responsibility, listening, working collaboratively, etc.) in addition to the appropriate subject area content. The institutional effectiveness of the developmental studies program, like that of any other academic unit, is dependent on the involvement of all the program stakeholders and the support of the administration. A successful program has the respect and the appreciation of the entire college community.

## Conclusion

The challenges that community colleges face in conducting an assessment program have much in common with the other segments of higher education. However, the array of missions and programs, the tradition of open-door admissions, the nature of the student population, and personnel systems of the two-year institutions exacerbate those challenges. Community colleges commonly hear from their external constituents about the extent to which their programs are achieving the desired learning outcomes. Less commonly, they have developed elaborate internal data-based systems to provide feedback about student performance and educational program effectiveness (Mundhenk, 2004).

As illustrated in the chapter, several entities external to the two-year institutions (governing boards, employers, transfer institutions, and professional groups) demand accountability, often in terms of explicit learning outcomes. Where the demand has been traditionally expressed in terms of student achievement (degrees and certificates awarded, transfers completed, success rates, etc.), there is some evidence of increasing interest in actual learning accomplishment. Several illustrations have been offered as to the ways in which those demands can be turned to useful sources of information to help the two-year faculty adjust the curriculum and pedagogy.

Faculty efforts to accomplish an assessment program using techniques internal to the institution have been offered as illustrations of the work being done in two-year schools. Perhaps the greatest challenge is to find ways to make these efforts explicit and systematic in order to make changes in a more comprehensive fashion. Much of the internal work of assessment appears rooted in courses rather than programs as a unit of analysis. Moving the insights gained from lesson and course assessment up to the program level continues to be a challenge for the faculty. Generally, vocational faculties, particularly

**Figure 89**

## *Two-Year College Developmental Studies Program – Three Columns*

**Expanded Statement of Institutional Purpose:**

**Institutional Mission Statement:** The purpose of Your Community College is to provide low-cost technical education..., college transfer, and ... that meet the needs of its students and community.

**Institutional Goal:**

To provide developmental education for students who need basic academic skills.

**Program Intended Educational Outcomes:**

1. Program completers will be prepared to perform successfully in college level composition courses.

2. Program completers will perform mathematical processes sufficiently to complete freshman college mathematics requirements.

3. Program completers will read at the collegiate level.

**Means of Program Assessment and Criteria for Success:**

1a. At least 70% of students will complete college composition on the first attempt.

1b. A faculty panel will use a rubric and rate at least 90% of completers as satisfactory (4 or 5) on a 5-point scale on each category of the exit writing sample.

2a. Seventy percent of completers will score 75% or higher on a locally devised test of pre-college mathematical competencies. Seventy percent of completers will score 75% or higher on each section (sub score) of the locally devised test.

3a. Eighty percent of completers will score 85% or better on a statewide reading comprehension exit test.

3b. Eighty percent of completers will score at or above the national average on the Nelson Denny post test sub-score for reading comprehension and for vocabulary. No completer will score below the 40th percentile.

# Figure 90

## *Two-Year College Developmental Studies Program – Five Columns*

| Expanded Statement of Institutional Purpose: | Program Intended Educational Outcomes: | Means of Program Assessment and Criteria for Success: | Summary of Data Collected: | Use of Results: |
|---|---|---|---|---|
| Institutional Mission Statement: The purpose of … Community College is to provide low-cost technical education…, college transfer, and … that meet the needs of its students and community. | 1. Program completers will be prepared to perform successfully in college level composition courses. | 1a. At least 70% of students will complete college composition on the first attempt. | 1a. Eighty-two percent (338 of 412 students) completed EN 101 | 1a. No action necessary. |
| | | 1b. A faculty panel will use a rubric and rate at least 90% of completers as satisfactory (4 or 5) on a 5-point scale on each category of the exit writing sample. | 1b. Percent of students who scored 4 or 5 on the 5 point scale: Organization - 92%; Reasoning - 91%; Grammar - 78%; Rhetoric - 89% | 1b. Faculty have added a grammar review with a major focus on using the grammar handbook. |
| | 2. Program completers will perform mathematical processes sufficiently to complete freshman college mathematics requirements. | 2. Seventy percent of completers will score 75% or higher on a locally devised test of pre college mathematical competencies. Seventy percent of completers will score 75 or higher on each section (sub score) of the locally devised test. | 2. Eighty-one percent of completers scored 75% or better. Percent of completers who scored 75 or higher: Linear Equations-92%; Inequalities-84%; Quadratic Equations-88%; Graphing 62%; Powers and Roots-86%; Proportions-78%. | 2. Criteria met but row and column analysis showed weakest areas were problem-solving and graphing. Faculty have developed new video tapes on graphing to strengthen out-of-class resources and provided adjunct faculty with development in teaching graphing concepts. |
| Institutional Goal: To provide developmental education for students who need basic academic skills. | 3. Program completers will read at the collegiate level. | 3a. Eighty percent of completers will score 85% or better on a statewide reading comprehension exit test. | 3a. Eighty-nine percent (213 of 239) of completers scored 85% or better. | 3a. Faculty have reviewed the state exit test and compared it to the Nelson Denny in content. Suggested to the statewide test development committee to add questions on reading comprehension. |
| | | 3b. Eighty percent of completers will score at or above the national average on the Nelson Denny post test sub-score for reading comprehension and for vocabulary. No completer will score below the 40th percentile. | 3b.62% scored at or above the national average on reading comprehension. 88% of students scored at or above average on the vocabulary. | 3b. Faculty have added two exercises on reading comprehension. |

those in programs that are externally accredited, appear to be ahead of others in assessment work. However, the overwhelming numbers of students granted degrees from two-year schools are in the liberal arts and sciences, general studies, and humanities. As noted above, large numbers of community college students are not awarded the associate degree before they transfer but have mastered the skills, competencies, and body of knowledge from the general education curriculum as a result of their studies. The major challenge to faculties at two-year institutions is to foster an internal system of assessment that will address this popular segment of curriculum. Some examples of successful efforts to accomplish that task have been offered in this chapter. The Five Column Model advanced in this book provides a framework for systematic assessment activities that can be and are being accomplished in two-year institutions across the nation.

## Works Cited

Adelman, Clifford. *Answers in the Tool Box: Academic Intensity, Attendance Patterns, and Bachelor's Degree Attainment*. OERI. U.S. Department of Education, 1999.

Adelman, Clifford. *Lessons of a Generation*. San Francisco: Jossey-Bass, 1994.

Alfred, Richard, Peter Ewell, James Judgins, and Kay McClenney. *Core Indicators of Effectiveness for Community Colleges* 2$^{nd}$ ed. Washington, D.C.: American Association of Community College Press, 1999.

Allen, Mary J. *Assessing Academic Programs in Higher Education. Bolton, MA:* Anker Publishing, 2004.

American Association of Community Colleges. *National Profile of Community Colleges: Trends and Statistics* 3$^{rd}$ ed. Washington, D.C.: American Association of Community Colleges Press, 2000.

American Association of Community Colleges. *Improving Access to the Baccalaureate*. Washington, D.C.: American Association of Community Colleges Press, 2004.

Banta, Trudy W. *Assessment in Community Colleges: Setting the Standard for Higher Education?* Boulder, CO: National Center for Higher Education Management Systems, 1999.

Baughin, Judith, Evelyn Brod, and Deboah Page. "Primary Trait Analysis: A Tool for Classroom-based Assessment." *College Teaching* 50:2 ( 2002):75-80.

Berkner, L., L Horne, and M. Clune. *Descriptive Summary of 1995-96 Beginning Postsecondary Students*. U.S. Department of Education, National Center for Educational Statistics. Washington, D.C.: U.S. Government Printing Office, 2000.

Bers, Trudy, B. Diane Davis, and Mary L. Mittler. "Assessing the Achievement of General Education Objectives in the Community College: A Project Across the Disciplines." *Journal of General Education* 49:3 ( 2000).

Bers, Trudy and Irene Kovala. *When the College (Not a Department) Assesses General Education*. Presentation at the Indiana University-Purdue University at Indianapolis Assessment Conference, 2003.

Borden, Victor. "Accommodating Student Swirl." *Change* 36:2 (March/April 2004): 10-17.

Brown, Karla. "Why Aren't Faculty Jumping on the Assessment Bandwagon and What Can Be Done to Encourage Their Involvement." *Assessment Update* 13:2 (2001):8-9.

Byland, Hunter. *What Works: Research-Based Best Practices in Developmental Education*. Boon, NC: National Center for Developmental Education, 2002.

Callan, Patrick. *Measuring Up 2002: A National Report Card on Higher Education. San Jose, CA:* National Center for Public Policy and Higher Education, 2002.

Callan, Patrick. *Measuring Up 2004: A National Report Card on Higher Education. San Jose, CA:* National Center for Public Policy and Higher Education, 2004.

Chaddock, Diane. "Closing the Feedback Loop: How An Outcomes Assessment Instrument Has Led to Positive Curricular Reform" *Assessment Update* 12:3 (2000): 5-6.

Cohen, Arthur M and Florence B. Brauer. *The American Community College*, 4th ed. San Francisco: John Wiley & Sons, 2003.

Chesla, Jim et. al. *We're Number Two: Using Curriculum Processes to Further Assessment."* Presentation at the American Association for Higher Education Assessment Conference, 2003.

Devier, David. "Corporate Partnership in Student Assessment: The Owens Community College Experience" *Assessment Update* 14:5 (2002): 9-10.

Dillon, Paul H. "Parameters of Multiple College Attendance." Paper presented at the California Association of Institutional Research, November 2000.

D'Allegro, Mary Lou. "Building Campus Support One Brick at a Time" *Assessment Update* 15:6 (2003): 4-5.

DeVito, Terry and Peggy Schyler. *Different Yet Similar.* Presentation to the American Association for Higher Education Assessment Conference, 2003.

Fukes, Janet. *Assessing Student Learning in Community Colleges.* Bakersfield College, 2004.

Geesamann, Jan, Peter Klassen, and Russell Watson. "Assessing General Education Using a Standardized Test: Challenges and Successful Solutions." *Assessment Update* 12:6 (2000): 11-12.

Goldman, Gloria. "Simulated Performance Assessment in a Community College Nursing Program." *Assessment Update* 11:3 (1999): 12-15.

Greene, Andrea. *Personal Correspondence.* Associate Dean, Director of Research and Planning. Mesa Community College, 2005.

Henderson, Carol. "Dyed in the Wool: Creating an Effective Culture of Assessment at the Community College." *Journal of Applied Research in the Community College* 9:2 (2002): 131-137.

Hunt, Scott. "Using A Capstone Course to Assess General Education Outcomes." *Assessment Update* 12:2 (2000): 3-4.

Iyengar, Shree. *Assessment of Learning Outcomes in General Education Courses: An Emerging Model for Community Colleges.* Presentation to the American Association for Higher Education Assessment Conference, 2002.

Jeffers, Robin. *Everybody's Job: Engaging the Faculty in Curricular Renewal.* Presentation at the American Association of Colleges and Universities Annual Meeting, March 2004.

Jensen, Victoria and Alan Wenzel (2001). *Creating a Sophomore Capstone Experience in the Community College.* Freeport, IL: Highland Community College. (ERIC Document Reproduction Service No. ED 451 906)

Kerr, Barbara A. "New Kid on the Block: Becoming A Culture of Assessment—A Work in Progress." *Assessment Update* 14:4 (2002): 12-13, 16.

Lee, Otto, Elizabeth Armstrong, and Constance Carroll. *Using Course-Embedded Assessment for Student Learning Outcomes.* Presentation to the Community College League of California Annual Convention, 2003.

McCord-Ito, Robin A. "Assessment in the Sciences: Challenges and Possible Solutions" *Assessment Update* 14:2 (2002): 8-9.

McCormick, A.C. "Swirling and Double-Dipping: New Patterns of Student Attendance and Their Implications for Higher Education," in J. E. King, E. L. Anderson, and M.E. Corrigan, eds. *Changing Student Attendance Patterns: Challenges for Policy and Practice, New Directions for Higher Education, No. 121.* San Francisco: Jossey-Bass, 2003.

Mee, Gail. "Learning Outcomes Assessment at Mesa College." Presentation at American Association for Higher Education Assessment Conference, 2002.

Mundhenk, Robert. "Communities of Assessment." *Change* 36:6 (November/December 2004): 36-41.

Peterson, Marvin et. al. *Designing Student Assessment to Strengthen Institutional Performance in Associate of Arts Institutions.* National Center for Postsecondary Improvement, 1999.

Rouseff-Baker, Holm Andrew. "Engaging Faculty and Students in Classroom Assessment of Learning," in Andrea Serban and Jack Friedlander, eds. *Developing and Implementing Assessment of Student Learning Outcomes.* San Francisco: Jossey-Bass, 2004 (No. 126, Summer 2004).

Roueche, John E. and Suanne D. *Between A Rock and a Hard Place: The At Risk Student in the Open-Door*

*College*. Washington, D.C.: Community College Press, 1993.

Scroggins, Bill. *Student Learning Outcomes Institute*. Modesto Junior College, 2004.

Serban, Andreea and Jack Friedlander, eds. *Developing and Implementing Assessment of Student Learning Outcomes*. San Francisco: Jossey-Bass, 2004 (No. 126, Summer 2004).

Seybert, Jeffrey A. "Assessing Student Learning Outcomes in Community Colleges," in T.H. Bers and H.A. Calhoun, eds. *New Directions for Community Colleges,* No. 117, 2002. San Francisco: Jossey-Bass.

Seybert, Jeffrey A. and K. A. O'Hara. "Implementation of a Performance-Based Model for Assessment of General Education." *Assessment Update* 9:4 (1997): 5-7.

Shoenbert, Robert. *General Education in an Age of Student Mobility*. Washington, D.C.: Association of American Colleges and Universities, 2001.

Smith, Cindra J. *Trusteeship in Community Colleges: A Guide for Effective Governance*. Washington D.C.: Association of Community College Trustees, 2000.

Sonandre, Debbie M. Ayres. "Assessment of Student Learning: How Two Paths Forge into One." *Journal of Applied Research in the Community College* 9:2 (2002): 117-124.

Speary, Phil. "The Butler Community College Individualized Student Assessment Pilot Project." *Assessment Update* 14:3 (2002): 5-6.

Speary, Phil. "Collegewide Assessment of General Education: The Butler County Community College Model." *Assessment Update* 13:6 (2001): 2-13.

Suskie, Linda. *Assessing Student Learning: A Common Sense Guide*. Bolton, MA: Anker Publishing, 2004.

Quantry, Michael, Richard Dixon, and Dennis Ridley. "A New Paradigm for Evaluating Transfer Success." *Assessment Update* 10:2 (1998): 12-13.

U.S. Department of Education, NCESa. *Condition of Education 2003 (NCES 2003-067)*. Washington, DC: U.S. Government Printing Office, 2003.

U.S. Department of Education, NCESb. *Community College Students: Goals, Academic Preparation, and Outcomes*. NCES 2003-164, by Gary Hoachlander, Anna C. Sikora, and Laura Horn. Project Officer: C. Dennis Carroll. Washington, D.C., 2003.

Walvoord, Barbara, Barbara Bodes, and Janice Denton. "Closing the Feedback Loop in Classroom-Based Assessment." *Assessment Update* 10:5 (1998): 9-10.

Watson, Russell and Peter Klassen. *General Education Assessment at a Large Community College Using ACT/CAAP*. Presentation at the American Association for Higher Education Assessment Conference, 2000.

Wilson, Cynthia D, C.L. Miles, R.L. Baker, and R.L. Schoenberger. *LearningOutcomes for the 21st Century: Report of a Community College Study*. Mission Viejo, CA: League for Innovation in the Community College, 2000.

Womack, Nancy. "The Emergence of Leadership as a By-Product of the Assessment Initiative at Isothermal Community College." *Assessment Update* 15:4 (2003): 12-13.

Zakel, Lori. *General Education Report*. Sinclair Community College, 1997.

CHAPTER TWELVE

# ASSESSMENT ISSUES IN GRADUATE AND PROFESSIONAL PROGRAMS

## Margie Hobbs, Author

*An often overlooked portion of the institution's journey toward comprehensive im-plementation of institutional effectiveness involves graduate or professional programs. There frequently exists a misconception that these types of programs are above such pe-destrian pursuits. "Bad news" is delivered to many institutions when they belatedly dis-cover that regional and professional accrediting associations are not of the similar opinion. The "good news" concerning this journey is that institutions who have devel-oped implementation first at the undergraduate level will find assessment implementation for graduate and professional programs to be relatively smooth traveling.*

The underlying principles for assessing graduate and professional education are the same as for those for assessing undergraduate education. The faculty must establish the de-sired student learning outcomes of the program, devise tools to assess these outcomes, conduct the assessment, analyze the resulting data, determine program adjustments needed based on the data analysis, and make these adjustments in the program. Then, faculty con-duct assessment activities iteratively to form a continuous cycle to ensure adjustments made in the program are achieving the desired results or assess entirely different out-comes. Assessing graduate and professional education is often much easier than assessing undergraduate programs because many of the tools needed to assess outcomes are already in existence as part of the graduate and professional programs' educational process.

### Differences in Assessing Undergraduate Programs and Graduate and Professional Programs

Faculties who teach both graduate and undergraduate classes are generally asked to develop assessment plans for undergraduate programs before developing plans for grad-uate and professional programs for several reasons. One reason is that the level of com-plexity of expected student learning outcomes in undergraduate programs is lower than the level of complexity of expected student learning outcomes in graduate and profes-sional programs.

In the early years of assessment, regional accrediting agencies focused requirements on assessing educational outcomes for undergraduate programs. Emphases in undergraduate programs focus on content knowledge and application of that knowledge in familiar settings. Emphases in graduate and professional programs focus on applying knowledge/ skills in unfamiliar settings and in creating new knowledge (research).

The bachelor's degree for most undergraduate programs is designed to give students a broad base of knowledge in the discipline. Master's degree programs usually have one of two emphases. Research-oriented programs emphasize preparing students for further study in doctoral programs where they will learn research skills that are designed to enable them to apply knowledge in new ways or to create new knowledge. Practice-oriented graduate programs prepare students to enter a professional practice and apply existing knowledge. For example: Graduates may become prepared to teach in the discipline at the high school level or the first two years of undergraduate education. Doctoral programs are noted for further specialization of the discipline's content, and such programs prepare their graduates for roles as researchers or college and university educators.

First professional degree programs such as law, medicine, and religion offer the student sufficient knowledge to enter the field as a general practitioner. Advanced training is often required for further specialization as seen in the medical field with residency programs that prepare doctors to practice in highly specific branches of medicine.

Thus, as students matriculate from undergraduate programs to master's, first professional, doctoral degrees, and post graduate study or residency practice, the degree of specificity changes from broad based knowledge to increasingly specialized knowledge. Benjamin S. Bloom's Taxonomy identifies three learning domains: (a) the *cognitive domain*, which involves knowledge and intellectual skills; (b) the *affective domain*, which includes the way in which we deal with emotional feelings, appreciation, enthusiasms, motivations, and attitudes; and (c) the *psychomotor domain,* which relates to physical movement, coordination, and use of motor skills to perform tasks. Intended outcomes at the undergraduate level generally focus on the lower end of the taxonomy for each domain, while intended outcomes for graduate and professional programs generally focus on the upper end of the taxonomy for each domain. These taxonomies provide a useful context for developing intended student learning outcomes for graduate and professional programs.

## Intended Educational Outcomes for Graduate and First Professional Level Programs

Graduate and professional programs have some common student learning outcomes that are important to any discipline. Graduates of these programs should be aware of ethical issues in the field and should demonstrate behavior that indicates they have internalized a value system that reflects appropriate ethical values in the field and is demonstrated by consistent and predictable behavior. Students should understand the central issues and current research in the field. Graduates should have broad and in-depth knowledge of the field. Graduates should be able to communicate their knowledge of the field. Graduates should be able to design and present a meaningful research proposal, while at the doctoral level the outcome might be that students should have developed their own specific research agenda, should be thoroughly knowledgeable of the specific area, and should be able to conduct a piece of significant research. Postdoctoral trainees should be able to conduct "cutting edge" research in the discipline.

Establishing intended student learning outcomes for graduate and professional level programs is a key component, as it is for the undergraduate program. These outcomes form the basis for developing a coherent curriculum. Often, the program curriculum designed previously is realigned once intended outcomes have been established for the program. These student learning outcomes become the cornerstone of all instructional activity, and they should be used to inform students, employers, accrediting agencies, and other stakeholders about the intentions of the faculty. Student learning outcomes form the basis for all program assessment.

Some possible categories of intended student learning outcomes for graduate and professional level programs include: (a) attainment of advanced knowledge, (b) acquisition of specialized skills, (c) attainment of licensure, (d) ability to teach, conduct research, or present or publish scholarly papers, (e) employment in the field, and (f) admission to programs of further study.

Graduates are expected to attain advanced knowledge in graduate degree programs and specialized knowledge in first professional degree programs. A master's degree student in mathematics, English, business administration or other discipline would be expected to attain advanced knowledge based on the major at the undergraduate level. Doctoral graduates in such programs would be expected to have specialized learning sufficient to be viewed as expert on a particular topic within the discipline.

A student in a first professional degree program such as law might have had an undergraduate degree in another field such as political science, English, or even mathematics. Such students are expected to use the learning skills and knowledge developed in undergraduate study to gain a general knowledge of problem solving and logic which they apply later in the professional field. Students entering a pharmacy doctoral degree program might have an undergraduate degree in chemistry, biology, or some related science field. Some students entering first professional degree programs do not earn a degree in that field at the undergraduate level but rather matriculate from a collection of undergraduate preparatory courses to study in the first professional degree program.

General examples of intended educational outcomes for graduate programs that address attainment of advanced knowledge include:

- Graduates will attain advanced knowledge in the field.
- Graduates will demonstrate mastery of one specialization within the field.

First professional programs should expect that "Graduates will exhibit a fundamental knowledge of all aspects of the field sufficient to enter practice in the field." Advanced professional degree programs, such as medical residencies, prepare graduates for practice in a specialized practice within the medical field.

Examples of intended educational outcomes for graduate programs that relate to the acquisition of specialized skills include:

- Graduates will conduct advanced research in the field.
- Graduates will demonstrate skills necessary to perform in their field of specialization.

Professional programs should expect that "Graduates will demonstrate the skills necessary to perform in general practice."

Many, if not most, professional programs require graduates to be licensed to practice in the field. Licensure, especially when sub-scores earned on the licensure test are available to faculty, can provide rich data to measure the effectiveness of a program of study. (Also see comments in Chapter Seven.) Thus, a measurable outcome for some professional programs and graduate programs could be: "Graduates will acquire sufficient knowledge/skills to receive professional licensure."

Many students complete graduate and professional programs with the intent to teach. Graduates of master's programs should be able to teach in lower division programs (two-year colleges or the first two years in the university) in their field, and graduates of doctoral programs should be able to teach in both undergraduate and graduate programs. Some graduates of professional programs also intend to teach. Graduates also are often expected to disseminate their knowledge though making presentations at professional meetings or publishing scholarly papers.

Examples of educational outcomes that pertain to teaching, research, and dissemination of scholarly work for graduate and professional programs include:

- Graduates will teach at the undergraduate or graduate level.
- Graduates will present results of research at professional meetings.
- Graduates will publish scholarly papers.

Most educators would agree that employment in the field is an expected outcome of graduate and professional education. Employment in the field should have the broadest possible definition, depending on the specific discipline. It should be expected that, especially in some disciplines, self-employment may be the norm rather than exception.

Examples of educational outcomes for both graduate and professional programs regarding employment in the field include:

- Graduates will find employment in the field.
- Graduates of the program will continue practicing in the profession.

Just as some undergraduate programs are designed to prepare students for further study, graduate and professional programs may also expect students to matriculate to further study. Some master's programs and first professional programs prepare students for further study. Doctoral and professional programs prepare students to take part in post-graduate study in the student's area of specialization. Examples of educational outcomes for both graduate and professional programs regarding admission to further study include:

- Graduates will be admitted to study for the terminal degree in the field.
- Graduates will participate in post-graduate study in their area of specialization.

Statements such as those regarding student retention, the qualifications of faculty, quality of preparation of students entering the program, national recognition of the program, and program funding are important aspects of a successful program. But they are *not* appropriate statements of student learning outcomes. Student opinions about the faculty and about their satisfaction with the program are also inappropriate measures of student learning. Student opinions about what they think they have learned from the program are *indirect* measures of student learning and should not be used in place of direct measures of student learning that use student work and artifacts as evidence. (See discussion in Chapter Seven.)

With the many responsibilities for which graduate faculty are accountable, assessment efforts must be kept simple but must consist of substantive work. Faculty should specify three to five educational outcomes to assess per assessment cycle. Programs that are establishing assessment programs for the first time should select three to five student learning outcomes that are amenable to assessment and that, in the view of the faculty, have potential for resulting in assessment findings that can be used to make program improvements. Further iterations of the assessment cycle can focus on increasingly more difficult outcomes to assess.

### Means of Assessment in Graduate and Professional Level Programs

The instruments used to assess graduate and professional level programs are much more clearly defined than for undergraduate programs. Data regarding only the successful completion of theses, oral seminars, dissertations, etc., do not provide evidence to identify strengths of the program nor areas of the program where learning could be improved. Graduate faculty may claim they "know effective graduate programs when they see them," but attention must be given to student learning outcomes. Assessment methods must be clearly linked to and flow from the statements of intended student learning outcomes, and the data gathered must give faculty the knowledge and ability to diagnose the program's strengths and weaknesses in order to devise improvements where needed. These data should be gathered across students to determine trends in learning for specified outcomes. To this extent, the "Column and Row Model" shown in Figure 33 in Chapter Seven is a useful tool to organize assessment data and delineate scores that can show where program improvements need to be made. The use of a rubric (Chapter Seven) is one method of organizing a scheme for collecting data for specific outcomes, especially those that are more qualitative in nature. Examine the sample "Column and Row Model" in Figure 91, individual student scores by faculty panel on graduate program psychology comprehensive exam.

Each student's score can be determined by focusing on an individual column. For example, Student 2 has scores of 5, 4, 5, and 3, respectively for each component and an overall score of 17, which results in a grade of *A*. To discern how well the program is pre-

**Figure 91**

*Relationship Between Individual Student Scoring and Educational Outcomes Assessment*

## Individual Students Comps Scored by Various Faculty or Faculty Panel

| Criteria | Student 1 | Student 2 | Student 3 | Student 4 | Student 5 | Criteria/Intended Educational Outcomes Average |
|---|---|---|---|---|---|---|
| Learning & Cognition | 2 | 5 | 3 | 2 | 5 | 3.4 |
| Neural Basis of Memory | 3 | 4 | 1 | 2 | 3 | 2.6 |
| Sensation & Perception | 4 | 5 | 2 | 3 | 4 | 3.6 |
| Behavior Therapy | 4 | 3 | 4 | 5 | 3 | 3.8 |
| TOTAL | 13 | 17 | 10 | 12 | 15 | |
| *Individual Student Score* | C | A | D | C | B | |

Total "Down the Columns" for Individual Student Scoring

Analyze "Across the Rows" for Assessment of Intended Educational Outcomes Accomplishment

Nichols, J.O. (1995). The departmental guide and record book for student outcomes assessment and institutional effectiveness. New York: Agathon Press.

paring students, examine the scores for each component across students, row by row. By viewing the total scores for each component, it should be immediately clear that the score for "Neural Basis of Memory" is the lowest of the four components. This information is an indicator to faculty that a close examination of the program curriculum concerning this component should reveal what changes need to be made in the program to improve student learning.

Theses, dissertations, dissertation defenses, comprehensive examinations, case studies, seminar papers and oral presentations, projects, etc., are examples of required student works that are embedded into the requirements for course or graduate and professional degrees. Using the "Column and Row Model," these tools can be used to assess individual student's learning and can be reexamined by components and across students to determine how well students are performing on a specified field. The component for assessment purposes should be explicitly stated. For example, what components constitute a dissertation that "passes"? What are the "traits" of an acceptable dissertation? These components or traits are what faculty care about and deem important for students to be able to accomplish when they have completed the program and are ideal subjects for the development of analytic rubrics.

Faculty expect students who are preparing a dissertation to be able to conduct feasibility studies to determine the topic, feasibility, and scope of conducting research on a particular topic. Once the topic has been selected and appropriately limited, students are expected to review the associated literature to determine what research has already been conducted on the topic and to aid in developing a design and methodology for the research. Students may also be expected to develop instruments needed to conduct the research on the selected topic. A pilot study also may need to be a part of the research methodology. Students are expected to carry out the research protocol, organize and analyze the data, and interpret the data in the context of the research questions. Then students are expected to show how their research relates to other research on the topic and to make recommendations for the implications of the research and for further research on the topic. The research topic itself is not the central focus of this assessment. Rather, the focus is upon the various components of the multi-stepped process of moving from selecting a topic for the research to completion of the research project and dissemination of the results. Integrated throughout the process is the student's ability to communicate effectively.

Graduate and professional programs often require students to complete a significant project or an advanced topics course or seminar just prior to completion of the program. These projects and seminars provide rich opportunities to assess educational outcomes within the course (known as course-embedded assessments.) The professor of record for the class evaluates each individual student's project by examining the project in view of the various components or traits that have been established. The professor assigns an overall grade to the student work based on findings for each of the components. A panel of faculty or experts also examines the work of this student and other students as well, using a list of commonly agreed upon components. A three-level or five-level rating scale is often used to indicate the degree of quality associated with this aspect of the project.

Such a rating scale with the descriptions of each of the ratings is called a rubric. Chapter Seven of this book includes an extensive discussion regarding the construction and use of rubrics to collect and organize data from student work. This rubric discussion is easily applied to assessment of graduate and professional programs.

Faculty should also set benchmarks or criteria for success for each of the components or traits related to the assessment artifact. These criteria may be determined by faculty knowledge of the past performance of successful students, standards set by the profession, or criteria for successful performance on licensure examinations, etc. If scores on licensure examinations are used as tools to assess program outcomes, the scores should be available from all or virtually all graduates. If only a small portion of the program's graduates take the licensure examination, the aggregate data may not be a valid reflection of program outputs regarding student learning. Licensure examination scores are most useful when (a) a substantial and representative proportion of graduates take them and (b) when sub scores are available to the faculty. When students are afforded multiple opportunities to complete a piece of work, such as oral or written comprehensive examinations or dissertations, the criteria also should specify the data will be gathered from students who are performing the work "on their first attempt." This methodology promotes reliability among all students' scores and more accurately reflects student learning in the curriculum.

## Issues in Assessing Graduate Education

Many graduate programs have very small numbers of graduates each year. Programs should not be expected to use assessment data from very small numbers of students to make program changes. In such cases, data should be collected for two or three years to provide reliable evidence of the need for improvement. Caution should be taken to ensure data from each year's graduates are comparable.

The length of time required for doctoral students to complete all requirements for the degree has wide variation. Graduate students often drop in and stop out to work or for other reasons. The dissertation may take longer to complete than the course work. This is one reason it is important to consider embedding assessment in courses that are taken near the end of the course of study. The use of comprehensive examinations, oral or written, can also be a useful source of assessment data.

## Concluding Comments

Regional accrediting associations continue to "raise the bar" with regard to assessment in graduate and professional programs. For example, note Comprehensive Standard 3.6.2 from the Southern Association of Colleges and Schools' Commission on Colleges, which states, "The institution ensures that its graduate instruction and resources foster independent learning, enabling the graduate to contribute to a profession or field of study."

Professional accrediting associations have increasingly influenced assessment in graduate and professional programs, and most, if not all, currently require assessment of intended student learning outcomes using direct measures of student work and "closing the loop" by making program improvements based on data analysis. Information prepared to satisfy professional accrediting agencies, in many instances, can be used to satisfy regional accreditation purposes. However, professional accreditation itself validates the program's *educational process* and **not** its intended student learning outcomes. Professional accreditation of a program is **not** a valid means of assessing intended student learning outcomes.

The Five-Column Models shown in Figures 92 to 94 are representative of implementation of assessment of student learning outcomes in graduate and professional level programs. However, the richness and variety of these fields enable faculty to construct plausible assessment structures that are effective in gathering data from student work and other sources that, when analyzed and interpreted, provide faculty the direction to make thoughtful and reflective improvements in the instructional program.

# Figure 92

## *Doctorate in Literature – Five Columns*

### Expanded Statement of Institutional Purpose

**Institutional Mission Statement:**
Our University offers master's and doctoral degree programs in selected areas that will prepare individuals for positions of leadership in their chosen careers.

**Institutional Goal Statement:**

Goal # 3: Our University will improve graduate education and research to attract and retain outstanding students and faculty.

### Program Intended Educational Outcomes:

**1.** Graduates will demonstrate a depth of knowledge in one of six specializations.

**2.** Graduates will exhibit strong literary analysis skills

**3.** Graduates will be highly competitive in the college teaching market.

### Means of Program Assessment and Criteria for Success:

**1a.** Each year 80% will pass the comprehensive exam in their specialized field on their first attempt.

**1b.** Over the past three years, the pass rate in each specialization will be at least 70% on the first attempt.

**2a.** 50% of the graduates will have a review of literary work accepted for publication within one year of graduation as indicated on an alumni survey.

**2b.** Based on a rubric used by a faculty panel, 95% of the dissertations reviewed will meet departmental requirements for literary analysis.

**3a.** Course evaluations in classes taught by graduates will be the same or better than the department, college, and university averages for similar courses.

**3b.** 80% of graduates who apply for teaching positions and were reached by phone one year after graduation will report employment in field teaching at a college or university.

### Summary of Data Collected:

**1a.** This year 9 of 10 students passed the comprehensive exam in their specialized field on their first attempt. Only two specializations tested this year.

**1b.** Over the last three years, 12 of 21 students in American Literature and 6 of 9 students in British Literature specialization passed on first testing.

**2a.** Two of ten graduates (20%) had such works accepted for publication.

**2b.** All dissertations were found to meet departmental requirements for literary analysis.

**3a.** Of the ten graduates, three found to exceed department and college averages. None, however, equaled university norms.

**3b.** One year after graduation 40% (four) of last year's doctoral graduates (ten) reported employment in field at college level.

### Use of Results:

**1a.** While choice of specialization was continued, faculty decided to implement a "breadth" requirement for entering class.

**1b.** Contemporary American Writers (Eng 755) now required of all in American Literature specialization.

**2a.** Requirements for students to submit publishable literary analysis for faculty review throughout program is more fully enforced.

**2b.** Departmental rubrics for literary analysis revised for more rigor.

**3a.** University instructional development seminar now required in students' first semester of graduate level enrollment.

**3b.** Improved publication record (2a) and instructional skills (3a) above required should lead to improved employment rate.

# Figure 93

## *Juris Doctorate in Law – Five Columns*

| Expanded Statement of Institutional Purpose | Program Intended Educational Outcomes: | Means of Program Assessment and Criteria for Success | Summary of Data Collected: | Use of Results: |
|---|---|---|---|---|
| **Institutional Mission Statement:** The University will continue to provide the initial professional education of those who formulate, interpret, and practice law. | 1. Graduates will have a fundamental knowledge of basic substantive law. | 1a. The primary means of assessment are the results on the "State" Bar Examination. 75% of graduates will pass the bar on the first attempt. On no individual scale will the failure rate be more than 35%. | 1a. For the current reporting period, 73% of our graduates who were first time takers passed the Bar. The failure rate on Constitutional Law was 37% | 1a. Results of the bar exam were distributed to all School of Law faculty and administrators, as well as to the University administration and alumni leaders. The faculty after much discussion modified the second year curriculum to include additional required class in Constitutional Law. |
| | | 1b. Preceptors in the intern program will give a composite rating of 3.0 or higher (on a 5 point scale) on each question of a survey of legal intern's knowledge of law and legal process. | 1b. The composite score on the first question was 4.52 and on the second it was 3.62. | 1b. Criteria was met but faculty decided the means of assessment was not giving useful information for improvement. More specific survey to be given next year. |
| | 2. Graduates will exhibit effective legal research skills. | 2a. A faculty panel will use a project completed in the capstone course to rate students' research skills on a scale of 1-4. Student's average score will be 3.8 or above. | 2a. Students in the most recent graduating class scored and average of 3.65. | 2a. The faculty have included a research component in Commercial Law 571. |
| | | 2b. No student will have a rating below 3.0 on any of the components of research skills. | 2b. No student scored below 3.0. | 2b. No action is required. But due to new course, staff wants to monitor again next year. |
| **Institutional Goal:** The University will concentrate graduate and professional education and research in areas consistent with the Focus Areas. | 3. Graduates will demonstrate ethical responsibility. | 3a. A composite score of 3.0 or above (on a 5 point scale) will be recorded by intern supervisors for students responding to question "The students' performance demonstrated an understanding of the profession and ethical duties of lawyers." | 3a. The composite score for this reporting period was 2.91. This was a decrease over the score last year of 3.2 | 3a. Faculty study concluded that d recent changes in faculty who teach the course in professional responsibility may be responsible. Faculty will closely monitor this area of the curriculum to determine if curricular modifications are needed. |
| | | 3b. On new ethical case study presented in LAW 673, 80% of students will choose ethical solution as determined by group of faculty. | 3b. 70% of the students chose the ethical solution. | 3b. Group of faculty re-evaluated the new case study and determined solution was indeed ethical solution. Will use the same case study next year before making decision regarding curriculum change. |

**Figure 94**

## Master of Science in Geology – Five Columns

| Expanded Statement of Institutional Purpose | Program Intended Educational Outcomes | Means of Program Assessment & Criteria for Success | Summary of Data Collected | Use of Results |
|---|---|---|---|---|
| **Institutional Mission Statement:** While recognizing that its primary role… educates students to assume leadership roles… through its nationally recognized programs of undergraduate, graduate, and professional study. | 1. Graduates of the MS Geology program will have acquired the necessary skills for a professional employment position in geology or a related discipline. | 1. 75% percent of students who complete the M.S. program in Geology and seek a professional position in geological engineering or a related discipline will be successful. | 1. Of the 3 graduates during this assessment period, 2 are employed in professional positions in geology and 1 has entered a Ph.D. program in geology. | 1. We propose to continue this pattern of success, with attention to achieving a balance between those graduates entering Ph.D. programs and those seeking employment. Because our enrollment is growing, we anticipate ties to alumni, industry, and graduates in appropriate professional positions. |
| **Institutional Goal:** The University will concentrate graduate education and research in areas of strength consistent with its mission. | 2. Graduates will have advanced knowledge of Geology. | 2a. Students will score 80% or above on each component of a comprehensive written exam for each of the various advanced sub-specialties at the end of the program of study. <br> 2b. Students will answer 75% of oral questions correctly in each of the components of their sub-specialty. | 2a. An analysis of student responses for each component show that all students scored above 80% of each component except the questions regarding exploration for oil and gas deposits where only 66% answered correctly. <br> 2b. Of the 3 graduates of during this assessment period, all answered more than 75% of the oral questions for his/her sub-specialty correctly. | 2a. GEO 624 has been revised to include more thorough coverage of oil and gas exploration techniques. <br> 2b. Staff was pleased with student success. A review of the rigor of the oral questions found that the questions were too basic for Master Level Students. New questions have been developed for next assessment cycle. |
| | 3. Graduates will have completed a research project of sufficient sophistication that it is published in a minor scientific journal. | 3. Fifty percent of students who complete the M.S. program in Engineering Science - Geology will publish the results of their master's program research in a minor scientific journal before they graduate or soon thereafter. | 3. Only 1 of the 3 graduates has prepared a manuscript that will soon be submitted for publication. However, this manuscript has been informally reviewed and judged to be publishable in a minor scientific journal. Accordingly, it has been submitted to the *American Association of Petroleum Geologists Bulletin*, which has an international circulation and can be found in just about any scientific library in the world. | 3. Increased emphasis has been placed on demonstrating the value and significance of our graduate student research thorough publication results. A seminar has been initiated for each fall semester that reviews the basics of manuscript presentation, the mechanics of peer review process, and describes ways to effectively respond to reviewer comments. |

CHAPTER THIRTEEN

# DOCUMENTING ASSESSMENT

Daniel A. Weinstein, Author

*From the earliest annals of history, we have learned much through reading the journals of previous travelers. In these journals the travelers were able to keep a record of their journeys and provide the stories of their accomplishments. The improvement of student learning and administrative services through assessment likewise provides evidence of accomplishments to others. The documentation within the institution of a consistent journal describing the journey toward improvement demonstrates to others outside the institution (regional accreditors) as well as to current and future colleagues within the institution the actions which have taken place. The following chapter describes a process that can be developed at an institution for recording program and unit accomplishments.*

This publication presents a pragmatic model of how to approach the science and method of doing outcomes assessment. While the science is simple, much of the meaning inherent in the assessment process will be lost if it is not well documented. Indeed, systematic and straightforward documentation of the assessment process is as important as engaging in the process itself. Walvoord (2004) warns against gathering data no one will use and making the assessment process too complicated. Quality documentation of assessment on college and university campuses not only maintains a permanent, easily accessible record, but substantiates clear evidence that an assessment process is in place and that the results of assessment are being used to drive program improvement.

### Keys to Effective Documentation

We know that the expanded statement of institutional purpose and the intended student outcomes and administrative objectives are the drivers of the Five-Column Model of assessment. Measurable, or ascertainable, criteria are our indicators of success for each outcome statement. Whatever our assessment results suggest to us will become the basis for planned change. It is to an institution's credit that it can document this process in a consistent format across campus. This "scholarship of assessment," as Banta (2002) refers to it, involves developing appropriate summaries of findings for effective sharing.

Effective documentation also creates a "road map," or linkage, of assessment activities to the use of results for improvement. It lays out graphically how change is implemented based on observations related directly to intended outcomes. For the documentation to be effective, it needs to be simple and easy for users to maintain. The computer, digital space, and the Internet are highly efficient vehicles for maintaining the documented assessment records for an institution. All that is needed is an effective and accessible template. Maki (2004) asserts that establishing reciprocal channels of the communication of assessment opens up the possibility for greater focus on improving areas of weak performance.

As the demands for accountability and for the establishment of a culture of evidence at colleges and universities intensify, there will be a need for increased order and centrality to the process. Even Astin in 1991 submitted a "theory of utilization" of assessment in which he posited that the role of assessment is to enhance the feedback available to faculty and staff in order to assist them in becoming more effective practitioners. Institutions will also benefit by establishing a campus clearinghouse where all assessment documentation is accessible or a centralized copy is housed. Such an enterprise for documentation provides organization and value for outcomes assessment and is impressive to reviewing teams at accreditation time.

## A Solution to Documentation Issues: The Assessment Record Book

The Assessment Record Book provides an easy-to-use template for documentation of program/unit level assessment. Each intended student learning outcome or administrative objective is tracked individually through the "use of results." A *title page* (Form A) lists the educational programs from a department for which an assessment report is attached. (See Figure 95.) A *linkage page* (Form B) connects the Expanded Statement of Institutional Purpose (ESIP) with intended student learning outcomes. (See Figure 96.) An *educational outcome report page* (Form C) shows the means of assessment, the summary of data collected, and the use of results to improve the program. (See Figure 97.) These forms are available at no cost to the institution at www.iea-nich.com.

The process of tracking one outcome at a time helps not only to highlight the completion of the assessment process but also allows the evidence of improvements as a result of the assessment process to be easily demonstrated to external reviewers. The forms that are available on the above mentioned web site are available for institutions to download and adapt to their own institution. A suggested adaptation is the inclusion of the institution's logo. The downloadable forms feature expandable text boxes in which to type, allowing the maintenance of detailed analyses of assessment results, if need be. The main point to remember is that there needs to be at the institution a consistent, simple, and manageable process known on campus for the documentation of the assessment process conducted. The point is to keep it a simple and manageable process. Suskie (2004) reminds us that the shorter the communication of assessment results, the more likely people will pay attention to them and put them to good use. The forms that are described in this chapter are easily adaptable to web-based documentation.

# Figure 95

## ASSESSMENT RECORD FOR

## DEPARTMENT

## OF

_____

(Academic Department Name)

_____             _____

(Assessment Period Covered)                       (Date Report Submitted)

Includes Assessment Reports for those Educational Programs listed below:

<u>Title of Educational Degree Program</u>                     <u>Degree Level</u>

                                                     (Associate, Bachelor's, Master's, etc.)

_____             _____

_____             _____

_____             _____

_____             _____

_____             _____

_____             _____

Submitted By: _____

(Department Chair or Faculty Assessment Representative)

*Form A-Title Page*

# Figure 96

## ASSESSMENT REPORT FOR

_____          _____

**(Educational Degree Program)**                     **(Degree Level)**


_____          _____

**(Assessment Period Covered)**                  **(Date Report Submitted)**

**Expanded Statement of Institutional Purpose Linkage:**

| |
|---|
| **Institutional Mission Statement Reference:** |

| |
|---|
| **Institutional Goal(s) Supported:** |

**Intended Educational (Student Learning) Outcomes:**

| |
|---|
| 1. |

| |
|---|
| 2. |

| |
|---|
| 3. |

| |
|---|
| 4. |

| |
|---|
| 5. |

*Form B-Linkage Page*

# Figure 97

## ASSESSMENT REPORT FOR

_____

(Educational Degree Program)

_____

(Assessment Period Covered)

_____

(Degree Level)

_____

(Date Report Submitted)

**Intended Educational (Student Learning) Outcome:**
*Note: There should be one Form C for each intended outcome listed on Form B. Intended outcome should be restated in the box immediately below and the intended outcome number entered in blank spaces.*

| |
|---|
| — |

**First Means of Program Assessment and Criteria for Success for Student Learning Outcome Identified Above:**

| |
|---|
| __ a.  Means of Program Assessment and Criteria for Success: |

| |
|---|
| __ a.  Summary of Assessment Data Collected: |

| |
|---|
| __ a.  Use of Results to Improve Educational Program: |

**Second Means of Program Assessment and Criteria for Success for Student Learning Outcome Identified Above:**

| |
|---|
| __ b.  Means of Program Assessment and Criteria for Success: |

| |
|---|
| __ b.  Summary of Assessment Data Collected: |

| |
|---|
| __ b.  Use of Results to Improve Educational Program: |

*Form C-Educational Outcome Report Page*

## Form A—Title Page

Form A is the cover page. It provides basic information about the educational department, including the title of the degree program and degree level for which assessment reports are forwarded. The title page also presents the assessment cycle period and date submitted. There is space at the bottom of the page for the name of the submitting, or contact, person.

As the institution completes more than one assessment cycle, the ability to identify the dates on the reports allows the units to demonstrate that the assessment process is indeed "systematic." The submitted date on the title page identifies any changes made by the department/unit within the assessment cycle. The title page is important for maintaining basic information about the program being assessed. It becomes crucial once there are multiple programs being assessed during a given cycle. They keep track of, but also differentiate between, programs being assessed at the same time.

## Form B—Linkage Page

Form B is the critical institutional linkage and intended outcomes page. Simply, this page presents institutional mission and institutional goal references with space for up to five intended outcomes for the given assessment cycle. Not only does the form present the program student learning outcomes efficiently, but it also shows their direct connection to institutional intentions. Banta and others (1996) support that assessment works best when programs have clear, explicitly stated purposes.

At the top of Form B is a reminder of the degree program title, degree level, period covered, and date submitted. Since intended student learning outcomes and administrative objectives are at the heart of the assessment process, Form B is an important representation of what the educational program is all about. Indeed, Form B sets the stage for systematic, step-wise assessment. It delimits and focuses assessment data collected and analyzed, rather than attempting to document collected data with no direct purpose.

## Form C – Educational Outcome Report Page

Form C is the report page. This form allows the educational program or AES unit to describe in detail what process took place in relationship to the individual student learning outcome. The form presents intended outcomes individually. Each "means of assessment," up to two, is fleshed out individually by the criteria for success, the summary of the data collected and the use of those results to improve the program. Form C effectively "closes the loop" on the assessment process by showing what has been done as a result of the information attained.

Also at the top of Form C is the reminder of the degree program title, degree level, period covered, and date submitted. Much of the information presented on Form C will be important to keep accessible for historical purposes. As changes happen in personnel, it may be important sometime in the future to know why certain changes were made and what outcomes they were tied to.

The examples presented so far are those to be used for the educational programs. Also available at the web site are forms for the AES units. The AES forms have the same appearance as the forms for the educational programs but allow for the differences between these two areas as outlined in Chapter Nine. Specifically, Form A, the *title page* is singular and is used for each individual unit, and Form B, *the linkage page*, provides a block for the AES unit to provide the unit mission statement. Form C, *the reporting page*, remains the same for both educational programs and AES units. Completed examples of both the educational and the AES forms are found in Appendix D.

## Maintaining the Documentation

It is important to keep in mind at this point in a chapter on the documentation of assessment that the assessment enterprise is much more than just completing forms. The bottom line is that any given educational program or AES unit needs to be genuinely self-reflective and document the assessment process pragmatically. While forms by themselves will not create a culture of evidence on a campus, how the documentation is maintained at the institutional level can have an effect. An "integrated assessment model" can promote positive change along the dimensions of the assessment (Sedlacek, 2004).

In order for assessment to truly thrive on a campus, efforts at accommodating the process at the institutional level can be crucial. The institutional research office and information technology are often called upon to provide campus leadership in this regard. All participating programs can have their assessment documentation forms stored on a local network or shared drive. It can be set up so the forms are accessible in-house only.

The Internet provides a myriad of options for form maintenance and showcasing. Suskie (2004) recommends posting a summary of assessment results on a departmental or institutional web site. Many institutions have used the Internet for this purpose and, therefore, have been able to initiate a culture of accountability and continuous improvement (e.g., Weber State University and University of South Florida). Again, forms, local networks, and the Internet are merely vehicles used to store and document assessment information. A thoughtful decision concerning how these vehicles are used will help to determine the course of assessment on a college or university campus.

It is also critical to understand the impact it will have on individuals, academic departments, and service units for sensitive assessment data and analyses to be out and in the open on the Internet. Many faculty and staff members will be reluctant to have this level of detail available to anyone at the click of the mouse. This is not the intent of posting assessment data and results on the Internet. Institutions and individual departments are at liberty to post their outcomes assessment information on the Internet, but to protect the privacy of the departments and units, it should be a password entry, accessible only to authorized personnel.

## Documenting Assessment: Issues to Consider

The regional accrediting bodies in the United States want to see evidence from colleges and universities that they are engaged in the process of improvement on a continual basis. Episodic efforts of outcomes assessment are no longer acceptable. A successful outcomes assessment program is ongoing and well maintained and presents every opportunity to the user for self-reflection. Good documentation will help make the difference. Among Gupta's (1999) tips for communicating assessment results are the inclusion of objectives, methodology, findings, conclusions, and recommendations in a formal report. The steps that an institution takes to streamline assessment documentation will communicate loudly to all stakeholders how much the process is valued and that the results are genuinely being used to effect important changes.

## Assessment Software Packages

Depending on the approach of your institution to assessment and the extent to which you will be doing in-depth analyses, you may want to consider one of many assessment software packages available. Such packages as TracDat and Exact-Data can help you with the organization of data, as well as uniform reporting across various departments. Not all assessment software packages are the same and not all are right for any one institution, so it's important to research each one thoroughly and decide which one is the best fit for your institution and assessment needs. Institutions should carefully consider the cost of such software, its fit with their region's assessment requirements, and the tendency at some institutions to focus attention on implementation of the software, as opposed to the substantive changes which it should document. Improvement of student learning and administrative services is not a software problem that can be handled by the information technology department.

## Summary

The choices that an institution makes regarding the documentation of assessment will have an effect on how the process is received and how effective the process will be. Assessment Record Book forms provide an easy-to-use template for the documentation of assessment activities—one intended outcome at a time. The establishment of a central "clearinghouse," as well as easy access to forms, will communicate to all stakeholders how much the institution values the process of outcomes assessment. Indeed, electronic, web-based vehicles are the future of assessment documentation.

## Works Cited

Astin, Alexander W. *Assessment for Excellence: The Philosophy and Practice of Assessment and Evaluation in Higher Education.* New York: Maxwell MacMillan International, 1991.

Banta, Trudy W., et. al. *Assessment in Practice: Putting Principles to Work on College Campuses.* San Francisco: Jossey-Bass Publishers, 1996.

Banta, Trudy W., et. al. *Building a Scholarship of Assessment.* San Francisco: Jossey-Bass Publishers, 2004.

Gupta, Kavita. *A Practical Guide to Needs Assessment.* San Francisco: Jossey-Bass Publishers, 1999.

Maki, Peggy L. *Assessing for Learning: Building a Sustainable Commitment Across the Institution.* Sterling: American Association of Higher Education, 2004.

Sedlacek, William E. *Beyond the Big Test: Noncognitive Assessment in Higher Education.* San Francisco:

Jossey-Bass Publishers, 2004.

Suskie, Linda. *Assessing Student Learning: A Common Sense Guide.* Bolton: Anker Publishing Co., 2004.

Walvoord, Barbara E. *Assessment Clear and Simple: A Practical Guide for Institutions, Departments, and General Education.* San Francisco: Jossey-Bass Publishers, 2004.

# RESOURCE SECTION
# STANDARDIZED ASSESSMENT TESTS

*compiled by Paul Cunningham*

| Test Name | Vendor |
|---|---|
| AREA CONCENTRATION ACHIEVEMENT TESTS (ACAT) | Project for Area Concentration Achievement Tests PACAT, Inc. |

### Brief Description

ACAT is a nationally standardized test used at 2- and 4-year institutions to assess basic knowledge acquisition in 11 different academic majors using a multiple-choice format to obtain specific curricular feedback for program evaluation. Departments may select the content areas which will appear on the instrument they use. The number of content areas to be selected for a particular major (e.g., psychology) appears as separate "curricular areas" (e.g., abnormal, animal learning and motivation, human learning and cognition, clinical and counseling, developmental, experimental design, history and systems, statistics, personality, physiological, sensation and perception, social, tests and measurements). Departments determine what they want to measure and select those curricular areas that correspond (e.g., 10 areas, 8 areas, 6 areas, or 4 areas in the major of psychology) and that will appear on the version of the test it uses. The exact combination may vary from department to department and from year to year.

### Field(s) Covered

Flexible content options are available for the following disciplines: Agriculture, Biology, Criminal Justice, Geology, History, Neuroscience, Political Science, Psychology, and Social Work (i.e., departments determine which areas appear on the instrument they use). Flexible content options are not available in: Art, Literature in English (i.e. curricular areas are pre-selected by ACAT).

### Score Reports

Two individualized copies of a score report are provided and include an overall standard score and percentile that indicates a student's overall performance compared to all students in the 5-year sample group taking a test with the same number of content areas. A "raw percent correct score" is provided indicating how well students did in a curricular area in terms of percent of items answered correctly. Interim reports may be produced containing any scores for the most recent group of students for whom answer sheets have been submitted. Annual summary reports are also available, including longitudinal records with end-of-year comparisons to individual departments' own cumulative group.

### Customized Results Processing

ACAT does not customize the test at the level of individual questions. Customization is done by including the requested content area components on the version of the test to be used. Departments may elect to change their test configuration once during any testing year (June-May). Departments may also use multiple versions of the ACAT to meet curricular needs. Score reports can contain change scores based upon the performance of the department's former students, correlational statistics relating content area scores to coursework and GPA, and individualized student scores either as standard scores or stanines. Score reports can also be provided on computer diskette.

### Norm Group

A 6-year national sample of institutions who took a test with the same number of content areas in most disciplines is provided to determine percentile ranks. Each content area has its own 6 year comparison group consisting of all students taking that particular content area test. In some disciplines, the comparison group size is different for each content area.

| Review Copy | Testing Time |
|---|---|
| No charge is made for sample tests. To request a sample, download a sample request form from the ACAT website. Specify the discipline and list the specific curricular areas to be included in the version of the test to be used. Custom administration manuals are provided with each version. Sample tests are available for a 90 day review. | The ACAT is administered by the department or institution at its convenience as a group, individual, or class test. Administration time depends upon the discipline and number of content areas selected, varying from 48 minutes (4 content areas selected) to 2 hours (10 content areas selected). |

| Cost | Turn Around Time |
|---|---|
| The fee for use of the ACAT varies from $6 to $15 per examinee depending upon the discipline and version used. Test fee includes the one-time use of that booklet, an answer sheet, administration manual(s), scoring, score report, and long term maintenance of score histories. All unused materials must be returned within 30 days of expiration date. | Scoring is conducted monthly and special scoring for a fee. ACATs are scored during the last full working week of the month. All answer sheets received prior to that time will be processed. Typically, the score reports are mailed during the first working week of each month. Special scoring which does not conform to this schedule can be accomplished upon request for a fee. |

### Contact Information

PACAT Inc.
P.O. Box 767, Clarksville, TN 37041
Telephone: (866) 680-2228 or (931) 552-9028
FAX: (931) 552-9167
Website: www.collegeoutcomes.com
E-mail: info@collegeoutcomes.com

| Test Name | Vendor |
|---|---|
| ASSET | American College Testing (ACT) Educational Services |

**Brief Description**

ASSET includes seven separate diagnostic tests in a multiple-choice format appropriate for use with college freshmen and transfer students and designed to provide placement information regarding reading, writing, numerical skills, and career skills (optional). ASSET provides a series of short placement tests of entering students' strengths in specific subject areas. Entering students take only the ASSET tests that will be most helpful in determining which courses are most appropriate for a student's current level of knowledge and skills. ASSET tests are often given during orientation to incoming freshmen who have been admitted to the school.

**Field(s) Covered**

ASSET has three tests of basic skills in writing, reading, and numerical reasoning, plus four more advanced mathematic tests in elementary algebra, intermediate algebra, college algebra, and geometry, and additional skills (up to five scores may be added by the institution, such as English essay sample, chemistry, or ACT assessment). Writing skills test measures knowledge of appropriate usage of grammar, punctuation, sentence structure, writing strategy, and writing style. Reading skills test measures ability to find specific information in text and make logical inferences beyond textual information. Numerical skills test measures knowledge and skills of basic mathematical operations and pre-algebra knowledge and skills. Elementary algebra test measures skills taught in 1st-year high school (hs) algebra. Intermediate algebra measures skills in 2nd year of hs algebra. College algebra measures skills in 1st year college algebra. Geometry test measures skills taught in hs geometry. The ASSET program also offers an Educational Planning Form which supplements ASSET test scores by providing information about students' educational needs and goals.

**Score Reports**

ASSET provides immediate scoring and reporting through the choice of three options: Option 1 with locally-scored answer sheets; Option 2 with ACT machine-scored answer sheets; Option 3 with microcomputer data base system providing software that scores answer sheets and prints an ASSET Student Report complete with localized course placement recommendations. There are no cut-off or "passing scores" used. ASSET scores indicate areas in which the students are strong and areas for improvement helpful in determining the courses each student should take. All three options provide immediate student advising reports, educational planning reports, and transfer planning reports.

**Customized Results Processing**

Six additional reports are available for ASSET users, including: Entering Student Descriptive Report (no charge), Returning Student Retention Report (no charge), Course Placement Service (10 analyses=$225), and Underprepared Student Follow-Up Report (5 pairs of courses=$225), College Outcomes Survey Report and CAAP Linkage Report (call for price information). ASSET makes available machine-scored (Scantron or NCS) and PC-scored answer sheets with software (annual license fee=$450) for an additional fee.

**Norm Group**

Since ASSET scores are criterion-referenced and used for placement and diagnostic purposes only, norm group data are not available

| Review Copy | Testing Time |
|---|---|
| The *ASSET Student Guide* can be downloaded from the ASSET web site to provide sample questions and instructions for all tests. | Each test consists of approximately 25-35 questions. 25 minutes is allowed for each test. |

| Cost | Turn Around Time |
|---|---|
| To implement ASSET, an institution must purchase both ASSET Test Booklets and ASSET Student Sets. Test booklets cost $36.75 (25/pkg) and are reusable. One ASSET Student Set (containing an Educational Planning Form and one self-scored or machine-scored answer sheet) is required for each student, costs $3.55 per student, and is not reusable. | Since ASSET is scored locally by hand or by optical scan, immediate scoring and reporting is provided. |

**Contact Information**
ACT Educational Services
500 ACT Drive, P.O. Box 168, Iowa City, Iowa 52243-0168
Telephone: (319) 337-1270
Website: www.act.org/asset
E-mail: outcomes@act.org

| Test Name | Vendor |
|---|---|
| CALIFORNIA CRITICAL THINKING SKILLS TEST (CCTST) | Insight Assessment (formerly The California Academic Press) |

### Brief Description

The CCTST is a 34-item assessment in a multiple-choice format for use with students at community college, undergraduate, graduate, and professional school levels to assess an individual's or group's critical thinking and inductive and deductive reasoning skills or to gather data from program evaluation and research on critical thinking development. Test items indicate the test taker's ability to draw inferences, make interpretations, analyze information, identify reasons for a conclusion, and evaluate those reasons using discipline-neutral content with statistically equivalent forms (Form A, 1990; Form B, 1992; Form 2000). On-line testing available.

### Field(s) Covered

The CCTST assesses a student's capacity to perform inductive reasoning, deductive reasoning, analysis, inference, and evaluation in relation to short problem statements and scenarios.

### Score Reports

Written reports with descriptive statistics as well as a computer file are provided. Score reports provide an overall critical thinking skills total score and norm-referenced percentile rankings, sub-scale scores of inductive and deductive reasoning, analysis, inference, and evaluation. Group descriptive statistics (i.e., mean, median, range, standard deviation) are provided. Results are presented in numerical form and with graphs. Overall scores and subscale scores for each test-taker are also provided: basic descriptive statistics based on choice of one or more demographic variables (gender, class level, ethnicity). Answer sheets allow for institutions to distinguish groups of test-takers from one another for purposes of comparing the scores of different groups.

### Customized Results Processing

Customized statistical analyzes can include inferential statistics (t-test, correlations, ANOVA) and additional analyses of interest to institution's research assessment projects. Test design specialists are available to assist institutions custom design their own critical thinking assessment instrument and assist with the entire instrument development process, even to the point of placing the institution's critical thinking test on-line. Pricing for custom services are negotiated on a case-by-case basis depending upon objectives, requirements, and time format.

### Norm Group

National norms and norms for several significant groups of test takers are available. Self-selected reference group norms can be developed at additional cost. *Critical Thinking in Nursing Education* (1997), for example, presents CCTST norms for undergraduate and graduate professions in that discipline.

| Review Copy | Testing Time |
|---|---|
| A Specimen Kit can be obtained by downloading the FAX form from the Internet. Specimen Kit contains one copy of each Form A and B and a Test Manual providing administration instruction, scoring keys, scale score interpretation, and percentile norms. Specimen kit costs $60. | The 34-item, multiple-choice CCTST takes 50 minutes to administer. |

| Cost | Turn Around Time |
|---|---|
| First 50 tests cost $20 per student. Use of 51-500 tests cost $15 per student. Over 500 tests cost $10 per student. Institutional discounts are available. Prices per test include batch scoring and data analysis of paper version. Since answer forms are analyzed in batches, splitting the batches by using separate mailing incurs additional "batch split fees." Phone for on-line testing price information. | Orders should be placed at least 20 working days, although rush orders (within three days, not including shipping time) are subject to additional fees. Allow 2 weeks for scanning, scoring, and statistical analysis of response forms. Rush order service is available for a fee |

### Contact Information

Insight Assessment
217 La Cruz Avenue, Millbrae, CA 94030
Telephone: (650) 697-5628
FAX: (650) 692-0141
Website: www.insightassessment.com
E-Mail: info@insightassessment.com

| Test Name | Vendor |
|---|---|
| COLLEGIATE ASSESSMENT of ACADEMIC PROFICIENCY (CAAP) | American College Testing (ACT) Educational Services |

### Brief Description

A postsecondary assessment consisting of five different tests in a multiple-choice format (except for essay) designed to measure reading, writing, math, science reasoning, and critical thinking to help community colleges, four-year public and private institutions measure learning outcomes of college sophomores or seniors who have completed at least 30 semester credits in general education areas of the curriculum.

### Field(s) Covered

CAAP module tests separately assess the following five academic areas: Reading, Writing Skills, Mathematics, Science, and Critical Thinking. Test modules are in a 52-item multiple-choice format (except in the writing skills component which includes an additional optional essay format) and may be used as a stand-alone exam or in combination with other exams. CAAP offers two options to measure writing skills: a 72-item multiple-choice indirect writing skills test assesses writing usage, mechanics, and rhetorical style skills, and a direct writing Essay Test consisting of two 20 minute essays scored centrally by ACT or locally. Essays are evaluated according to how well, in a timed draft composition, the student formulates and executes a response to issues raised in the essay prompt.

### Score Reports

A total score is provided for each CAAP exam and subscores are given for Writing, Reading, and Math tests. The following reports and certificate are sent directly to the institution:

* Institutional Summary Report for 25 or more students provides mean scores for each demographic area, a summary of student self-reported motivation, and national and local percentile distributions.
* Two copies of Student Score Reports and a basic interpretative guide for each student.
* Certificate of Achievement for all students earning scores at or above the national mean.
* Student Roster Report that reports scale scores, including local and natural percentiles, academic major, educational level, and performance effort on the test.
* National sophomore norms are reported based on the type of institution (2-year or 4-year).

If ACT scores the Writing Essay Test, a composite score and scores for each essay are reported on a modified, holistic basis on a 1-6 scale, reflecting ability to perform a prompted, timed, first draft composition.

### Customized Results Processing

Opportunity is provided to collect responses to nine locally developed questions; frequency distributions are provided for each item. In addition to the local questions, institutions may be provided special subgroup breakdown reports for subsequent analysis or to identify a special subset of students (e.g., RN, LPN, other majors). An institution may request up to 3 student subgroup reports at no charge. Each student subgroup report follows the same format as the Institutional Summary Report. Additional subgroup reports are available for a fee. There is a $50 set-up charge for the following reporting services: (a) Electronic File of data on diskette/CD-Rom, (b) Supplemental Roster Report provides supplementary data on all students reported in the basic report, (c) Linkage Report documents change in academic performance over time for an intact cohort of students who have taken one of ACT's Placement Testing Programs (COMPASS, ASSET, ACT Assessment), (d) Trend Analysis (compares progress across several years for total students tested and for specific student subgroups) with normative data.

### Norm Group

A user norms booklet containing a full description of the most recent norms for freshmen through seniors is available for community college, four-year public, and four-year private institutions. Local and national normative information is reported as percentile ranks by type of institution (e.g., 2-year, public) and level of student (e.g., sophomore).

| Review Copy | Testing Time |
|---|---|
| To review CAAP material contact ACT. | Actual testing time for each CAAP test is 40 minutes (including two 20-minute essays). |

| Cost | Turn Around Time |
|---|---|
| Annual institutional fee of $350. Use of 1-500 tests for each student taking a single objective test = $11.55. Each student taking 2-5 objective tests responding on the same answer sheet = $17.85. Test local scoring guide, standard reporting package, and research reports ($48). Essay test: local scoring with purchase of objective test = $3.45, alone = $5.25, ACT scored = $11.55. | Institutions should order CAAP tests at least 2 weeks prior to administration and shipped to arrive 7 days prior to first day of testing. Upon completion of the 2-week testing period, both used and unused test booklets must be returned to ACT. Score reports are sent 3-4 weeks after receipt by ACT. |

### Contact Information

ACT Outcomes Assessment
500 ACT Drive, P.O. Box 168, Iowa City, Iowa 52243-0168
Telephone: 1-800-294-7027, FAX: (319) 337-1790
Website: www.act.org/caap
E-mail: outcomes@act.org

| Test Name | Vendor |
|---|---|
| College Basic Academic Subjects Examination (COLLEGE *BASE*) | Assessment Resource Center University of Missouri-Columbia |

### Brief Description

A criterion-referenced subject test assessment utilizing a combination of multiple-choice/essay question formats that evaluates knowledge and skills in four subject areas - English, mathematics, natural science, and social studies. Designed to assess students who have completed college-level general education curriculum, emphasizing concepts and principles derived from course material in the four above-mentioned subject areas and evaluate performance in three higher-order reasoning skills: Interpretive Reasoning, Strategic Reasoning, and Adaptive Reasoning. Tests are available on audiocassette, in large print, and Braille to meet the special needs of students with disabilities.

### Field(s) Covered

College *Base* is a 180 multiple-choice test and optional essay that assesses general education knowledge in each of the following four subject areas (and sub-areas) including: (a) English (reading and literature, writing) using a combination of multiple-choice and essay questions; (b) Mathematics (general mathematics, algebra, geometry); (c) Natural Science (laboratory/field work and fundamental concepts); and (d) Social Studies (history and social sciences). College *Base* also assesses capability in three cognitive processing skills (Interpretive, Strategic, and Adaptive Reasoning) as they apply to all subject areas. Institutions may choose to administer any single subject test or administer up to four subject tests, depending upon their needs. The English writing essay test may be administered alone, or with 1-4 subject tests (one subject must be English).

### Score Reports

Three score report options are available: (a) Standard Subjects option provides testing in 1-4 subject areas with all students taking the same subject test. Essay test may also be included; (b) College Base 1:1 option provides institutional summary data for all 4 subject areas but each student takes only 1-2 subject tests; (c) Basic Skills option: assesses certain populations for basic skills including English, Math, and/or Writing. The essay may also be included.

Student Score Report and Institutional Summary Report are provided. Students receive individualized score reports; institutions receive summary of scores in all subjects administered, and copies of all student score reports. The Institutional Summary Report represents aggregate scores for all examinees. Scores are presented in two categories of achievement: Four Subject Scores (English, Math, Science, Social Studies) and three Competency Scores (Interpretive, Strategic, and Adaptive Reasoning). Subject Scores and Competency Scores gives the frequency and percentage of examinees who achieved a high rating, medium rating, and low rating in subject area knowledge and reasoning skills regardless of particular content. A Composite Score gives the average composite score achieved by the group of examinee.

### Customized Results Processing

Customized results processing is available, at an additional fee, and includes: Comparative/comparable institutional reports, summaries by year in school, gender, and ethnicity, and institution-wide administration student rosters, special statistical analyses, special institutional summaries, item analysis. Electronic data files available on compact diskette or CD. Local item option is not available.

### Norm Group

College *Base* is a criterion-referenced examination. Custom reports are available to provide norm-referenced data at an additional fee, if requested.

| Review Copy | Testing Time |
|---|---|
| A review copy may be downloaded off the Internet that provides detailed descriptions of the subject areas and the reasoning competencies, as well as sample questions. | The administration time per subject test is approximately 45 minutes, plus 40 minutes for the optional essay test. The battery of four subject tests (including essay) may be administered in 3.75 hours. |

| Cost | Turn Around Time |
|---|---|
| Price per examinee varies depending on number of subject tests ordered. Manual free with materials. A minimum order requires 20 answer booklets with 3-4 subjects, 30 answer booklets with 1-2 subjects, or a total invoice of at least $150. Fifty test booklets with Examiner's Manual ($69). | Institutional and student results are generally mailed within 2-4 weeks of receipt at the Assessment Resource Center. If testing includes m/c sections only, score reports will be returned in 2-3 weeks. If testing includes essays, score reports will be returned in 3-4 weeks. |

### Contact Information

College *Base* Coordinator, Assessment Resource Center
University of Missouri-Columbia, 2800 Maguire Boulevard, Columbia, Missouri 65201
Telephone: (800) 366-8232; FAX: 573-882-8937
Website: www.arc.missouri.edu/collegebase
E-mail: collegebase@missouri.edu

| Test Name | Vendor |
|---|---|
| Computerized Placement and Assessment and Support System (COMPASS/ESL/e-Write) | American College Testing (ACT) Educational Services |

### Brief Description

COMPASS is an untimed, flexible, computerized adaptive testing system utilizing the Internet or Windows 95/98 NT-based software (available for stand-alone or networked systems) for placement and diagnostic purposes in the areas of mathematics, reading and writing that can be scored and returned immediately following submission. COMPASS/ESL includes placement testing for English as a Second Language (ESL). COMPASS/ESL assists institutions in placing entering students into appropriate developmental or preparatory courses and can be utilized in conjunction with an institution's advising, course placement, and retention services. COMPASS e-Write is a direct writing assessment delivered via the Internet that evaluates a student's writing sample using an analytical rubric.

### Field(s) Covered

COMPASS offers three placement measures in the areas of math, reading, and writing that provide up to seven possible scores: One in Writing Skills (usage/ mechanics and rhetorical skills), one in Reading and up to five in Mathematics (numerical skills/pre-algebra, algebra, college algebra, geometry, trigonometry). The measures may be used individually or in different combinations. In addition to the placement scores, COMPASS also offers 15 mathematic diagnostic tests (seven in pre-algebra and 8 in algebra), three reading diagnostic scores, and eight writing skills diagnostic scores. A student may start a placement test and if performance is low, diagnostics can be used to determine the specific areas in which the student is proficient or needs additional work. The math and reading tests are in a multiple-choice format. The writing test asks students to find and correct errors in essays, inserting examinee's selected revisions into the original test and giving the student an opportunity to make further editing changes.

### Score Reports

A sample COMPASS student score report provides information about student background and educational plans, local demographics, academic areas for which the student has requested assistance, and refers the student to resources recommended by the institution. Score reports summarize results for the placement measure(s), reporting scores, testing times, and recommended course placements. Reports also summarize results for the diagnostic measure(s), providing more detailed information about the student's algebra skills, reading, and writing skills. All academic advisors connected to the network can access individual student records in the system with full review. The institution determines which tests are administered on computer, defines cut-off scores, and placement messages. COMPASS e-Write reports a single overall score and proficiency in focus, content, organization, style, and mechanical conventions.

### Customized Results Processing

Six additional reports are available for COMPASS users, including: Entering Student Descriptive Report (no charge), Returning Student Retention Report (no charge), Course Placement Service (10 analyses=$225), and Underprepared Student Follow-Up Report (5 pairs of courses=$225). Call for price information for the following: College Outcomes Survey Report and CAAP Linkage Report (i.e., connects with the results of other ACT services such as ACT Assessment, ASSET, CAAP). Capability exists for institutions to create up to 30 local interest questions, create bulletin boards, and additional multiple student record options for use in uploading comparisons, and inputting ESL data to an institution's student information system. Institutions can select additional variables to be included and can generate a placement summary report to describe the recommended placements for groups of students. COMPASS e-write offers hand scoring of a paper-and-pencil version of the writing sample.

### Norm Group

COMPASS provides total college local norms for all measures.

| Review Copy | Testing Time |
|---|---|
| Institutions may download from ACT's website PDF versions of the sample questions for COMPASS placement measures (math, reading, writing) along with sample screen shots, and detailed information about content areas and samples of the diagnostic measures and sample student score report. | The three placement tests can take approximately 60-90 minutes to complete. Since the computerized adaptive format adjusts the level of the test to the skills and expertise of the individual test taker, most examinees will complete a different number of items, so that individualized start and finish times are the norm. |

| Cost | Turn Around Time |
|---|---|
| To implement COMPASS/ESL/e-Write, an institution must secure the right to use the software through purchase of an annual license ($450). COMPASS/ESL requires the purchase of "Administrative Units" ($1.30 per unit). | Student reports can be printed immediately or on a delayed basis at the discretion of the institution, displayed on the computer screen, or sent to a disk for storage or transfer to another computer system. |

### Contact Information

ACT Educational Services
500 ACT Drive, P.O. Box 168, Iowa City, Iowa 52243-0168
Telephone: (319) 337-1054 or (319) 337-1000
FAX: (319) 337-1790 or (319) 339-3020
Website: www.act.org/compass
E-mail: compass@act.org

| Test Name | Vendor |
|---|---|
| ENGINEERING TECHNOLOGIST CERTIFICATION EXAMS | National Institute for Certification in Engineering Technologies (NICET) |

### Brief Description

NICET offers a variety of highly specialized open-book style, multiple choice examinations on categories of typical job tasks in the engineering field to certify job skills and knowledge based on industry standards for up to four progressively more demanding levels according to exam performance, work experience, and third-party evaluations. Level I certification is designed for trainees and entry-level technicians who perform limited job tasks under frequent supervision. Level II is for technicians who perform routine tasks under general daily supervision. Level III is for intermediate-level technicians who, under little or no supervision, work with plans and specification. Level IV is for independent, senior-level technicians whose work includes supervising others.

NICET Certification Exams are used to identify those technicians who have acquired a minimum amount of relevant work experience and have demonstrated their knowledge by meeting a rigorous exam requirement. NICET written exams are usually designed for individuals who have already performed the work elements on a routine basis associated with the certification area. The typical job duties and associated responsibilities of engineering technicians have been broken down into discrete work elements which form the basis for an evaluation of the candidates' knowledge.

### Field(s) Covered

NICET provides Technician Certification in more than 30 specialty areas including: Fire Protection, Low Voltage Electric communication Systems, Industrial Instrumentation, Transportation, Construction Materials Testing, Geotechnical, Underground Utilities Construction, Building Construction, Land Management and Water Control, Geosynthetic Materials Installation and Inspection. NICET also provides Technologist Certification (no testing required) that requires a bachelor's degree in an engineering technology program accredited by TAC/ABET.

### Score Reports

The score report lists the numerical score achieved for each work element ("test module") that appears on the exam and whether that score is "pass" or "fail" based on a nationally established cut-off score. A sample score report is included in every program detail manual. A certification of achievement is included. NICET keeps an individual's score history as long as certification is active.

### Customized Results Processing

Applicants select level of certification desired and indicate the number of work elements (general, core, and special) required for certification. NICET prepares individualized examinations for each applicant based on the work elements identified on the application form (no more than 34 work elements).

### Norm Group

Each certification test is standardized based on industry standards for the specialty area and provides a "cut-off" pass/fail score based on those standards.

| Review Copy | Testing Time |
|---|---|
| Download *the Program Detail Manual* from NICET's website to find a detailed description of each work element ("test modules"), examination requirements chart, and other resources. | After application and fee is submitted to NICET, confirmation notice and directions to nearest test center is provided. NICET's exam schedule is divided into a series of four cycles (Jan-Mar, Apr-June, July-Sept, Oct-Dec), scheduling one exam per date per cycle at most test centers around the U.S. Seats at test centers are on first-come, first-served basis. Depending upon certification area, written examinations may be in two parts, each part 3 hours duration. |

| Cost | Turn Around Time |
|---|---|
| Examination fee: $180. Exams administered at times and places different from scheduled test require additional fees. Once certified, a yearly fee of $40 is required to maintain certification. Other fees may apply for recertification and application review for any level of certification that does not require paid testing. | Initial score reports are generally mailed to candidates within 2-3 weeks of the test date. |

### Contact Information

National Institute for Certification in Engineering Technologies (NICET)
1420 King Street, Alexandria, VA 22314-2794
Telephone: (888) 476-4238 or (703) 548-1518
Website: www.nicet.org
E-mail: test@nicet.org

| Test Name | Vendor |
|---|---|
| GRADUATE RECORD EXAMINATION (GRE)<br><br>General Test and Subject Tests | Educational Testing Service (ETS) |

**Brief Description**

The GRE consists of two types of tests: General Test and Subject Tests.

The GRE General Test is designed to assess analytical writing, verbal skills, and quantitative skills in either a traditional pencil-and-paper or adaptive computerized format (paper-based tests are available where computer-based testing is not available).

The GRE Subject tests are currently available in a pencil-and-paper format only and are designed to assess undergraduate students' knowledge of the subject matter emphasized in specific disciplines.

**Field(s) Covered**

The GRE General Test measures three skills: analytical writing, verbal skills, and quantitative skills. The analytical writing section is a performance test that consists of two writing tasks (45-minute "Present Your Perspective on an Issue" task and a 30-minute "Analyze an Argument" task. The "Writing" tasks assess a student's ability to express complex ideas, analyze and evaluate arguments, and write a coherent first-draft essay. The verbal skills section assesses the ability to analyze, evaluate, and synthesize written passages. The quantitative skills section assesses knowledge of basic mathematical concepts in arithmetic, algebra, geometry, and ability to reason quantitatively.

The GRE Subject Tests are currently available in eight disciplines: Biochemistry, Cell and Molecular Biology, Biology, Chemistry, Computer Science, Literature in English, Mathematics, Physics, and Psychology.

**Score Reports**

Three scores are reported for the GRE General Test: a verbal score reported on a 200-800 score scale, a quantitative score reported on a 200-800 score scale, and a holistic analytical writing score reported on a 0-6 score scale. A single total score reported on a 200-900 score scale is provided for each individual GRE Subject Test.

In addition to the total score, some Subject Tests provide sub-scores that indicate test taker's strengths and weaknesses in specific content areas. All scores earned during a 5 year period will be reported to all designated recipients

**Customized Results Processing**

Examinees may choose to send only General Test scores, only Subject Test scores, only Writing Assessment scores or any combination of the above. Scores may be obtained by telephone ($10 fee). Additional score reports may be ordered ($15). Criterion On-Line Writing Evaluation service is available through ETS's web-based service. Undergraduate Institution Summary Report ($75), Graduate Institution Summary Report ($100) are available to authorized individuals.

**Norm Group**

Scores permit percentile ranking comparisons of students from different institutions with different undergraduate populations.

| Review Copy | Testing Time |
|---|---|
| Free GRE Subject Test can be downloaded from the GRE website when registering for a GRE Test. GRE General Test Practice Books can be ordered from GRE website ($21). The Practice Book describes the test in detail, recommends test-taking strategies, and offers a full-length test with answer key. | GRE General Test can take up to 4 hours to complete (actual testing time is 2 hrs. 15 min.).<br><br>GRE Subject Testing can take up to 3.5 hours to complete (actual testing time is 2 hrs. 50 min.). |

| Cost | Turn Around Time |
|---|---|
| GRE General Test (both computer-based and paper-based) costs $115. GRE Subject Test fee is $130. Rescheduling fee ($40). Standby registration ($35). GRE fee waivers are available to qualified individuals. | GRE General Test computer-based scores mailed within 10-15 days after the test. Pencil-and-paper scores mailed within 6 weeks. Score reports are mailed within 6 weeks after the GRE Subject Test is taken. |

**Contact Information**

GRE-ETS, P. O. Box 6000, Princeton, New Jersey 08541-6000
Telephone: 1-866-473-4373
FAX: (609) 771-7906
Website: www.gre.org
E-mail:  gre.info@ets.org

| Test Name | Vendor |
|---|---|
| JOB READY SERIES OF TESTS | National Occupational Competency Testing Institute (NOCTI) |

### Brief Description

A series of standardized technical tests in a multiple-choice format designed to measure basic knowledge and skills in a variety of occupational fields of individuals who have completed training/education in an occupation (i.e., senior at a career/skill center or community college program graduate) Student/job ready occupational assessments can be used diagnostically to determine if a graduating student will be successful in the workplace, to measure the quality of educational and training programs, to evaluate the effectiveness of curriculum and instructional methods, to identify which students need additional training to master a new procedure or technology, to measure an individual's ability to complete specific jobs required by industry standards, and to obtain a certificate of competency for job credentials.

### Field(s) Covered

Offers over 170 written and performance assessments in a variety of occupational fields based on industry standards, including the areas of business/office, drafting and design, electrical and electronics, trade and industrial, health occupations, and vocational home economics.   Institutions may choose to use written tests, performance tests, or both.

### Score Reports

Separate scores are provided for written and performance assessments for each individual. Score reports include: Group Composite Scores, Individual Participant Scores, Certificate of Completion for each participant, and materials for interpreting the data. Each institution determines the passing or cut-off score for each test. Written and performance tests provide for separate pretest and posttest scores, cut-off scores, and school, state, and national percentiles for job tasks associated with each job category.

### Customized Results Processing

Customized assessments for specific needs are available. If the NOCTI standardized test battery does not include a test, the Whitener Group can work with your school to develop a customized assessment. Local item option is not available.

### Norm Group

NOCTI supplies statistical information for comparison with school, state, and national scores. Self-selected reference groups are not available.

| Review Copy | Testing Time |
|---|---|
| Sample assessments in all occupational areas are available from the NOCTI website. Sample assessments include a list of critical core competencies, along with other information (e.g., number of questions on written test, number of jobs for performance test, administration time, and sample questions). | Written assessment: Approx. 3 hours. Performance assessment: Approx. 30 minutes – 4 hours depending on job category. |

| Cost | Turn Around Time |
|---|---|
| Written test = $17.50 per student; Performance test = $17.50 per student. Both written + performance test = $20.00. Price includes test booklets, evaluator's guide, detailed administration instructions, answer sheets, return labels, and demographic booklet. Shipping is not included.  Also Test Center Coordinator training is required (offered every year at the ACTE Conference, every other year at the NOCTI Conference). NOCTI also provides on-site workshops to train performance test administrators. | Orders should be placed at least 4 weeks before a scheduled test date. Rush shipping available for additional fees. Score reporting for student testing is within 2 weeks of receipt. |

### Contact Information

NOCTI (and the Whitener Group)
500 North Bronson Ave., Big Rapids, MI 49307
Telephone: (800) 334-6283 or (231) 796-4695
Fax: (231) 796-4699
Website: www.nocti.org
E-mail: nocti@nocti.org

| Test Name | Vendor |
|---|---|
| | Educational Testing Service (ETS) |
| MAJOR FIELD TESTS (MFT) | |

**Brief Description**

The MFTs, based on the Graduate Record Examinations (GRE) Subject Tests, are 120-minute, 140 multiple-choice examinations in 15 disciplines appropriate for 4-year institutions for assessing basic knowledge of concepts and principles expected of senior-level undergraduates who have completed the majority of courses in an academic major.

**Field(s) Covered**

Biology, Business, Chemistry, Computer Science, Criminal Justice, Economics, Education, History, Literature in English, Mathematics, Music Theory and History, Physics, Political Science, Psychology, Sociology, and MBA.

**Score Reports**

Three types of scale scores are provided for the MFT (not every test reports all three types of scores):
- Total Scores that characterize performance on the test overall are reported for each individual student and mean (average) total score for the group.
- Sub-scores representing achievement in broad areas within the field of study are reported for each student and for the group as a whole.
- Assessment Indicators reflecting the performance pertaining to sub-areas within the major field of study are reported as mean (average) percent correct for the group of students. Assessment Indicators are not reported for individual students.
- Percentile tables for all seniors taking the current version of the test are also provided.

Summary of demographic information (gender, ethnicity, educational level, transfer status, enrollment status, English Best Communication Language, undergraduate GPA, education planned, major field GPA) is also provided. In addition to the standard report, departments may request (for an additional fee) reports for up to five subgroups of students (a minimum of five students is required for each subgroup)

**Customized Results Processing**

Special Score Reports are available for an additional fee. Duplicate score reports may be purchased for $50.00 each. A group of reports from different report dates may be combined into a single summary report from the same form of a single test for $150.00. Subgroup Reports may be ordered for $25.00 per Subgroup. A special departmental report that displays item level data (i.e., the percentage of test takers who provide the correct response to each question) from one administration of a test or combined from several administrations is also available. Up to 50 optional, locally written multiple-choice questions (items) gives the institution an opportunity to assess distinctive aspects of its program with a report provided of the number and percentage of students choosing each response to each item. No charge for scoring optional items. Custom Comparative Data Reports are available with which institutions may compare their departmental scores to those of other institutions of their choosing. Call or Email ETS for current fee listing.

**Norm Group**

Comparative group data, updated periodically, consist of tables with percentile ranks of institutional and individual student total scores, average subscores, and average assessment indicators of all senior-level students who have taken the most recent form of the test. A list of participating institutions, by test, is provided along with demographic makeup of each comparative group. The data is comparative, rather than normative.

| Review Copy | Testing Time |
|---|---|
| Institutions can obtain a review copy of any of the tests by sending a signed copy of a Confidential Review Copy Request Form to ETS. This form is available by calling ETS or printing the form from the ETS web page | The MFAT tests are two hour multiple-choice tests. |

| Cost | Turn Around Time |
|---|---|
| $26 each test, except MBA. Single orders of 100 tests or more: $25 each test. MBA Test ONLY: $30.00 each test. Single orders of 100 tests or more: $25.00 each test. Shipping charges are in addition to the cost of the books. | Approximately 3-4 weeks turn-around time. Reports are mailed to institutions according to a "Scoring/ Reporting Schedule" cycle established by ETS. Answer sheets received after the "Answer Sheets Received By" date are held until the next scoring cycle, thus test date(s) need to be planned accordingly. Scoring/Reporting Schedule is posted on ETS Website. |

**Contact Information**

Major Field Tests

Educational Testing Service, Rosedale Road, Princeton, NJ 08541

Telephone: (800) 745-0269 or (609) 921-9000

FAX: (609) 734-5410

Website: www.ets.org/hea/mft

E-Mail: hea@ets.org

| Test Name | Vendor |
|---|---|
| MEDICAL COLLEGE ADMISSIONS TEST (MCAT) | Association of American Medical Colleges (AAMC) |

### Brief Description

The MCAT is a standardized multiple-choice examination designed to assess problem solving, critical thinking, and writing skills in addition to knowledge of science concepts and principles requisite to the study of medicine. The MCAT is used to identify medical school candidates who are broadly educated in the social sciences and humanities, natural and physical sciences. The MCAT assesses mastery of biology, chemistry, and physics concepts, and facility with scientific problem solving, critical thinking, and writing. Offered in paper test and computer-based test format.

### Field(s) Covered

The MCAT assesses verbal reasoning, knowledge of basic concepts in physical sciences and biological sciences, and writing skill. Verbal reasoning section of the MCAT uses a multiple-choice format to assess the ability to understand, evaluate, and apply information and arguments presented in prose text. Physical and biological science sections of the MCAT uses a multiple-choice format to assess the ability to use prior knowledge in the physical and biological sciences to solve problems derived from basic principles in biology, chemistry, and physics. The writing section of the MCAT consists of two writing prompts, each composed of a brief topic statement and sets of writing tasks calling for a combination of expository writing and argumentative writing designed to assess the ability to write a timed, coherent, first-draft essay.

### Score Reports

Four separate scores are reported based on the four sections of the MCAT exam: Verbal reasoning (60 questions), physical sciences (77 questions), biological sciences (77 questions), and the writing sample (2 questions). Raw scores on the three multiple-choice sections of the exam are based on the number of questions answered correctly and are reported as scaled scores ranging from 1 (lowest) to 15 (highest). Raw score on the writing sample is based on the total rating of two different readers on the two writing responses holistically scored and converted to an alphabetic scale for reporting ranging from J (lowest) to T (highest). Scaled score means and standard deviations for each area, percentages of students achieving each scaled score, and percentile rank ranges are provided in each score report.

### Customized Results Processing
Not available.

### Norm Group

Scale scores can be interpreted as percentile rank ranges based on the performance of all students taking a test during a given administration or in a given year.

| Review Copy | Testing Time |
|---|---|
| Free access to a full-length practice test similar to that used in an actual test administration is available from the MCAT website, including instructions, an answer sheet, and answer key. Free practice test on-line is available at www.e-mcat.com. | The MCAT is a 5-3/4 hour test. Two sections are given in the morning followed by the remaining two sections after a lunch break. Verbal reasoning takes 85 minutes. Physical science takes 100 minutes. Biological science takes 100 minutes. Writing sample takes 60 minutes. |
| **Cost** | **Turn Around Time** |
| Cost = $200. Late fee = $50. Change of test site fee = $20. Fee assistance available for those with extreme need. | The MCAT is administered in April and August of each year at established test centers. Admission tickets for the MCAT are sent within 3 weeks of receipt of registration materials. Score reports are available approximately 60 days after each test date. |

### Contact Information
MCAT Program Office
Association of American Medical Colleges, 2450 N St. N.W., Washington, DC 20037-1127
Telephone: (202) 828-0416 or (319) 337-1354
Website: www.aamc.org/mcat
E-mail: mcat@aamc.org

| Test Name | Vendor |
|---|---|
| WATSON-GLASER CRITICAL THINKING APPRAISAL (WGCTA) | Harcourt Brace/ The Psychological Corporation |

### Brief Description

The WGCTA measures five aspects of verbal reasoning ability, including: drawing sound inferences, recognizing assumptions, reasoning by deduction, interpretation, and evaluating the logic of arguments. The test requires consideration of a series of propositions (either an inference, assumption, conclusion, or argument) relating to a given statement and requires the test taker to evaluate how appropriate or valid these propositions are. Two equivalent, 80-item forms (Form A and Form B) and an abbreviated 40-item version (Form S) are available in a multiple-choice/true-false format. The WGCTA is an untimed test that can be administered individually or in groups and is available in both traditional pencil-and-paper and Internet-based on-line computer versions. The WGCTA is appropriate for grade 9-12, college students, preprofessional, and professional adults. Suitable for individual or group settings

### Field(s) Covered

The WGCTA assesses five aspects of critical thinking: (1) ability to judge the validity of inferences; (2) ability to recognize presuppositions and assumptions that are implicit in statements made by others; (3) ability to recognize whether particular conclusions necessarily follow from the evidence given by particular propositions; (4) ability to weigh evidence and decide if generalizations or conclusions based on given evidence are logically warranted; (5) ability to distinguish between arguments that are strong and those that are weak and irrelevant to a given issue.

### Score Reports

The WGCTA may be scored by hand or by machine. A total raw score based on assessment of the five critical thinking skills (inference, recognition of assumptions, deduction, interpretation, evaluation of arguments) is provided that can be related to specifically defined comparison groups. Raw scores that identify the total number of items answered correctly on each of the five aspects of critical thinking can be obtained from hand-scored answer sheets for Form A and Form B.

### Customized Results Processing

Not available.

### Norm Group

Percentile norms corresponding to total score for a variety of groups is available including: high school students (Grades 9-12), college students (2-year and 4-year), preprofessional students (education, nursing, MBA, medical), police officers, sales representatives, and state trooper applicants.

| Review Copy | Testing Time |
|---|---|
| Examination Kit for Forms A, B, and S costs $63 and includes Test Booklet, Answer Sheet, and Manual (does not include answer key). | Form A and Form B (80 items) can be completed in 40-60 minutes. Form S (40 items) can be completed in 45 minutes. |

| Cost | Turn Around Time |
|---|---|
| Forms A and B: Test booklets (pkg/25, includes Manual) = $137; Answer Sheets (pkg/25) = $42; Key for Hand Scoring = $31. Short Form S Test Booklets (pkg/25, includes directions for administering) = $112; Answer Sheets (pkg/25) = $40; Key for Hand Scoring = $31. Manual = $55. | Since test is locally scored (not scored by Harcourt Brace/Psychological Corporation), feedback of results may obtained immediately. |

### Contact Information

The Psychological Corporation
Order Service Center, P.O. Box 708906, San Antonio, TX 78270-8906
Telephone: (800) 228-0752 or (800) 872-1726.
FAX: (800) 232-1223
Website: www.psychcorp.com
E-mail: customer_care@harcourt.com

# RESOURCE SECTION
# ATTITUDINAL ASSESSMENT SURVEYS

*compiled by Daniel Weinstein*

| Student Attitudinal Survey Listing | | | |
|---|---|---|---|
| **Instrument Name** | **Survey Category** | **Purpose** | **Vendor** |
| ACT Evaluation Survey Services (ESS) can help postsecondary institutions obtain comprehensive information about their students' attitudes, opinions, needs, and development. | Post secondary students and alumni | ACT offers 17 standardized instruments for secondary institutions:<br>- Adult Learner Needs Assessment Survey<br>- Alumni Outcomes Survey<br>- Alumni Survey (Four-year & Two-year College Form)<br>- College Outcomes Survey<br>- College Student Needs Assessment Survey<br>- Entering Student Survey<br>- Faces of the Future Survey<br>- Financial Aid Student Services Survey<br>- Student Opinion Survey (Four-year and Two-year College Form)<br>- Survey of Academic Advising<br>- Survey of Current Activities and Plans<br>- Survey of Postsecondary Educational Plans<br>- Survey of Student Opinions<br>- Withdrawing/Nonreturning Student Survey (Long Form)<br>- Withdrawing/Nonreturning Student Survey (Short Form) | ACT- ESS Evaluation Survey Series http://www.act.org/ess/postsec.html |
| (ALS) Adult Learner Survey | Adult UG students | Assessment for adult students completing undergraduate programs. It is a Web-based survey that shows how satisfied your students are and what's most important to them. | Noel-Levitz http://www.noellevitz.com/NLCOM/Our+Services/Retention/Tools/ |
| (ASPS) Adult Student Priorities Survey | Students age 25 or older | For graduate students, continuing education students, and evening/weekend learners. Measures satisfaction of students age 25 and older | Noel-Levitz http://www.noellevitz.com/NLCOM/Our+Services/Retention/Tools/ |
| (ASQ) Admitted Student Questionnaire & Admitted Student Questionnaire Plus (ASQ Plus) | UG admitted students | Admitted Student Questionnaire (ASQ) and Admitted Student Questionnaire PLUS (ASQ Plus) ask admitted students to tell you what they really think of your programs, recruitment literature, financial aid packages, competition, and more. | The College Board http://www.collegeboard.org/aes/asq/html/index000.html |
| (CAAS) Comprehensive Alumni Assessment Survey | Alumni | Measures evidence of institutional effectiveness and reports on alumni personal development and career preparation | NCHEMS http://www.nchems.org/surveys/caas.htm |
| (CCSEQ) Community College Student Experiences Questionnaire | All enrolled students | Measures students' progress and experiences.  Community college version of CSEQ. | The University of Memphis http://www.people.memphis.edu/~coe_cshe/CCSEQ_main.htm |
| (CCSSE) Community College Survey of Student Engagement | All enrolled students- given during randomly selected classes | A tool for assessing quality in community college education. *CCSSE* results help colleges focus on good educational practice — defined as practice that promotes high levels of student learning and retention — and identify areas in which community colleges can improve their programs and services for students. | http://www.ccsse.org/ |
| (CIRP) Freshman Survey | Entering Freshmen | The CIRP Freshman Survey is designed to be of immediate use to institutions. Participating institutions receive a detailed profile of their entering freshman class, as well as national normative data for students in similar types of institutions. | HERI - Cooperative Institutional Research Program http://www.gseis.ucla.edu/heri/freshman.html |
| (CSS) College Student Survey – Designed as a follow-up survey to the CIRP | UG enrolled students | The College Student Survey (CSS) helps institutions respond to the need for assessment and accountability data by providing information on a broad range of student outcomes. The CSS offers valuable feedback on your students' academic and campus life experiences. | HERI - Cooperative Institutional Research Program http://www.gseis.ucla.edu/heri/css.html |

| Student Attitudinal Survey Listing | | | |
|---|---|---|---|
| **Instrument Name** | **Survey Category** | **Purpose** | **Vendor** |
| (CRS) College Results Survey | Alumni | Identifies personal values, abilities, occupations, work skills, and participation in lifelong learning of college graduates. Uses alumni responses to establish a unique institutional profile | Peterson's http://www.petersons.com/ |
| (CSEQ) College Student Experiences Questionnaire | UG enrolled students | Assesses the quality of effort students expend in using the resources and opportunities provided by the institution for their learning and development | Center for Postsecondary Research and Planning, Indiana University http://www.indiana.edu/~cseq/csxq_about.html |
| (CSXQ) College Student Expectations Questionnaire | UG entering students | Assesses new students' expectations upon matriculation. Findings can be compared with student reports of their actual experiences as measured by the College Student Experiences (CSEQ) | Center for Postsecondary Research and Planning, Indiana University http://www.indiana.edu/~cseq/csxq_about.html |
| (FCPS) Freshman Class Profile Service | UG entering students | The Freshman Class Profile Service provides a comprehensive summary of a college's entering freshman class and a parallel description of ACT-tested students who were admitted but did not enroll. | ACT http://www.act.org/research/services/freshman/index.html |
| (NSSE) National Survey of Student Engagement | UG first-year and senior students | Designed to obtain, on an annual basis, information from scores of colleges and universities nationwide about student participation in programs and activities that institutions provide for their learning and personal development. | Indiana University Center for Postsecondary Research & Planning http://www.indiana.edu/~nsse/ |
| (PSAS) Program Self-Assessment Service and Graduate Program Self-Assessment Service (GPSA) | Students majoring in the program, recent graduates, and faculty members | The Program Self-Assessment Service (PSAS) is designed to help college and university programs carry out program review at the undergraduate level. Faculty members, students majoring in the program, and recent graduates have the opportunity to respond to questions grouped into 16 Program Characteristics. | ETS http://www.ets.org/hea/sas/psas.html |
| (SACQ) Student Adaptation to College Questionnaire | UG enrolled students | Helps determine how well a student is handling the demands of college. Assesses overall adjustment to college, as well as adjustment in four specific areas: Academic Adjustment/ Personal-Emotional Adjustment/ Social Adjustment/ Attachment (to the institution) | http://wbarratt.indstate.edu/dragon/saroi/sa-sacq.htm |
| (SOIS) Student Outcomes Information Survey | 6 surveys according to student type: Entering students, continuing students, former students, graduating students, recent alumni, and long-term alumni | Collects information about students' needs and reactions to their educational experiences | NCHEMS http://www.nchems.org/Surveys/sois.htm |
| (SSI) Student Satisfaction Inventory | UG enrolled students | First survey of its kind to measure student satisfaction **and** the importance of campus issues to students. | Noel-Levitz http://www.noellevitz.com/NLCOM/Our+Services/Retention/Tools |
| (YFCYS) Your First College Year Survey | First Year students | Designed as a follow-up survey to the CIRP Freshman Survey. Assesses student development during the first year of college. | Higher Education Research Institute, UCLA Graduate School of Education and Information Studies http://www.gseis.ucla.edu/heri/yfcy/index.html |

## General Information for Entire ACT 17 Survey Instruments for Postsecondary Students and Alumni

| Survey Name<br>Act Survey Services – Assessment for Postsecondary Students and Alumni | Vendor<br>ACT – ESS Evaluation Survey Services |
|---|---|

| Brief Description |
|---|
| For Individual Survey information – see follow-up pages.<br><br>ACT's Evaluation Survey Services (ESS) can help postsecondary institutions obtain comprehensive information about their students' attitudes, opinions, needs, and development. |

| Norm Group | Intended Audience<br>Post secondary Students and Alumni |
|---|---|
| Postsecondary Students and/or Alumni at Institution | ACT offers 17 standardized instruments for use in postsecondary institutions:<br><br>- Adult Learner Needs Assessment Survey<br>- Alumni Outcomes Survey<br>- Alumni Survey (Four-year & Two-year College Form)<br>- College Outcomes Survey<br>- College Student Needs Assessment Survey<br>- Entering Student Survey<br>- Faces of the Future Survey<br>- Financial Aid Student Services Survey<br>- Student Opinion Survey (Four-year and Two-year College Form)<br>- Survey of Academic Advising<br>- Survey of Current Activities and Plans<br>- Survey of Postsecondary Educational Plans<br>- Survey of Student Opinions<br>- Withdrawing/Nonreturning Student Survey (Long Form)<br>- Withdrawing/Nonreturning Student Survey (Short Form) |

| Address<br>Act Evaluation Survey Services<br>2727 Scott Blvd.<br>PO Box 1008<br>Iowa City, Iowa 52243-0168<br><br>Website<br>http://www.act.org/ess/postsec.html<br><br>Email<br>outcomes@act.org<br><br>Telephone<br>(319) 337-1053 | Cost<br>$17 per pack of 25. $1.00 per survey scanning fee and $70 handling/set-up fee (if reporting package is ordered, this fee is waived.)<br><br>**Basic Reporting Package** $200 includes Handling/Setup fee; Summary Report; Graphics Report; Normative Data Report<br>**Extended Reporting Package** $340 includes Basic plus 15-Subgroup Report and Data Diskette<br>**Extended Reporting Package for Student Opinion Survey** $410 (available only for Student Opinion Survey and 2-4-year college forms) includes Basic and Extended plus Statistical Comparison Report<br><br>**Reporting Services**<br>Summary Report $70<br>15-Subgroup Report $110<br>Graphics Report $80<br>Statistical Comparison Report $80<br>Data Diskette of scanned survey $45<br>Normative Data Report for individual surveys $45 |

**Attitudinal Assessment Survey**
**Adult Learner Needs Assessment Survey**

| Survey Name | Vendor |
|---|---|
| ACT- Adult Learner Needs Assessment Survey | ACT- ESS Evaluation Survey Services |

| Brief Description |
|---|
| Explores the perceived educational and personal needs of adult students at your institution, or of prospective adult students in the community. 25 minutes to complete |

| Example Questions | Intended Audience |
|---|---|
| Educational Plans and Preferences<br>Are you currently planning to continue your education?<br>10 categories<br>Personal and Educational Needs<br>For each of the items listed in this section, select the oval that best indicates your educational or personal needs:<br>Developing independence<br>Learning how to better concentrate - 66 items | -Postsecondary adult students at participating college or university<br>-Prospective adult students in the community |

| Option for Local Questions | Cost and Contact Information |
|---|---|
| Each survey also contains a section for up to 30 additional questions (which can be added by local personnel), a section for background and demographic information, and a place where students can write additional comments. | See ACT General Information Cover Sheet. |

| Norm Group | Standard Results |
|---|---|
| Normative data report provides user norms based on data from institutions that have used the survey. | A summary report contains summary statistics for the total group for each item on the survey.<br>15-Subgroup Report contains one page of data for every item on the instrument.<br>Data Diskette provides raw data. |

| Customized Results | Separate Peer Groups |
|---|---|
| Special consultation services and technical report preparation available on a contractual basis. | Subgroup and Summary Composite Reports-<br>Two or more institutions/campuses can administer the same ESS survey form and request that a report be produced for each institution and that a composite report containing the combined data for all participating institutions be produced. |

## Attitudinal Assessment Survey
## Alumni Outcomes Survey

| Survey Name | Vendor |
|---|---|
| ACT- Alumni Outcomes Survey | ACT- ESS Evaluation Survey Services |

| Brief Description |
|---|
| Assesses alumni's perceptions of your institution's impact on their personal and professional growth and development and provides a detailed employment and education history. 25 minutes to complete. |

| Example Questions | Intended Audience |
|---|---|
| Employment History and Experiences<br>In what field/major was your first, full-time job after completing your first program at this school?  8 categories<br>Educational Outcomes<br>Level of importance to you:<br>Developing original ideas and/or products. 19 items<br>Educational Experiences<br>Rate these factors:<br>High quality of academic programs. 7 categories<br>Activities and Organizations<br>Indicate your level of involvement:<br>Professional; religious – 11 items | Postsecondary alumni from the institution |

| Option for Local Questions | Cost and Contact Information |
|---|---|
| Each survey also contains a section for up to 30 additional questions (which can be added by local personnel), a section for background and demographic information, and a place where students can write additional comments. | See ACT General Information Cover Sheet. |

| Norm Group | Standard Results |
|---|---|
| Normative data report provides user norms based on data from institutions that have used the survey. | A summary report contains summary statistics for the total group for each item on the survey.<br>15-Subgroup Report contains one page of data for every item on the instrument.<br>Data Diskette provides raw data.<br>Graphics Report contains graphical information for selected demographic and Likert scale items for local data and in comparison with national user norms. |

| Customized Results | Separate Peer Groups |
|---|---|
| Special consultation services and technical report preparation available on a contractual basis | Subgroup and Summary Composite Reports-<br>Two or more institutions/campuses can administer the same ESS survey form and request that a report be produced for each institution and that a composite report containing the combined data for all participating institutions be produced. |

## Attitudinal Assessment Survey
## Alumni Survey (Four-year)

| Survey Name | Vendor |
|---|---|
| ACT- Alumni Survey (Four-year College Form) | ACT- ESS Evaluation Survey Services |

| Brief Description |
|---|
| Helps four-year institutions evaluate the impact of their programs, services, and experiences on students by assessing the perceptions of its graduates; also provides a detailed employment and education history. 25 minutes to complete. |

| Example Questions | Intended Audience |
|---|---|
| College Experiences<br>How much did your education at this college contribute to your personal growth in each of the following areas: Working independently – 24 items; 8 categories.<br><br>Employment History<br>How long did it take you to obtain your first fulltime job after leaving this college? 15 categories | Postsecondary alumni from a four-year institution. |

| Option for Local Questions | Cost and Contact Information |
|---|---|
| Each survey also contains a section for up to 30 additional questions (which can be added by local personnel), a section for background and demographic information, and a place where students can write additional comments. | See ACT General Information Cover Sheet. |

| Norm Group | Standard Results |
|---|---|
| Normative data report provides user norms based on data from institutions that have used the survey. | A summary report contains summary statistics for the total group for each item on the survey. 15-Subgroup Report contains one page of data for every item on the instrument. Data Diskette provides raw data. Graphics Report contains graphical information for selected demographic and Likert scale items for local data and in comparison with national user norms. |

| Customized Results | Separate Peer Groups |
|---|---|
| Special consultation services and technical report preparation available on a contractual basis | Subgroup and Summary Composite Reports-Two or more institutions/campuses can administer the same ESS survey form and request that a report be produced for each institution and that a composite report containing the combined data for all participating institutions be produced. |

## Attitudinal Assessment Survey
## Alumni Survey (Two-year)

| Survey Name | Vendor |
|---|---|
| ACT- Alumni Survey (Two-year College Form) | ACT- ESS Evaluation Survey Services |

| Brief Description |
|---|
| Helps two-year institutions evaluate the impact of their programs, services, and experiences on students by assessing the perceptions of its graduates; also provides a detailed employment and education history. 25 minutes to complete. |

| Example Questions | Intended Audience |
|---|---|
| Educational Experiences<br>What was your primary reason for attending this 2-year college? 10 categories<br><br>Employment History<br>How long did it take you to obtain your first full-time job after leaving this college? 15 categories | Postsecondary alumni from a two-year institution. |

| Option for Local Questions | Cost and Contact Information |
|---|---|
| Each survey also contains a section for up to 30 additional questions (which can be added by local personnel), a section for background and demographic information, and a place where students can write additional comments. | See ACT General Information Cover Sheet.. |

| Norm Group | Standard Results |
|---|---|
| Normative data report provides user norms based on data from institutions that have used the survey. | A summary report contains summary statistics for the total group for each item on the survey. 15-Subgroup Report contains one page of data for every item on the instrument. Data Diskette provides raw data. Graphics Report contains graphical information for selected demographic and Likert scale items for local data and in comparison with national user norms. |

| Customized Results | Separate Peer Groups |
|---|---|
| Special consultation services and technical report preparation available on a contractual basis | Subgroup and Summary Composite Reports- Two or more institutions/campuses can administer the same ESS survey form and request that a report be produced for each institution and that a composite report containing the combined data for all participating institutions be produced. |

**Attitudinal Assessment Survey**
**College Outcomes Survey**

| Survey Name | Vendor |
|---|---|
| ACT- College Outcomes Survey | ACT- ESS Evaluation Survey Services |

| Brief Description |
|---|
| Assesses enrolled students' perceptions of the importance of, progress toward, and college contribution to a variety of college outcomes; assesses satisfaction with selected aspects of the institution's programs and services. 30 minutes to complete. |

| Example Questions | Intended Audience |
|---|---|
| College Outcomes<br>Indicate level of importance:<br>Becoming an effective team or group member. 6 categories with 62 items<br>Satisfaction with Given Aspects of This College<br>Indicate level of importance:<br>Faculty respect for students; Quality of instruction<br>39 items<br>Your Experiences at This College<br>How large a contribution do you feel your educational experiences at this college have made to your growth and preparation in the following areas: 6 items | Postsecondary students enrolled at institution |
| **Option for Local Questions**<br>Each survey also contains a section for up to 30 additional questions (which can be added by local personnel), a section for background and demographic information, and a place where students can write additional comments. | **Cost and Contact Information**<br><br>See ACT General Information Cover Sheet. |

| Norm Group | Standard Results |
|---|---|
| Normative data report provides user norms based on data from institutions that have used the survey. | A summary report contains summary statistics for the total group for each item on the survey.<br>15-Subgroup Report contains one page of data for every item on the instrument.<br>Data Diskette provides raw data.<br>Graphics Report contains graphical information for selected demographic and Likert scale items for local data and in comparison with national user norms. |

| Customized Results | Separate Peer Groups |
|---|---|
| Special consultation services and technical report preparation available on a contractual basis | Subgroup and Summary Composite Reports-<br>Two or more institutions/campuses can administer the same ESS survey form and request that a report be produced for each institution and that a composite report containing the combined data for all participating institutions be produced. |

**Attitudinal Assessment Survey**
**College Student Needs Assessment Survey**

| Survey Name | Vendor |
|---|---|
| ACT- College Student Needs Assessment Survey | ACT- ESS Evaluation Survey Services |

| Brief Description |
|---|
| Helps identify the perceived personal and educational needs of students enrolled at your institution. 20 minutes to complete. |

| Example Questions | Intended Audience |
|---|---|
| Career and Life Goals<br>Indicate how important it is to you to accomplish each of the following career and life goals:<br>To have a steady, secure job. 20 items<br><br>Educational and Personal Needs<br>Indicate how much help you need in each of the following educational and personal areas<br>Deciding what to do with my life; Identifying career areas that fit my current skills. 59 items | Postsecondary students enrolled at institution. |

| Option for Local Questions | Cost and Contact Information |
|---|---|
| Each survey also contains a section for up to 30 additional questions (which can be added by local personnel), a section for background and demographic information, and a place where students can write additional comments. | See ACT General Information Cover Sheet. |

| Norm Group | Standard Results |
|---|---|
| Normative data report provides user norms based on data from institutions that have used the survey. | A summary report contains summary statistics for the total group for each item on the survey.<br>15-Subgroup Report contains one page of data for every item on the instrument.<br>Data Diskette provides raw data.<br>Graphics Report contains graphical information for selected demographic and Likert scale items for local data and in comparison with national user norms. |

| Customized Results | Separate Peer Groups |
|---|---|
| Special consultation services and technical report preparation available on a contractual basis | Subgroup and Summary Composite Reports-<br>Two or more institutions/campuses can administer the same ESS survey form and request that a report be produced for each institution and that a composite report containing the combined data for all participating institutions be produced. |

**Attitudinal Assessment Survey**
**Entering Student Survey**

| Survey Name | Vendor |
|---|---|
| ACT- Entering Student Survey | ACT- ESS Evaluation Survey Services |

| Brief Description |
|---|
| Collects a variety of demographic, background, and educational information about the institution's students as they enter school. 20 minutes to complete. |

| Example Questions | Intended Audience |
|---|---|
| Educational Plans and Preferences<br>Indicate whether each of the following was a major, minor, or not a reason for continuing your education:<br>To become a better educated person. 9 categories<br>College Impressions<br>How important was each of the following in your decision to attend this college:<br>Academic reputation of the college. 5 categories with 37 items | Postsecondary students entering institution. |

| Option for Local Questions | Cost and Contact Information |
|---|---|
| Each survey also contains a section for up to 30 additional questions (which can be added by local personnel), a section for background and demographic information, and a place where students can write additional comments. | See ACT General Information Cover Sheet. |

| Norm Group | Standard Results |
|---|---|
| Normative data report provides user norms based on data from institutions that have used the survey. | A summary report contains summary statistics for the total group for each item on the survey.<br>15-Subgroup Report contains one page of data for every item on the instrument.<br>Data Diskette provides raw data.<br>Graphics Report contains graphical information for selected demographic and Likert scale items for local data and in comparison with national user norms. |

| Customized Results | Separate Peer Groups |
|---|---|
| Special consultation services and technical report preparation available on a contractual basis | Subgroup and Summary Composite Reports-<br>Two or more institutions/campuses can administer the same ESS survey form and request that a report be produced for each institution and that a composite report containing the combined data for all participating institutions be produced. |

## Attitudinal Assessment Survey
## Faces of the Future Survey

| Survey Name<br>ACT- Faces of the Future Survey | Vendor<br>ACT- ESS Evaluation Survey Services |
|---|---|
| **Brief Description**<br>Collects a variety of information from community college credit and noncredit students, as well as their assessments of the institution's programs, services, and climate. 25 minutes to complete. | |
| **Example Questions**<br>Employment Background<br>How many jobs do you currently hold?  8 categories<br><br>Educational Background<br>What is the highest academic degree you have earned? 10 categories<br><br>Current College Experience<br>On a scale of 1-5 how much have your experiences at this college contributed to your growth in each of the following areas:<br>Enriching my intellectual life. 3 categories | **Intended Audience**<br>Students enrolled at community college, both credit and noncredit students. |
| **Option for Local Questions**<br>Each survey also contains a section for up to 10 additional questions (which can be added by local personnel), a section for background and demographic information, and a place where students can write additional comments. | **Cost and Contact Information**<br><br>See ACT General Information Cover Sheet. |
| **Norm Group**<br><br>Normative data report provides user norms based on data from institutions that have used the survey. | **Standard Results**<br>A summary report contains summary statistics for the total group for each item on the survey.<br>15-Subgroup Report contains one page of data for every item on the instrument.<br>Data Diskette provides raw data.<br>Graphics Report contains graphical information for selected demographic and Likert scale items for local data and in comparison with national user norms. |
| **Customized Results**<br>Special consultation services and technical report preparation available on a contractual basis | **Separate Peer Groups**<br>Subgroup and Summary Composite Reports-<br>Two or more institutions/campuses can administer the same ESS survey form and request that a report be produced for each institution and that a composite report containing the combined data for all participating institutions be produced. |

## Attitudinal Assessment Survey
## Financial Aid Student Services Survey

| Survey Name | Vendor |
|---|---|
| ACT- Financial Aid Student Services Survey | ACT- ESS Evaluation Survey Services |

| Brief Description |
|---|
| Addresses the informational needs of the financial aid office. 20 minutes to complete. |

| Example Questions | Intended Audience |
|---|---|
| Financial Aid Background Information<br>When did you first initiate or file a financial aid application at this college? 3 categories<br>Financial Aid Services<br>Based on your experiences at this college, to what extent do you agree or disagree with each of the following statements:<br>I found the Financial Aid counselor to be friendly and easy to talk with. 5 categories | Postsecondary students at institution -- Financial aid information. |

| Option for Local Questions | Cost and Contact Information |
|---|---|
| Each survey also contains a section for up to 30 additional questions (which can be added by local personnel), a section for background and demographic information, and a place where students can write additional comments. | See ACT General Information Cover Sheet. |

| Norm Group | Standard Results |
|---|---|
| Normative data report provides user norms based on data from institutions that have used the survey. | A summary report contains summary statistics for the total group for each item on the survey.<br>15-Subgroup Report contains one page of data for every item on the instrument.<br>Data Diskette provides raw data. |

| Customized Results | Separate Peer Groups |
|---|---|
| Special consultation services and technical report preparation available on a contractual basis | Subgroup and Summary Composite Reports-<br>Two or more institutions/campuses can administer the same ESS survey form and request that a report be produced for each institution and that a composite report containing the combined data for all participating institutions be produced. |

## Attitudinal Assessment Survey
## Student Opinion Survey (Four-year)

| Survey Name | Vendor |
| --- | --- |
| ACT- Student Opinion Survey (Four-year College Form) | ACT- ESS Evaluation Survey Services |

| Brief Description |
| --- |
| Explores enrolled students satisfaction with programs, services, and other aspects of their college experience. 20 minutes to complete. This survey is also available in a web-based version. |

| Example Questions | Intended Audience |
| --- | --- |
| College Services<br>For each service listed below, indicate its level of importance to you:<br>Academic advising; Career planning - 23 items.<br>College Environment<br>Indicate your level of satisfaction with:<br>Testing/grading system; Course content in your major field - 42 items. | Postsecondary students at four-year institution<br>Satisfaction with:<br>Programs<br>Services<br>Other aspects of college experience |

| Option for Local Questions | Cost and Contact Information |
| --- | --- |
| Each survey also contains a section for up to 30 additional questions (which can be added by local personnel), a section for background and demographic information, and a place where students can write additional comments. | See ACT General Information Cover Sheet. |

| Norm Group | Standard Results |
| --- | --- |
| Normative data report provides user norms based on total scanned, survey question with rank and average. | A summary report contains summary statistics for the total group for each item on the survey.<br>15-Subgroup Report contains one page of data for every item on the instrument.<br>Data Diskette provides raw data.<br>Graphics Report contains graphical information for selected demographic and Likert scale items for local data and in comparison with national user norms. |

| Customized Results | Separate Peer Groups |
| --- | --- |
| Special consultation services and technical report preparation available on a contractual basis | Subgroup and Summary Composite Reports-<br>Two or more institutions/campuses can administer the same ESS survey form and request that a report be produced for each institution and that a composite report containing the combined data for all participating institutions be produced.<br><br>Statistical comparison report provides statistical comparisons between local survey results and those for comparable institutions from the national user norms. |

**Attitudinal Assessment Survey**
**Student Opinion Survey (Two-year)**

| Survey Name | Vendor |
|---|---|
| ACT- Student Opinion Survey (Two-year College Form) | ACT- ESS Evaluation Survey Services |

| Brief Description |
|---|
| Explores enrolled students satisfaction with programs, services, and other aspects of their college experience. 20 minutes to complete. This survey is also available in a web-based version. |

| Example Questions | Intended Audience |
|---|---|
| College Impressions<br>What is your overall impression of the quality of education at this 2-year college – 4 categories with 32 items<br>College Services<br>Indicate whether or not you have used the service and level of satisfaction:<br>Academic advising/course planning services- 20 items<br>College Environment<br>Mark your level of satisfaction with:<br>Testing-grading system - 44 items | Postsecondary students at two-year institution. Satisfaction with:<br>Programs<br>Services<br>Other aspects of college experience |
| **Option for Local Questions**<br>Each survey also contains a section for up to 30 additional questions (which can be added by local personnel), a section for background and demographic information, and a place where students can write additional comments. | **Cost and Contact Information**<br><br>See ACT General Information Cover Sheet. |
| **Norm Group**<br><br>Normative data report provides user norms based on total scanned, survey question with rank and average. | **Standard Results**<br>A summary report contains summary statistics for the total group for each item on the survey.<br>15-Subgroup Report contains one page of data for every item on the instrument.<br>Data Diskette provides raw data.<br>Graphics Report contains graphical information for selected demographic and Likert scale items for local data and in comparison with national user norms. |
| **Customized Results**<br>Special consultation services and technical report preparation available on a contractual basis | **Separate Peer Groups**<br>Subgroup and Summary Composite Reports-<br>Two or more institutions/campuses can administer the same ESS survey form and request that a report be produced for each institution and that a composite report containing the combined data for all participating institutions be produced.<br><br>Statistical comparison report provides statistical comparisons between local survey results and those for comparable institutions from the national user norms. |

## Attitudinal Assessment Survey
## Survey of Academic Advising

| Survey Name | Vendor |
|---|---|
| ACT- Survey of Academic Advising | ACT- ESS Evaluation Survey Services |

| Brief Description |
|---|
| Obtains students' impressions of the institution's academic advising services. 20 minutes to complete. |

| Example Questions | Intended Audience |
|---|---|
| **Advising Information** <br> How well does the academic advising system currently offered by this institution meet your needs?  4 categories <br> **Academic Advising Needs** <br> Indicate whether or not you and your current advisor have discussed the following and your satisfaction: My academic progress. 18 items <br> **Impressions of Your Advisor** <br> Level of agreement with the following items: Expresses interest in me as a unique individual. 36 items <br> **Additional Advising Information** <br> Have you changed advisors since enrolling in this institution? 5 categories | Postsecondary students at institution. |

| Option for Local Questions | Cost and Contact Information |
|---|---|
| Each survey also contains a section for up to 30 additional questions (which can be added by local personnel), a section for background and demographic information, and a place where students can write additional comments. | See ACT General Information Cover Sheet. |

| Norm Group | Standard Results |
|---|---|
| Normative data report provides user norms based on data from institutions that have used the survey. | A summary report contains summary statistics for the total group for each item on the survey. <br> 15-Subgroup Report contains one page of data for every item on the instrument. <br> Data Diskette provides raw data. <br> Graphics Report contains graphical information for selected demographic and Likert scale items for local data and in comparison with national user norms. |

| Customized Results | Separate Peer Groups |
|---|---|
| Special consultation services and technical report preparation available on a contractual basis | Subgroup and Summary Composite Reports- Two or more institutions/campuses can administer the same ESS survey form and request that a report be produced for each institution and that a composite report containing the combined data for all participating institutions be produced. |

**Attitudinal Assessment Survey**
**Survey of Current Activities and Plans**

| Survey Name | Vendor |
|---|---|
| ACT- Survey of Current Activities and Plans | ACT- ESS Evaluation Survey Services |

| Brief Description |
|---|
| Identifies why prospective students accepted for admission chose not to matriculate. 25 minutes to complete. |

| Example Questions | Intended Audience |
|---|---|
| Impressions of This College<br>Indicate your level of agreement with each statement about this college:<br>Has high-quality academic programs. 8 categories<br>Educational Plans and Activities<br>How would you describe the institution you are now attending? 7 categories<br>Employment Plans<br>If you are employed full-time or part-time or are self-employed, indicate your area of employment. 4 categories | Prospective postsecondary students at institution. |

| Option for Local Questions | Cost and Contact Information |
|---|---|
| Each survey also contains a section for up to 30 additional questions (which can be added by local personnel), a section for background and demographic information, and a place where students can write additional comments. | See ACT General Information Cover Sheet. |

| Norm Group | Standard Results |
|---|---|
| Normative data report provides user norms based on data from institutions that have used the survey. | A summary report contains summary statistics for the total group for each item on the survey.<br>15-Subgroup Report contains one page of data for every item on the instrument.<br>Data Diskette provides raw data. |

| Customized Results | Separate Peer Groups |
|---|---|
| Special consultation services and technical report preparation available on a contractual basis | Subgroup and Summary Composite Reports-<br>Two or more institutions/campuses can administer the same ESS survey form and request that a report be produced for each institution and that a composite report containing the combined data for all participating institutions be produced. |

## Attitudinal Assessment Survey
## Survey of Postsecondary Educational Plans

| Survey Name | Vendor |
|---|---|
| ACT- Survey of Postsecondary Educational Plans | ACT- ESS Evaluation Survey Services |

| Brief Description |
|---|
| Identifies the educational plans and preferences of prospective students while they are still enrolled in secondary school. 20 minutes to complete. |

| Example Questions | Intended Audience |
|---|---|
| Occupational Plans after High School<br>How well do you feel your high school is preparing your for your chosen occupation? 4 questions<br>Educational Plans after High School<br>Which type of postsecondary school do you prefer to attend? 11 questions<br>Impressions of This College<br>This college has high-quality academic programs.  24 questions. | Prospective postsecondary students still in secondary school. |

| Option for Local Questions | Cost and Contact Information |
|---|---|
| Each survey also contains a section for up to 30 additional questions (which can be added by local personnel), a section for background and demographic information, and a place where students can write additional comments. | See ACT General Information Cover Sheet. |

| Norm Group | Standard Results |
|---|---|
| Normative data report provides user norms based on data from institutions that have used the survey. | A summary report contains summary statistics for the total group for each item on the survey.<br>15-Subgroup Report contains one page of data for every item on the instrument.<br>Data Diskette provides raw data. |

| Customized Results | Separate Peer Groups |
|---|---|
| Special consultation services and technical report preparation available on a contractual basis | Subgroup and Summary Composite Reports-<br>Two or more institutions/campuses can administer the same ESS survey form and request that a report be produced for each institution and that a composite report containing the combined data for all participating institutions be produced. |

## Attitudinal Assessment Survey
## Survey of Student Opinions

| Survey Name | Vendor |
|---|---|
| ACT- Survey of Student Opinions | ACT- ESS Evaluation Survey Services |

| Brief Description |
|---|
| Assesses students' perceptions of the importance of, and satisfaction with, a full range of programs, services, and environmental factors at the college they are attending. Also included are an extended set of background items and a set of items related to students' impressions of, and experiences at, the college. 30 minutes to complete. |

| Example Questions | Intended Audience |
|---|---|
| College Services<br>Indicate level of importance for:<br>Academic Advising – 21items<br>Aspects of College Environment<br>Indicate level of importance for:<br>Testing grading system – 43 items<br>College Impressions<br>Indicate the extent to which you agree with the following statements:<br>If you could start college all over, would you choose to attend this college? 4 categories | Postsecondary students at institution. |

| Option for Local Questions | Cost and Contact Information |
|---|---|
| Each survey also contains a section for up to 30 additional questions (which can be added by local personnel), a section for background and demographic information, and a place where students can write additional comments. | See ACT General Information Cover Sheet. |

| Norm Group | Standard Results |
|---|---|
| Normative data report provides user norms based on data from institutions that have used the survey. | A summary report contains summary statistics for the total group for each item on the survey. 15-Subgroup Report contains one page of data for every item on the instrument. Data Diskette provides raw data. |

| Customized Results | Separate Peer Groups |
|---|---|
| Special consultation services and technical report preparation available on a contractual basis | Subgroup and Summary Composite Reports- Two or more institutions/campuses can administer the same ESS survey form and request that a report be produced for each institution and that a composite report containing the combined data for all participating institutions be produced. |

## Attitudinal Assessment Survey
## Withdrawing/Nonreturning Students (Long Form)

| Survey Name | Vendor |
|---|---|
| ACT- Withdrawing/Nonreturning Students (Long Form) | ACT- ESS Evaluation Survey Services |

| Brief Description |
|---|
| Provides an in-depth look at students' reasons for leaving college before completing a degree or certificate program. 20 minutes to complete. |

| Example Questions | Intended Audience |
|---|---|
| Reasons for Leaving This College<br>Learned all I wanted to learn at this time- 48 items<br><br>College Services and Characteristics<br>Indicate your level of satisfaction with: Job placement services. 46 items | Postsecondary students at institution who withdrew or did not return. |

| Option for Local Questions | Cost and Contact Information |
|---|---|
| Each survey also contains a section for up to 30 additional questions (which can be added by local personnel), a section for background and demographic information, and a place where students can write additional comments. | See ACT General Information Cover Sheet. |

| Norm Group | Standard Results |
|---|---|
| Normative data report provides user norms based on data from institutions that have used the survey. | A summary report contains summary statistics for the total group for each item on the survey.<br>15-Subgroup Report contains one page of data for every item on the instrument.<br>Data Diskette provides raw data. |

| Customized Results | Separate Peer Groups |
|---|---|
| Special consultation services and technical report preparation available on a contractual basis | Subgroup and Summary Composite Reports-<br>Two or more institutions/campuses can administer the same ESS survey form and request that a report be produced for each institution and that a composite report containing the combined data for all participating institutions be produced. |

**Attitudinal Assessment Survey**
**Withdrawing/Nonreturning Students (Short Form)**

| Survey Name | Vendor |
|---|---|
| ACT- Withdrawing/Nonreturning Students (Short Form) | ACT- ESS Evaluation Survey Services |

| Brief Description |
|---|
| Provides an in-depth look at students' reasons for leaving college before completing a degree or certificate program. 10 minutes to complete. |

| Example Questions | Intended Audience |
|---|---|
| Reasons for Leaving This College<br>Indicate the reason as major, minor, or not a reason:<br>Learned all I wanted to learn at this time.<br>Wanted a break from my college studies. 48 items | Postsecondary students at institution who withdrew or did not return. |

| Option for Local Questions | Cost and Contact Information |
|---|---|
| 20 optional questions | See ACT General Information Cover Sheet. |

| Norm Group | Standard Results |
|---|---|
| Normative data report provides user norms based on data from institutions that have used the survey. | A summary report contains summary statistics for the total group for each item on the survey.<br>15-Subgroup Report contains one page of data for every item on the instrument.<br>Data Diskette provides raw data. |

| Customized Results | Separate Peer Groups |
|---|---|
| Special consultation services and technical report preparation available on a contractual basis | Subgroup and Summary Composite Reports-<br>Two or more institutions/campuses can administer the same ESS survey form and request that a report be produced for each institution and that a composite report containing the combined data for all participating institutions be produced. |

## Attitudinal Assessment Survey
## Adult Learner Survey

| Survey Name | Vendor |
|---|---|
| Adult Learner Survey | Noel-Levitz |

| Brief Description | |
|---|---|
| Assessment for adult students completing undergraduate programs. It is a Web-based survey that shows how satisfied your students are and what's most important to them. | |

| Example Questions | Intended Audience |
|---|---|
| | Adult UG students |

| Option for Local Questions | Cost |
|---|---|
| | $125 processing and setup fee plus $1.65-$2.10 per survey depending on how many ordered.<br>Optional:<br>Comparison Report $75<br>Target report $45<br>Data CD $125 |

| Norm Group | Standard Results |
|---|---|
| | |

| Customized Results | Separate Peer Groups |
|---|---|
| | |

| Address | Website |
|---|---|
| | http://www.noellevitz.com/NLCOM/Our+Services/Retention/Tools/ |

## Attitudinal Assessment Survey
## Adult Student Priorities Survey

| Survey Name | Vendor |
| --- | --- |
| ASPS - Adult Student Priorities Survey | Noel-Levitz |

| Brief Description | |
| --- | --- |
| Ratings on importance of and satisfaction with various aspects of campus. The survey is specific to the experience of adult students 25 years and older. Takes 25-30 minutes. Paper and web version. | |

| Example Questions | Intended Audience |
| --- | --- |
| The content of the courses within my major is valuable.<br>Importance to me rate 1-7; Level of satisfaction rate<br>1-7.<br><br>I am able to register for classes by personal computer, fax or telephone.  Importance to me rate 1-7; Level of satisfaction rate<br>1-7. | For graduate students, continuing education students, and evening/weekend learners. Measures satisfaction of students age 25 and older. |

| Option for Local Questions | Cost |
| --- | --- |
| None | $125 processing and setup fee plus $1.65-$2.10 per survey depending on how many ordered.<br>Optional:<br>Comparison Report $75<br>Target report $45<br>Data CD $125 |

| Norm Group | Standard Results |
| --- | --- |
| Adult learners 25 years of age and older | The standard campus report includes the mean data for all students alongside national averages. The national comparison group includes data from four-year and two-year institutions and is updated twice a year. |

| Customized Results | Separate Peer Groups |
| --- | --- |
| You can request customized benchmark comparison scores by region or for a hand-picked set of institutions. | Results are compared with scores from a national database along with institution's student scores. |

| Address | Website |
| --- | --- |
| Noel-Levitz<br>Noel-Levitz Office Park<br>2101 ACT Circle<br>Iowa City, IA 52245-9910 | http://www.noellevitz.com/NLCOM/Our+Services/Retention/Tools/ |

| Telephone | Email |
| --- | --- |
| 1-800-876-1117 | info@noellevitz.com |

## Attitudinal Assessment Survey
## Admitted Student Questionnaire

| Survey Name<br>ASQ – Admitted Student Questionnaire | Vendor<br>The College Board |
|---|---|
| **Brief Description**<br>Studies admitted students' perceptions of their institution and its admissions process. Paper and web version available. | |

| Example Questions<br>Including our college, to how many institutions did you apply?<br><br>Including our college, to how many of these institutions were you admitted?<br><br>Were you offered financial aid by any college? | Intended Audience<br><br>Admitted students at institution assessment of:  programs, admissions procedures, literature, institutional image, financial aid packages, common acceptances, comparative evaluations. |
|---|---|
| Option for Local Questions<br><br>Yes- additional $250 fee for paper; or $475 for web | Cost<br>ASQ $675; ASQ Plus $1000.<br>Questionnaire Printing Fee: ASQ $.61 per form; ASQ Plus $.66 per form. Min. order $250/$275<br>Processing Fee: ASQ $2.10 per form returned-$1.85 web; ASQ Plus $2.55 per form returned- $2.30 web.<br>Additional $200 fee for web version. |
| Norm Group<br><br>Norms report with national data for admitted students at institutions. Facilitates competitor and overlap comparisons. | Standard Results<br><br>Highlight Report (executive summary), detailed report with all data, data file also available. |
| Customized Results<br>ASQ Plus provides specific institutional comparisons. ID for Tracking is Available | Separate Peer Groups<br>Highlights and detailed reports can be ordered for subgroups of students. |
| Address<br>Admitted Student Questionnaire<br>The College Board<br>11911 Freedom Dr., Ste. 300<br>Reston, VA 20190-5602 | Website<br><br>http://www.collegeboard.org/aes/asq/html/index000.html |
| Telephone<br><br>Phone:  (800) 626-9795<br>Fax: (703) 707-5599 | Email<br><br>enrollmentsolutions@collegeboard.org |

## Attitudinal Assessment Survey
## Comprehensive Alumni Assessment Survey

| Survey Name | Vendor |
|---|---|
| CAAS – Comprehensive Alumni Assessment Survey | NCHEMS—SOIS Student Outcomes Information Services |

**Brief Description**

NCHEMS Comprehensive Alumni Assessment Survey (CAAS), in both two and four-year versions, measures evidence of institutional effectiveness and reports on alumni personal development and career preparation.

| Example Questions | Intended Audience |
|---|---|
| What is your current employment status? Was your first job related to your major field of study at our college? Your current job? | Alumni from 2 or 4-year institution. Questions cover: Employment and continuing education; undergraduate experience; development of intellect; achievement of community goals; personal development and enrichment; community participation; demographic and background information. |
| **Option for Local Questions**<br><br>Up to 20 local questions are available for a data entry fee of $1.25 per question. | **Cost**<br>$.85 per questionnaire plus shipping and handling. $200 for analysis (includes one analytical report)<br><br>Additional copies of Analytical Report--$20.00 each<br>Flat ASCII file containing your institutional data on tape or diskette--$75.00<br>SPSS portable file on tape or diskette--$75.00<br>Both the Flat ASCII file and SPSS portable file--$100.00 |
| **Norm Group**<br><br>Alumni at institution. No national data available. | **Standard Results**<br>Analytical report with data diskette available. Helps clarify the institutional mission and goals and even assist in the development of new institutional goals as they are identified by the graduates. |
| **Customized Results**<br>Local questions analyzed with the entire instrument. | **Separate Peer Groups**<br>No- only alumni from the institution. |
| **Address**<br><br>NCHEMS - SOIS<br>P.O. Box 9752<br>Boulder, CO 80301-9752 | **Website**<br><br>http://www.nchems.org/surveys/caas.htm |
| **Telephone**<br><br>(303) 497-0390<br>Fax: (303) 497-0338 | **Email**<br><br>info@nechems.org |

## Attitudinal Assessment Survey
## Community College Student Experiences Questionnaire

| Survey Name | Vendor |
|---|---|
| CCSEQ – Community College Student Experiences Questionnaire | Indiana University Center for Postsecondary Research and Planning |

| Brief Description |
|---|
| Community college version of CSEQ. A versatile tool that assesses the quality of effort students expend in using the resources and opportunities provided by the community college for their learning and development. Takes 20 minutes or less. |

| Example Questions | Intended Audience |
|---|---|
| "In your experience at this institution during the current school year, about how often have your done each of the following?" Completed the assigned readings for class; talked with your instructor about information related to a course you were taking<br><br>"In thinking about your college or university experience up to now, to what extend to you feel you have gained or made progress in the following areas?" Acquiring knowledge and skills applicable to a specific job or type of work; Understanding yourself, your abilities, interests, and personality | Students enrolled in community college. Focuses on four elements: (1) Who are the community college students and why are they attending the community college? (2) Which facilities and opportunities at the community college to students use productively and extensively? (3) What are the students' impressions of the community college? (4) What progress have students made toward their important goals? |

| Option for Local Questions | Cost |
|---|---|
| Up to 20 additional questions. | Test Manual: $12 each<br>Instrument cost per form: Paper- $0.75<br>Scanning/Processing per form: Paper- $1.50<br>$125 for print report and data on diskette |

| Norm Group | Standard Results |
|---|---|
| Administered to part-time and full-time students; to traditional and non-traditional students; to students whose aim is to transfer to a four-year institution, to seek a degree, or to acquire training for a specialized job or occupation. | A diskette which contains institution data; a frequency distribution readable by SPSS is prepared for the data. In addition, hard copies of two reports: a frequency distribution of the data and any identification numbers the students have selected. |

| Customized Results | Separate Peer Groups |
|---|---|
| Consultation and additional analyses available at reasonable rates. The *CCSEQ Test Manual and Comparative Data* publication also reports statistical analyses of the measures used in the CCSEQ Instrument. | Results can be compared with the normative scores and percentages reported in the ***CCSEQ Test Manual and Comparative Data***. This publication contains the responses of over 18,000 students from over 60 community colleges. |

| Address | Website |
|---|---|
| Center for the Study of Higher Education<br>The University of Memphis<br>308 Browning Hall<br>Memphis, TN 38152 | http://www.people.memphis.edu/coe_cshe/CCSEQ_main.htm |

| Telephone | Email |
|---|---|
| (901) 678-2775<br>Fax: (901) 678-4291 | ccseqlib@memphis.edu |

## Attitudinal Assessment Survey
## Community College Survey of Student Engagement

| Survey Name | Vendor |
|---|---|
| CCSSE – Community College Survey of Student Engagement | Community College Leadership Program at The University of Texas at Austin |

| Brief Description |
|---|
| The survey is administered directly to community college students at *CCSSE* member colleges during randomly selected classes. The survey asks questions about institutional practices and student behaviors that are highly correlated with student learning and retention.  Can be taken online also. |

| Example Questions | Intended Audience |
|---|---|
| In your experiences at this college during the current school year, about how often have you done each of the following? (20 questions – see sample) <br> 1=Never; 2=Sometimes; 3=Often; 4=Very often <br> -Asked questions in class or contributed to class discussions <br> -Made a class presentation <br><br> Which of the following have you done, are you doing, or do you plan to do while attending this college? (11 questions— see sample). 1=I Have Not Done, Nor Plan To Do; 2=I Plan To Do; 3=I Have Done <br> -Internship, field experience, co-op experience, or clinical assignment <br> -Coursework in a foreign language other than English | Students enrolled at community college. Asks students about their college experiences — how they spend their time; what they feel they have gained from their classes; how they assess the quality of their interactions with faculty, counselors, and peers; what kinds of work they are challenged to do; how the college supports their learning; and other important indicators. |

| Option for Local Questions | Cost |
|---|---|
| None | Enrollment less than 1,500 (call for more information) <br> Enrollment 1,500–4,499  $4,500 <br> Enrollment 4,500–7,999  $6,000 <br> Enrollment 8,000–14,999  $7,500 <br> Enrollment 15,000 or more $9,000 <br><br> Upon request, the college's sample size can be increased at a cost of $2 per student surveyed if administration is managed by CCSSE or $1.50 per student if the survey is administered by the college. |

| Norm Group | Standard Results |
|---|---|
| -Frequencies and means for the items that make up each benchmark. <br> -Frequencies and means for all other survey items. <br> - Compares performance of like institutions | -An institutional profile of survey results <br> -Aggregated comparative data for similar colleges <br> -National benchmarks <br> -The complete electronic data file of your students' responses, for use in your own institutional research |

| Customized Results | Separate Peer Groups |
|---|---|
| Results are public, and they are presented for the full *CCSSE* population, various subgroups within the full population, and individual colleges.* Beginning in fall 2003, results will include national benchmarks and institutional benchmark scores for five key areas of engagement. | Comparative data for similar colleges. |

| Address | Website |
|---|---|
| Community College Survey of Student Engagement <br> The University of Texas at Austin <br> 2609 University Avenue <br> Building UA9, Suite 3.104 <br> Austin, TX 78712 | www.ccsse.org |

| Telephone | Email |
|---|---|
| Telephone: (512) 471-6807 <br> Fax: (512) 471-4209 | info@ccsse.org |

## Attitudinal Assessment Survey
## CIRP Freshman Survey

| Survey Name | Vendor |
|---|---|
| CIRP Freshman Survey | Higher Education Research Institute, UCLA - Cooperative Institutional Research Program |

| Brief Description |
|---|
| The CIRP Freshman Survey is administered to first-time, full-time freshmen, part-time and transfer students at participating institutions. The survey provides important data that is useful in a variety of program and policy areas: admissions and recruitment; academic program development and review; institutional self-study and accreditation activities; public relations and development; institutional research and assessment; retention studies; and longitudinal research about the impacts of campus policies and programs. |

| Example Questions | Intended Audience |
|---|---|
| Is this college your: First Choice; Second Choice; Third Choice; Less than third choice<br><br>What is the highest academic degree you intend to obtain: Mark Highest Planned and Highest Planned at This College- None; Vocational certificate; Associate; Bachelor's degree; Master's degree; Ph.D. or Ed.D; MD/DO/DDS/DVM; LLB/JD; BD OR M.DIV; Other | Entering students at university or college. Questions cover:<br>- Demographic characteristics<br>- Expectations of the college experience<br>- Secondary school experiences<br>- Degree goals and career plans<br>- College finances<br>- Attitudes, values, and life goals<br>- Reasons for attending college |

| Option for Local Questions | Cost |
|---|---|
| None | Participation fee of $400 plus $1.50 per returned survey up to 1000, then $1.00 per survey<br>Data file- $75 + 0.10 per student record<br>Report on Spreadsheet- $15 per report<br>Additional Comparison Groups- $5 per each group up to four |

| Norm Group | Standard Results |
|---|---|
| Although the normative data provided with the institutional reports are based on the population of first-time, full-time freshmen, participating institutions also receive separate reports for their part-time and transfer students. Survey questions are benchmarked against similar schools' results. | Participating institutions receive a detailed profile of their entering freshman class, as well as national normative data for students in similar types of institutions. Provides an in-depth profile of freshmen men, women and all freshmen, plus separate profiles of transfer and part-time students. |

| Customized Results | Separate Peer Groups |
|---|---|
| Participating campuses can obtain supplemental reports profiling students by various subgroups (for example, by intended major or career, by academic ability, by home state) as part of the basic participation costs. Data file and spreadsheet reports available. | National normative data for students in other similar types of institutions. |

| Address | Website |
|---|---|
| Higher Education Research Institute<br>UCLA -- CIRP<br>3005 Moore Hall - Box 951521<br>Los Angeles, Ca 90095-1521 | www.gseis.ucla.edu/heri/cirp |

| Telephone | Email |
|---|---|
| (310) 825-1925<br>(310) 206-2228 (fax) | heri@ucla.edu |

## Attitudinal Assessment Survey
## College Results Survey

| Survey Name | Vendor |
|---|---|
| CRS - College Results Survey | Peterson's, a Thomson Learning Company |

| Brief Description |
|---|
| Identifies alumni personal values, abilities, occupations, work skills, and participation in lifelong learning of college graduates. Web-based survey comprised of four sections: lifelong learning; personal values; confidence; occupation and income; and work skills. Takes 15 to 20 minutes to complete. |

| Example Questions | Intended Audience |
|---|---|
| How are you putting your degree to work?<br><br>Have you continued on for more school?<br><br>How has your life changed? | Alumni from bachelor-degree-granting institution, preferably four to 10 years following degree attainment. Alumni visit web site to complete survey. Institutions identify alumni cohorts, whom Peterson's then contacts and directs to the online instrument. |

| Option for Local Questions | Cost |
|---|---|
| | There is no respondent cost to complete the online CRS. |

| Norm Group | Standard Results |
|---|---|
| Alumni from institution. No national data available. | Uses alumni responses to establish a unique institutional profile.<br>Institutions receive data file of responses in spreadsheet format for analyses. |

| Customized Results | Separate Peer Groups |
|---|---|
| Models for working with individual institutions are under development.<br>Costs for institutional applications of the CRS are being explored as collaborative models are identified. | Analytic tools for peer comparisons have been developed and are available to participating institutions at a secure web site. |

| Address | Website |
|---|---|
| Peterson's, a Thomson Learning Company<br>Princeton Pike Corporate Center<br>2000 Lenox Drive<br>P.O. Box 67005<br>Lawrenceville, NJ 08648 | http://www.petersons.com/ |

| Telephone | Email |
|---|---|
| 800-338-3282 ext. 3250<br>Fax: 609-896-4535 | rocco.russo@petersons.com |

**Attitudinal Assessment Survey**
**College Student Experiences Questionnaire**

| Survey Name | Vendor |
|---|---|
| CSEQ - College Student Experiences Questionnaire | Indiana University Center for Postsecondary Research and Planning |

| Brief Description |
|---|
| A versatile tool that assesses the quality of effort students expend in using the resources and opportunities provided by the institution for their learning and development. Quality of effort is a key dimension for understanding student satisfaction, persistence, and the effects of attending college. The more students engage in educational activities the more they benefit in meaningful ways in their learning and development. Takes 20-30 minutes to complete. Available paper and online. |

| Example Questions | Intended Audience |
|---|---|
| "In your experience at this institution during the current school year, about how often have your done each of the following?" Completed the assigned readings for class; talked with your instructor about information related to a course you were taking<br><br>"In thinking about your college or university experience up to now, to what extend to you feel you have gained or made progress in the following areas?" Acquiring knowledge and skills applicable to a specific job or type of work; Understanding yourself, your abilities, interests, and personality | Undergraduate college students' experiences within institution. |

| Option for Local Questions | Cost |
|---|---|
| Online – additional questions, up to 20 | Administration fee: Paper or Online- $200<br>Instrument cost per form: Paper- $2.00; Online- $2.75<br>Online additional questions: $40 per question or $500 for a set of up to 20 questions.<br>Special Analysis per hour: $150<br>Student Advising Report: $500 |

| Norm Group | Standard Results |
|---|---|
| Frequencies and means listed for undergraduate students at institution for all survey questions.<br><br>If requested, frequencies and means compared with other institutions with the same Carnegie classification. | Report of frequencies and means for all survey questions. Codebook describing all survey questions, variable names, and response options<br>Currently available norms tables from national database<br>Disk containing raw data, SPSS Output, SPSS Syntax, and an electronic copy of the codebook |

| Customized Results | Separate Peer Groups |
|---|---|
| Special data analysis can be performed for institutions desiring information beyond the basic frequencies and descriptive statistics provided in the results package. | The *Student Advising Report* is an individualized display of CSEQ results showing a student's responses alongside the average responses of his or her peers.<br>Special data analysis compared with other institutions with the same Carnegie classification. |

| Address | Website |
|---|---|
| CSEQ Research Program<br>Center for Postsecondary Research<br>Indiana University<br>1900 East 10th Street<br>Eigenmann Hall 419<br>Bloomington, IN 47406-7512 | http://www.indiana.edu/cseq/ |

| Telephone | Email |
|---|---|
| (812) 856 – 5825 | cseq@indiana.edu |

**Attitudinal Assessment Survey**
**College Student Survey**

| Survey Name | Vendor |
|---|---|
| CSS - College Student Survey | Higher Education Research Institute, UCLA |

| Brief Description |
|---|
| The College Student Survey (CSS) provides valuable feedback on the institution's students' academic and campus life experiences--information that can be used for student assessment activities, accreditation and self-study reports, campus planning, and policy analysis. Takes approx. 45 minutes. |

| Example Questions | Intended Audience |
|---|---|
| Since entering college, indicate how often you: Worked on independent study projects; took interdisciplinary courses; discussed course content with students outside of class ... During the past year, how much time did you spend during a typical week doing the following activities: Studying/homework; attending classes; socializing with friends ... | Students enrolled at university or college. Covers: - Satisfaction with the college experience - Student involvement - Cognitive and affective development - Student values, attitudes, and goals - Degree aspirations and career plans - Internet, electronic mail, and other computer uses |

| Option for Local Questions | Cost |
|---|---|
| Optional questions can be used to gather data on topics of importance to individual campuses- up to 30 local questions. | Participation fee of $400 plus $1.50 per returned survey up to 1000, then $1.00 per survey Data file- $75 + 0.10 per student record Report on Spreadsheet- $15 per report Additional Comparison Groups- $5 per each group up to four |

| Norm Group | Standard Results |
|---|---|
| Students enrolled at university or college. | Printed report for students at the institution grouped by number of responses, gender, and by survey question. |

| Customized Results | Separate Peer Groups |
|---|---|
| *The CSS Campus Profile Report.* A report describing the results of the CSS for all respondents at your institution broken out by gender. Also included are comparative results for all schools similar to yours. *The CSS Longitudinal Report.* This report compares responses made on the CSS to responses students made as students (if available). *Data files.* A diskette containing individual item responses to the CSS (and Freshman Survey, if available) for each CSS respondent at your institution. *Reports on Spreadsheet.* Each report in your profile can be duplicated as an EXCEL or Lotus spreadsheet. *Special Breakout Reports.* Up to 190 sub-reports for separate groupings of students can be produced to your specifications. | *Special Comparison Reports.* This report permits you to compare your institution's responses to any two of the seven available comparison groups. *Consortium Reports.* The report shows aggregate profiles based on the CSS responses from five or more participating institutions. |

| Address | Website |
|---|---|
| Higher Education Research Institute UCLA-- CIRP 3005 Moore Hall - Box 951521 Los Angeles, Ca 90095-1521 | http://www.gseis.ucla.edu/heri/css.html |

| Telephone | Email |
|---|---|
| (310) 825-1925 (310) 206-2228 (fax) | heri@ucla.edu |

## Attitudinal Assessment Survey
## College Student Expectations Questionnaire

| Survey Name | Vendor |
|---|---|
| CSXQ - College Student Expectations Questionnaire | Center for Postsecondary Research and Planning, Indiana University |

| Brief Description |
|---|
| Assesses new students' expectations upon matriculation. Findings can be compared with student reports of their actual experiences as measured by the College Student Experiences (CSEQ). Information collected: background information; expectations for involvement in college activities; predicted satisfaction with college; and expected nature of college learning environments. Four-page paper survey and web version available. Takes 10-15 minutes to complete. |

| Example Questions | Intended Audience |
|---|---|
| During the coming year in college, how often do you expect to do the following? Complete the assigned readings before class: Very often; Often; Occasionally; Never<br><br>Ask an instructor or staff member for advice and help to improve your writing? Very often; Often; Occasionally; Never | Four-year public and private institutions/Incoming students. Most institutions administer the survey during fall orientation. To compare student expectations with actual experiences, colleges administer the CSEQ to the same students the following spring. |

| Option for Local Questions | Cost |
|---|---|
| Online additional questions- up to 20. | Administration fee:  Paper or Online- $200<br>Instrument cost per form:  Paper- $2.00; Online- $2.75<br>Online additional questions: $40 per question or $500 for a set of up to 20 questions.<br>Special Analysis per hour: $150<br>Student Advising Report: $500 |

| Norm Group | Standard Results |
|---|---|
| Entering students' norms reports will include relevant comparison group data by Carnegie type. | Computer diskette containing raw institutional data file and output file with descriptive statistics. Schools also receive a hard copy of the output file. |

| Customized Results | Separate Peer Groups |
|---|---|
| Additional analyses available for a fee. Comparison with CSEQ data to identify areas where the first-year experience can be improved. | Compared to other groups at similar institutions. |

| Address | Website |
|---|---|
| College Student Experiences Questionnaire<br>Center for Postsecondary Research and Planning<br>Indiana University<br>Ashton Aley Hall Suite 102<br>1913 East 7th St.<br>Bloomington, IN 47405-7510 | http://www.indiana.edu/cseq/csxq_generalinfo.htm |

| Telephone | Email |
|---|---|
| 812-856-5825<br>Fax: 812-856-5150 | cseq@indiana.edu |

## Attitudinal Assessment Survey
## National Survey of Student Engagement

| Survey Name | Vendor |
|---|---|
| NSSE - National Survey of Student Engagement | Indiana University Center for Postsecondary Research & Planning |

| Brief Description ||
|---|---|
| NSSE assesses the extent to which first-year and senior students engage in educational practices associated with high levels of learning and development. The survey itself (also referred to as "The College Student Report") covers student behaviors in college, institutional actions and requirements, student reactions to college and student background information. The 30-question survey takes students 15-20 minutes to complete. ||

| Example Questions | Intended Audience |
|---|---|
| "In your experience at your institution during the current school year, about how often have you asked questions in class or contributed to class discussions?"<br><br>"To what extent has your experience at this institution contributed to your knowledge, skills and personal development in acquiring a broad general education?" | - Administrators, faculty and staff at participating colleges and universities.<br>- Prospective students and parents.<br>- Multiple stakeholders in higher education. |

| Option for Local Questions | Cost |
|---|---|
| Participating institutions may join the NSSE Consortium to add up to 20 local questions for an additional $150-$450, depending on student enrollment. | $300 participation fee. The cost depends on the number of students enrolled at the participating institution. The total cost includes the instruments, respondent sampling, data processing, and a comprehensive report.<br>  - Less than 4,000 students   = $3,500<br>  - 4,000-15,000 students   = $5,250<br>  - More than 15,000 students = $7,300 |

| Norm Group | Standard Results |
|---|---|
| For each item, the institution is compared to<br>  - All other participating institutions with the same Carnegie classification and<br>  - All other participating institutions | A binder holds comprehensive results including:<br>  - Respondent characteristics<br>  - Mean comparisons<br>  - Frequency distributions<br>  - Additional NSSE information<br>  - Data CD/informational video |

| Customized Results | Separate Peer Groups |
|---|---|
| Customized results processing (e.g. , comparisons by school or major) is available from NSSE at the cost of $150/hour. | Special analyses with a minimum of eight other participating institutions is available for $300. |

| Address | Website |
|---|---|
| Ashton Aley Hall Suite 102<br>1913 East Seventh Street<br>Bloomington, IN 47405-7510 | www.iub.edu/nsse |

| Telephone | Email |
|---|---|
| (812) 856-5824 – office<br>(812) 856-5150 - fax | nsse@indiana.edu |

## Attitudinal Assessment Survey
## Program Self-Assessment Service

| Survey Name | Vendor |
|---|---|
| PSAS – Program Self-Assessment Service | ETS- Educational Testing Service |

| Brief Description |
|---|
| Assesses enrolled students' opinions on undergraduate programs. Used by departments for self-study and as additional indicators of program quality for accreditation purposes. |

| Example Questions | Intended Audience |
|---|---|
| Part I- To what extent do you agree with the following statements at the program/department in which you are majoring:<br>Most faculty members are genuinely interested in the welfare and professional development of departmental majors. 16 items<br>Part II- Please rate each of the following aspects of your department or program:<br>Intellectual environment. 31 items<br>Seven Sections, Part I-Part VII | Undergraduate and students at college or university. Information collected: Quality of teaching; scholarly excellence; faculty concern for students; curriculum; students' satisfaction with programs; resource accessibility; employment assistance; faculty involvement; departmental procedures; learning environment. |

| Option for Local Questions | Cost |
|---|---|
| Local questions are available. | $40 for 25 questionnaires plus shipping and handling (minimum purchase of 75 questionnaires). $4.00 per booklet processed.<br>$75 for summary data report<br>$75 for subgroup report (optional)<br>$75 for data diskette (optional) |

| Norm Group | Standard Results |
|---|---|
| No national data available. Undergraduate and students enrolled at college or university. | Summary data report includes separate analyses for faculty, students, and alumni. |

| Customized Results | Separate Peer Groups |
|---|---|
| Optional subgroup reports and data file available for a fee. | No- self study only. |

| Address | Website |
|---|---|
| Program Self-Assessment Service (PSAS)<br>Educational Testing Service<br>Rosedale Road<br>Princeton, NJ 08541 | http://www.ets.org/hea/sas/psas.html |

| Telephone | Email |
|---|---|
| 609-683-2273<br>Fax: 609-683-2270 | ETSinfo@ets.org |

**Attitudinal Assessment Survey**
**Student Adaptation to College Questionnaire**

| Survey Name | Vendor |
|---|---|
| SACQ- Student Adaptation to College Questionnaire | Western Psychological Services |

| Brief Description |
|---|
| The Student Adaptation to College Questionnaire (SACQ) was designed to measure student adjustment to college. Takes approx. 20 minutes. |

| Example Questions | Intended Audience |
|---|---|
| Not available. | Enrolled students at university or college. Measures:<br>- Academic adjustment<br>- Social adjustment<br>- Personal-Emotional Adjustment<br>- Goal Commitment/Institutional Attachment |

| Option for Local Questions | Cost |
|---|---|
| None | Sample set (Manual) - 45.00<br>Kit (25 questionnaires, 1 manual, and 2 prepaid answer sheets for computer scoring and interpretation) - $100<br>Questionnaire (hand scored) - $35 per pkg (25)<br>2-9 packages - 31.50/pkg.<br>10 or more packages - 29.90/pkg.<br>SACQ answer sheet (for computer scoring and interpretation)<br>1-9 sheets - 11.50 ea; 10-99 sheets - 10.35 ea.<br>100-999 sheets - 9.90 ea.<br>SACQ microcomputer disk for administration, scoring and interpretation (25 uses per disk)<br>1 disk - 195.00; 2+ disks – 182.50 ea.<br>Processing fees - no fee; Report of results - no fee<br>Shipping and handling - 10% |

| Norm Group | Standard Results |
|---|---|
| Normative data for the instrument is based on data from only one college. The instrument can be utilized at any time during a student's college career. | Computerized scoring and interpretation for the SACQ includes a 6-page printout report which includes: (a) the student's background information, (b) an introduction to the questionnaire, (c) a graphic display of full scale and subscale scores, (d) arrangement of responses into item clusters for counseling use, and (e) a display of the actual item responses given. A Group Report is also printed which lists the raw scores for the five SACQ scales for each student, provides the means and standard deviation for the group, and identifies students with extremely low scale scores. |

| Customized Results | Separate Peer Groups |
|---|---|
| The SACQ provides a framework for follow-up counseling. Ninety percent of the students with low SACQ scores accept offers of post-test interviews and counseling. | Comparability must be established independently or by the collection of local norms. |

| Address | Website |
|---|---|
| Western Psychological Services<br>12031 Wilshire Blvd.<br>Los Angeles, CA 90025-1251 | http://wbarratt.indstate.edu/dragon/saroi/sa-sacq.htm |

| Telephone | Email |
|---|---|
| (310) 478-2061<br>(310) 478-7838 (fax) | N/A |

## Attitudinal Assessment Survey
## SOIS Student Outcomes Information Surveys

| Survey Name | Vendor |
|---|---|
| SOIS Student Outcomes Information Surveys<br>-Entering Student Questionnaire<br>-Continuing Student Questionnaire<br>-Former Student Questionnaire<br>-Graduating Student Questionnaire<br>-Recent Alumni Questionnaire<br>-Long-term Alumni Questionnaire | NCHEMS – National Center for Higher Education Management Systems |

| Brief Description |
|---|
| NCHEMS' Student Outcomes Information Services (SOIS) is one of the nation's oldest and most comprehensive college student survey systems. It is designed to help colleges and universities gain up-to-date information on student needs and reactions to their educational experiences. All six questionnaires (available in both two-year and four-year college versions) contain a set of common questions that allow an institution to collect information at different stages in a student's college career. Takes 20 minutes. |

| Example Questions | Intended Audience |
|---|---|
| ESQ- How did you learn about our college? Was our college your first choice?<br>CSQ- Do you plan to enroll at our college next term? When would you prefer to take your classes?<br>GSQ- Which of the following degrees are you receiving from our college? What are your current employment plans?<br>FSQ- What degree were you seeking when you attended our college? Why did you leave our college?<br>RAQ- What was the most recent certificate or degree received from our college? Since completing your program at our college, have you enrolled at another college?<br>LTAQ- Since completing your program at our college, have you undertaken further formal study? How well did our college prepare your for your additional formal education? | Students at university or college. Six core areas:<br>-Background<br>-Personal goals and career aspirations<br>-Factors influencing choice of college<br>-Satisfaction with college experience<br>-Activities while in college<br>-Career choices and career successes |

| Option for Local Questions | Cost |
|---|---|
| Up to 15 local questions | Surveys- $0.30 each<br>**NCHEMS SOIS Analysis Service**<br>Data entry with student ID -- $1.25 each<br>Analysis Service (includes one Analytical Report) -- $150.00<br>Additional Copies of Analytical Report -- $20.00 each<br>Flat ASCII file or SPSSX file containing your institutional data on tape or diskette -- $75.00<br>Both the flat ASCII file and SPSSX portable file -- $100.00 |

| Norm Group | Standard Results |
|---|---|
| Longitudinal and/or periodic assessment of students' experiences and opinions at or from the institution. | Data for students at institution by gender, ethnicity, age at entry, and current residence. |

| Customized Results | Separate Peer Groups |
|---|---|
| Analysis Service includes one analytical report. | Comparison of the students at the institution at various stages of their college life. |

| Address | Website |
|---|---|
| NCHEMS - SOIS<br>PO Box 9752<br>Boulder, CO 80301-9752 | http://www.nchems.org/Surveys/surveys.htm |

| Telephone | Email |
|---|---|
| (303) 497-0390<br>Fax: (303) 497-0338 | clara@nchems.org |

**Attitudinal Assessment Survey**
**Student Satisfaction Inventory Survey**

| Survey Name | Vendor |
| --- | --- |
| SSI - Student Satisfaction Inventory Survey | Noel-Levitz |

| Brief Description |
| --- |
| The Student Satisfaction Inventory measures students' satisfaction and the importance of campus issues to students. It helps identify where the institution needs to focus retention efforts to improve student retention. Can be taken online. |

| Example Questions | Intended Audience |
| --- | --- |
| Faculty care about me as an individual: importance to me (rated 1-7); Level of satisfaction (rated 1-7).<br><br>I am able to register for classes I need with few conflicts: importance to me (rated 1-7); Level of satisfaction (rated 1-7). | Students enrolled in a four-year institution; community, junior or technical college; or two-year career/private school.<br>-Measures the satisfaction of students on a wide variety of topics.<br>-Ranks the importance of each item of concern, using a 12-scale system. |

| Option for Local Questions | Cost |
| --- | --- |
| None | Survey- $2.10 per student (100-999); $1.90 (1000-2499); $1.65 2500-<br>Online Survey- price depends upon number of completed surveys<br>Processing and Set-up Fee- $125 ($175 online)<br>Optional – Campus Report on CD- $75<br>Comparison report- $65; Year-to-year $75<br>Comparative Summary Analysis- $45; Single analysis $80<br>Data Diskette $125 |

| Norm Group | Standard Results |
| --- | --- |
| Students enrolled at institution. Shows composite scores for 12 scales.  The findings are presented with three scores for each item: importance mean, satisfaction mean, and performance gap mean. | Hard copy campus report that includes national IPS comparison group data and data isolated for faculty, administrators, and staff in a 12 scale system. |

| Customized Results | Separate Peer Groups |
| --- | --- |
| You can request customized benchmark comparison scores by region or for a hand-picked set of institutions. | Results are compared with scores from a national database along with institution's student scores. |

| Address | Website |
| --- | --- |
| Noel-Levitz<br>Noel-Levitz Office Park<br>2101 ACT Circle<br>Iowa City, IA 52245-9910 | http://www.noellevitz.com/NLCOM/Our+Services/Retention/Tools |

| Telephone | Email |
| --- | --- |
| 1-800-876-1117 | info@noellevitz.com |

## Attitudinal Assessment Survey
## Your First College Year Survey

| Survey Name | Vendor |
|---|---|
| YFCYS -- Your First College Year Survey | HERI- Higher Education Research Institute, UCLA Graduate School of Education and Information Studies |

| Brief Description |
|---|
| Designed as a follow-up survey to the CIRP Freshman Survey. Assesses enrolled students development near the end of the first year of college. Available as a web or paper-based survey. YFCY also may be used as a stand-alone instrument. |

| Example Questions | Intended Audience |
|---|---|
| Since entering this college, how successful have you felt at: Understanding what your professors expect of your academically. Answer: Completely; somewhat; unsuccessful<br><br>Since entering this college, how often have you: Used the Internet for research or homework. Answer: Frequently, Occasionally, Not at all | First year students at the institution. One-third of items are CIRP post-test items. Remaining questions address students' various experiences; self-concept and life goals; patterns of peer and faculty interaction; adjustment and persistence; degree aspirations; and satisfaction. |

| Option for Local Questions | Cost |
|---|---|
| Yes- up to 30. | Cost: Institutional participation fee: $475.00<br>Cost per scanned survey: $2.00<br>These fees cover all costs for the surveys, data processing, and preparation of three campus reports.<br><br>Electronic Data File, Reports on Spreadsheet, Peer Group Reports, Data Merges available at extra fees. |

| Norm Group | Standard Results |
|---|---|
| First year students at institution. Students' responses to the survey are compared to national and institutional peer group aggregates, participating institutions can determine where their first-year cohort "stands" relative to the experiences of first-year students at large. | Three reports: Profile Report, Means Report, and Follow-up Report Paper. A Factor Analysis of the YFCY National Aggregate Data is also available. |

| Customized Results | Separate Peer Groups |
|---|---|
| Space for institution-specific supplementary questions offers additional opportunities to conduct within-institution analyses.<br>*Trends Analyses* - The YFCY Survey repeats items from previous years. As such, institutions are able to start to assess trends in the characteristics, attitudes, values, classroom practices, personal behaviors, satisfaction, and adjustment of their entering freshmen.<br>*Future Analyses* - YFCY data benchmark student characteristics for the second year of college. Therefore, YFCY not only serves as a follow-up to data collected at college entry but also serve as baseline data for future analyses of student development and institutional impact. | Ability to conduct comparisons between up to 190 various subgroups of students. For example, it is possible to compare first-year outcomes such as adjustment or retention based on participation in a learning community, academic "cluster" program, or a first year seminar. It is also possible to analyze the data by gender, race/ethnicity, or place of residence. |

| Address | Website |
|---|---|
| Your First College Year<br>HERI - UCLA<br>3005 Moore Hall - Box 951521<br>Los Angeles, CA 90095-1521 | http://www.gseis.ucla.edu/heri/yfcy/index.html |

| Telephone | Email |
|---|---|
| 310-825-1925<br>Fax: 310-206-2228 | yfcy@ucla.edu |

# Our University Statement of Institutional Mission

Our University is an independent, nonsectarian, coeducational institution, in the tradition of the liberal arts and sciences. Seeking to be faithful to the ideals of its heritage, Our University is committed, in all of its policies and practices, to the unrestricted and rigorous pursuit of truth, to the centrality of values in human life, and to a respect for differing points of view.

Our mission is to provide an outstanding education for a relatively small number of talented and highly motivated students from a diversity of geographic, ethnic, and socioeconomic backgrounds. To achieve this end, we recruit and retain outstanding faculty members who are dedicated to the art of teaching and advising; to the search for and dissemination of truth through scholarship, research, and creative endeavor; and to service to the university and the larger community. We also seek to provide a supportive and challenging environment in which students can realize the full potential of their abilities and come to understand their responsibility for service in the human community.

The principal focus of Our University's curricular programs is undergraduate education in the liberal arts and sciences, combined with a number of directly career related and preprofessional fields. Relations between the liberal arts and the career related and preprofessional fields are carefully nurtured to provide mutually reinforcing intellectual experiences for students and faculty. Our University also offers master's and doctoral degree programs in selected professional areas that will prepare individuals for positions of leadership in their chosen careers. In addition, recognizing its responsibility to the larger community, Our University provides a variety of carefully selected programs of continuing education and cultural enrichment. Finally, Our University recognizes its responsibility in maintaining a position of excellence and leadership in research.

In its recruitment and retention of members of the University community, Our University, consistent with its academic and institutional heritage, maintains an openness to all qualified persons.

### OUR UNIVERSITY STATEMENT OF INSTITUTIONAL GOALS

**I. Introduction**

- The "Statement of Institutional Mission" on the preceding page expresses a vision of what our institution intends to be and do. The purpose of the present document is to set forth specific goals for each major area of the university for the next 5 years, with the conviction that the achievement of these goals will lead to the fulfillment of Our University's stated mission.

- It must be recognized that such achievement is contingent upon a number of circumstances, including the availability of adequate financial and other resources. Indeed, decisions regarding essentially academic matters must sometimes be based, at least in part, on factors that are themselves not specifically academic in nature. What immediately follows in this introduction, therefore, is a summary of certain economic assumptions (i.e., matters over which the university has little or no control), planning parameters, and implications that are presupposed in the following sections of the document.

A. *Economic Assumptions*
   1. Inflation will remain approximately at 3% to 4% over the next 5 years.
   2. Financial support to private institutions and students by state and federal agencies will tend to be reduced in the next 5 years.
   3. The annual income from the current unrestricted endowment sources will remain relatively fixed over the next 5 years.

B. *Planning Parameters*
   1. The student-faculty ratio (FTE students to FTE faculty) will stabilize at 13 to 1 by 2008-2009.
   2. The Education and General (E & G) Budget (the basic operating budget) will increase between 7% and 8% each year in the next 5 years and will reach approximately $50 million in the 2008-2009 academic year.
   3. Annual giving will increase moderately between now and 2007.
   4. Adequate fiscal reserves should be created or enlarged to allow for the timely renovation of campus buildings and other facilities.
   5. Annual tuition rate increases will be approximately 7% in each of the next 5 years.

C. *Implications*
   1. By the 2008-2009 academic year, the total number of undergraduate students will stabilize at approximately 4,000.
   2. The number of entering freshmen will increase by approximately 30 per year and will reach a class size of approximately 1,200 by the 2008-2009 academic year.
   3. Efforts will be made to increase the number of applications for admission each year so that we obtain 3,200 applications from highly qualified students by 2008-2009.

4. The proportion of the undergraduate students who attend on a full-time basis will increase by approximately 1% per year for the next 5 years.

5. The six year attrition rate will be reduced by .5% per year for each of the next 5 years.

6. The increasing number of undergraduate students will create the need for a new residence hall in the 2008-2009 academic year.

7. To accommodate more undergraduate students, funds should be dedicated to development of more playing/athletic fields.

8. To accommodate the needs of our changing student body, we will need to renovate/add to the University Center.

## II.  ACADEMIC AFFAIRS

- The goal of Our University is to be one of the leading independent liberal arts and sciences universities in the nation, as measured by the quality of its faculty, the strength of its curriculum and academic programs, the effectiveness of its support services, the excellence of its graduates, and the accomplishment of its intended outcomes. Significant steps already have been taken toward achievement of this goal through continued offering of both liberal arts programs designed to impart a depth of understanding in the major field and preprofessional programs preparing the graduate for employment upon graduation. Although the following goals do not represent the totality of intellectual and administrative activity within academic affairs, they do represent focal points for action in the near future.

### A. *Curriculum and Academic Programs*

- Our University is committed to offering all students a distinctive and challenging academic foundation in liberal studies in order to enhance their communication and analytic skills; to provide an understanding of their intellectual and cultural heritage; and to assist them in the development of self-awareness, responsible leadership, and the capacity to make reasoned, moral judgments. Our University will continue to offer the range of disciplines basic to a liberal education and will maintain a balance in the undergraduate curriculum among the humanities, fine arts, behavioral sciences, natural sciences, and selected preprofessional programs. The following goals are of high priority:

1. Study the university's general education program to determine whether revisions are desirable.

2. Initiate more varied forms of instruction for entering students, such as freshman seminars.

3. Establish a process to identify systematically those academic programs that should be targeted for qualitative enhancement and/or numerical growth. The principal criteria to be employed in making these judgments should be centrality to our mission, quality of the existing program, demand, cost-effectiveness, and comparative advantage in offering the program.

4. Encourage new academic program initiatives, particularly of an interdisciplinary nature, that reflect emerging intellectual perspectives and that are appropriate to the mission of Our University.

5. Encourage the development of new minors and areas of concentration that complement existing degree programs and are responsive to student interests and societal needs.

6. Be responsive to the continuing education needs of local business and industry in areas in which Our University is academically strong.

B. *Graduate and Research Programs*
- Although the primary academic thrust of Our University will continue to be its undergraduate program of instruction, graduate education and research will play an increasing role in support of the institution and its attraction and retention of outstanding students and faculty. Within this secondary academic role, Our University will seek during the next 5 years to:

1. Develop a limited number of additional graduate-level programs in areas in which the institution maintains a strong undergraduate program, sufficient student demand is evidenced, and local or regional demand for graduates is identified.

2. Review current graduate programs to determine the academic and economic feasibility of their continuation.

3. Increase the level of organized or sponsored research expenditures by 5% per year for the next 5 years.

4. Focus the development of proposals for externally funded or organized research on subjects directly related to local/regional industries or those subjects of particular interest to foundations with which Our University has enjoyed a continuing relationship.

C. *Continuing Education/Public Service*
- While maintaining primary commitments to teaching and research, Our University is also committed to helping to meet the continuing education and cultural enrichment needs of our surrounding community. In the next 5 years Our University's goals are to:

1. Offer noncredit instruction targeted to meet the continuing education needs of Our University's faculty, staff, and surrounding community. Such programs should not duplicate the efforts of two- and four-year postsecondary institutions within a 25-mile radius of Our University.

2. Provide cultural enrichment opportunities for the university and surrounding community through an artist/lecture/concert series.

3. Offer in-service specialized short courses and seminars for local business and industry.

D. *Faculty*
- Persons who combine a love of teaching with a continuing curiosity and a passion for learning, scholarship, research, and creativity are the most important resources of the university. Excellent teaching and advising are essential to the fulfillment of the mission of Our University, as is the conduct of both basic and applied research that contributes to the advancement of knowledge and to the consideration of important societal problems. Various steps have already been taken to develop and maintain an excellent faculty, and the following goals are particularly important:
  1. Maintain salaries at highly competitive levels in order to attract a diverse faculty noted for its teaching excellence, scholarly achievements, and dedication to the highest standards of professional activity.
  2. Continue to emphasize research and scholarly activity through research assistants' support, travel funds, library materials, adequate access to computer facilities, and other forms of faculty development such as academic leaves and summer stipends.
  3. Continue to develop the emphasis placed on advising and working directly with individual students.

E. *Students*
- Our University will remain an institution of modest size with a total enrollment of no more than 4,000 students. In the recruitment of all students, emphasis is placed on potential for the very highest in academic achievement; leadership, special talents, and abilities; and diversity in geographic origin, ethnicity, and socioeconomic status. Appropriate scholarships and need-based financial aid programs will be administered to facilitate recruitment and retention of these students, continuing the significant advances already made.
  1. Our University seeks to make it possible for each student to experience the academic and cultural diversity of the university, and the following academic goals for the composition of the student body directly address this commitment:
     a. Continue to increase the number of academically talented students attending Our University, achieve by 2009 an average SAT score for entering freshmen of 1200, and maintain this level as a minimum throughout the rest of the planning period.
     b. Continue to increase the number of out-of-state students attending Our University, so that this group will comprise 50% of the student body by 2009, and maintain this percentage as a minimum for the rest of the planning period.
     c. Give increased emphasis to recruitment of minority students (Hispanic, Black, Asian, and Native American) and increase their representation in the overall student population.
     d. Strive to have an equal number of men and women in the student body.

2. Each graduate of Our University will be treated as an individual, and all graduates of baccalaureate-level programs at the university will have developed a depth of understanding in their major field and been afforded the opportunity to prepare for a career or profession following graduation. Additionally, they will be able to

   a. Express themselves clearly, correctly, and succinctly in writing.
   b. Make an effective verbal presentation of their ideas concerning a topic.
   c. Read and offer an analysis of periodical literature concerning a topic of interest.
   d. Complete accurately basic mathematical calculations.
   e. Demonstrate a sufficient level of computer literacy.
   f. Utilize basic scholarly modes of inquiry.

F. *Academic Support Services*
- Services in direct support of academic programs must be both effective and efficient in the accomplishment of their assigned activities. Our University will strive for excellence in the following goals:

   1. Continue to increase library acquisitions so that the number of bound volumes will reach 650,000 by 2008.
   2. Improve the quality of library materials supporting instruction by acquiring the most advanced audiovisual equipment and by judiciously purchasing periodicals applicable to a liberal arts and sciences curriculum, as well as the limited number of graduate programs offered.
   3. Increase accessibility of computer facilities at the university for both students and faculty through expansion of microcomputer laboratories and enhancement of computer support.
   4. Develop more systematic data concerning the outcomes of each student's educational experiences.
   5. Plan and modify the existing classroom and laboratory space to meet the evolving needs of the new curriculum.

## III.   STUDENT AFFAIRS

- The function of the Student Affairs Office is to establish an environment at Our University that supports and encourages students in their academic progress and to assist those students in their personal and social development. Student Affairs prepares Our University graduates for adult life by teaching them to appreciate quality, to develop values, to accept responsibility for their decisions and actions, and to know how and when to compromise.
- To accomplish this mission, the following specific goals must receive continuing and expanded attention:

A. *Environment*
   1. Provide a comfortable and secure living environment in the residence halls.

2. Encourage development of appropriate attitudes and conduct for a communal academic environment.
3. Expand and encourage supplemental cultural and intellectual enrichment opportunities outside the classroom.
4. Explore the possibility of offering more options in housing.
5. Provide opportunities in an informal atmosphere for interaction of faculty with students outside the classroom.
6. Include in the University Center, which is being redesigned, a bookstore offering excellent academic support materials and current literature, as well as appropriate notions, supplies, and services needed by students, faculty, and staff.
7. Provide a variety of options for nutritional meals in comfortable and attractive settings for resident as well as commuting students, faculty, staff, and guests.

B. *Development*
1. Offer opportunities for self-evaluation and self-knowledge through administration and interpretation of standardized tests.
2. Provide comprehensive career planning for all students and career counseling for seniors and graduate students, prepare students to conduct effective job searches, and coordinate employment interviews on the campus.

## IV. FISCAL AFFAIRS

- The purpose of the university's Fiscal Affairs operations is to provide an environment that enables faculty, staff, and students to concentrate on their appropriate tasks, which are essentially educational.
- Fiscal Affairs has two major areas of responsibility: (1) the management of, and accounting for, financial resources (the handling of funds, endowments, investments, and expenditures for salaries and wages); and (2) the operation of support services (physical plant, purchasing, security, personnel, and other areas). These two essential areas provide a base upon which the institution can accomplish its mission.

A. *Financial Resources*
1. To achieve expansion and growth in financial assets, Our University will:
   a. Manage the budget prudently.
   b. Encourage and assist its faculty in seeking university-administered grants and contracts from external sources.
   c. Price its auxiliary enterprise services so that they are self-sustaining and do not draw from other resources of the institution.
2. In allocating funds for its academic and economic needs, the university will emphasize the following goals:
   a. Maintaining a level of salaries that will attract and retain competent professionals.

    b. Providing adequate funding for scholarships to attract exceptional students.

    c. Purchasing and replacing equipment in support of the instruction and research needs of the university.

    d. Building adequate plant-fund reserves in order to protect against deferred maintenance.

B. *Support Services*

    1. To achieve maximum utilization of its resources, our University will:

        a. Use its personnel, equipment, structures, and funds efficiently and effectively to provide a safe and comfortable environment for all faculty, staff, and students.

        b. Fund support services at a level that provides for the most efficient operation consistent with a scholarly environment.

    2. In personnel matters, the university will

        a. Improve communications between support services and all employees to ensure that applicable fiscal and personnel procedures are understood.

        b. Maintain a vigorous affirmative action program that will include specific goals and a systematic review of procedures and progress.

## V.  UNIVERSITY RELATIONS AND DEVELOPMENT

- The University Relations and Development function manages the closely related areas of fund raising, alumni activities, and public relations. Most of the activities and programs take place for the ultimate purpose of increasing gift income for the university and attracting qualified students and faculty to the university.

- Within this context, the University Relations and Development function has established the following integrated goals:

A. *Fund Raising*

    1. Build a permanent university endowment of $150 million to $155 million by 2009.

    2. Achieve a level of annual giving (unrestricted annual fund) of at least $750,000 per year by 2009.

    3. Achieve 35% participation among alumni in the annual giving program.

B. *Alumni Activities*

    1. Have 5% of all alumni return to campus for various programs such as Alumni Weekend, Alumni College, class reunions, etc.

    2. Develop an active national alumni association with chapters in all cities where 100 or more alumni reside.

C. *Public Relations*

    1. Achieve a national image of the university as a high-quality, selective-admissions liberal arts and sciences institution that is among the best of its type in the nation.

    2. Maintain a positive relationship with the community in which the institution is located.

# Your Community College Mission

Your Community College is an open-admission, community-based comprehensive college designed to provide inexpensive, quality educational opportunities to residents of a five-county service area in the central portion of the Magnolia State. The college was formed early in 1971 by the joint action of the Smith, Lawrence, Karnes, Neuceuss, and Willow county governments and recognized by the legislature and the State Board of Community Colleges later in that year. The college replaced a former branch of Magnolia State University and has developed an educational mission characterized by diversification, growth, and community orientation.

Your Community College operates in the belief that all individuals should be

a. Treated with dignity and respect,
b. Afforded equal opportunity to acquire a complete educational experience,
c. Given an opportunity to discover and develop their special aptitudes and insights,
d. Provided an opportunity to equip themselves for a fulfilling life and responsible citizenship in a world characterized by change.

Finally, the college functions as an integral part of the five-county area that it serves and has a responsibility to provide educational and cultural leadership to this constituency.

### Institutional Goals

Your Community College seeks to:

A. Serve students in the first 2 years of instruction leading to a bachelor's degree.
   1. Recipients of the Associate of Arts (AA) or Associate of Science (AS) degree will be readily accepted at all public universities in the Magnolia State.
   2. The majority of graduates with the AA or AS degree attending four-year institutions on a full-time basis will complete their bachelor's degrees within 3 years of enrollment at the four-year institution.
   3. Courses offered at the college as a foundation or prerequisite for courses at public four-year colleges will be fully accepted for that purpose.
B. Serve persons of all ages in preparing for job entry and careers in a variety of fields.
   1. Recipients of an Associate of Applied Science (AAS) degree will be well prepared for their first or entry-level position in a career field.
   2. The great majority of AAS graduates will find employment in the five-county service area.
   3. College AAS programs will be focused on career-related opportunities for graduates in the five-county area.
C. Insure that all recipients of an associate (AA/AS or AAS) degree will be able to:
   1. Express their thoughts clearly and correctly in writing.
   2. Read and understand literature and current event articles commonly found in the print media.

3. Perform the basic mathematical calculations required to function in society.
D. Assist students in overcoming deficiencies and acquiring skills fundamental to further academic and career achievement.
   1. Prior to entry into AA/AS or AAS degree programs, all students will hold a high school diploma or GED certificate.
   2. The college will provide a noncredit college preparatory curriculum for students seeking to receive their GED certificate.
   3. Students completing noncredit occupational/technical training programs will be offered assistance with obtaining their GED certificate if they have not completed high school.
E. Provide a broad range of student services, including counseling, career planning, placement, and financial assistance.
   1. Counseling and career planning services will support both transfer (AA/AS) and career/technical (AAS) students.
   2. Placement services will be oriented toward the support of career/technical (AAS) graduates and focused in the five-county area.
   3. Every effort possible will be pursued to provide financial assistance for those in need of such support to attend the college.
F. Serve constituents who need additional training for advancement in their current field or retraining for employment in new fields.
   1. Continuing career education classes will be offered annually at night in each field in which the college offers an AAS.
   2. In conjunction with Magnolia State University, continuing professional education opportunities will be offered in business and other professional areas.
   3. Opportunities for retraining will be made available to all citizens of the five counties and be intensified, should economic circumstances warrant.
G. Provide educational programs to meet the needs of employers in the five-county area.
H. Serve persons who want to take special classes and workshops, as well as regular credit classes for personal development or cultural enrichment.
I. Cooperate with community agencies in community development activities.

# Expanded Statement of Institutional Purpose — University of Mississippi, Oxford Campus

The University of Mississippi Statement of Academic Focus and Goals for the 1990s contained in the following pages constitute the central core values that will guide the University's actions during the balance of the 1990s. These statements provide the over-arching framework of institutional aspirations, concepts, and ideals upon which the University's plans and expected results are to be based and against which its accomplishments must ultimately be judged or assessed.

The following Statement of Academic Purpose for the University is intended to serve as the foundation for University decision making concerning its academic offerings, the basis for its existence. It identifies the "core" or "essential" areas of academic endeavor in which the University will be engaged throughout the balance of this century.

## Statement of Academic Focus for the 1990s

The University of Mississippi is the oldest public institution of higher learning in the state. Its fundamental purpose is the creation and dissemination of knowledge. Throughout its long history the University has enhanced the educational, economic, and cultural foundations of the state, region, and nation. As a comprehensive, doctoral-degree granting institution, the University offers a broad range of undergraduate and graduate programs as well as opportunities for continuing study.

While recognizing that its primary role is to serve the state of Mississippi, the University educates students to assume leadership roles in both the state and nation through its nationally recognized programs of undergraduate, graduate, and professional study. Its teaching, research, and service missions are characterized by equal access and equal opportunity to all who qualify. Within this framework, the University will focus its resources on:

1. **Science and Humanities**. The University will continue its traditional leadership in the Liberal Arts by emphasizing existing programs of strength in the sciences and humanities and programs that sustain nationally important centers of research and service.

2. **Health**. The University will continue to provide the professional education of those who deliver and administer human health services and those who perform research aimed at improving the efficiency, effectiveness, quality, and availability of healthcare.

3. **Legal Education**. The University will continue to provide the initial and continuing professional education of those who formulate, interpret, and practice law.

4. **Business Development and Economic Growth**. The University recognizes that economic growth and business development are essential to the future of Mississippi in the increasingly integrated world economy. The University will enhance the development of entrepreneurial, financial, managerial, and information pro-

cessing activities through existing preprofessional, professional, and public service programs.

5. **Communications and Related Technologies**. The University recognizes that communications technology will be one of the most important growth areas of the next century. The University will continue developing programs that sustain the communication and telecommunication industries. The area of focus crosses disciplinary boundaries and incorporates expertise from specialties such as foreign languages, journalism, engineering, computing, and distance learning.

**University of Mississippi Oxford Campus—Goals for the 1990s**

**Goal 1**. The University will improve undergraduate education, especially in lower-division courses.

**Goal 2**. The University will concentrate graduate education and research in areas of strength consistent with the Focus Areas.

**Goal 3**. The University will increase employee compensation to the Southern University Group (SUG) average in order to attract and retain a highly qualified faculty and staff.

**Goal 4**. The University will improve educational support services (library, computer networking, database availability, instructional support, etc.) to increase access to information and communication on the campus.

**Goal 5**. The University will disseminate its expertise and knowledge to nonacademic communities throughout the state of Mississippi and the Midsouth region.

**Goal 6**. The University will continue to develop leadership and to instill in its students a sense of justice, moral courage, and tolerance for the views of others.

**Goal 7**. The University will maintain efficient and effective administrative services to support the University's instructional, research, and public service programs.

**Goal 8**. The University will increase faculty and staff involvement in University planning.

**Goal 9**. The University will increase its efforts to secure support from federal, state, and private sources.

# Outline of Twelve-Month Sequence of Events for Preparation of Expanded Statement of Institutional Purpose

**I. Doing the Homework (September through December)**

    A. Appoint Broad-Based Constituent Group—The group should be composed of faculty (probably the majority), administrators, student leaders, and representatives of the governing board. The purpose of the group is to serve as the overall steering committee that will review and discuss important issues related to the mission or purpose of the institution. This group may become somewhat large due to the need to involve various constituencies; however, most of the work done will be accomplished by several staff members appointed to support the work of the representative group.

    B. Review Current Statement of Purpose—The current statement of purpose should be reviewed for several reasons. First, it represents the official policy of the institution as of the beginning of the process. Second, from a political standpoint, it may be that this existing statement cannot be entirely discarded due to legal ramifications or other circumstances and will need to be incorporated into the ESIP or circumvented.

    C. Gather Input from Constituents—The attempt to involve the greater campus community in consideration of the ESIP should involve a broad canvassing of faculty, administrators, student leaders, and the governing board members for their opinions concerning the future development of the institution. The Institutional Goals Inventory from the Educational Testing Service has proven to be a useful tool for this purpose and is a relatively easy way to gain maximum participation with minimum effort and cost.

    D. Determine External Opportunities and Constraints—The term **environmental scanning** conjures up massive efforts by a substantial staff to describe every detail of the environment in which the institution operates. On the contrary, an abbreviated environmental scan can not only be a valuable source of relatively easily obtained information but also provide an opportunity for participation by faculty experts in the different areas. It is possible to conduct an abbreviated environmental scan within 2 to 3 months and to present to the institution a summary of the political, economic, educational, and social issues forming the context within which it operates.

E. Consider Analysis of Internal Strengths/Weaknesses—It is highly unlikely (though possible) that the institution has the "intestinal fortitude" necessary to identify its weaknesses on paper. In most instances, institutions can go about the task of identifying those areas widely regarded on the campus as strengths. In this case, areas not identified as strengths should be considered as either generally acceptable or as weaknesses of the institution.

## II. Conducting Meaningful Deliberations (January through April)

A. Establish Issues to Be Addressed

1. Identify Key Issues/Topics—The product of "Doing the Homework" should suggest a number of issues or topics (clientele, programs, research, etc.) that need to be addressed in the ESIP. It is important both to identify these topics as early as possible and to leave time for further topics to be developed during this second portion of the process.

2. Determine Relative Priorities—Some of the topics identified initially will obviously be of greater importance to the institution than others. As early as possible, these topics should be identified and sequenced for consideration, leaving several periods of time open for consideration of topics developed during this second phase.

B. Follow the Sequence of Deliberations

1. Schedule Meetings with Topics—The number of topics identified will determine, to a great extent, the number and frequency of meetings to be scheduled. It is important, however, that these meetings be scheduled in advance so that members will know what topic is to be considered at which meetings and, accordingly, can arrange their calendars well in advance.

2. Assign Responsibilities for the Drafting Component of Mission and Goals Statements—Each topic to be discussed should have a "floor manager" appointed to consider the information provided during the "Doing the Homework" phase and to frame initial components of the ESIP consideration by the group.

3. Target Draft Completion by March 31—Preparation of the draft ESIP in the 3 months from January 1 to March 31 will doubtlessly require a number of meetings to discuss the topics identified and the original draft of the ESIP. The staff members supporting the broad-based constituent group can be expected to bear primary responsibility for logistical aspects of the completion of the initial draft.

C. Distribute Draft ESIP on Campus for Review/Comment and Hold Open Meeting—During early April, the draft ESIP prepared should be widely distributed on the campus for comment and review by faculty, administrators, student leaders, and members of the governing board. An open meeting will need to be held, at which widely differing viewpoints will no doubt be aired.

D. Complete Revised Draft of ESIP by the End of April—By the end of April, a revised ESIP should be forwarded to the chief executive officer for his or her review and potential modification.

## III. Seek Approval and Complete Publication (May through August)

A. Have Final Review/Modification by Chief Executive Officer—The constituent groups' proposed ESIP should not come as a surprise to the CEO, since he or she should have been kept informed of progress throughout their deliberations. The CEO should have the authority to adjust and refine the statement presented to him or her; however, major or substantive changes of the proposed ESIP should be discussed with the broad-based constituent group prior to forwarding them to the governing board.

B. Gain Approval of Governing Board—Ultimately, the governing board of the institution should approve the ESIP. Chief executive officers who have accomplished this indicate that it is not among the most "comfortable" experiences they have "enjoyed." As members of the governing board, many for the first time, they are asked to play a meaningful role in charting the course of the future of their institution. However, following discussion, modification, and approval of the ESIP, the governing board should be more supportive of the CEO's implementation of the concepts contained as representative of their collective will.

C. Publish Statement in Catalog—The ESIP should be published in the college catalog. In addition, the complete ESIP should be widely disseminated on the campus so that faculty, administrators, and student leaders are knowledgeable concerning the directions for future growth of the institution.

D. Present Document to the Institution as the Basis for Institutional Effectiveness Implementation/Self-Study—Finally, the ESIP should be presented to the faculty at the beginning of the following academic year as the basis for implementation of outcomes assessment, institutional effectiveness, and, in many cases, the self-study process.

# APPENDIX C

## President's Insert for Letter to Faculty and Staff Concerning the Implementation of Institutional Effectiveness and the Use of Results

As you are aware _____ (college/university) is developing a comprehensive program for the improvement of student learning and institutional services. This Institutional Effectiveness/Assessment program is among the most important initiatives which the college/university has implemented in recent years. For the process to be successful and the institution to benefit from the efforts, it is vitally important that everyone take part in the process and understand its purpose.

The purpose of the process is to gather information which will allow us to make improvements in student learning and services. Each program and unit will do assessment to gather information about their current levels of student learning and services to determine what needs to be improved. The results of these assessment efforts will not be utilized in any manner to evaluate individuals, services, or instructional programs. In specific, such information will not be utilized regarding individuals' promotions, salary increases, tenure, or continuing contract (if appropriate) status. The information regarding student learning and the quality of our services is for the program or unit's use in making improvement in its functioning. The information collected from assessment is not for supervisors to use to make judgments about you, the instructional program, or unit services.

On the other hand, I believe this Institutional Effectiveness process to be of sufficient importance that I am asking all supervisor personnel, through existing individual and program evaluation processes, to ensure that all campus employees are taking part in these activities and that improvement based upon assessment results is documented. While it is unreasonable to expect that every attempt to improve learning and services will be successful, it is not unreasonable to expect each of us to make a genuine effort to identify intended program/unit outcomes, take part in the assessment effort, and then seek to improve student learning and services based upon collected assessment results.

We are all privileged to serve at a great educational institution, and through this process it will accomplish even more service to students and our community.

# ASSESSMENT RECORD BOOK
# INSTRUCTIONAL AND ADMINISTRATIVE
# AND EDUCATIONAL SUPPORT
# UNIT EXAMPLES

# ASSESSMENT RECORD FOR

# DEPARTMENT

# OF

## Composite Technology Department

### (Academic Department Name)

Current Assessment Cycle                                   September 15, Assessment Cycle

**(Assessment Period Covered)**                                   **(Date Report Submitted)**

**Includes Assessment Reports for those Educational Programs listed below:**

| **Title of Educational Degree Program** | **Degree Level** |
| --- | --- |
| | **(Associate, Bachelor's, Master's, etc.)** |
| Automotive Technology | AS |
| Paralegal Technology | AS |
| Office Technology | AS |
| Criminal Justice | AS |
| | |
| | |

**Submitted By:** _____

**(Department Chair or Faculty Assessment Representative)**

*Form A-Title Page*

# ASSESSMENT REPORT FOR

Automotive Technology                                              AS
_____                    _____

**(Educational Degree Program)**                        **(Degree Level)**

Current Assessment Cycle
_____                    _____

**(Assessment Period Covered)**                     **(Date Report Submitted)**

**Expanded Statement of Institutional Purpose Linkage:**

> **Institutional Mission Statement Reference:** _____ Community College is an open-admission, community-based, comprehensive college.

> **Institutional Goal(s) Supported:** Serve persons of all ages in preparing for job entry and careers in a variety of fields.

**Program Intended Educational (Student Learning) Outcomes:**

> **1.** Graduates of the Automotive Technology Program will be successfully employed in the field.

> **2.** Graduates of the Automotive Technology Program will be technically proficient.

> **3.** Employers of the Automotive Technology Program graduates, in the five-county service area, will be pleased with the education received by their employees.

> **4.**

> **5.**

*Form B-Linkage Page*

# ASSESSMENT REPORT FOR

Automotive Technology

AS

**(Educational Degree Program)**

**(Degree Level)**

Current Assessment Cycle

**(Assessment Period Covered)**

**(Date Report Submitted)**

**Intended Educational (Student Learning) Outcome:**
*Note: There should be one Form C for each intended outcome listed on Form B. Intended outcome should be restated in the box immediately below and the intended outcome number entered in blank spaces.*

1. **Graduates of the Automotive Technology Program will be successfully employed in the field.**

**First Means of Program Assessment and Criteria for Success for Student Learning Outcome Identified Above:**

**1a. Means of Program Assessment and Criteria for Success:** 50% of the responding graduates of the Automotive Technology Program will report employment in the field on the Graduating Student Survey administered at the time of program completion.

**1a. Summary of Assessment Data Collected:** 73% reported employment.

**1a. Use of Results to Improve Educational Program:** Revised criteria for success to 70%

**Second Means of Program Assessment and Criteria for Success for Student Learning Outcome Identified Above:**

**1b. Means of Program Assessment and Criteria for Success:** 80% of the responding graduates of the Automotive Technology Program will report employment in the field on the recent Alumni Survey administered one year after graduation.

**1b. Summary of Assessment Data Collected:** 81% reported employment one year after graduation.

**1b. Use of Results to Improve Educational Program:** No action necessary at this time, however, will continue to monitor.

*Form C-Educational Outcome Report Page*

# ASSESSMENT REPORT FOR

Automotive Technology

AS

---

**(Educational Degree Program)**

**(Degree Level)**

Current Assessment Cycle

---

**(Assessment Period Covered)**

**(Date Report Submitted)**

**Intended Educational (Student Learning) Outcome:**
*Note: There should be one Form C for each intended outcome listed on Form B. Intended outcome should be restated in the box immediately below and the intended outcome number entered in blank spaces.*

---

2. **Graduates of the Automotive Technology Program will be technically proficient.**

---

**First Means of Program Assessment and Criteria for Success for Student Learning Outcome Identified Above:**

---

**2a. Means of Program Assessment and Criteria for Success:** At the close of their final term, 90% of the graduates will be able to identify and correct within a given period of time all of the mechanical problems in five test cars that have been "prepared" for the students by Automotive Technology Program faculty. No single automotive malfunction will fail to be identified and corrected by more that 20% of students.

---

**2a. Summary of Assessment Data Collected:** 79% overall success rate. Electrical system malfunction undetected by 39% of students.

---

**2a. Use of Results to Improve Educational Program:** Expanded electrical trouble-shooting component of AT 202 to include automotive electrical systems.

---

**Second Means of Program Assessment and Criteria for Success for Student Learning Outcome Identified Above:**

---

**2b. Means of Program Assessment and Criteria for Success:** 80% of Automotive Technology Program graduates will pass the National Automotive Test. On no subscale will participants average missing 30% or more of the items

---

**2b. Summary of Assessment Data Collected:** Pass rate on National Automotive Test was 83%; however, on "hydraulic theory" sub-scale students missed an average of 34% of questions.

---

**2b. Use of Results to Improve Educational Program:** Modified means of teaching hydraulic theory during AT 102 (Basic Auto Systems) by use of automated simulation model.

---

*Form C-Educational Outcome Report Page*

# ASSESSMENT REPORT FOR

Automotive Technology

AS

**(Educational Degree Program)**

**(Degree Level)**

Current Assessment Cycle

**(Assessment Period Covered)**

**(Date Report Submitted)**

**Intended Educational (Student Learning) Outcome:**
*Note: There should be one Form C for each intended outcome listed on Form B. Intended outcome should be restated in the box immediately below and the intended outcome number entered in blank spaces.*

**3. Employers of the Automotive Technology Program graduates, in the five-county service area, will be pleased with the education received by their employees.**

First Means of Program Assessment and Criteria for Success for Student Learning Outcome Identified Above:

**3a. Means of Program Assessment and Criteria for Success:** 80% of the respondents to an Employer Survey conducted every 3 years by the college will respond that they would be pleased to employ future graduates.

**3a. Summary of Assessment Data Collected:** 90% reported willingness to employ graduates, but only 50% of body shops.

**3a. Use of Results to Improve Educational Program:** Added body shop representative to Advisory Committee and subsequently established separate Auto-Body certificate Program.

Second Means of Program Assessment and Criteria for Success for Student Learning Outcome Identified Above:

**__b. Means of Program Assessment and Criteria for Success:**

**__b. Summary of Assessment Data Collected:**

**__b. Use of Results to Improve Educational Program:**

*Form C-Educational Outcome Report Page*

# ASSESSMENT RECORD FOR

# DEPARTMENT/UNIT

# OF

_____

(Name of Administrative or Educational Support Department/Unit)

_____     _____
(Assessment Period Covered)                              (Date Submitted)

Submitted By: _____
(Unit Assessment Representative)

*Form A-Title Page*

# ASSESSMENT RECORD FOR

# DEPARTMENT/UNIT

# OF

CAREER CENTER

**(Name of Administrative or Educational Support Department/Unit)**

Current Assessment Cycle                    September, Current Assessment Cycle

**(Assessment Period Covered)**                    **(Date Submitted)**

**Submitted By:** _____
**(Unit Assessment Representative)**

*Form A-Title Page*

# ASSESSMENT REPORT FOR

_____

(Administrative or Educational Support Unit)

_____                    _____

(Assessment Period Covered)                           (Date Report Submitted)

Expanded Statement of Institutional Purpose Linkage:

| |
|---|
| Institution Mission/Goal Statement Reference: |

| |
|---|
| Unit Mission Statement: |

Intended Administrative Objectives/Outcomes:

| |
|---|
| 1. |

| |
|---|
| 2. |

| |
|---|
| 3. |

| |
|---|
| 4. |

| |
|---|
| 5. |

*Form B-Linkage Page*

# ASSESSMENT REPORT FOR

## CAREER CENTER

**(Administrative or Educational Support Unit)**

| Current Assessment Cycle | September, Current Assessment Cycle |
|---|---|
| **(Assessment Period Covered)** | **(Date Report Submitted)** |

**Expanded Statement of Institutional Purpose Linkage:**

**Institution Mission/Goal Statement Reference:** (Goal 6) ... The University will continue to develop leadership and to instill in its students a sense of justice, moral courage, and tolerance for the views of others ... improve admissions, academic, *career and placement counseling.*

**Unit Mission Statement:** ... to assist students in transition from academia to the world of work by preparing students for life after graduation ... Career Center offers services which include: career counseling; three classes for academic credit; workshops and seminars on career related subjects; assistance with resume writing and interviewing; and opportunities for part-time jobs, internships, and full-time jobs.

**Intended Administrative Objectives/Outcomes:**

1.  **Students attending Career Center resume workshops will produce quality resumes.**

2.  **Career Center will provide job search assistance.**

3.  **Graduates will be satisfied with services provided by the Career Center.**

4.

5.

*Form B-Linkage Page*

# ASSESSMENT REPORT FOR

_____

**(Administrative or Educational Support Unit)**

_____                    _____

**(Assessment Period Covered)**                    **(Date Report Submitted)**

**Intended Administrative or Educational Support Objective/Outcome:**

*Note: There should be one Form C for each administrative objective/outcome listed on Form B. Administrative objective/outcome should be restated in the box immediately below and the administrative objective/outcome number entered in blank spaces.*

| |
|---|
| — |

**First Means of Assessment for Objective/Outcome Identified Above:**

| |
|---|
| __ a. Means of Unit Assessment and Criteria for Success: |

| |
|---|
| __ a. Summary of Assessment Data Collected: |

| |
|---|
| __ a. Use of Results to Improve Unit Services: |

**Second Means of Assessment for Objective/Outcome Identified Above:** *(If available)*

| |
|---|
| __ b. Means of Unit Assessment and Criteria for Success: |

| |
|---|
| __ b. Summary of Assessment Data Collected: |

| |
|---|
| __ b. Use of Results to Improve Unit Services: |

*Form C-Administrative Objective/Outcome Report Page*

# ASSESSMENT REPORT FOR
## CAREER CENTER
### (Administrative or Educational Support Unit)

Current Assessment Cycle                           September, Current Assessment Cycle

**(Assessment Period Covered)**                          **(Date Report Submitted)**

**Intended Administrative or Educational Support Objective/Outcome:**

*Note: There should be one Form C for each administrative objective/outcome listed on Form B. Administrative objective/outcome should be restated in the box immediately below and the administrative objective/outcome number entered in blank spaces.*

> **1.  Students attending Career Center resume workshops will produce quality resumes.**

**First Means of Assessment for Objective/Outcome Identified Above:**

> **1a. Means of Unit Assessment and Criteria for Success:** Using the checklist describing the five quality components of a resume, the CC staff will analyze resumes submitted for company referrals. The resumes of 80% of students who attended a current resume workshop will receive greater than 4 rating on checklist. No indicator will be below 3.0.

> **1a. Summary of Assessment Data Collected:** 536 resumes were reviewed. 316 resumes were from students who attended workshops. 213 resumes received quality score of 5 (67%); 89 scored 4 (28%); 14 received a 3. The quality indicator consistently missed by students was "use of action verbs."

> **1a. Use of Results to Improve Unit Services:** While quality resumes were produced by students who attended the workshops, CC staff decided all students who submit resumes for referrals should be required to attend workshop. The idea has been submitted to Vice Chancellor for consideration. The CC staff developed a skit for the workshops stressing the importance of using action verbs. Decided to use checklist again next year to compare results. Focus groups scheduled to further evaluate content of workshop.

**Second Means of Assessment for Objective/Outcome Identified Above:** *(If available)*

> **1b. Means of Unit Assessment and Criteria for Success:** On survey given to recruiters regarding quality of resumes reviewed, recruiters will rank student resumes as 3.5 or higher overall. No indicator will be consistently below 3.1.

> **1b.  Summary of Assessment Data Collected:** Recruiters rated the quality of the resumes at 3.1. No indicator was consistently below 3.0.

> **1b.  Use of Results to Improve Unit Services:** Although the criteria was met, the CC staff examined the survey given to recruiters and decided the information from it gave nothing that could be used to help students with resume writing. Decided to redesign survey.

*Form C-Administrative Objective/Outcome*

# ASSESSMENT REPORT FOR

## CAREER CENTER

**(Administrative or Educational Support Unit)**

Current Assessment Cycle

September, Current Assessment Cycle

**(Assessment Period Covered)**

**(Date Report Submitted)**

**Intended Administrative or Educational Support Objective/Outcome:**

*Note: There should be one Form C for each administrative objective/outcome listed on Form B. Administrative objective/outcome should be restated in the box immediately below and the administrative objective/outcome number entered in blank spaces.*

> **2. Career Center will provide job search assistance.**

**First Means of Assessment for Objective/Outcome Identified Above:**

> **2a. Means of Unit Assessment and Criteria for Success:** At the end of the year, CC will evaluate five of the job search assistance programs. Records will indicate each of the areas had an increase in numbers of students attending this year over last.

> **2a. Summary of Assessment Data Collected:** Overall there was an increase in attendance at job search programs of 43. Resume workshops + 27; Interview workshops +21; Mock Interviews +8; Job Search Techniques +6; and On-Campus Recruiting (-19).

> **2a. Use of Results to Improve Unit Services:** Career Center staff is satisfied with three of the five job search programs offered. Staff decided to offer additional Job Search Techniques program each semester. Staff is concerned with On-Campus Recruiting as this is second year for a decline in student interest. Staff compiled a focus group of recent graduates to meet in the fall. Topic is "Determining Effective Ways of Increasing Interest in On-campus Recruiting.

**Second Means of Assessment for Objective/Outcome Identified Above:** *(If available)*

> __b. Means of Unit Assessment and Criteria for Success:

> __b. Summary of Assessment Data Collected:

> __b. Use of Results to Improve Unit Services:

*Form C-Administrative Objective/Outcome Report Page*

# ASSESSMENT REPORT FOR

## CAREER CENTER

### (Administrative or Educational Support Unit)

Current Assessment Cycle                                September, Current Assessment Cycle

**(Assessment Period Covered)**                          **(Date Report Submitted)**

## Intended Administrative or Educational Support Objective/Outcome:

*Note: There should be one Form C for each administrative objective/outcome listed on Form B. Administrative objective/outcome should be restated in the box immediately below and the administrative objective/outcome number entered in blank spaces.*

---

**3. Graduates will be satisfied with services provided by the Career Center.**

---

**First Means of Assessment for Objective/Outcome Identified Above:**

---

**3a. Means of Unit Assessment and Criteria for Success:** Respondents will indicate on Graduating Student Survey an average rating of 3.3 or higher as to satisfaction with Career Center.

---

**3a. Summary of Assessment Data Collected:** Graduates rated satisfaction with Career Center as 3.4. However; the international students only indicated a 1.4 satisfaction rating.

---

**3a. Use of Results to Improve Unit Services:** While criteria for success was met, workshops have been held by Career Center staff in conjunction with International Services to provide direct services to international students. Collecting material from nationally know programs.

---

**Second Means of Assessment for Objective/Outcome Identified Above:** *(If available)*

---

**3b. Means of Unit Assessment and Criteria for Success:** 95% of students completing a point-of-contact survey will be "very satisfied" or "satisfied" with their "overall experience" with the Career Center. No service will receive "Not Satisfied" by more than 30% of the students responding.

---

**3b. Summary of Assessment Data Collected:** 91% of students completing a point-of-contact survey indicated "very satisfied" or "satisfied" with "overall experience" with Career Center. However, 47% of students indicated "not satisfied" rating with computer/Internet Job Search Sources.

---

**3b. Use of Results to Improve Unit Services:** Career Center staff have located several new internet sources of career information. Six additional work stations were established using computer hardware denoted by Kroger and International Paper.

---

*Form C-Administrative Objective/Outcome Report Page*

# APPENDIX E

# COMMENT SHEET FOR COMMITTEE REVIEW OF ASSESSMENT PLANS AND REPORTS

## Check List

Program/Unit Reviewed: _____  Reviewing Team: _____  Date Reviewed: _____

<u>Relationship to University Mission</u>

|  |  | Strongly Agree | | | | Strongly Disagree |
|---|---|---|---|---|---|---|
| 1. | The Record utilizes the University's *Statement of Purpose* (University Goal(s) for instructional units;  University goal(s) and unit mission for administrative and educational support (AES) unit(s). | 1 | 2 | 3 | 4 | 5 |

<u>Statement of Intended Educational (Student) Outcomes or Administrative Objectives</u>

| | | | | | | |
|---|---|---|---|---|---|---|
| 2. a. | The Record states 3-5 outcomes or 2-3 objectives that seem appropriate to assess. | 1 | 2 | 3 | 4 | 5 |
| b. | The Record states 3-5 outcomes or 2-3 objectives that seem measurable for purpose of assessment. | 1 | 2 | 3 | 4 | 5 |
| 3. | Instructional Units:  The statements are formulated in terms of what students should be able to think, know, or do. | 1 | 2 | 3 | 4 | 5 |
| 4. | Educational Support and Administrative Units:  The statements relate to current services and describe services provided to its clients or what its clients would think, know or do after the provision of the service. | 1 | 2 | 3 | 4 | 5 |

<u>Means of Assessment and Criteria for Success</u>

| | | | | | | |
|---|---|---|---|---|---|---|
| 5. | The *means of assessment* appear to measure the accomplishment of the intended outcome or objective/service. | 1 | 2 | 3 | 4 | 5 |
| 6. | The *means of assessment*  appear feasible and appropriate in terms of resources. | 1 | 2 | 3 | 4 | 5 |
| 7. | Multiple *means of assessment* are described for most outcomes or objectives. | 1 | 2 | 3 | 4 | 5 |
| 8. | *Criteria for success* are established by the unit for each of the *means of assessment.* | 1 | 2 | 3 | 4 | 5 |

------------------------------------------------------------------------

<u>Assessment Results</u>

| | | | | | | |
|---|---|---|---|---|---|---|
| 9. | The Record includes sufficient data to determine whether assessment actually took place. | 1 | 2 | 3 | 4 | 5 |
| 10. | There was sufficient analysis or reflection for the unit to judge the success of outcomes or objectives. | 1 | 2 | 3 | 4 | 5 |

<u>Use of Assessment Results</u>

| | | | | | | |
|---|---|---|---|---|---|---|
| 11. | There is evidence of unit faculty/staff involvement in deciding how to use assessment results. | 1 | 2 | 3 | 4 | 5 |
| 12. | The described uses of assessment results appear reasonably likely to foster the intended outcome or objective. | 1 | 2 | 3 | 4 | 5 |

P
L
A
N  — brackets "PLAN" for items 1–8

R
E
P
O
R
T  — brackets "REPORT" for items 9–12

**COMMENT SHEET FOR COMMITTEE REVIEW OF ASSESSMENT PLANS AND REPORTS**

## Narrative Report

**The Committee believes the following comments and suggestions may help you strengthen the assessment record for your department/unit.**

**Relationship to University Mission**

**Intended Educational (Student) Outcome or Administrative Objectives**

**Means of Assessment and Criteria for Success**

**Assessment Results**

**Use of Assessment Results**

# ISSUES RELATING TO ASSESSMENT OF DISTANCE LEARNING

Educational program or individual classes taking place without the instructor being in direct proximity to the student are normally described as distance learning. While this type of instructional style has existed for a number of years, the term distance learning is now popularly utilized to describe those electronically facilitated modes of instruction in which the student is separate from the instruction. The term does not apply to classes offered through the traditional mode of classroom instruction, but at a location other than the institution's main campus.

Without going into the specific electronic technology (which changes daily) in this mode of instruction, among the most common modes of electronic support feature:

* One way video (from instructor to student) and two way audio (between instructor and student)
* Two way video and audio (from instructor to student and from student to instructor)
* Internet facilitated
* Computer facilitated (through use of separate disks)

Of course, a combination of these modes and between these modes and the more traditional classroom instruction exists. These include video/audio facilitated courses in which students attend traditional laboratory sessions which rotate among remote site locations, as well as other combinations.

The primary differences between distance learning and traditional classroom instruction were noted by Daniel Weinstein during the 14th Annual Institutional Effectiveness Workshop. In the traditional classroom the student (a) is face-to-face with the instructor, (b) has social contact with other students, (c) has campus life and resources, (d) has a proctored test taking environment, and (e) receives immediate feedback. On the other hand, in the distance learning environment, the student is (a) away from the instructor, (b) isolated from other students, (c) has a home environment and personal resources, (d) has uncontrolled test taking environment, and (e) has delayed feedback.

Many representatives of the public sector (legislators, governors, governing boards, etc.) view distance learning as the "education mode of tomorrow." Distance learning offers educational opportunities previously not available otherwise to isolated populations. It can be scheduled at the convenience of the individual student and on a "self-paced" basis. In addition, colleges see distance learning as a relatively low cost per student mode of instruction once the development costs are recovered.

There are many challenges associated with distance learning, but the most often voiced by its opponents are (a) relative lack of security in proctoring student evaluation, (b) the cost and compatibility of hardware, (c) inability to develop human relations and inter-personal skills, and (d) the provision of support services (library, counseling, or computer resources).

As a campus considers the consequences of developing a distance learning program, another concern often emerges from the traditional faculty. Traditional faculty often sees distance learning as a threat. Their concern is that the institution will be able to produce relatively inexpensive education with fewer instructors. The faculty are aware of the growing educational programming now offered by proprietary institutions as well as existing institutions of higher learning. Distance learning is often questioned by more traditional academics based upon "quality" when, in the author's opinion; the actual basis of their concern is frequently the competitive threat of greater efficiency, which is not seen as "arguable" in a public setting. These questions concerning the "quality" of student learning lead to the subject of outcomes assessment as a basis for the judgment of the extent of "quality."

Several years ago the concern regarding the "quality" of distance learning and the fact that these educational programs were quickly overlapping regional accrediting association geographic boundaries led the regional accrediting associations to jointly endorse a statement regarding "Best Practices for Electronically Offered Degree and Certificate Programs" originated by the Western Cooperative for Educational Tele-communications. This statement is available at www.wiche.edu/telecom/. Among the best practices cited are the following:

- First time offerings will be subject to review prior to their conduct.
- Assessment of distance learning will be accomplished as part of each comprehensive review.
- Institutions are expected to conduct self-evaluations of distance learning programs.
- Deficiencies or concerns noted in reviews will be aggressively monitored.
- When justified, actions will be taken to close individual distance learning programs.

Each regional accrediting association has incorporated these "Best Practices" into its requirements for institutions. Individual institutions should identify the requirements for assessment of distance learning in their particular region.

The simple processes outlined in this publication form a basic foundation for assessment of any educational program, including those electronically facilitated. It is important that as an institution strives for institutional effectiveness that the differences in the various unique components of the institution are addressed. Distance learning exhibits several such characteristics which differ from assessment of education offered in the more traditional settings. *First*, because distance learning offerings often are more fragmented to the individual class level, course level assessment is practiced more often and, due to the limited number of courses is frequently more feasible. *Second*, the appropriateness of the particular electronic mode utilized to teach the class is also among the assessment topics covered, as well as student learning. *Third*, due to the difficulty in proctoring examinations/projects and providing support services, client satisfaction information is somewhat more readily accepted (though in the author's opinion its exclusive use remains a considerable gamble).

The ultimate assessment of distance learning at the course and program level must be in relation to the question, "Are students learning an equivalent amount through the distance learning mode as they would be in a more traditional classroom setting" This "Equivalency of Learning" concept calls, whenever feasible, for a comparison of the groups being educated through electronic means and those through more tradition classroom based instructional modes, utilizing to the extent possible the same means of assessment. Differences in assessment results are routinely accepted when factors such as differences in student academic preparation, age, time since high school graduation, etc., are utilized to justify differences. However, when such matters which are largely beyond institutional control cannot be utilized to justify disparities, institutions are expected to bring about changes in the mode of instruction.

This subject is now and will continue to develop as a highly visible issue in higher education. The Five Column-Model and means of assessment described earlier in this publication should provide the basis upon which adaptations are fashioned to assess the effectiveness of this growing aspect of higher education.

# ASSESSMENT GLOSSARY EXAMPLE

**Accreditation**—the designation that an institution functions appropriately in higher education with respect to its purpose and resources. (Regional accrediting agencies accredit an entire institution; The University is accredited by the Commission on Colleges of the Southern Association of Colleges and Schools. Professional accrediting agencies accredit professional programs. For example, the Department of Chemistry is accredited by the American Chemical Society.)

**Administrative or Educational Support Unit Mission Statement**—the part of the administrative department's unit mission statement that best (1) fits the linkage to the university's mission and purpose and (2) fits with the *Intended Administrative Objectives* being assessed

**ARB**—the *Assessment Record Book*

**Assessment**—the process of determining whether an *Intended Educational (Student Learning) Outcome* or *Intended Educational Support or Administrative Objective* has been achieved and to what degree

**Assessment Period**—the two academic years covered by the *Assessment Record* (see *Cycle A, Cycle B*)

**Assessment Plan**—the initial assessment document in all *Assessment Record Books* that describes the assessment strategy for a department or unit of the University

**Assessment Record**—the collection of *Assessment Reports* submitted annually by each department and unit to the *University Assessment Committee* documenting assessment activities during the *Cycle A* or *Cycle B Assessment Period*

**Assessment Record Book**—a binder that each department and unit on campus will have copies for filing the *Assessment Records*

**Assessment Record Forms**—the various *Form A*s, *Form B*s, and *Form C*s that make up an *Assessment Record*

**Assessment Report**—the *Form B*s and *Form C*s that make up an *Assessment Record* for an *instructional department*

**Assessment Results**—the section of a *Form C* in which the department describes the results of its *assessment* of an *intended educational (student learning) outcome* or *administrative objective*

**College/University Goal(s) Supported**—the goal(s) from the college/university's planning document that best fit(s) the instructional department's function or the administrative/educational support unit's function.

*Column and Row Model*—an evaluation format used by *Instructional Departments* to assess student demonstration of knowledge, skills, and abilities

**Criteria for Success**—the numeric level (e.g., 80%)—the benchmark—in the department's assessment of an *Intended Outcome* or *Objective* used with *Means of Assessment* and necessary to assess the degree to which the outcome or objective was achieved

**Cycle A**—the group of *educational support/administrative departments/units* and instructional programs assessed in the academic period September through August of even-numbered years (e.g., 1998-2000)

**Cycle B**—the group of *educational support/administrative departments/units* and instructional programs assessed in the academic period September through August of odd-numbered years (e.g., 1999-2001)

*Departmental Guide*—a publication by Dr. James O. Nichols used as a reference for the *Institutional Effectiveness* programs

**Description of Data Collection**—a description of the source of data and the discussion of the results of assessment (data analysis) in an *Assessment Record*

**Educational Support/Administrative Department/Unit**—any department of the college/university that is not instructional but supports the educational and operational functions of the University

**Evaluation**—to determine the value of an instructional program, educational support service, or student learning outcome; interchangeable with *Assessment*

**Expanded Statement of Institutional Purpose Linkage** - the part of an Assessment Record that is necessary to establish the department's, unit's, or program's link to the college/university's purpose

**First Means of Assessment for Outcome/Objective Identified Above** - the section of a Form C where the primary means for assessing the intended outcome or objective is documented

**Form A**—the first page of an *Assessment Record* that is the title page of the document

**Form B**—the second page of an *Assessment Record* where the *Expanded Statement of Institutional Purpose Linkage* and the *Intended Educational (Student Learning) Outcomes* or the *Intended Administrative Objectives* are initially listed

**Form C**—the template from the IEA web page <www.iea-nich.com> for an *Assessment Record* where two *Means of Assessment* can be described for an outcome or objective

*Goals for the College/University*—a part of the college/university planning document that gives the goals

**Institutional Effectiveness**—the process of improving quality by assessing achievement of goals and adjusting services to achieve future goals

**Institutional Mission Reference**—the focus area from college/university planning document that best fits the *instructional department*'s function

**Institutional Mission/Goal(s) Reference**—the goal(s) from college/university planning document that best fit(s) the *instructional departments* or *administrative or educational support department*'s function

**Instructional or Academic Department**—any department of the University of Mississippi that is responsible for the educational functions of the institution

**Intended Educational (Student Learning) Outcome**—the three to five goals (what students will be able to think, know, or do because of their educational experiences) the instructional department intends to assess during an *Assessment Period*

**Intended Administrative Objective**—the three to five outcomes the *educational support* or *administrative unit* intends to assess during an *Assessment Period*

**Means of Program Assessment**—the tool used to assess the intended outcome or objective

**Second Means of Assessment for Outcome Identified Above**—the section of a Form C2 or C3 where a secondary means for assessing the intended outcome or objective is documented

**Principles of Accreditation**—New document describing the minimum standards of quality expected from higher education institutions contains 73 must statements

**Quality Enhancement Plan (QEP)**—Required plan for improvement required by SACS

**SACS**—Southern Association of Colleges and Schools; the accrediting agency of higher education institutions in Alabama, Florida, Georgia, Kentucky, Louisiana, Mississippi, North Carolina, South Carolina, Tennessee, Texas, and Virginia

**Student Learning Outcomes**—the results (i.e., knowledge, skills, abilities) of education

**University Assessment Committee**—the group of faculty and staff selected each fall to review and evaluate the *Assessment Records* for the departments and programs in that *Cycle*

**Use of Results to Improve Instructional Program**—how the *Assessment Results* will be used by the *instructional department* to improve its student learning outcomes

**Use of Results to Improve Unit Services**—how the *Assessment Results* will be used by the *educational support* or *administrative unit* to improve the services it provides to its customers

# Index